D0902118

A Region of Regimes

A volume in the series

Cornell Studies in Political Economy
Edited by Peter J. Katzenstein

A list of titles in this series is available at cornellpress.cornell.edu.

A Region of Regimes

Prosperity and Plunder
in the Asia-Pacific

T. J. Pempel

Cornell University Press
Ithaca and London

Copyright © 2021 by Cornell University

All rights reserved. Except for brief quotations in a review, this book, or parts thereof, must not be reproduced in any form without permission in writing from the publisher. For information, address Cornell University Press, Sage House, 512 East State Street, Ithaca, New York 14850. Visit our website at cornellpress.cornell.edu.

First published 2021 by Cornell University Press

Library of Congress Cataloging-in-Publication Data

Names: Pempel, T. J., 1942– author.
Title: A region of regimes : prosperity and plunder in the Asia-Pacific / T.J. Pempel.
Description: Ithaca [New York] : Cornell University Press, 2021. | Series: Cornell studies in political economy | Includes bibliographical references and index.
Identifiers: LCCN 2021006020 (print) | LCCN 2021006021 (ebook) | ISBN 9781501758799 (hardcover) | ISBN 9781501758805 (paperback) | ISBN 9781501758829 (pdf) | ISBN 9781501758812 (epub)
Subjects: LCSH: East Asia—Economic conditions—Regional dispari- ties. | Southeast Asia—Economic conditions—Regional disparities. | East Asia—Economic policy—20th century. | East Asia—Economic policy—21st century. | Southeast Asia—Economic policy—20th century. | Southeast Asia—Economic policy—21st century.
Classification: LCC HC460.5 .P44 2021 (print) | LCC HC460.5 (ebook) | DDC 330.95—dc23
LC record available at https://lccn.loc.gov/2021006020
LC ebook record available at https://lccn.loc.gov/2021006021

For my wife, Kaela,
whose unwavering support has been invaluable

Contents

Preface

Anyone who has attempted to write a book has experienced the frustrating sense of powerlessness that arises when the book starts to take control of its own movements. Initially reactive to the author's slightest touch, the manuscript mutates into a runaway eighteen-wheeler on ice defying the most daunting authorial efforts to regain control. This book has been no exception. I originally conceptualized a more constricted set of problems and a more limited geography. Yet every exploration demanded closer attention to an expanding universe of cognate issues and unexplained variations. This book reflects the resulting interplay between my best efforts at control and the book's self-assertiveness. It is the product of long periods puzzling over a wide range of regional political, economic, and security problems.

The book has its deepest roots in the fertile soil of political economy. Three related puzzles have driven my analysis. First, what are the most insightful similarities and differences in the ways that individual nations have fused politics and economics? Second, how have domestic and external forces interacted in the shaping of those differences? Third, how has the Asia-Pacific region as a whole influenced and reflected the ongoing interactions among different national political economies?

I address these questions by analyzing the dramatic economic advances that unfolded in successive waves among multiple countries of East Asia. The book argues that understanding such successes requires attention to more than economics per se. Instead, it demonstrates the interpenetration of political, socioeconomic, and international forces that undergirded diverse national experiences. While the book focuses on consistent patterns over long periods, it also underscores key inflection points and transitions over time. Yet, the book is not solely a story of successes; it analyzes as well several conspicuous cases in which national political economies, though exceptionally lucrative to a narrow few, have failed the many.

As I sought to grapple with the interactions between politics and economics among the multiple countries in East Asia and to understand why countries develop in such starkly different ways, certain patterns became clear. Yet understanding the most compelling patterns demanded attention not only to domestic dynamics but also to external forces, both global and regional. How the internal and external interacted became essential to my understanding of national patterns. Adding to the complexity, I came to realize that any satisfactory analysis of the broader regional tableau necessitated an examination of the shifting nexus between a nation's economics and its security. The result is a book that is self-consciously synthetic but that seeks to offer a fresh prism through which to view what I see as the most defining continuities and changes in the postwar political economy of the Asia-Pacific.

Throughout its evolution, this book has benefited enormously from the questions, thoughts, and ideas of a large number of scholars, business and civic leaders, government officials, and policymakers across the Asia-Pacific who have generously shared their knowledge and insights with me. Even when we disagreed, their challenges and insights forced me to deepen my investigations and to sharpen my thinking in weaving the intellectual tapestry of this book. I have done my best to acknowledge my debts through the standard academic references; however, I acknowledge that one or two such citations can by no means capture the depth of my dependence on so many others.

I owe a particularly rich debt to the numerous colleagues who generously read and commented on iterations and segments of this book. Their critiques have been bracing jolts of criticism and encouragement. I owe a great debt to Greg Chin, John Delury, Rick Doner, Steph Haggard, Chris Hughes, Paul Hutchcroft, Peter Katzenstein, Greg Noble, Seung-youn Oh, Tom Pepinsky, John Ravenhill, Michael Shalev, Yul Sohn, Richard Stubbs, Joe Wong, and Steve Vogel. Two anonymous readers also offered extremely helpful comments. I have done my best to take account of their myriad suggestions and criticisms; however, as always, responsibility for the final product is mine alone.

Perhaps the greatest joy of an academic career is the ongoing interaction with inquisitive and talented students. As this project evolved, a number of such students provided me with exceptional research assistance. I wish to give particular thanks to Charles Faulkner Ayers, Raj Bhargava, Sean Diament, Kristi Govella, Joon Lee, Seung-youn Oh, Chris Reinhardt, Matthew Stenberg, William Li Wong, Sharon (Jiaming) Yang, Noah Young Kwon Yu, and Fengyang Zhou. I also benefited enormously by presenting iterations of my evolving ideas to seminars of strikingly talented and critical undergraduate and graduate students in the Charles and Louise Travers Department of Political Science here at Berkeley. All posed probing questions and well-crafted essays that continually forced me to refine my initial ideas.

I received generous funding for my research from the Institute of East Asian Studies, the Department of Political Science, and the Jack M. Forcey Chair at the University of California, Berkeley. Even more valuable than financial support, U.C. Berkeley has also provided an intellectually vigorous and administratively supportive base from which to work. Particularly helpful have been the faculty colloquia in comparative politics and international relations. Lynne Bush and Charlotte Merriwether gave me invaluable help in preparing the manuscript.

I also wish to acknowledge my explicit appreciation to several institutions that have welcomed me as a visiting scholar—the Graduate School of International Studies at Yonsei University and the ASAN Institute in Seoul, the S. Rajarathnan School of International Studies at Nanyang University in Singapore, and the Graduate Research Institute of Policy Studies (GRIPS) in Tokyo. Each provided me with time and intellectual stimulation that enriched my understanding of the issues central to this project.

Like many others who have been fortunate to have their books included in Cornell University Press's Cornell Series in Political Economy, I am most especially indebted to the ongoing editorial and intellectual guidance of Peter Katzenstein and Roger Haydon. Over decades of deep friendship, both have continually managed to leaven personal warmth with professional rigor. Each has demonstrated that the best friends are the most empowered to offer the harshest criticisms. Through multiple projects, but particularly this one, Peter and Roger in their own ways have pressed me to probe more deeply, organize more clearly, and write more crisply. If the final product fails to reflect the lessons they sought to impart, I know it is vastly superior to my multiple earlier drafts. Their ongoing counsel encouraged me to treat such versions as merely the test flights needed before launching on a more arduous journey.

My deepest thanks go to my wife, Kaela Kory. She has been saintly in her unfailing tolerance of my unceasing requests to jettison vacations, skirt household chores, or renege on prior commitments in the service of "just one more" spur of the moment research trip or the need to "grab a few hours" to develop some new "insight." It is hardly adequate payback but I lovingly dedicate this book to her.

A Region of Regimes

Introduction

On July 13, 2001, the International Olympic Committee (IOC) awarded the 2008 Summer Olympics to Beijing. Such an international laurel would have been unimaginable three decades earlier. The People's Republic of China (PRC, hereafter China) was then under Maoist control, isolated from Western institutions, and mired in a pervasive poverty that left per capita GDP (gross domestic product) at a dismal $113 per year. Winning the right to hold the 2008 Olympics was a global triumph that underscored China's turbocharged political, social, and economic transformation. Much the same adulation surrounded South Korea (hereafter Korea) as Seoul hosted the Summer Olympics in 1988. The Korean achievement, too, capped an equally inconceivable political and economic metamorphosis. The 1964 Tokyo Olympics was acknowledgment of an equally dramatic success for a Japan that only twenty years earlier was politically fragmented, internationally castigated, and economically prostrate as the consequence of its disastrous performance in World War II.

These laurel-laden vignettes are congruent with the popular perception of rapid and sustained economic improvement among multiple countries across East Asia in the decades since World War II. Most had to overcome numerous obstacles predicted to impede such growth: the economic and political chaos of war, an array of military challenges, pervasive poverty, the social divisions bequeathed by colonialism, and the sociopolitical struggles endemic to newly independent states, to highlight only the most obvious. A gimlet eye is not required to appreciate the bold outlines of the region's transformation. Since the 1960s, eight of the world's ten most rapidly growing economies have been located in East Asia. East Asia accounted for 19 percent of world GDP in 1950, 37 percent by 1998,[1] and 47 percent by 2020.

Such a shared regional transformation presents one of the most puzzling geographic anomalies in contemporary political economy. How, despite the mélange of impediments, were so many countries as diverse as South Korea,

China, and Indonesia able to achieve decades of consistent macroeconomic growth, particularly in comparison with the far less impressive economic score-cards of the majority of countries in South Asia, Africa, Latin America, and the Middle East? The famous 1993 World Bank study addressed this issue and concluded: "If growth were randomly distributed, there is roughly one chance in ten thousand that success would have been so regionally concentrated."[2] The geographical pervasiveness of such economic success turned "the Asian Economic Miracle" into a media and academic trope.

There is no shortage of attempts to explain such successful economic trans-formation across East Asia. Competing explanations cluster into several key cat-egories: Asian culture, neoliberal economics, state power, and international relations, to name but a few.[3] In most, the search is for some single macroexpla-nation for "all" of East Asia's collective growth.

The region as a whole has unquestionably flourished; however, attention to only East Asia's macroregional economic success risks overlooking several anomalies that demand to be unpacked. One of these involves several conspic-uous despotic failures such as the Democratic People's Republic of Korea (DPRK, or North Korea) or Myanmar that cast a political and economic shadow over regional achievements. Complicating any bifurcation between a story of rags to riches and another of riches to rags are several additional incongrui-ties. One involves a distinctive group of countries that achieved partial suc-cess in ways that hindered further advances. Another complication emerges in trying to understand a number of baffling reversals by previously unidirec-tional successes. Finally, a geographical focus on East Asia forces attention to how diverse interactions of national political economies link to the fluctuat-ing dynamics across the Asia-Pacific as a whole. In an effort to unravel such puzzles, this book analyzes the relationship among politics, economics, and policy. It advances six central conclusions.

First, the overarching East Asian narrative is not a sequence of national gal-lops along some single path to homogeneously high growth. Rather, individual political economies trod several distinctive pathways, some of which resulted in success while others spawned failure. Japan, Taiwan, and Thailand, for exam-ple, enjoyed several decades of 8 to 9 percent annual GDP growth. In striking contrast, for equally long periods, Myanmar and the DPRK, among others, rarely topped 3 percent annually and were more often negative.

Second, a detailed analysis of ten different countries over several decades demonstrates that East Asian political economies form at least three distinct clusters. Countries in each cluster share key similarities to one another that differentiate them in critical ways from countries in the other two. I use the term *regimes* to summarize the interactions among each cluster's common po-litical, socioeconomic, and international properties.

Third, distinct regime types fuse with different economic paradigms. For example, although South Korea, Taiwan, Malaysia, and Thailand all achieved commonly high exports and GDP growth, the South Korean and Taiwanese advances rested on high value-added and domestically capitalized firms, while Malaysia and Thailand succeeded by relying on foreign direct investment to produce component parts for global supply chains.

Fourth, regime structures are influenced by both domestic and international forces. In particular, during the Cold War, robust security and economic nurturance from the United States was endemic to the domestic sociopolitical configurations and economic policy paradigms pursued by Japan, Korea, Taiwan, and the Philippines. In contrast, for decades the United States orchestrated extensive economic boycotts and containment constraints against the PRC, the DPRK, and periodically, Myanmar, that in turn shaped their domestic political economies. More broadly, global financial, trade, and monetary institutions have inescapably facilitated or constricted the structural and policy options of every country in the region, particularly since the mid- to late 1980s.

Fifth, even the most ostensibly entrenched regime patterns shift over time. Historical pathways, to be sure, structure political economies and policy paradigms in indelible ways. However, radical shifts in domestic or external forces, or both, have periodically upended even long-standing patterns. This was most dramatic in the major modifications in the political economies and policies of Japan, Korea, and Taiwan in the aftermath of their great economic transformations. Equally striking was the PRC's break with Maoism and (quite possibly) the embryonic breaks with deleterious past patterns possibly unfolding in Myanmar.

Sixth, and finally, there is a reciprocal interaction among the shifting mixes of domestic regimes, their policy paradigms, and the Asia-Pacific order as a whole. When multiple prominent countries in the region are achieving rapid economic growth, military tensions recede. In addition, the focus on growth can become regionally contagious, spurring emulation. Conversely, when such a collective pursuit fades, diplomatic and security frictions gain traction and the regional order as a whole becomes more fraught.

I address these anomalies through an analytic framework that examines distinct configurations among state institutions, socioeconomics, and external forces on the one hand and economic trajectories on the other. I use the term *regime* as the conceptual umbrella to capture the specific configurations of political, socioeconomic, and external forces that have prevailed across ten East Asian countries for sustained and instructive periods during the postwar era. Among those ten, I identify three discrete *regime types* that, in turn, correspond to particular economic paradigms. The analysis in these chapters demonstrates that rather than one unvarying East Asian model and common advances in growth, the region has consisted of distinct regime types advancing discrete economic policy paradigms with varying economic consequences. This analysis forms the core of part 1 of the book.

In part 2, I analyze two important variations from these three types. First, I assess the sharp shifts that took place in Japan, Korea, and Taiwan following their most remarkable growth spurts. Second, I explore China's regime and its related economic development to show that while China combines aspects of each of the three principal regime types outlined in part 1, it mirrors no single type exclusively even though its economic success is analogous to that of Japan, Korea, and Taiwan. The final chapter examines how shifting combinations of regimes and economic paradigms have interacted with and shaped alternate regional orders in the Asia-Pacific.

In combination, this analysis provides an innovative pathway between region-wide but inevitably partial similarities and the uniqueness of individual countries, while also providing a much-needed comparative perspective on China. The result, I believe, is a richer analytic understanding of East Asia's metamorphosis.

This analysis has more than historical and academic significance. As the Asia-Pacific entered the third decile of the twenty-first century, the previous regional feel-good story of widespread economic success has taken on a downbeat plot turn dominated by maritime tensions, renewed nationalisms, weaponization of a global pandemic, and rising anxieties about the increased danger of state-to-state conflict. The analysis in this book will show that current security frictions, far from being independent from the earlier growth experiences, are its intimate by-product.

Regimes and Their Components

Like most core concepts in the social sciences, the term *regime* emerges in a multiplicity of guises.[4] Thus, although many analysts of comparative politics restrict the usage to a bifurcation between democratic and authoritarian regimes, a number of studies in comparative political economy (CPE) develop more fine-grained distinctions. For example, Esping-Andersen uses the concept of regime to differentiate his "three worlds of welfare capitalism."[5] Collier and Collier analyze labor mobilization patterns to categorize a host of Latin American regimes.[6] Following a path-dependent logic, Mahoney distinguishes regime types in Central America.[7] Lensen and Wantchekon examine the relationship between resource wealth and regime varieties across Africa.[8] Juan Linz isolates differences among categories of nondemocratic regimes.[9] Elsewhere, I have analyzed democratic regimes in which a single party manages to retain decades of political dominance.[10]

This book adopts a similar approach by identifying discrete regime types that have close empirical approximations across postwar East Asia. In this book, *regime* refers to the fused interactions of three components pivotal to a country's political economy. Those three are its state institutions, its socioeconomic forces, and such external forces as are integral to domestic functioning. The three share what Max Weber (following Goethe) labeled "elective affinities." Their clustering is not random, but neither one nor another component is determinative of their affinity.

Previous analyses have linked each of these three as integral to economic policy paradigms in general and to East Asian economic development in particular. Rather than parsing the respective contribution of each individually, the book examines their mutual interdependence and links the mutually reinforcing combination as a whole to economic paradigms. It is well to examine each component in the context of their interrelationships and their respective links to economic development.

State Institutions

A substantial body of scholarship in comparative political economy privileges state institutions as decisive in shaping a country's socioeconomic structures and its economic paradigm. Certainly, countries vary widely in the effectiveness of their state institutions. To the extent that its institutions function with coherence, competence, and control, a state can mobilize available resources in pursuit of a common state-defined set of economic goals. The opposite is equally true. States plagued by inefficiency, fracture, and sporadic control usually generate policies that are indecisive and ineffective. To be sure, these two represent extreme end points on a continuum of connections between state institutions and economic development.

Efficient and well-functioning state institutions have definitely provided a key explanation for key East Asian transformations, with Japan, Korea, and Taiwan valorized as characterized by "developmental states."[11] Common to such analyses is the contention that rapid economic transformations for all three came as the deliberate by-product of focused and consequential actions by state institutions. The developmental state epitomizes coherent, competent, and controlling political institutions. Endemic to each is a pilot agency, staffed by a merit-based civil service that is technically competent and deft at manipulating an array of administrative tools in the furtherance of rapid economic transformation. The contributions of state institutions to economic growth is hardly limited to East Asia, however, with scholars such as Kohli and Acemoglu and Robinson, for example, making the more expansive claim that state institutions are the principal historical source of cross-country differences in economic success.[12]

The analytic power of the "developmental state" concept led to its broad application to a variety of other countries, particularly in East Asia. The result, in the words of Linda Weiss, is that the developmental state "become[s] virtually synonymous with 'the state in East Asia.'"[13] Regrettably, as Fine notes, however, the concept too often morphed into "a blanket buzz term for any circumstance in which there is state involvement in some aspect of development."[14]

Competent and self-assertive state institutions may appear to be self-evident ingredients for forward-looking policies. Yet more fine-grained analysis of diverse patterns of state-directed development shows how historically uncommon the coherent, competent, and controlling state institutions of Northeast Asia actually were.[15] Far more prevalent are politicians and civil servants who hold their posts by virtue of ethnicity, religion, regional origin, or family ties. Technical competence is in short supply. The instruments of control are absent or wielded ineffectively. Such institutional drawbacks are more common than not. Stephen Krasner notes that "most developing countries have very weak domestic political institutions," while Samuel Huntington decades ago pointed out that in many developing countries, "governments simply do not govern."[16]

A particular complication of the relationship between state institutions and economic development arises with the military. Many national military leaderships are dubious about rapid economic transformation if it threatens to reallocate scarce budgetary resources to civilian industrializers, to generate peace with traditional enemies, or to constrain senior officers' control of economic rents in the localities under their command. For many countries, including several in East Asia, the progrowth versus antigrowth predispositions of the senior officer corps exerted determinative influence over state institutions with corresponding consequences for the national economy.

State institutions are critical to a country's economic paradigm because of their ability to shape the incentives, rewards, and punishment available to key socioeconomic actors. Thus, state institutions rarely operate in a socioeconomic vacuum. That leads to the question of which socioeconomic hands control the levers of state institutions. Into whose pockets does the silver and gold most smoothly flow?[17] Therefore, considerable analysis has linked socioeconomic forces, their specific coalitions, and their interface with the state to different economic patterns.[18]

Socioeconomic Forces

Most analyses of socioeconomic forces emphasize less the dichotomy between "state" and "society" and more their interactions. As Woo-Cumings noted, a state that is successful in spurring rapid economic transformations is rarely "an imperious entity lording it over society but a partner with the business sector in a historical compact of industrial transformation."[19] Similarly, Peter Evans demonstrated that most regimes carrying out successful economic transformations benefit from state institutions that are deeply "embedded" in their societies and their economies.[20]

That state institutions and socioeconomic forces interact is beyond question; however, debates continue about the relative influence of one upon the other. While influential analyses have focused on state institutions as the key driver of economic policies, an equally strong focus assesses a country's socioeconomic forces as determinative of its economic paradigm. Barrington Moore laid a compelling foundation for such analysis with his powerful argument about the pivotal role of socioeconomic forces in shaping national political and economic development.[21] Plausible accounts exist, of course, for reversing the arrow of causality; however, the key insight of both lies in their demonstration of the interactive linkages of one to the other and how distinctive linkages connect to discrete paths of economic development. This interaction is integral to my use of *regime*. In this context, my use of the term regime resonates with common usages in much of the CPE writing, as noted above.

A key factor in the influence of socioeconomic forces hinges on the degree of unity versus division in a country's socioeconomic composition. What are a country's most salient social and economic cleavages? Deep ethnic, regional, religious, or sectoral divisions foster national fragmentation; their absence facilitates coherence. When deep socioeconomic divisions seriously impede state efficiency, the results can be economically disastrous, as Joel Migdal demonstrates in his analysis of the deleterious combination of "strong societies and weak states."[22]

Late developing nation-states that achieve rapid economic development are most often devoid of such powerful ethnic, regional, or linguistic divisions. Instead, national sociocultural homogeneity is strong and dominant socioeconomic cleavages fall largely along the classic lines of land-labor-capital, rather than tribe, religion, or territory. Anti-industrial forces such as landowning compradors exert minimal influence. Progrowth coalitions dominate and populist social groups such as labor or consumers have little capacity to blunt the high-growth paradigm. Furthermore, within that broad framework, the ways specific socioeconomic sectors cooperate or clash can determine national economic preferences and policies. As different socioeconomic groups and coalitions enjoy greater or lesser influence, the resultant political-socioeconomic arrangements give broad and distinguishing shape to distinctive national economic paradigms.[23] Such treatments of socioeconomic forces and state institutions, either separately or in congruence, are integral to uses of the term regime in comparative politics.

Regimes form as the consequence of the interdependence between socioeconomics and the institutions of government. What holds these regimes together is less often clear. It is there that studies of regimes by analysts of international relations (IR) resonate in valuable ways. IR studies of regimes accept that individual states are the central actors within international politics; however, they underscore how international regimes provide a matrix of constraints and opportunities within which the regime's members (i.e., states) maneuver.[24] For instance, investment, trade, and monetary regimes limit the discretion of constituent units of the particular international regime.[25] At the same time, by deferring short-term relative gains, member cooperation within such regimes has engendered long-term absolute and collective gains for cooperating regime participants in areas as diverse as the environment,[26] nuclear weapons reduction,[27] national security,[28] and fishing.[29] Regimes are effective to the extent that they can foster cooperation among members, reduce intraregime conflicts,[30] and generate sustained and predictable patterns, norms, rules, and behaviors that guide member behavior. These insights from IR studies of regimes are equally applicable to the components of domestic regimes. Most important for this study, participants in any regime bond to-gether around a shared conviction about the long-term benefits of continued collaboration in the face of jointly perceived threats and challenges.

Examples of such synchronicities between regime types and policy paradigms are widespread in the CPE literature. Exemplars include Esping-Andersen's al-ready noted "three worlds of welfare capitalism,"[31] Katzenstein's "liberal" versus "social" corporatism,[32] Steinmo's tax regimes,[33] or Hall and Soskice's dichoto-mization between "liberal market economies" (LMEs) and "coordinated mar-ket economies"(CMEs).[34] More recently, Thelen reformulated the Hall and Soskice framework to distinguish two different CME trajectories: dualization exemplified by Germany and embedded flexibilization exemplified by Sweden and Denmark.[35] In all such instances, key regime components bond around their elective affinity for a particular set of domestic structures and policy paradigms.

Understanding a specific country's regime and its economic paradigm, how-ever, is problematic if the focus is exclusively on domestic state institutions and domestic socioeconomic forces. Rarely do such domestic forces operate in a global or regional vacuum. As noted, there is an elective affinity between domestic state institutions and socioeconomic forces. Equally, there is an elec-tive affinity between such domestic affinities, on the one hand, and particu-lar external forces, on the other. Beyond structuring broad constraints and opportunities, external forces can become endemic elements in national re-gimes. This was true for the ten cases analyzed in this book; hence, it is es-sential to include, rather than to marginalize, such external forces.

External Forces

The third element integral to any regime involves nondomestic influences. Do-mestic political and socioeconomic arrangements invariably fluctuate within a matrix of global and regional forces that present domestic forces with a va-riety of constraints and opportunities. Thus, the modern nation-state, like the mythological Janus, wears two faces, one looking inward, the other eyeing pros-pects and challenges that lie outside. Robert Putnam analyzed this duality as forcing national policymakers continually to engage in "two level games" in their ongoing effort to steer the ship of state between domestic and foreign demands and opportunities.[36] Theda Skocpol also captures this dual perspec-tive: "States necessarily stand at the intersections between domestic sociopo-litical orders and the transnational relations within which they must maneuver for survival and advantage."[37] Likewise, George Tsebelis shows how domestic–international relationships involve "nested games" with political actors playing domestic and international games simultaneously, the conflicts and payoffs from one influencing opportunities in the other.[38]

Numerous studies demonstrate the hurdles individual countries confront in navigating tempestuous global waters. Alexander Gerschenkron established the shaping power that preexisting markets and technologies have over late developing states.[39] All must overcome the prevailing international market hierarchy in which already rich countries enjoy technological leads and have strong incentives to retain that dominance by constricting the opportunities available to poor countries below them. The latter provide the inexpensive raw materials and cheap labor essential to the functioning and expansion of manufacturing, finance, technology, and ever-rising productivity and standards of living in a limited number of sophisticated economies. In the metaphor of Ha-Joon Chang, power holders in countries that have climbed the ladder of economic success have every incentive to "kick away the ladder" to prevent potential competitors from replicating their climb.[40] These difficulties in advancing national development are further confounded when an authoritarian state, a domestic military, and an anti-industrial upper class receive external reinforcement from rapacious foreign governments or corporations.[41]

Equally impactful external forces arise from the infrequent but powerful global shocks that force substantial reassessments of domestic coalitions and economic strategies.[42] Too often, however, this perspective, while invaluable in examining differentiated national responses to collective shocks, treats external forces primarily as a pool cue periodically striking a unified domestic ball and observing where it rolls. While not denying the tumultuous impact episodic external forces can exert over nation states as a whole, my analysis starts from the premise that rather than providing only occasional disruptive catalysts of change, certain nondomestic forces are often integral and constant components of a national regime.

The substantive analysis in this book highlights at least three distinct features of the integral nature of external forces for the character and policy options of any regime. First, the United States exerted overwhelming and intrusive influence in domestic sociopolitical arrangements and policy choices across East Asia for at least the first four decades following World War II. It is impossible to understand state institutions, socioeconomic forces, and the economic policy paradigms in Japan, Korea, and Taiwan without taking into account the intimate and enduring influence of the United States and its Cold War strategy.[43] Yet even toward US allies, American influence has not always been economically benevolent (witness the recurring insistences of radical exchange rate demands and trade restrictions). Moreover, if American engagement during the Cold War was broadly consistent with a grand strategy of anticommunist containment and support for alliance partners, no such consistency has been evident since at least the 1990s. Instead, successive US administrations from different political parties have swung wildly between contrastive foreign policy priorities, often upending entrenched domestic arrangements in East Asia.

The United States is not the only external influencer. Other counties have also emerged to exert powerful external sway over neighbors. China, for example, has long been a protector of the DPRK; Japan served as a major source of aid, technology, and investment for China and a host of Southeast Asian countries. ASEAN's (the Association of Southeast Asian Nations) member states have been a strong force behind Myanmar's shifting regime.

Second, regimes across East Asia operate under the pervasive shadow of global institutions such as the World Bank, the IMF (International Monetary Fund), and the WTO (World Trade Organization), in whose creation none had a decisive hand. Beyond such generic influence, changing global monetary and trade pressures contributed powerfully to deep alterations in the Japanese, Korean, and Taiwanese regimes, most notably during the 1980s and 1990s (see chapter 4). Likewise, surging and retreating hot money from foreign investors and global currency speculators forced similar reshaping of the prevailing regimes in Malaysia, Indonesia, Thailand, and Korea as was most obvious during the Asian financial crisis (AFC).[44] A flurry of ASEAN-initiated regional institutions have enhanced regional adjustments and cooperation on a host of functional issues, from crime to the environment to fishing, while the rising number of bilateral and multilateral free trade pacts have catalyzed the restructuring of prior economic paradigms. It is plausible that surges in new regional financing from China and institutions such as the Belt and Road Initiative (BRI) and the Asian Infrastructure Investment Bank (AIIB) will exert similarly influential restructurings.

Powerful as such globalizing forces have been, this book does not contend that global finance has acquired unchecked power to trump hitherto meaningful national distinctions. Such distinctions, many argue, blur into insignificance in the face of pressures from an increasingly globalized economy. Such views have gained particular force since the global financial crisis of 2007–2009.[45] Though the analysis below underscores the power of global finance, such financial impacts have not blotted out vital national distinctions.

A third point to note is simply that external forces endemic to East Asian regimes have not always been impediments to economic development. A variety of strategic or other considerations have oftentimes led external forces to advocate, not oppose, economic development in various East Asian regimes. This was obvious, for example, in US support for the economic development of Japan, Korea, and Taiwan. In addition, the global financial and trade order not only set constraints but also presented opportunities to much of developing East Asia. Furthermore, as scholars such as John Ravenhill, Richard Stubbs, and Henry Wai-chung Yeung outline, international corporations' vast capital infusions across much of the region forged regional production networks that have been vital components in the economic advances of several regimes in Southeast Asia, as well as in China.[46]

This book demonstrates how particular combinations of domestic state and socioeconomic forces navigated the strong tailwinds or headwinds emanating from powerful international forces to propel themselves in alternative economic directions. The regimes discussed in this book all sought to navigate in ways that would minimize their permanent inferiority and consignment to the global periphery. Those that succeeded found what Haggard labelled "pathways from the periphery" and escaped the rocky economic shoals that impaled so many other late developing countries.[47]

Consistent and mutually beneficial relationships within regimes are conducive to steadiness in economic policy paradigms. A sustained policy paradigm is vital for the continuity and reinforcement of any regime. Such a policy paradigm is akin to what Antonio Gramsci called a "hegemonic project," that is, the broad thrusts or biases in national policies. The hegemonic project bonds a regime's constituent components together in pursuit of a shared venture, the pursuit and achievement of which results in ongoing and outsized benefits for the regime and its components, along with the disproportionate disadvantaging of potential regime opponents. Regime consistency and policy consistency become mutually reinforcing. A regime and its policy paradigm thus reflect what David Easton describes as a national "gestalt," "system," or "weltanschauung," or what E. E. Schattschneider has dubbed a prevailing "mobilization of bias."[48]

As noted above, this book examines the ongoing interdependence among the specific state institutions, socioeconomic forces, and external influences of ten East Asian countries. It demonstrates that these individual regimes separate into three distinct constellations, each associated with a particular economic policy paradigm. The relationship between regime and policy is preponderantly symbiotic: regimes generate and change broad economic policies, but those policies in turn feed back to the regime, ideally reinforcing intraregime cohesion, reaffirming the logic for sustained collaboration and enhancing long-term regime coherence and persistence.[49]

Any consistent and coherent regime is thus constantly in the process of reinvigorating itself through economic policy.[50] When effective, the result is a "virtuous cycle" in which the policy paradigm reinforces and enhances intraregime relations, attracts and retains regime supporters, and marginalizes erstwhile regime challengers. Regime coherence, in turn, allows for a continuation and reinforcement of the underlying policy paradigm. Figure I.1 provides a diagrammatic sketch of the key elements I treat as constituting a regime and the regime's congruence with its overarching economic paradigm.

Categorizing Regimes and Policy Paradigms

The first three chapters in part 1 examine nine country cases, each closely approximating one of three idealized regime types as well as their corresponding economic policy paradigm. I label these three regime types "developmental," "ersatz developmental," and "rapacious." Each chapter analyzes the common features of one regime type, their concrete elaboration in three distinct countries, and their corresponding economic paradigms. Japan, Korea, and Taiwan offer the clearest examples of developmental regimes (chapter 1). Analogous in some ways, but critically distinct in crucial fundamentals, are ersatz

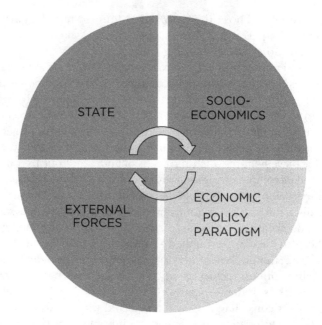

Figure I.1 Regimes and their key components.

developmental regimes. Malaysia, Indonesia, and Thailand are exemplars (chapter 2). Undeniably integral to the East Asian region but often ignored in the emphasis on economic successes is a third category I label rapacious regimes. The DPRK, Myanmar, and the Philippines under Marcos represent prototypical examples (chapter 3). Table I.1 summarizes the key regime traits and their corresponding economic policy paradigm.

Part 2 extends the analysis of part 1 in three additional directions. First, it examines how a succession of domestic and international challenges triggered fundamental changes in the underpinnings of the developmental regimes. All three responded by reconfiguring core elements of their regimes and essential aspects of their policy paradigms leaving them looking quite different than they did at their developmental peaks (chapter 4). Second, I examine the PRC as a tenth country case (chapter 5). Following the same regime logic used in part 1, I show that China, despite sharing various features with each of the three idealized types, combines them in distinct ways.[51] Furthermore, the Chinese regime, with far less disruption, is accommodating challenges that upended the developmental regimes and their policy paradigms. Third, and finally (chapter 6), the book examines the back-and-forth interactions between diverse regime combinations and the Asia-Pacific regional order as a whole. Such interactions have gone through several kaleidoscopic tumblings reflecting individual regime shifts and interactions. At the same time, the chapter also examines how prevailing regional trends have shaped certain regimes.

Table 1.1 Key regime variables

	Developmental (Japan, Korea, Taiwan)	Ersatz (Malaysia, Thailand, Indonesia)	Rapacious (Philippines under Marcos, DPRK, Myanmar)	Reconstructed developmental (Japan, Korea, Taiwan)	China
State institutions	Concentrated Meritocratic/talented bureaucracy	Fragmented Ethnic/patronage Lower-skilled bureaucracy	Concentrated Politically chosen Low skilled bureaucracy	Partisan fragmentation Bureaucracy subject to partisan goals	Concentrated Talented Political-merit mix
Socioeconomics	Cohesive and comprehensive Strong business support	Fragmented Fragmented business	Minimal Limited independent business	Fragmented Business global	Party-state control Minimal independent business
External forces	Strong US military and economic support	Investment support	Differs by regime	Pressures from globalization Loss of easy markets	Global support for growth and trade FDI-dependent
Economic policy paradigm	Embedded mercantilism Rapid sophistication Human skills training	Dependent development Low human skills training Middle-income trap	Predatory Minimal Low human skills training	Mercantilism challenged Innovation impeded	Selective globalization Rapid sophistication High human skills

Notes: DPRK = Democratic People's Republic of Korea; FDI = foreign direct investment.

Table I.2 Average GDP growth rates over time

	1950s	1960s	1970s	1980s	1990s	2000s	2010s
Developmental							
Japan	8.4	10.7	5.3	4.3	1.5	0.5	1.3
South Korea	6.3	8.1	9.7	7.9	7.1	4.7	3.3
Taiwan	8.2	9.1	10.2	8.2	6.6	3.8	3.2
Ersatz							
Indonesia	3.9	3.1	7.4	5.1	4.8	5.3	5.4
Malaysia	2.1	5.9	8.1	5.9	7.3	4.7	5.4
Thailand	5.6	8.4	6.9	7.2	5.3	4.3	3.7
Rapacious							
Myanmar	5.7	3.1	4.2	1.9	6.1	11.2	6.3
DPRK	9.3	3.7	4.5	2.7	−3.7	0.7	1.9
Philippines	7	4.7	5.8	2	2.8	4.5	6.3
China	11	3	7.4	9.7	10	10.3	7.6

Source: Data from the Conference Board Total Economy Database, "Output, Labor and Labor Productivity, 1950–2019" (original version), April 2019, https://conference-board.org/data /economydatabase/total-economy-database-archive.

Notes: GDP = gross domestic product; DPRK = Democratic People's Republic of Korea.

Decade averages of GDP growth rates. Rounding to one decimal place before averaging took place. GDP statistics based on 2018 US dollars. GDP growth statistics begin in 1951. Chinese statistics are official and begin in 1953.

Tables I.2, I.3, and I.4 present time series data for all ten countries on GDP growth, GDP per capita, and per capita energy use (a proxy for the depth of each country's industrialization). Each table demonstrates how collectively the three examples of each regime type resemble one another while differing sharply from those in the other two groups. All three tables show that the three developmental regimes—Japan, Korea, and Taiwan—experienced more impressive economic figures far earlier than any of the others. The rapacious regimes consistently trail the others, particularly on GDP per capita and energy use. The three ersatz regimes, starting later, subsequently achieved levels of annual GDP growth and GDP per capita that rival the very early performances of Japan, Korea, and Taiwan; however, their levels of energy use continue to lag further behind. Although China's upward trajectory started later, the country displays far more rapid growth over a longer period than even the developmental regimes even though it continues to lag in GDP per capita and energy use. Before proceeding, it is useful to highlight the broad outlines that form the main arguments the book will flesh out more fully.

The Developmental Regimes

Prototypical examples of developmental regimes include Japan, Korea, and Taiwan during their peak economic growth spurts. All enjoyed coherent, cohesive,

Table I.3 GDP per capita over time

	1950s	1960s	1970s	1980s	1990s	2000s	2010s
Developmental							
Japan	4,711	10,491	19,771	27,409	36,236	39,411	42,526
South Korea	1,604	2,244	4,746	8,698	17,600	28,226	38,118
Taiwan	2,028	3,159	6,535	12,479	23,522	36,068	49,770
Ersatz							
Indonesia	1,851	2,000	2,989	4,028	6,197	7,567	11,738
Malaysia	3,519	4,209	6,501	9,955	15,919	20,844	28,480
Thailand	1,480	2,154	3,295	5,138	9,621	12,830	17,633
Rapacious							
Myanmar	600	768	875	1,115	1,219	2,868	5,429
DPRK	787	925	1,002	1,150	884	788	799
Philippines	2,565	3,160	3,976	4,305	4,309	5,108	7,290
China	340	402	625	1,212	2,754	6,522	14,938

Source: Data from the Conference Board Total Economy Database, "Output, Labor and Labor Productivity, 1950–2019" (original version), April 2019, https://conference-board.org/data/economydatabase/total-economy-database-archive.

Notes: GDP = gross domestic product; DPRK = Democratic People's Republic of Korea.

Decade averages of per capita GDP measured in nominal 2018 US dollars. Chinese statistics are official and begin in 1952. DPRK statistics come from Byung-Yeon Kim and begin in 1954 and end in 2013; these may not be directly comparable for the 1950s and 2010s. Kim's statistics estimated GDP per capita in 2012 dollars; the database uses 2018 dollars. As such, averaged DPRK values were converted from 2012 to 2018 US dollars using https://stats.areppim.com/calc/calc_usdlrxdeflator.php. Averaging took place before currency conversion.

and efficient state institutions; integrated and cohesive progrowth socioeconomic coalitions; and unstinting economic, security, and geopolitical sustenance from the United States. Each advanced an economic policy paradigm devoted to catch-up industrialization and domestic economic transformation. In this, they benefited from a global financial system tolerant of undervalued currencies and a trading system conducive to their expanding exports.

Significantly, natural resources and foreign capital played no more than marginal roles in their early development. All three were devoid of natural resources and each explicitly eliminated the economic and social power of large landowners, a group typically antagonistic to industrialization and economic transformation. Moreover, none of the three developmental regimes experienced deep ethnic, religious, or linguistic fissures. In addition, although many national militaries oppose investments in industrial improvement, the officer corps in Japan had lost meaningful political influence with the Japanese defeat in World War II and the American Occupation's demilitarization campaign. In turn, within the far more militarized regimes in both Taiwan and Korea, following some initial resistance, the armed forces actively supported economic growth as congruent with, if not central to, enhanced national security. Consequently, with regime strength solid and enjoying multiple

Table I.4 Energy use per capita

	1970s	1980s	1990s	2000s	2010s
Developmental					
Japan	2837	3016	3824	3978	3616
South Korea	743.5	1363	3026	4339	5206
Taiwan	NA	1866	3124	4601	4995
Ersatz					
Indonesia	326.1	410	630	781	862.3
Malaysia	632.1	1007	1685	2427	2787
Thailand	414.7	499	978	1434	1864
Rapacious					
Myanmar	276.4	275.4	262	293	310.5
DPRK	1424	1802	1105	848	564.6
Philippines	439.9	451.8	478	457	445.6
China	532.2	655.4	823	1319	2129

Sources: World Bank World Development Indicators, https://datacatalog.worldbank.org/dataset/world-development-indicators except for 1980–2014 data for Taiwan, which was from US EIA (Energy Information Administration) and converted into per capita data using population statistics from the University of Grongingen and UC Davis, Penn World Table, https://cid.econ.ucdavis.edu/pwt.html; this data was then averaged and converted from quadrillion BTUs to kg of oil equivalent.

Note: DPRK = Democratic People's Republic of Korea.
Decade mean of primary energy consumption in kg of oil equivalent per capita (1971–2014).

tailwinds, all three turned to enhancing essential industries as the logical keystone to their developmental policy paradigms.

Each of the three advanced their technological sophistication through a mixture of domestic capital accumulation, deferred gratification, indigenous adaptation and innovation, human capital skill development, and ever-more sophisticated export products. The most prominent companies in these countries remained predominantly under indigenous ownership as they generated extensive forward and backward linkages domestically that in turn created integrated and dynamic economies capable of self-sustaining growth.[52] Both governments and private corporations systematically upgraded the quality of their workforces in ways that further boosted the national capacity for more refined production.[53] External support, in the form of US military and economic assistance, as well as access to valuable technologies and overseas markets, were integral to the economic success of all three. I label their economic paradigms "embedded mercantilism."[54] Eventually, their multiyear successes lit the way for neighboring countries to discover pathways for their own economic development.

It is worth noting that the three developmental regimes contributed more than just templates for others to model. Their ever more sophisticated economies demanded more natural resources, low cost land and labor, access to advantageous transportation networks, and markets for their own lower-end exports. All three therefore joined the moves toward regional production networks. These, in turn, became critical shapers of the regime types and economic paradigms of many neighboring countries. Economic interdependence across national borders surged. Yet, as the chapters devoted to the ersatz developmental regimes (chapter 2) and to China (chapter 5) will demonstrate, these regimes took on substantially different characteristics from those of the developmental regimes.

The Ersatz Developmental Regimes

The second type of regime is what I label "ersatz developmental regimes." The prime examples are Malaysia, Indonesia, and Thailand. In those regimes, state institutions displayed bouts of efficiency that contributed to advancing economic politics and resulted in high levels of GDP growth and expanding exports. Yet in contrast to the developmental regimes, state institutions in all three were rarely as cohesive or as competently staffed. Moreover, the incisive tools of state control wielded in Japan, Korea, and Taiwan were either unavailable or less well utilized. In addition, powerful and often anti-industrializing militaries in Thailand and Indonesia compromised any singular pursuit of a cohesive national development agenda. Further impeding moves toward a comprehensive transformative economic paradigm, divisive ethnic and regional loyalties pervaded all three, compromising both state cohesion and technical competence. As a result, government institutions were rarely capable of consistent long-term planning and direction in the service of self-sustaining economic transformation.

Regional, religious, and ethnic cleavages were pervasive. Islam exerted particularly outsized influence in Indonesia and Malaysia. In all three regimes, moreover, numerous holders of capital enjoyed secure incomes from property investments or quasi-monopolistic control over key products or resources. These sunk economic costs combined with political volatility to incentivize most to avoid the high costs and riskiness of deep industrial investments. Instead, most sought fast exit options to protect their accumulated wealth.

Malaysia, Thailand, and Indonesia, nonetheless, did achieve laudable economic successes in total growth and exports, in this way resembling the developmental regimes. In contrast to resource-poor Japan, Korea, and Taiwan, however, the three Southeast Asian countries were resource rich, allowing them to rely more heavily on resource and agricultural exports, with fewer incentives to advance industrialization for export success and government funding.

Most critically, most ersatz developmental advances into sophisticated manufacturing resulted from dependence on foreign direct investments searching for low cost labor. Supplying that workforce, in turn, required only minimal skill development and motivated little local innovation. State and corporate failure to enhance domestic workforce skills left these regimes plugged into the production of highly sophisticated products principally as subordinates within regional and global supply chains.

Equally, the dependence on outside capital left all three regimes highly vulnerable to the swift currents of fast moving money. Foreign investors, with minimal political stake in any of these countries but a mandate to search for the highest possible returns for their investments, moved money in and out of these regimes with flicks of a computer keyboard. This had disastrous effects on all three regimes during the AFC in 1997–98.

Because of such outside dependence on foreign capital, indigenous owners and managers garnered far smaller portions of the profits from the high value-added products that passed through their borders. In combination, such conditions reduced the ability of the ersatz regimes to generate and sustain a trajectory of industrial deepening. They risked enmeshment in a "middle income trap" that would prevent them from moving beyond moderately sophisticated economic levels as they remained ever vulnerable to other locations offering cheaper workers and marginally higher returns to globally mobile foreign investors.[55]

The Rapacious Regimes

Chapter 3 analyzes a third distinct assemblage, namely East Asia's rapacious regimes, most conspicuously the DPRK, Myanmar, and the Philippines under Marcos. The attention-grabbing economic advances achieved by both the developmental and the ersatz developmental regimes (as well as Hong Kong, Singapore, China, and Vietnam) make it easy to lose sight of such conspicuous regional exceptions.

These three stand as antitransformational contrasts that pose the question of why, despite enjoying among the best "objective" conditions for economic success in the 1950s and 1960s, these three languished for decades while neighboring countries raced ahead. Strong as the rip tide of the Asian economic miracle was, it stirred little more than limp ripples in several of the region's backwaters. Rather than floating along with the regional tide, regimes in these countries swam against the current, rejecting economic transformation while exploiting their populations rather than improving their lot. Understanding the regional mix behind such rejection reflects valuable light back on the regime arrangements supporting regional successes.

State institutions in the rapacious regimes were typically internally cohesive and in possession of powerful tools of control. Yet those institutions rarely exhibited much that an outside observer would acknowledge as competence beyond the recurrently heavy hammer of state repression in service of nationally draconian ends. Moreover, in the DPRK, Myanmar, and in the Philippines under Marcos, state institutions were suffused with patronage, corruption, and (for at least the latter two) intense agency infighting.

Ethnic and geographic fragmentation were especially prominent in Myanmar and the Philippines where linguistic and religious tensions overlapped with ethnic separatism. In addition, in the Philippines a powerful landowning comprador class with close ties to American agricultural importers provided an additional phalanx that favored state predation and mitigated against rapid industrialization. Compounding these impediments to rapid economic improvements, antitransformational militaries played key roles in all three, with military budgets dwarfing allocations beneficial to economic transformation in the DPRK and Myanmar.

Despite the periodic incantation of developmental aspirations—in accord with socialist principles in the DPRK and Myanmar, and capitalist verbiage under President Marcos—these regimes surrendered to the blandishments of pervasive plunder. Instead of delivering growth and improved livelihoods, these regimes ruled through intimidation, preyed on citizens, pillaged national resources, and provided minimal citizen improvements.[56] Despite facing a diversity of regional and global conditions over different periods, all three regimes resembled what Charles Tilly labeled organized crime families.[57] State officeholders used official institutions to forge protection rackets, monetizing their offices to promote illicit activities and/or to extract public resources for the benefit of themselves, their families, and their narrow circles of personal support. Predatory aggrandizement superseded extensive national developmental as the regimes' hegemonic project.[58]

Extending Regime Logic

Drawing on the analysis of these three regime types in part 1, part 2 advances into three other areas. First, chapter 4 analyzes how the previously successful fusion of regime and economy in Japan, Korea, and Taiwan moved away from embedded mercantilism and into relative economic slowdown, greater global openness, and regime reorganization. Recurrently explosive gains in GDP and repeatedly expanding shares of world exports are, of course, no more plausible than for a world record holder in the 400-meter dash to sustain that same pace over the 26.2 miles of a marathon. Slowing growth rates are logical as countries move closer to the technological frontier. Yet the developmental regimes in Japan, Korea, and Taiwan all confronted compounding difficulties under radically altered global conditions that impeded continued regime coherence and economic momentum. The results were dramatic regime reconfiguration accompanied by drops in their rates of growth, declines in productivity per capita, drop-offs in shares of world GDP, and noteworthy reductions in the market shares within many previously dominated manufacturing sectors.

Schumpeterian "creative destruction" contends that economic dynamism requires that the new continually supplant the old. Although the specific and unusual constellations endemic to these regimes during developmentalism ultimately fractured in ways that deconstructed the developmental regimes, powerful forces also minimized comprehensive regime collapse and rapid abandonment of entrenched arrangements that had previously worked well. This mix of old and new made it difficult for each country to advance into technologically sophisticated sectors of the global economy such as artificial intelligence, Internet software, genomics, or synthetic biology.

Chapter 5 offers a second extension. The Chinese regime and its economic policy paradigm represent still another national chapter in the Asia-Pacific growth story. In the late 1970s, China broke free from the constrictive cage of Marxist-Leninist-Maoism, catalyzing four decades of rapid economic transformation. Between 1978 and 2018, China averaged 10 percent growth in GDP, in the process surpassing Japan as the world's second largest economy. It advanced its share of global GDP from 5 percent to 17 percent. By the second decade of the twenty-first century, China was the fulcrum around which East Asia's overall regional development was pivoting.

After abandoning the Maoist developmental model, the Chinese regime and its policy paradigm reflected a mix of traits found in each of the three regime types examined in part 1. For much of the period from the late 1970s until about 2008, the regime presented something of a hybrid of each of the three regime types. The Chinese regime mirrored many of the structural features integral to the rapid growth and transformation in Japan, Korea, and Taiwan, most notably strong and cohesive state institutions, the marginalization of opposition forces, targeted capital allocations, and heavy investment in the improvement of human capital. Yet, while benefiting from the generic global order and generous grants and loans from Japan and other foreign investments, the Chinese regime benefited from little of the explicit and generous external support that the United States had lavished on Japan, Korea, and Taiwan during their developmental heydays.

At the same time, beginning its trajectory in an era of deepened globalization, China shared the openness of Malaysia, Indonesia, and Thailand to infusions of foreign capital and an initial reliance on low-cost labor to assemble and package goods for foreign multinationals. Furthermore, although Chinese state institutions displayed much of the cohesion and efficiency found in the developmental regimes, and though they had localities and civil societies with more autonomy, they nonetheless exercised many of the repressive tools of social control used by the rapacious regimes.

Over four decades, a powerful party-state retained strict control over key elements of both socioeconomic forces and economic policy, and as China's economy flourished, state efficiency and a nationalist predisposition allowed the regime to steer a course away from the dependent and low-end development of the ersatz developmental regimes. Heavy government investments in human capital, mandatory partnerships between foreign investors and domestic firms, and a state-led clawing back of the advantages previously enjoyed by foreign firms allowed the regime to reclaim greater national control of key industrial sectors. In conjunction, the party-state laid plans to bolster indigenous innovation within advanced industries in a quest to dominate the world's most cutting-edge technologies. China thus appears, at present, to have a good chance of reversing some of its external dependence, and in the process, escaping the middle-income trap.

Recent developments in the Chinese regime open up the question of whether China will continue to forge its own distinct regime type or whether instead it will take on characteristics that approximated one of the region's existing ideal types and if so, which one. Two alternative possibilities for China seem most likely if the developmental regimes' experiences are considered. Is dramatically slower growth and regime reconfiguration likely to emerge as the future price for past successes? Alternatively, can China continue its economic successes and regime cohesion while adjusting in ways that avoid such slowdowns and restructuring?

The concluding chapter widens the perspective to assess the interplay between these multiple regime clusters and the broader Asia-Pacific region over time. It examines how regime combinations shaped the regional order but also how prevailing regional trends reverberated to influence different regimes. Altered global conditions favored the emergence of particular types of regimes while precluding others. Yet the chapter also analyzes how different mixes of regimes reshaped the Asia-Pacific regional order in defining ways.

To presage that chapter's general message, I argue that the regional order has gone through three discrete phases. The first was predominantly shaped and reinforced by American hegemony and Cold War bipolarity. That order contributed to the sustenance and early economic successes of the developmental regimes while also reinforcing the predatory nature of the rapacious regimes and contributing to China's economic isolation. The persistence and economic successes of the developmental regimes, however, helped to trigger the erosion of the bipolar regional order. So did the American defeat in Vietnam and China's moves away from the Soviet Union, Maoism, and toward a new economic paradigm. Meanwhile, American policymakers lost their earlier tolerance of embedded mercantilism and economic globalization triggered outgoing FDI (foreign direct investment) in ways that spurred countries such as Malaysia, Indonesia, Thailand, and China to embrace interdependent economic development.

This second regional order saw the advance of regional economic synergies as the Asia-Pacific shifted from hostile bipolarity into an order characterized by peace and prosperity. Regional economic interactions and interdependence blossomed, as did formal governmental moves to enhance regional interactions through numerous trade agreements and regional institutions. Hard security clashes diminished and cooperation on a host of nontraditional security matters advanced.

A third regional order has been taking shape roughly since the global financial crisis (2008–9). It radiates an increase in national assertiveness, a rise in territorial contestation, and an increase in geostrategic competition. How the different domestic regimes have stimulated and reacted to such changes will, of course, influence how regionally definitive such shifts will be. Structural pressures toward geopolitical competition need not swamp the powers of agency and choice available to policymakers through the region. Many regimes are now far more muscular than decades ago and regime maintenance in a host of countries favors retention of a less confrontational global and regional order. It is not clear, however, whether their efforts to balance regime maintenance and adjustment will work to quell or exacerbate rising regional tensions.

PART ONE

PART ONE

Chapter 1

Developmental Regimes

Japan, Korea, and Taiwan

The stunning economic transformations of Japan, Korea, and Taiwan constituted the first waves in the subsequent tsunami of national economic successes that swept across East Asia. Each of the three overcame daunting barriers left from World War II (and for Korea, the conflict of 1950–53) to deliver decades of sequential GDP growth rates that were roughly double that of the industrialized world. Each accumulated capital, invested heavily in domestic production facilities and national infrastructure, and created forward and backward linkages among sophisticated corporations and sectors, laying strong foundations for ongoing product innovation and industrial deepening. In the process, each also gained steadily larger shares of world exports, stronger currencies, and ballooning foreign reserves.

Increased economic sophistication brought broad-scale citizen inclusion and patterns of income distribution that, by international standards, were quite egalitarian. Of critical significance, heavy reliance on indigenous capital and national ownership ensured that the bulk of the benefits from increased productivity would redound predominantly to locals rather than escaping to foreign coffers.

This chapter argues that such economic achievements arose in tandem with a specific type of regime in Japan, Korea, and Taiwan, and a particular economic paradigm. The three national experiences, though not identical, were sufficiently analogous in a number of fundamentals to treat them as a group.[1] They provide empirical manifestations of what I label "developmental regimes."

All three had strong and cohesive state institutions; each had concentrated and dominant progrowth socioeconomic coalitions; all received extensive security and economic support from the United States and enjoyed the benefits of global financial and trade institutions. Each regime bonded around what Slater has labelled "protection pacts." Driven by a shared sense of existential threat, foreign and domestic elites joined together to advance an economic policy paradigm that I label "embedded mercantilism." Core components included industrial policy, undervalued currencies, export expansion, and rapid industrialization, all advancing behind institutional bulwarks against the perceived threats.[2]

As their national economies took flight, growth provided positive feedback that reinforced cohesion among key regime components while marginalizing potential regime opponents and alternative economic paradigms. Each regime gained greater internal cohesion, legitimacy, and institutional enmeshment. Stronger regimes, in turn, reinforced the economic paradigm, the two continuously buttressing one another in a "virtuous cycle."

Considerable analysis has stressed the centrality of state institutions, particularly the civil service, in the economic transformations of Japan, Korea, and Taiwan. Strong and coherent state institutions were undoubtedly necessary for that transformation, yet state institutional strength alone was by no means sufficient. Equally critical was the nature of two other key regime components, notably cohesive progrowth socioeconomic coalitions and consistent and powerful external backing. All three cohered to form what I categorize as "developmental regimes" that in turn steadily advanced transformative national economic paradigms. The result was radical and rapid industrial transformation.

State Institutions

Although many states might have the intention to achieve economic development, far fewer show a capacity to do so. An exchange in Shakespeare's *Henry IV* captures the distinction. Glendower, touting his alleged powers, announces, "I can call spirits from the vasty deep." The response from Hotspur punctures such arrogance, "Why, so can I, or so can any man, but will they come when you do call for them?"[3]

To forge and implement an economic policy paradigm capable of calling forth the spirits critical for development, cohesive state institutions designed for decisiveness are an invaluable asset. Unlike the more fragmented state structures found in much of Latin America, Africa, and the Middle East,[4] Japan, Korea, and Taiwan had state institutions designed for decisive action rather than for minority voice, extensive representation, and compromise. State authorities could focus with unblinking eyes on the lodestar of economic catch-up so that it became what Linda Weiss categorized as the nation's "transformative project"[5] and Bob Jessop branded its "hegemonic project."[6]

Strong and cohesive state institutions had deep historical roots in Japan, Korea, and Taiwan.[7] In the late nineteenth century, the Japanese ruling elite, anxious to escape the colonial depredations forced on most of the nonwhite world, took a constitutional leaf from Bismarck's Germany to configure governmental structures that concentrated, rather than dispersed, political power.[8] Citizen duties were extensive; their rights were few. Unsurprisingly, political parties and Parliament had to cope with elaborately constructed barriers denying them the influence many of their counterparts enjoyed in parts of Western Europe, Latin America, and the United States.

Without gainsaying the imbalance in power between colonizer and colonized, decades under Japanese imperial rule bequeathed state institutions to Korea and Taiwan that replicated those of their colonizer; trained and talented indigenous officials became the norm in all three countries.[9] The postwar governmental structures of all three continued the predisposition toward state institutional strength.

A substantial body of scholarship on Japan, Korea, and Taiwan privileges state institutions as the key to their economic success. Under the collective label of developmental states, these three each had a "pilot agency," composed of technically competent civil servants chosen through meritocratic processes who oversaw extensive mechanisms of control.[10] They used those institutional tools with cohesion, capacity, and disposition to advance a consistent agenda.[11]

Yet state bureaucrats were hardly autonomous operatives.[12] No matter their talents, they did not operate in a political vacuum; rather, they were at most valuable flywheels in a more extensive machinery of state institutions, rarely free to generate their own policy agendas. Nor were the goals they pursued self-evident.[13] Indeed, as Weber's analysis of bureaucracy makes clear, the rules by which bureaucrats operate are not self-generated but emanate from outside the bureaucrat cubicles.

At the apex of all three state systems was a more extensive and cohesive executive authority. In Japan's case, that ultimate authority controlling state institutions was the electorally dominant Liberal Democratic Party (LDP).

Japan, unlike Taiwan and Korea, began the postwar years as a constitutional democracy with a panoply of guarantees concerning citizen sovereignty, parliamentary power, and competitive elections together with press freedom and citizen rights.[14] For the first decade or so following World War II, Japanese state institutions struggled for direction amid brutal street battles and wide-ranging social and political uncertainties. A succession of coalition governments rotated into and out of Parliament and the prime minister's office, focused far more on geopolitical and security issues than on economic transformation.[15]

Finally, in 1955, several previously separate conservative parties, under strong pressure from the powerful business sector as well as the US government, combined forces to form the Liberal Democratic Party. Over the next four decades, the LDP consistently secured twice as many parliamentary seats as the second largest party. Electoral supremacy, in turn, gave the party sole control of all cabinet posts until 1993, marking Japan as one of a limited number of democracies manifesting one-party dominance.[16]

As a result, although Japanese economic bureaucrats enjoyed considerable tactical flexibility, they remained subject to strategic direction from the LDP.[17] The LDP retained that institutional superiority only by consistent victories at the ballot box. Consequently, the LDP was not free from constraints in advancing the country's policy paradigm; it also had to be an effective vote-mobilizing machine. Electoral effectiveness was essential if the LDP was to control the state apparatus for long enough periods to orchestrate a full-fledged economic transformation. Indeed, the long-ruling LDP was primarily a political machine organized to win elections and less one to govern the country. The LDP consequently off-loaded far more details of governance to the national bureaucracy than was true in the other two developmental regimes.

Neither the KMT (Kuomintang) nor the Korean military junta faced such electoral constraints. Instead, for the first decades of their economic transformations both Korea and Taiwan were under tight military control, authoritarian regulations, and extensive citizen surveillance. In Taiwan, a pervasive and powerful KMT bolstered bureaucratic actions while in Korea the personal support parties of successive autocratic presidents did the same.[18]

In Korea, state institutional cohesion became consolidated following the 1961 coup that brought Park Chung-hee and his military junta to power. For the next three decades, there was little doubt about the strength and cohesion of Korean state institutions. The military chain of command, combined with extensive constitutional powers afforded the president, ensured pointed and hierarchical cohesion across state institutions. Furthermore, the KCIA (Korean Central Intelligence Agency) and a shadow cabinet bolstered both state cohesion and citizen control.

Soon after he took power in May 1961, Park made it clear that the military would play the lead role in the regime. Only the military, he argued, had the organizational cohesion and hierarchical clarity to purge the country of what he saw as its two major problems—corruption and poverty. By arresting numerous leaders from the business community on corruption charges, Park established the unmistakable dominance of state over society, of politics over profits. Only after receiving business assurances of its willingness to cooperate with his political goals were chaebol leaders permitted to run their business operations with some measure of independence.[19] Until his assassination in 1979, Park exerted iron-fisted oversight of economic development policies, labeled "The Big Push." This combination of military and presidential power continued with only minimal challenge until the introduction of free elections in 1988.

Security concerns were hardly subservient to economic growth; however, Park and his followers concluded that national security necessitated economic transformation. Steel, shipbuilding, electronics, and infrastructure were essential for the production of weapons and the deterrence of aggressors, particularly the menacing regime to the North. The political leadership thus fused the two goals of military security and economic development, treating them not as trade-offs but as intimate partners, even though that intimacy resulted in major cuts to the military's share of the national budget.[20]

Economic bureaucrats remained subject to presidential commands. Park's inspiration was a logical outgrowth of his background: the top graduate in his class at a Japanese military academy; an officer trained at the Tokyo Military Academy; and subsequent service in Manchuria, where he participated in advancing economic development under Japanese military rule and industrial planning. In addition, Park had seen the ease with which North Korea in 1950 swept over the hapless Rhee Syngman government, as well as Rhee's reliance on a social coalition of absentee landowners and corrupt import-substituting industrialists, a point developed below.[21]

Korea's concentration of decision-making authority in hierarchical state institutions, along with the systematic suppression of opposition forces, continued into the late 1980s (and even after the military gave way to civilian rule, presidential predominance remained daunting). In Korea under Park, the president appointed roughly one-third of the Assembly members. Opposition politicians confronted legal bans on their political activity and a government-run media that impeded citizen support and funding for opposition parties. Between 1948 and the mid-1980s, one hundred or more political parties rose and fell. Most lacked money and influence, serving largely as transient entities cobbled together as the personal networks of prominent figures, rather than as cohesive, popularly anchored, and programmatic political parties.[22] Few played any meaningful part in checking state institutions, a situation that contrasted with both Japan and Taiwan.

In Taiwan following the takeover by Chiang Kai-shek's forces in 1949, state institutions centered on alignments among Chiang personally, his supportive KMT, and the military. From the time of his arrival on the island in 1949 until his death in 1975, "generalissimo" Chiang dominated the KMT, after which his son, Chiang Ching-kuo, exercised almost equal power. The civil service was talented but subordinate, particularly to the KMT. Replicating the CCP's (Chinese Communist Party) structures on the Communist mainland and continuing its own long-standing pattern, the KMT instituted parallel party and state structures to ensure the firm command of what Tun-jen Cheng identified as a "quasi-Leninist" party.[23] Despite their separate functions, the party and state marched largely in lockstep. The original KMT goal after taking control of Taiwan was the chimerical promise to reconquer the mainland. From the 1960s onward, however, economic growth gained enhanced justification as supporting, though not supplanting, retaking the mainland.[24]

KMT party components generated, or at least approved, all major policy decisions, including those integral to economic strategy. Local elections existed in Taiwan, as did national elections in Korea. Yet in both cases, authoritarian state structures prevented such elections from posing truly meaningful curbs. At the same time, elections in Taiwan provided state authorities with periodic feedback and an ability to scout for and recruit local talent into the KMT or into state institutions, thus developing a cadre of electorally savvy politicians who ultimately retained KMT goals following their respective democratizations.[25]

State institutions in Korea and Taiwan had one additional key component, namely, the professional military. The military ensured the maintenance of state authority and checked business autonomy and popular outbursts. Periods of martial law in both Taiwan and Korea enhanced state power, nascent elite cohesion, and policy coherence while suppressing potential opponents. Mandatory male conscription, strict regulation over assembly and free speech, and extensive citizen surveillance operations in both countries reinforced the power of political authorities. Even in democratic Japan, police and intelligence services carried out extensive monitoring of potential regime challengers.[26]

In all three cases, relations between top political and/or military officials and senior civil servants were hardly zero sum. More often, all allied to advance the shared hegemonic project of national economic growth. Such differences as arose were most often over tactics, instrumentalities, and degrees; rarely were they divisions over the policy paradigm itself. The KMT, the Park presidency, and the LDP, aided by talented and loyal administrative staffs, pursued consistent grand strategies. Political leaders in all three countries periodically undertook administrative reforms to enhance efficiency and cohesiveness in state institutions, largely in furtherance of economic goals.[27]

It is worth noting that not all state institutions radiated such coordinated commitment to economic development. For example, even as Korea's Park Chung-hee forged a highly efficient and technocratic set of state economic institutions, he prioritized patronage considerations in ministries dealing with public works, agriculture, and loan allocations.[28] The same was true in Japan as the LDP often used its control over top civil service appointments to ensure the steady provision of pork projects to favored constituencies and well-connected corporations, often in disregard of any potential contributions to rapid economic growth.[29]

A final note on state institutions concerns executive structures. Both Taiwan and Korea concentrated extensive authority in the office of the president. Each presidential office had sweeping authority over hierarchically structured state institutions and the policymaking process. Both regimes thus escaped the executive ambiguity that characterized the Japanese prime ministers' office during the country's developmental period. Japanese prime ministers consistently needed to balance their notional primacy against intra-LDP political machinations and the need for regular electoral validation. Japanese state institutions—clearly more cohesive than in many countries—thus still displayed less hierarchical cohesion and control than those in Korea or Taiwan.[30]

As subsequent analysis of other East Asian regimes will show, Japan, Korea, and Taiwan thus stand as striking contrasts to countries with more fragmented state institutions, often rife with ineptitude and patronage, or advancing policies antagonistic to economic transformation. In furthering their national economic policy paradigms, however, state institutions in each of the three developmental regimes benefited from the robust support of cohesive, pro-growth, socioeconomic coalitions. State institutions did not rule in pursuit of some abstract "national interest"; rather, those institutions defined the "national interest" in terms explicitly beneficial to a particular coalition of socioeconomic supporters.

Socioeconomic Forces

As competent, cohesive, and controlling as state institutions were, an exclusive focus on those institutions creates a thin politics that misses the ways state institutions in the developmental regimes depended on broader social support.[31] State institutions do, of course, determine the rules governing socioeconomic competition, and thus can bias its outcome.[32] Yet in return for critical support, state actions "reward the friendly, exclude the hostile, and disorganize the dangerous."[33] In short, the relationship between state institutions and socioeconomic forces is highly political. Which socioeconomic groups provide critical support for state institutions and the policies they advance, and what are the rewards for such support? In this regard, each of the three regimes included another key component, notably, a strong and cohesive pro-growth socioeconomic coalition.

All three of the developmental regimes included a fused collaboration between state institutions and socioeconomic forces. The latter added their own commitment and resources to the common economic project. The most central socioeconomic element in all three instances was big business with ancillary but essential contributions coming from agriculture and smaller businesses. The cumulative melding of these socioeconomic forces bolstered the regime and facilitated the advance of their jointly favored economic paradigm. Decades of joint political-socioeconomic collaboration allowed that alliance to surf successfully atop the waves of day-to-day political fluctuations and short-term setbacks.

Important to the dominance of that particular socioeconomic coalition in Japan, Korea, and Taiwan was the fortuitous absence of several lines of cleavage so often divisive in other countries, namely, high levels of ethnic, religious, linguistic, or racial cleavages. Such divisions militate against the psychological and emotional preconditions conducive to what Benedict Anderson called the "imagined community" that undergirds the modern nation-state.[34] Japan, South Korea, and Taiwan benefitted instead from rarely questioned national identities.[35]

Beyond the fact that both Korea and Taiwan existed as the partial residues of civil wars that left the original countries divided, territorial boundaries raised few driving questions within any of the three. In Japan and Korea, there was broad agreement on the bonds of nationhood. Taiwan, in partial contrast, confronted a cleavage between the indigenous population and the superimposed rulers from the mainland who began their rule lacking an endogenous socioeconomic power base and hence relied on greater levels of suppression of a distinctive ethnic minority.[36]

Initially, the KMT allowed the 15 percent of the population identified as "mainlanders" to ride roughshod over the fortunes of the remaining 85 percent identified as "Taiwanese."[37] Not surprisingly, top down state-KMT control confronted a restive civil society, a division that played out brutally in the February 28,

1947, incident when local Taiwanese rose up against mainlander controls.[38] The government responded with an indiscriminate killing of thousands of locals, thereby entrenching the deep fissure between locals and mainlanders that continues to the present. A subsequent KMT policy of Taiwanization softened the initial fracture, but this division continued to distinguish Taiwan in one important respect from the ethnically less fissiparous Japan or Korea. Nonetheless, social cleavages were sufficiently fuzzy or manageable in all three countries to minimize the ascriptive bases of socioeconomic alignments that so often prevail elsewhere.

Of special significance to socioeconomic relations in all three regimes was the early elimination of previously powerful large landowners. As noted in the introduction, landowning classes have historically resisted rapid industrialization as a threat to their profits and political influence. Industrial development transforms their lands into prime targets for taxes or expropriation; it also beckons local workers to flee their rural hustings for better-paying jobs in urban factories. In the process, previously responsive political powers shift their sensitive ears and their authority to the petitions of industrialists and entrepreneurs.

In the aftermath of World War II, major land reforms in all three countries eliminated such wealthy landowners as a cohesive and potentially anti-industrializing force. Prewar Japan had undergone some minor land reform measures; however, US Occupation authorities imposed a sweeping program that set strict limits on the size of all holdings. American actions decimated rich landowners as a socioeconomic force, thereby eliminating a potentially major opponent of industrial advances. At the same time, with agriculture still a powerful contributor to GDP, and farming families quite numerous, land reform simultaneously created what became an influential agricultural interest group composed of thousands of small holding farmers, knitted together through a powerful network of agricultural cooperatives.[39] Taking advantage of the green revolution and new technologies to enhance agricultural production, these small holders gained economic well-being for themselves while enabling the government to extract agricultural surpluses for industrial development.

Organized into cooperative structures and benefiting from an extensive government program of agricultural protection and price supports, small farmers became politically loyal supporters of the ruling LDP. Though costly in absolute terms, support for small-scale farmers became progressively less budgetarily draining since tax revenues from industrial transformation expanded and the number of farming families declined. Politically, the replacement of prewar absentee landowners with an owner-cultivator class was of great benefit to the LDP and the regime more broadly in that the cooperatives organizing small farmers were electorally invaluable in keeping the LDP in charge of state institutions.

In Taiwan, when the invading Nationalists took control, one-third of the island's GDP came from agriculture dominated by a numerically small but powerful proprietor class. The KMT had resisted land reform within mainland areas under its control due to the entrenched powers of regional warlords and the party's own land-holding members; however, such resistance had facilitated the Communist mobilization of impoverished peasants in the civil war. The lesson was not lost on the Nationalists when they fled to Taiwan. There they had few political constraints against extensive land reform since almost none of the incoming KMT members owned land on Taiwan, while most of the resident large landowners carried the stain of prewar collaboration with Japanese occupiers. Equally motiving was the successful, if draconian, land reform carried out across the straits.

In consequence, soon after fleeing the mainland, the KMT undertook an extensive rural reform program that freed the party from any incentive to protect landowners while simultaneously eviscerating a potential opponent to their takeover. Agricultural resources proved essential to the funding of industrialization. In addition, land reform and political inclusion generated valuable support among the farming population while reducing the likelihood of any peasant uprising against the KMT arrivistes.

Approximately one-quarter of Taiwan's territory underwent land reform with redistributed land going principally to entrepreneurial peasants.[40] The government then organized such peasants into some 340 KMT-controlled farmers associations that, like the cooperative in Japan, delivered a bevy of services from credit to technology to marketing and wove the small-holding farmers into an organization providing regime support.[41]

In South Korea, like Taiwan, about 70 per cent of all farmers were tenants in 1945. Absentee owners made up a small but wealthy and influential aristocracy that had great influence over early postwar governments.[42] As in Taiwan, that landed aristocracy had a long history of collaboration with, and profitability from, the Japanese occupation that left them, as it did their Taiwanese counterparts, with tarnished credentials as nationalists. Furthermore, just as Taiwan's political leaders saw its mainland counterparts advancing land redistribution, so South Korean leaders needed to look only across the 38th parallel for similar motivation.

Beginning in 1946–48, American authorities began pressing Korean land reform as a preemptive anti-Communist measure. In 1950, the government undertook policies designed to placate peasant restiveness during a period marked by intense ideological contestation and simmering regional conflicts.[43] Land controlled by owner-operators increased from 36 percent to 73 percent.[44]

Politically, such land reforms not only removed a potential roadblock to industrialization but also eliminated a major source of peasant grievance and incentivized newly enriched peasants to cooperate with conservative political forces. In these respects, all three regimes navigated socioeconomic conditions quite distinct from those prevailing in much of Latin America, the Philippines, South Asia, or Africa.[45]

In addition to eliminating a comprador class and including small farmers as regime supporters, the developmental regimes also benefited from a

reduced capability for collective action by popular sectors, most notably organized labor. All three countries faced formidable labor demands in the
penurious aftermath of World War II. Yet before labor gained much traction, Taiwan, South Korea, and Japan used all the tools available to state institutions, in conjunction with actions by business owners in their own spheres
of control, to suppress organized labor and other mass movements. The fears
of communism offered ideological legitimation to conservative politico-
economic concords that further restricted leftist and labor groups.[46]

State repression combined with entrepreneurial paternalism had kept Japanese labor organization limited through the prewar period.[47] The American
Occupation initially facilitated unionization, and union participation rates
rocketed to 56 percent in 1949. The outbreak of the Cold War and shifts in
US domestic politics, however, triggered a reverse course that included crackdowns on the nascent labor movement. The Americans banned numerous
strikes, purged labor leaders, and eliminated collective bargaining by public
sector workers. Once sovereignty returned, a sequence of Japanese governments followed suit, systematically breaking the most radical of the country's
unions. Unionization rates plunged into the 30 percent range from the 1950s
through the 1970s, after which they dropped steadily.

Within Japan's larger firms, the peculiarities of enterprise unions facilitated
a fusion of worker interests more with their employer than with workers nationwide. Further reducing its collective power, organized labor divided its loyalties
between two or three left-of-center parties, none of which ever gained more
than one-third of the seats in Parliament. Until 1993 (with the exception of a
six-month interregnum in 1947–48, when all government policies were subject
to veto by the American Occupation), Japan stood alone among the industrialized democracies in never having had a labor-backed government.

If labor was politically weak in Japan, it was even less potent as a national
force in Korea or Taiwan. Until as late as the early 1990s, state laws in both
countries limited the benefits enjoyed by workers even as some of the larger
SOEs (state-owned enterprises) and private firms in Taiwan began to offer benefits approaching those of their Japanese counterparts. Union membership
stood at approximately 10 percent of the workforce in Korea; there were no
minimum-wage standards, and Korean law banned strikes and closed shops.
The labor movement was consistently subject to a range of state controls, such
as limits on organization and strike activity, informal penetration, and government participation in the settlement of disputes. Those repressions increased under the government of Chun Doo-hwan in 1980.[48] Even political
liberalization following 1987 did not prevent massive police interventions from
breaking up strikes in the 1990s or the passage of new antilabor laws in 1996.
Not until the election of Kim Dae-jung in 1997 did Korean labor gain an official presidential ally.

In Taiwan, the incoming nationalist government brought with it the repressive labor legislation enacted on the mainland.[49] As in Korea until 1987, strikes

and collective bargaining were illegal, and unions remained subject to strong KMT controls, including veto power over leadership selection and all union activities.[50] Like Japan, some softening of oppressive conditions occurred via firm-level paternalism, but this was a long way from collective political influence.

Both Taiwan and Korea introduced state-led corporatist arrangements to strengthen political control over workers along with small businesses. Adopting many of the prewar Japanese patterns of state-led corporatist organization, the KMT in Taiwan wove farmers, labor organizations, religious bodies, small businesses, professional associations, and the like into hierarchical, noncompetitive, and exclusive networks subject to direct KMT control. These corporatist bodies received fixed quotas of seats in the National Assembly and the Legislative Yuan, both toothless bodies that existed mostly to legitimate the regime.[51] Taiwan proved a classic case of state-led economic corporatism.[52]

Similarly, in 1963, Korea introduced legislation requiring all unions to acquire legal recognition by the government and stipulating that they merge under a single union for each industrial sector, with state institutions given the power to intervene in their operations. In both countries, these corporatist union federations remained ineffectually quiescent and inactive.[53] Meanwhile, independent NGOs and influential citizens' groups remained limited in number and constricted in influence.

In contrast to sectors excluded from the developmental regimes, all wove in large domestic businesses and their organizations. Jointly fearful of existential threats in the form of military challenges on the one hand and labor and populist demands on the other, state institutions and powerful business groups cooperated on the hegemonic project of "catch-up economic transformation" as the joint objective motivating cooperation and shared commitment. State institutions set the rules structuring economic conditions and business incentives. In turn, key business groups and corporations provided corporate information essential to efficient state functioning. To prevent state institutions from garnering their assets, holders of capital and productive capacity had incentives to curry political favor. As David Kang argued for Korea, relatively tightly organized powerful firms and industrial groups nurtured their political connections as an important component of business strategy. At the same time, state actors labored to avoid capture by vested business interests.[54]

The boundaries between business and politics in all three regimes were consequently porous. Extensive networks of advisory committees, joint meetings, reciprocal favors, and easy access to one another's top power holders brought senior business leaders and government representatives into sustained and reciprocally influential contact. South Korea and Taiwan long relied on the peak associations of business—the Federation of Korean Industries (FKI) and the Chinese National Federation of Industries (CNFI). In Japan, the analogues were Keidanren and the Keizai Dôyûkai. In all three regimes, a latticework of informal channels of mutual access kept both political power holders and corporate power holders operating in harness to one another.[55] The networks for back-and-forth communication were many and well utilized, and often sector specific.[56] Money and favors flowed back and forth as the internal coherence and shared agenda of the state and the business sector prevented either from dictating events.

Richard Samuels captures the nature of the state–business relationship, labeling it one of "reciprocal consent."[57] In separate studies, Michael Young and Frank Upham emphasize the ongoing information exchanges between business and government as vital to their cooperation and to national economic success.[58] Meredith Jung-en Woo, examining the relationship between Korean state institutions under Park and the large business conglomerates (chaebol) underscores a similar interdependence.[59] In Taiwan, the KMT dominated the heights of the industrial economy, but in the 1960s took a major political risk and "created a business climate to stimulate private local and foreign investments" in an effort to integrate private sector businesses into a KMT-business alliance that would undergird economic development.[60]

The developmental regimes thus rested, not on blind dirigiste state power, but on a synergistic connection between state institutions and a mostly market system, the outputs of each becoming inputs for the other.[61] The collaboration mirrored what Migdal underscores as the mutual dependence of the "state in society," Linda Weiss views as "governed interdependence," Underhill and Zhang identify as a "state-market condominium,"[62] and Wade characterizes as state institutions that "govern the market."[63] During periods of high-speed national growth, all three of the developmental regimes valorized the broad interests of big domestic capital as congruent with long-term national interest. State and business entities pulled oars on opposite sides of the economic vessel, powering it forward stroke for stroke.

As state institutions and big businesses in all three countries carried out a combination of strategic repression and systematic exclusion of national organizations of labor and other popular sectors, a substantial openness to individual mobility counterbalanced collective restrictions. Thus, significant investments in human capital, job training, broad-scale public education, virtually universal male employment, relatively low levels of income inequality, and steady advances in GDP opened up individual opportunities that mitigated traditional class boundaries.[64] Vast numbers of citizens became "partners in growth" by virtue of such individual mobility.[65] Moreover, the constant enhancement of human skills provided the regimes with increasingly well-trained working populations to meet the demands of ever more sophisticated production.

In combination, state institutions and the progrowth coalition in the developmental regimes benefited from a global liberal trading order that welcomed their exports and a bipolar system that spurned communism and its economic ideology. Consequently, the combined forces also found affinity with the Cold War policies and economic predispositions of the United States. In return, the United States reciprocated by providing enormous external support to keep state institutions and their supporting socioeconomic coalitions together and favorable to the United States. Such US assistance provided the third leg of the developmental regimes' tripod.

External Forces

A peculiar, and largely advantageous, combination of external conditions was integral to the developmental regimes of Japan, Korea, and Taiwan, and to their economic transformations. Most critical was the unstinting decades-long support provided by the Asia-Pacific's security and economic hegemon, the United States, which proved to be an essential third component of the developmental regimes.

Initial US strategy for the post–World War II order presumed great power cooperation with its other victorious allies—Britain, France, the USSR, and China. The outbreak of the Cold War and the Communist victory in China's civil war vaporized that vision and created a dynamic in which, as John Ikenberry put it, "America needed allies and allies needed America."[66] Following the logic advanced by George Kennan, the US National Security Council (NSC) responded in April 1950 with NSC-68,[67] the Truman Doctrine, and a grand strategy of Communist containment and the development of an alliance structure. The United States scrambled for reliable East Asian partners.[68]

The United States sought to ensure militarily secure and economically robust allies. What followed was the mobilization, empowerment, and defense of anti-Communist forces in Japan, Korea, and Taiwan. That Japan and Korea were under direct US military occupation facilitated this effort, and when the KMT retreated from the mainland to Taiwan, American naval protection rescued the Chiang forces from complete annihilation.

What followed was bountiful American support for anti-Communist political and socioeconomic forces and economic policies favoring stabilization and growth. Japan, Korea, and Taiwan became indispensable links in America's hub and spoke alliance structure in East Asia. US military forces occupied an extensive network of bases in all three countries, allowing all three to off-load portions of their defense costs and to redirect such monies to other policies, including economic development. Indeed, Patrick and Rosovsky estimate that Japan's economy would have been 30 percent smaller by 1976 had it shouldered its own defense expenses.[69]

The ostensible existential threats posed by neighboring Communist regimes and their domestic sympathizers magnified the attractiveness of strong state institutions and socioeconomic forces promising to propel economic growth. All three regimes advanced the common message that national security demanded unquestioned anti-Communism, cohesive regime support, American foreign policies, and the promises of rapid economic transformation.[70] Domestic proclivities dovetailed with the United States' grand strategy of treating security and economics as "two halves of the same walnut."[71] Japan, Korea, and

Taiwan became cornerstones in the American defense architecture while their eventual economic successes validated the America-led liberal global order.[72]

Economic aid, both overt and covert, military and civilian, was an essential American regime contribution.[73] Between 1948 and the early 1970s, Korea received some $13 billion in American assistance and Taiwan received about $5.6 billion ($600 per capita in Korea], $425 per capita in Taiwan).[74]

Meanwhile, more than two-thirds of Japan's imports in 1947 were dependent on US aid. Subsequently, the United States' wars in Korea and Vietnam generated military procurements that provided Japan, in particular, with a further economic boost; indeed, those two wars proved key catalysts to its subsequent and uninterrupted growth.[75]

To appreciate the dimensions of American infusions, comparative figures are helpful. The ROK's (Republic of Korea's) total of nearly $6 billion in US economic grants and loans between 1946 and 1978 compares to a total for all of Africa of $6.89 billion and for all of Latin America of $14.8 billion; only India, with a population seventeen times that of South Korea, received more ($9.6 billion). US military deliveries to Taiwan and the ROK in 1955–78 (i.e., excluding the Korean War) totaled $9.05 billion. All of Latin America and all of Africa received $3.2 billion; only Iran got more, and most of that came after 1972 (the figure is $10.01 billion). Soviet economic aid to all less developed countries in the years 1954–78 was $7.6 billion, that is, little more than American aid to the ROK alone. Total aid for developing countries from all socialist countries during the same period was $13.4 billion, about 25 percent greater than the total for Taiwan and the ROK. Soviet military deliveries to developing countries totaled $25.3 billion, about 280 percent of the total for Taiwan and the ROK alone.[76] Furthermore, during the war in Vietnam, Korean provision of troops redounded to the benefit of Korean exporters of cement, fertilizer, petroleum products, textiles, shoes, and plywood, earning over $2 billion as a result and representing about 19 percent of the country's total foreign exchange earnings during the period.[77] Beyond such direct American assistance, the US Export-Import Bank along with the World Bank provided liberal low interest rate loans further assisting growth.

Until the late 1970s or early 1980s, and in some respects with continuing remnants long after, the anti-Communist mantra proved sufficiently sweeping to smother organized labor and the political Left domestically, in many instances including democratic activists and independent NGOs (nongovernmental organization). Castigating opponents as existential threats to national security became second nature among political and economic elites. As Meredith Woo-Cumings deftly phrased it, the genius of the conservative state–societal alliance at the heart of the developmental regimes lay in "harnessing the very real fears of war and instability toward a remarkable developmental energy, which in turn could become a binding agent for growth."[78] Domestic ideological biases in Taiwan and Korea gained added force from the undeniable immediacy of the military threats each faced from the Communist-led regimes controlling their "other halves," the PRC and the DPRK. For Japan, anti-Communism dovetailed with the country's long-standing geostrategic competition with the USSR/Russia.

Military and economic rationales reinforced one another within all three of America's allies. For example, Taiwan's KMT-state used the nearly perpetual state of national emergency from 1949 onward to justify a variety of luxury and special war taxes that kept the price of imported goods high.[79] Korean government–business cooperation used anti-Communism as the principal justification for heavy national industrialization projects in steel, chemicals, metal, machine building, plastics, shipbuilding, and electronics. Indeed, in 1972 Park Chung-hee declared, "steel equals national power."[80] Combining national security with industrial deepening generated increasingly sophisticated exports.[81] Japan adapted much of the transferred American military technology to commercial use. The braking system on Japan's super express trains came from the F-104 fighter jet. Fire truck hoses used the hydraulic technology of the F-86F. Japan Aviation Electronics Industry Ltd. adapted a gyroscope to bowling alley equipment, horse racing starting gates, and seismographs, while Nissan Motors used a version of the F-86F engine for shock resistance testing in autos and resistance measurement for skyscrapers.[82]

Equally significant, Japan, Korea, and Taiwan confronted relentless US pressure to shun economic transactions with Communist regimes, most critically to avoid trade or investments with the PRC. Such economic isolation from erstwhile enemies was integral to the broader US goal of containing communism not just through military force but also economically and ideologically. The United States had a strong stake in continued generous economic, political, and diplomatic support for its "democratic capitalist" allies; their economic success would project them as conspicuous non-Western economic successes, countering the appeals of communism across much of the developing world.

Had the United States prioritized its domestic and foreign policies differently, the success of the economic paradigms of Japan, Korea, and Taiwan would have been inconceivable.[83] Certainly, Taiwan's KMT benefited from the unflagging support of the US Seventh Fleet combined with help in avoiding capital flight. Similarly, as Carter Eckart phrased it, "Korea's nascent capitalist class, tainted by colonial collaboration, would in all likelihood have been severely purged or swept away in the politics of liberation, and the capitalist system itself would, at the very least, have been greatly modified."[84]

American support for Korea and Taiwan eventually gained supplementary injections from Japan as the latter achieved its own economic vitality.[85] The 1965 Treaty on Basic Relations between Japan and the ROK infused the latter with $800 million for economic cooperation that unleashed a wave of technical assistance, investment, and trade. Japan also provided critical dollops of ODA (official development assistance) to Taiwan, and for years served as Taiwan's second largest trading partner and the main source of its foreign capital and technology. Japan also provided critical injections of heavy industry as it off-loaded its outdated equipment to its two neighbors during their industrial start-up phase.[86]

One more major American contribution was crucial to the developmental regimes. Japanese, Korean, and Taiwanese export success depended heavily on the GATT (General Agreement on Tariffs and Trade) system of tariff reductions generally and the openness of the US market more specifically. During the period when the developmental regime was most dominant, Japan sent 30 to 35 percent of its exports to the United States. Its second largest export market rarely took more than 5 to 6 percent of its exports. In turn, Korea and Taiwan were even more dependent on the American market that took in 38 to 45 percent of both countries' exports with Japan typically taking an additional 12 to 20 percent.[87]

American goals remained consistent into at least the 1980s. Nor was that support unidirectional. As economic growth advanced within the developmental regimes, each created its own market for US intermediate goods, provided cheaper products for American consumers, and enhanced the global order fostered by, and favoring, the United States.[88] The early regional appeals of communism and anticapitalism dimmed as well. In short, the United States was an integral contributor to, and beneficiary of, the three developmental regimes.

Economic Policy Paradigm

The developmental regimes underwent phenomenal economic transformations. Leaps in GDP were merely the headline beneath which unfolded three to four decades of structural transformations that enhanced their manufacturing sophistication and deepened their capacity for indigenous adaptation and innovation. Furthermore, continual improvements in human skills and organizational sophistication facilitated ongoing expansion into more knowledge-based sectors.[89]

In their respective quests for national economic catch-up, each of the three developmental regimes created a nexus of reinforcing policies that elsewhere I have labeled embedded mercantilism. The term emphasizes both the domestic economic focus and the reinforcing state institutional structures that bolstered it.

Embedded mercantilism rested on four pillars. First. industrial policies restructured and upgraded specific firms and selected sectors deemed vital for long-term national growth. Second, upgrading advanced through the mobilization of vast amounts of closely targeted capital. Third, firms in key industries received domestic market protection. Fourth, the products of restructured firms competed successfully in overseas markets from which they generated foreign reserves. All four in combination were vital to the economic paradigm allowing each country to scale the technological ladder.

Embedded mercantilism defied neoliberal economic doctrines encouraging countries to develop by building on their comparative global advantage. Comparative advantage presumes that any region or country has discrete natural endowments making it logical to produce certain goods rather than others. Foreign imports allow the easy acquisition of goods in which it has less advantage. If large numbers of economies operate through a system of unencumbered free trade, all will benefit, given the diversity of the commodities each produces.[90] National efforts to resist will result in an inefficient use of scarce capital and prove counterproductive. Implicit in this logic is the assumption that late developing countries should be content with, and make the most of, their existing assets. Most frequently, these are land and labor, thus propelling them into agriculture and light industry.

Political and economic elites in Japan, Taiwan, and Korea initially accepted that logic, opting for periods of import substitution industrialization (ISI) protected behind high tariff walls designed to afford infant industries sufficient time and domestic profitability to modernize, expand the scale of their production, and gain valuable experience inside protected domestic economic greenhouses. Yet firms benefiting under ISI tend to be oligopolies characterized by excess capacity, inefficiency, high mark-up, and low-quality output.[91] Consequently, most resist foreign challenges to their profitable positions, instead demanding that state institutions provide them "just a bit more time" behind walls of state protection. Too often, graduation to globally competitive production remains perpetually "just around the corner."

The path of slow and gradual, albeit "low-risk," advances under ISI was soon rejected by all three developmental regimes as likely to confine their respective countries to permanently inferior global positions within sophisticated, capital-intensive, and high payoff industries, such as steel, shipbuilding, electronics, banking, and the like. State policymakers and corporate leaders in all three regimes saw little benefit in contributing to global economic efficiency at the expense of advancing their own national economies. Thus, after dabbling for periods in ISI (Korea until 1964; Taiwan until 1960), all three opted for policies aimed at creating competitive advantage rather than accepting the limitations of comparative advantage.

Gaining competitive advantage necessitated a focus on generating long-term dynamic efficiency rather than static efficiency. This meant directing scarce capital resources to industries promising multiple forward and backward linkages that would trigger ongoing technological improvements, long-term advances, higher productivity per capita, and sustainable capital returns. It also meant boosting global market shares for domestic industries while rejecting most foreign entry into home markets. Foreign competition in domestic markets was seen less a spur to the efficiency of indigenous firms and more an impediment to enhanced global competitiveness by local corporations. The benefits of competition could advance instead by restricting corporate rivalry to oligopolistic competition among domestic giants.[92] All three regimes thus permitted market coordination among domestic firms to reduce transaction costs, provide some degree of competitive market incentives, and ensure long-term economic transformation.[93]

The unwavering goal was advancing domestically owned and domestically operated industries in increasingly knowledge-based and skill-intensive industries. As such, profits and market shares for domestic firms took priority over lower prices and expanded choice for domestic consumers. Ultimately, improvements in citizen well-being might follow, but only as a second order consequence of rapid growth. Protecting domestic markets was key.

A series of multiyear economic plans laid out frameworks for transformations from agriculture, light industry, and labor-intensive industries into more sophisticated industrial exporters at the intersection of upstream and down-stream connections that would be able to gain enhanced global market shares. Central to that transition was access to critical technologies and processes in such sectors as synthetic fibers, electronics, petrochemicals, earth-moving equipment, and steel furnaces. An amalgam of licensing, buying, borrowing, forced joint ventures, reverse engineering, and intellectual property theft provided the desired infusions. In addition, state institutions devoted extensive public resources to research and development in targeted sectors. In Taiwan, national research centers, strategic hubs, and technology parks spawned extensive, non-firm-specific research, development, and cross-fertilization.[94] A typical requirement was that several domestic firms share acquired technologies to foster national advances while still ensuring a measure of intrafirm competition.

Critical to such industrial restructuring was a second component, namely, the mobilization and selective allocation of vast amounts of indigenously controlled capital. That hinged on intimate ties among state institutions, finance, and business. Finance was the coupling hinge binding the state to industrialists; finance represented the nerves of the state.[95] Bank lending rather than equity markets provided the primary source of capital for business borrowers. Such lending flowed in accord with direction from state institutions. Such directed capital went into the beckoning hands of companies anxious to acquire the financing needed to expand production, gobble up market shares, and work with the state to advance development.[96]

The particular techniques used to generate the needed capital differed among the three regimes. In Japan, the majority of banks were private with long-standing and intimate relations to one or another of the country's large industrial groups; however, the keystone of the entire financial system, the Bank of Japan, remained under direct control of the Ministry of Finance. In addition, the national postal system recycled vast sums of citizen savings into a second budget that channeled funds into politically privileged infrastructure and public works projects.[97] Available domestic capital allowed the state to limit borrowing from abroad that might compromise domestic retention of corporate profits.

In Taiwan, the ruling KMT had multiple financial anxieties, most of them stemming from attendant political risks, including the dangers of inflation, foreign dominance of capital and monetary markets, and countervailing business pressures, any of which might limit KMT authority. Fearful that any over-concentration of capital in the hands of indigenous forces could lead to state capture by regime opponents, the KMT limited the amounts of capital controlled by local Taiwanese bankers in favor of ex-mainlander dominance. Finance and industry remained in separate spheres, further constricting corporate muscularity. In addition, the state monopolized the banking sector through the institutions it brought from the mainland and the majority shares confiscated from Japanese partners in private local banks. Bankers in Taiwan were thus state employees ensuring that financial actions adhered closely to state policies.[98] At the same time, high domestic interest rates, designed to check inflation, stimulated high personal savings that in turn afforded the government substantial available capital. As in Japan, foreign borrowing remained minimal.

Minimal social safety nets in all three regimes led to domestic savings rates being uniformly high and thus providing vital sources of capital in all three regimes. In Taiwan, these increased from about 5 percent in the 1950s to over 30 percent in the late 1970s, one of the highest in the world. Japan at 25 percent and Korea at 17.5 percent were not far behind.[99] Such penury contrasted with gross domestic savings below 10 percent in South Asia and Sub-Saharan Africa.[100]

Corporate access to capital in Taiwan was contingent on exporting the resultant products. Large exporters gained substantial concessionary loans through the bigger banks, but small- and medium-sized firms, in contrast, could rarely borrow more than trifling sums requiring them to turn to several banks at once or to family and friends, thus constraining smaller domestic firm size. The result was a much lower debt–equity ratio in Taiwan than in Korea and small and equity-based enterprises were more significant than in Japan or Korea. Yet Taiwan still had forty or so extremely large conglomerates, either state-owned or KMT-controlled, and a "tripartite economy of upstream state- and party-owned enterprises, midstream family-owned diversified business groups, and downstream private small- and medium-sized firms."[101]

In all three cases, however, state institutions or their loyal surrogates exerted considerable influence over the taps through which scarce capital needed to flow, ensuring that targeted industries would acquire essential resources at low cost, ideally generating exportable products. State capital investments additionally acquired the aura of an official imprimatur of promised success for particular firms or sectors that often spurred further private investment.

In both Japan and Korea, the major beneficiaries of industrial policy and capital allocation were the large conglomerates, Japanese keiretsu and Korean chaebol. The huge Japanese groups borrowed heavily, rolling over loans systematically. In Korea, no comparable banks provided such a steady injection of funds, leaving the Korean chaebol and their component companies more dependent on overseas borrowing and more highly leveraged by debt.[102] Yet as in Japan, Korean state institutional oversight was integral in channeling the incoming monies to governmentally favored sectors.[103] Japanese companies were also debt driven in the 1960s and 1970s, leaving them vulnerable to manipulation by financial officials. By the 1980s, however, Japanese companies, then largely profitable, began to self-fund through retained earnings and equity financing, giving them far more autonomy from state and bank controls.

The third key element in the mix of embedded mercantilism was protection of domestic markets, particularly in advanced manufacturing. In much of Europe and Latin America during the early years after World War II, US multinationals invested heavily in key sectors and capital markets were substantially internationalized. In contrast, Japan, Korea, and Taiwan retained far greater national control over incoming and domestic investment capital. Since the nineteenth century, Japan had long eschewed foreign investment and foreign borrowing; it hardly threw out the welcome mat in the postwar years.[104] Sharing a similar skepticism about foreign firms, Korean state policymakers and corporate elites restricted such entry, thus creating safe spaces for the domestic expansion of the chaebol.

At least until the Cold War began winding down, US strategic and economic interests led to tolerance of such domestic favoritism by its East Asian allies. Transnational corporations entered Korea and Taiwan only in the mid-1960s, by which time worldwide norms governing relations between less developed countries and those transnationals were quite different from what they had been when US firms entered Latin America.[105] As a result, Korea and Taiwan avoided many of the most baleful effects associated with transnational corporations.

In the Japanese case, domestic protection took multiple forms. Like the currencies in Taiwan and Korea, the yen–dollar exchange rate created an undervalued and export-enhancing yen, initially at the rate of ¥360 to the dollar. The Foreign Exchange and Control Law of 1949 provided the legal basis for keeping out foreign companies if they wished to repatriate profits in dollars (as most did). The law also allowed the Japanese government to reward or punish domestically based exporters by granting permission to access foreign currencies. When GATT-driven liberalization posed a challenge in the mid-1960s, Japanese companies received permission from state institutions to circumvent antimonopoly regulations and to engage in extensive cross holding of one another's stocks as a way to prevent hostile foreign buyouts. Like many other policy components, this one required close coordination between state institutions and segments of the business community, reinforcing their interdependence.[106]

Meanwhile, in contrast to the high interest rates paid in Taiwan, insulation of Japan's capital markets kept interest rates low for savers who thus underwrote the exceptionally low borrowing rates for favored users of capital. Within this context, the Bank of Japan systematically offered over-loans and window guidance aimed at encouraging industrial expansion and exports.[107]

Security dependence on the United States gave firms in all three countries access to loan capital on favorable terms; to a lesser extent, Korea and Taiwan gained similar access to Japanese capital markets.[108] In Korea, the Economic Planning Board (EPB) controlled access to and usage of these foreign funds. The EPB also had veto power over all proposals for foreign direct investment and technology transfer agreements, which was used initially to protect infant industries and later to fund heavy and chemical industries, all the while restricting Korean citizens from purchasing foreign consumer goods.

In Taiwan, the KMT initially owned many of the most prominent firms, but responding to demands accompanying incoming US aid packages, large-scale divestment took place in the 1950s. Always more liberal than Japan or South Korea, Taiwan became an early advocate of the export-free zone, setting up East Asia's first such configuration at Kaohsiung in 1965. Such parks allowed select foreign firms to use Taiwan's low-cost labor for assembly and packaging their products but only for subsequent export; foreign firms were restricted from selling in Taiwan. Taiwan also had local content requirements for a limited range of goods that enabled it to make successful demands for local sourcing.[109]

Taiwan was thus more "semi-international" than were its two counterparts, particularly regarding information technologies where Taiwan created internationally competitive local firms though alliances with technology-rich multinationals.[110] Such alliances generated local jobs and transferred midlevel skills that ultimately allowed many Taiwanese entrepreneurs to develop their own firms. Taiwan's Investment Commission controlled joint ventures and, like Japan's MITI (Ministry of International Trade and Industry) during much of the 1950s and 1960s, often put a heavy state thumb on the economic scales to favor national businesses.[111]

State control over foreign direct investment by South Korea and Taiwan complemented diplomacy. For Taiwan in particular, the threat of international isolation became more acute after most countries transferred their diplomatic recognition to the PRC. Yet by opening up various investment opportunities to select multinational companies from major North American and European corporations, the Taiwanese government created economic hostages that provided the otherwise isolated government with valuable foreign allies. South Korea followed much the same strategy after President Carter in 1977 raised the specter of withdrawing US troops from the peninsula.

Boosting exports, the fourth component of developmental regime strategy, centered on incentivizing domestic producers to create products that would appeal beyond the tastes of domestic buyers and find favor in the discriminating global marketplace. Engagement with global trade was bifurcated, however. While all three restricted imports that might compete with domestic products, their firms took advantage of reduced global tariffs resulting from GATT negotiations to sell domestically manufactured goods abroad. In the mid-1970s, 95 percent of Japan's exports were manufactured goods, compared with only 31 percent of its imports. In contrast, manufacturing made up 50 to 68 percent of other industrialized economies' imports.[112]

Encouragement of exports led the three regimes to pursue a deliberate strategy of what Alice Amsden famously called "getting the prices wrong." Domestic consumers paid higher prices than might have been the result of open markets, thus creating profitable home market havens for domestic corporations that further enhanced their competitiveness abroad.[113] Common to all three regimes was a sequence in which firms developed products first for the protected domestic market and sold them indigenously at relatively high prices, and only after products were relatively bug free would they export, often at lower prices, to the larger world. Japanese companies benefited further by the large size of the domestic market. Taiwan and Korea protected their domestic markets, but since their home markets were smaller, they had even stronger incentives to advance their exports.

Exporters, however, faced pressures from both domestic and overseas competitors. Garnering larger global market shares demanded that exporting corporations continue to drive costs down and quality up. In this, many proved greatly successful. Thus, whereas exports accounted for only 20 percent of Japanese car production in 1970, by 1980 that figure was 54 percent, with half of those export sales going to North America.[114]

By the early 1990s, Japan accounted for 14 percent of the world's manufactured exports, while Taiwan and Korea together accounted for another 8 percent. Mexico, by way of contrast, accounted for only 0.4 percent. Taiwan and Korea, along with Hong Kong, accounted for more manufactured exports than did all of Latin America combined.[115] Export-oriented development became so linked in the public mind with the hypergrowth of Japan, Korea, and Taiwan that it acquired the aura of a new development orthodoxy.[116]

An important political and economic offset to the anticonsumerist biases built into macroeconomic policies was the consistent state and corporate emphasis on improving human skill levels. Skilled workers were essential for continued advances into higher-quality and more knowledge-intensive industries. Universal public education, along with widespread skills training within corporations, created increasingly sophisticated workforces. As human skills improved, industry benefited, but so did the assets and employment opportunities of individuals, thereby generating higher levels of socioeconomic well-being and, over time, substantial middle classes.

The resultant low levels of income inequality distinguished Japan, Taiwan, and Korea from most other countries at similar stages of economic development, as well as most industrialized economies. It put them on a par with the social democratic regimes of Scandinavia.[117] All exemplified conservative-led growth with equity, a critical by-product of which was the gradual reduction in the incentives for radical populism and class-driven opposition to the national economic policy paradigm. Notably, all three regimes achieved high levels of per capita income and low levels of inequality largely by avoiding pressures to become social welfare states.[118] This latter was largely the consequence of avoiding the political inclusion of organized labor in one or another form of societal corporatism.[119] Until the late 1980s, none showed more than limited inclinations toward socioeconomic pluralism and the state provision of an extensive safety net.

Embedded mercantilism, in summary, meant robust state institutional gate-keepers determining what came into and what left each country through an interlaced mixture of tariffs, corporate collaboration, oligopolization, state regulatory discretion, rigid restriction over foreign ownership, and strict limitations on imports. The result was three greenhouse economies within which domestic finance and manufacturing firms took root and flourished, largely insulated from the chilling winds of international competition swirling outside. An invaluable by-product of such economic policy paradigms was that indigenous firms and local citizens retained the vast bulk of the gains from sustained economic transformation; those benefits did not flow out to foreign financiers or multinational corporations.

This chapter has argued that the stunning economic transformations in all three regimes was the consequence of the interweaving of the interests and resources of several discrete political and socioeconomic forces. Domestic political and socioeconomic components of these developmental regimes cooperated to their mutual benefit in a host of ways, with successive successes reinforcing those bonds. Both in turn benefited from sustained and robust assistance from beyond their national borders, most notably from the United States, while their domestic cooperation advanced US strategic goals. These three legs of these developmental regimes, in turn, fostered an economic policy paradigm benefiting all three and resulting in transformative national economic projects.

The mutually reinforcing nature of each regime's components is critical. Uninterrupted cohesion and control by state institutions depended on a positive relationship with a progrowth socioeconomic coalition. That coalition, in turn, relied on state authorities to generate policies that would protect and enhance their own resources. Yet this domestic fusion of economic and political forces alone would have been insufficient without the added support stemming from the United States' unstinting security commitments, economic infusions, and open markets.

A major corollary of this reinforcing fusion was, of course, the economic paradigm and its successes that fed back to reinforce the interdependence among all three regime components and the regime's broader legitimacy and strategies, and over time, marginalized regime challenges lost their existential aura. Each of the three developmental regimes consequently thrived for relatively long periods, its component parts humming in tandem. In these ways, the regime whole was greater than the sum of its constituent parts.

All three regimes succeeded, not only in catch-up, but also in creating dynamic competitive advantage. While planners in Japan, Korea, and Taiwan originally viewed the more sophisticated economies of North America and Western Europe as distant targets for emulation, ultimately, many became vanishing objects in their rearview mirrors.

Yet the atypical configuration behind these three cases was the product of an unusual set of fortuitous global and domestic circumstances. The peculiar combination of factors that came together to form and sustain these developmental regimes and to support their transformative economic paradigms makes it almost certain that such experiences depended on a particular time and geography. Potential emulators of the developmental regimes in Japan, Korea, and Taiwan face enormous hurdles impeding any facile replication of such a fortuitous combination, particularly under radically different global circumstances. Indeed, as chapter 4 demonstrates, it was impossible even for these three to sustain the regime coherence and economic paradigms they enjoyed for so long.

Chapter 2

Ersatz Developmental Regimes

Malaysia, Indonesia, and Thailand

From roughly the mid-1960s until the 1997–98 Asian financial crisis (AFC), the period marking their greatest economic transformations, Malaysia, Indonesia, and Thailand (MIT) operated with regimes that shared a number of traits with one another. Their respective economic paradigms resonated as well. This chapter analyzes these similarities and demonstrates how their combination of regime plus paradigm distinguished them from the three developmental regimes.

Masking these deep differences, however, were the similarly rapid GDP growth rates and expanded export markets experienced by all six countries. Thus, for a full thirty years, starting in the mid-1960s, Thailand's GDP rose an average of 7.8 percent per year.[1] Malaysia and Indonesia did not lag far behind. From 1965 to 1980, Malaysia's annual GDP growth averaged 7.3 percent, while that of Indonesia was 7.0 percent; for 1980–90, those figures were 5.4 percent for Malaysia and 6.1 percent for Indonesia; for the 1990s, they were 8.7 percent and 7.6 percent, respectively.[2]

During these economic runs, all three countries diversified, industrialized, and became more externally oriented. Manufacturing locations, the range of goods produced, and the diversity and volume of exported products all soared. Such performances give the MIT regimes a surface-level similarity to the developmental regimes of Japan, Korea, and Taiwan and this is the usual basis for grouping all six together. Yet the MIT regimes diverged in critical ways from key elements common to the developmental regimes to their north. Regimes in all three countries were the result of a fundamentally different mixture of state institutions, socioeconomics, and international forces that in turn generated a quite different economic paradigm. Politically, state institutions were never as coherent or controlling as were those in the developmental regimes. They were socioeconomically more fragmented making the creation of a pro-growth coalition more problematic. Nor did these three countries enjoy the same advantages from external forces as those provided, particularly by the United States, to Japan, Korea, and Taiwan.

Their combination of regimes and economic paradigms did allow Malaysia, Indonesia, and Thailand to begin manufacturing in advanced economic sectors. That penetration, however, came without the industrial deepening and sophistication that required more technically skilled work forces and comprehensive structural transformations. As such, national producers failed to capture controlling positions in complex production networks. Instead, foreign investors rather than domestic businesspersons gleaned the lion's share of the benefits from expanded manufacturing exports and jumps in GDP.[3] In the terminology of Dani Rodrik, these countries failed to move "from a low-income equilibrium to a state of rapid growth."[4] Their vulnerability to foreign investors was on painful display when all three writhed during the Asian financial crisis.

This is not to deny that the national economies and general populations of Malaysia, Indonesia, and Thailand became far better off than before they began their rapid ascents. Yet their contributions to any Asian economic miracle came as supportive acolytes rather than as prime movers. As such, despite unquestioned epochal successes by all three, I label them "ersatz developmental regimes."

State Institutions

State institutions in the three MIT regimes approximated Levitsky and Way's "competitive authoritarianism."[5] Autocratic leaders submitted themselves to formal democratic institutions, such as parliaments, parties, and elections; however, abuses of democratic principles were frequent. Occupants of top state positions enjoyed outsized advantages; however, they nonetheless periodically faced greater checks by daunting oppositions than did state officeholders in the developmental regimes. Of particular consequence, state officeholders lacked the shared perception of epistemic threats to their wealth and well-being that energized the developmental regimes. Consequently, even though coalitions of political and socioeconomic elites in Malaysia, Indonesia, and Thailand retained sustained and robust grips over state institutions, they rarely displayed the same strength, inner cohesion, and ability to marginalize regime opponents in service of the same levels of ambitious economic transformations as drove the developmental regimes.[6]

Further impeding ambitious transformation, state institutions in all three countries had staffs that were less well educated and less technically capable than were their counterparts in Japan, Korea, and Taiwan. Communal divisions, most conspicuously those surrounding geography, religion, and ethnicity, further undercut state efficiency, with vast numbers of civil servants holding their positions as the consequence of ethnicity or personal patronage rather than demonstrated talent. Moreover, although official corruption was hardly unheard of in the developmental regimes, it was particularly corrosive in Indonesia and Thailand.[7] State institutions in all three countries were thus structurally less well equipped than were their counterparts to the north, either to help form and partner with a progrowth socioeconomic coalition or to generate, mobilize, and concentrate state resources in a singular commitment to an elaborate industrialization effort.

Indonesian state institutions were decidedly concentrated. Between 1945 and 1997, Indonesia had only two presidents, Sukarno and Suharto. Under both, the military exercised inordinate political and security authority. Suharto toppled Sukarno in a 1967 coup during and after which a series of massacres emasculated the remaining political parties and depoliticized the mass public.[8] Following two years of systematically purging the military of Communist and left-wing influences, Suharto went on to exert brutal effectiveness in eliminating alternative power centers, centralizing power, and achieving de facto harmony among the political elite.[9]

To reflect, represent, and mobilize support for state policies responsive to his personalist rule, Suharto turned to the army's Sekretariat Bersama Golongan Karya (Golkar for short), which, though underdeveloped at its center, included a broad network of affiliated organizations.[10] By 1969, Suharto had turned Golkar into a sweeping state-led corporatist instrument that afforded him a commanding fusion of party and state not unlike Taiwan's KMT. Similar to state corporatist networks elsewhere, far more influence flowed down from the top than up from below.

Golkar claimed nearly three hundred societal groups, including farmers, students, workers, civil servants, fishers, business leaders, professionals, intellectuals, and workers, as well as uniformed members of the armed forces. Each formed a single component allegedly reflecting the common good of the full sector.[11] In addition, membership in Golkar was mandatory for new appointees to the civil service, all of whom received material rewards as payback for party loyalty. Many local political figures received Golkar leadership positions, transforming their local credibility into state assets.[12] In this way, Golkar ensured that local authority bolstered rather than hindered central authority.[13] As Suharto's tenure lengthened, Golkar became Indonesia's only meaningful political party, contesting elections and occupying parliamentary seats as loyal supporters of the executive office. Golkar sidelined other political parties, prescribed a narrow range of acceptable political participation, and channeled societal groups into the extensive network of state-sponsored organizations. Central to the Indonesian regime's longevity was its ability to hold its supportive socioeconomic coalition together while incorporating potential political opponents into Golkar. Not until the early 1990s was there meaningful loosening of this authoritarian corporatism.[14]

Important as both Golkar and the military were, Suharto himself stood as the singular Colossus astride the party as the personalization of his "New Order." Exercising tight control over decisions on any influential ruling, his was the final and decisive vote.[15] Yet Suharto's singular control had a deleterious effect on technocratic influence over policy. As Pepinsky phrased it, "Suharto was the New Order's sole veto player, and only through personal access to Suharto were technocrats able to influence policy; technocratic influence existed only with Suharto's blessing and only to the extent that it did not interfere with the demands of the regime's other political supporters."[16] Consequently, as MacIntyre notes, the Indonesian state was not "strong" or "hard," as those terms are typically used. Instead, state institutions operated by reliance on patrimonial distribution networks linking state officials and businesspeople.[17]

Less all-inclusive than Indonesia's Golkar, Malaysia's Barisan Nasional (BN, or National Front), and its key component UMNO (United Malays National Organization), exerted similar dominance over top state institutions. A vastly oversized coalition, BN aggregates three ethnically anchored parties, an organizational form with roots in British colonial rule.[18] UMNO, the largest element in BN, is a strictly Malay party whose political influence derives from the numerical dominance of Malay citizens (about 62% of the population). The Malaysia Chinese Association (MCO) focuses on Chinese citizens (about 23%), while the Malaysian Indian Congress (MIC) does the same for Indians (about 6%).[19] Several smaller parties complete these consociational arrangements. BN's strength stems from its ability to organize and channel both political and socioeconomic elites in each of the three ethnic communities.[20]

UMNO has more than 2 million members (roughly a quarter of adult Malays) and 16,500 branch organizations reaching into every corner of the country.[21] Despite occasional losses in local or regional elections, recurring electoral successes usually delivered two-thirds majorities in Parliament, allowing BN to function as a unitary actor with UMNO as its predominant drive shaft. From 1969 until at least 2003, BN enjoyed political hegemony over state institutions, giving BN/UMNO virtually uncompromising control over the national policy paradigm.[22]

The one serious multiethnic opposition challenger, the Democratic Action Party (DAP), did exceptionally well in the May 1969 elections resulting in UMNO and BN losses. Racially based riots that killed several hundred Chinese prompted UMNO to initiate its New Economic Policy (NEP) (discussed below) in an effort to boost Malay support while pushing back against any subsequent cross-communal political vehicles such as DAP that might again challenge UMNO's ethnically anchored political preeminence.

Furthering top-down UMNO control was the personality of Mahathir Mohammed, who led UMNO to five consecutive electoral wins and who served as prime minister from 1981 to 2003 (and who returned in 2018 as the leader of the anti-UMNO Malaysian United Indigenous Party). Mahathir personified strong and focused leadership, an individual able to resist pulls toward regional fragmentation and national disintegration. Under Mahathir, Malaysia enjoyed its greatest economic advances, with his governments overseeing a number of bold infrastructure plans. Yet Mahathir and UMNO confronted vastly more complex bargaining problems than did Suharto and Golkar. Mahathir was never a one man ruler equivalent to Suharto.

Malaysian state institutions, nonetheless, enjoyed a battery of authoritarian powers to restrict opposition activities.[23] The 1948–60 British-led counterinsurgency had forged a sophisticated coercive machine inherited by UMNO. This included a strong and reliable army, a highly effective police force, and one of the most efficient intelligence services in the region. Security agencies monitored political activities throughout the country and their capacity to put down protest was beyond question.[24] The state used selective repression to combat threats to UMNO dominance, whether panethnic challengers such as labor movements or Malay-based challengers such as the Pan-Malaysian Islamic Party (PAS).[25]

At the same time, Malaysian authoritarianism was soft. Violent repression was rare; more often, the regime balanced repression with responsiveness to marginalize or coopt potential regime opponents.[26] Intra-UMNO divisions were always a risk, as was clear when a ruling party split in the October 1990 elections allowed an opposition coalition to topple UMNO in Kalamantan after it had already increased its control of Sabah just before that election.[27]

In comparison to the tightly honed and cohesive institutions in Indonesia and Malaysia, state institutions in Thailand were more fragmented, leaving centralized political authority correspondingly weaker and less effective; Thai state institutions were particularly less adept than those in Indonesia or Malaysia at marginalizing or coopting potential regime opponents.[28] Instead, as Dan Slater characterized them, Thai political power arrangements involved "factionalized fighting forces."[29] Frequent displays of such fragmentation among elites, however, represented squabbles within a commonly understood set of political and economic parameters. Consequently, as Rock has argued, "Thai governments were particularly unstable, but governments and the bureaucracy hewed to a stable set of development policies."[30]

Thailand is nominally a constitutional monarchy. The monarchy's historical roots run deep and popular respect for Bhumibol Adulyadej, who served as monarch from 1946 until his death in 2016, was widespread, enhanced by his generous royal patronage. As a result, the monarchy was widely courted by political elites who jockeyed to ensure that they and the king avoided conflicting trajectories. Periodically, the king made clear that he opposed a particular administration or course of action, usually foreshadowing its termination. Overall, however, the monarchy rarely exercised direct intervention into pivotal policies, preferring more subtle moral suasion. Real political control rested in the hands of party politicians and the military.

During most of Thailand's high-growth period, an ever-shifting mélange of as many as a dozen political parties jockeyed for pivotal positions in the Parliament and the cabinet. Parliamentary majorities of up to six parties were common and party agendas rarely overlapped.[31] Yet, as noted, policy differences were narrow and stayed closely responsive to the urban or rural socioeconomic elite. So long as Parliaments and elections were not stymied by the military, parties in the majority coalition took turns "presenting shopping lists of infrastructure projects, investment incentives, or industrial liberalization measures."[32] Blackmail by parties threatening to leave the ruling coalition left most administrations swirling amidst unending dramas and political instability.

Meanwhile, the military was a perennial specter in the shadows. A coup in 1947 solidified its role as the ultimate arbiter of Thai politics, and between 1947 and 2006, at least eight successful coups led to changes in government.[33] Military interventions strongly compromised political freedoms and basic human rights. Soon after World War II, military officers responded to labor protests over inflation and food shortages by destroying radical labor organizations while legalizing moderate unions and adopting legislation to improve working conditions. By the mid-1950s, with growing US military support and a fear of the political Left, the Thai military tightened its control over the country, cracking down on dissent from rural areas, intellectuals, and leftist students. They outlawed unionism completely.[34] Again, in the 1980s, the military mobilized national resources against indigenous Communist guerrillas and the external threat from Communist Vietnam.[35]

Widespread media censorship and oligarchic media ownership channeled the information available to citizens, further enhancing elite control. That said, the military never fully consolidated its rule. Party politicians, invariably waiting for their opportunities, persistently challenged military rule, demanding a return to democracy. While party politicians and military officers were in accord on their collective right to rule and on the need to suppress popular sectors, Thailand never had sufficient political consensus to forge the strong state institutions vital to the pursuit of a developmental economic paradigm. The most that could be said was that Thailand operated under political arrangements in which the "political-military elite was factionalized when it came to the pursuit of economic rents but united behind the country's economic and political strategies."[36] As Slater put it, "Flimsy coalitions produced flimsy institutions."[37] The Thai state thus remained less cohesive and powerful than that of Malaysia under UMNO or the military-Golkar regime in Indonesia, and all three were less unified and authoritative than those in Japan, Korea, and Taiwan.[38]

Meanwhile, in all three regimes, the administrative apparatus typically fell short of the cohesiveness, competence, and technical wherewithal needed to forge and implement a transformative paradigm of economic policies. None of the three regimes had an elite service that succeeded in attracting the most highly trained and motivated graduates.[39] Technical sophistication was rare; clientelistic appointees were pervasive. Although pockets of talent were scattered within the higher ranks, the broader reality was that well-educated officials were in short supply and received low salaries, leaving them prone to petty corruption.[40] Indeed, corruption was sufficiently pervasive in Indonesia that Quah identified it as the country's most serious problem.[41] Not surprisingly, in all three countries administrative staff were hesitant to generate independent policy options and anemic in directing broad policy initiatives that might threaten politically generated rent extraction.

Ironically, given the fragmentation of state institutions, Thai technocrats enjoyed episodic policy predominance, most notably following the shift to exports in the mid-1980s under Prime Minister Prem, and again from the late 1980s to mid-1990s under Anand. Both men were themselves neither party members nor military officers but technocrats. As such, they valued expertise. Even under these governments, however, technocratic preeminence remained limited to macroeconomic policy initiatives. Western trained officials in the National Economic and Social Development Board (NESDB), the Bank of Thailand, the Ministry of Finance, and the prime minister's office became influential players behind the national economic success.[42] These technocrats also benefited from the fact that military officers, when assigned to oversee government agencies, rarely grasped the technicalities of economic policymaking. Most relied instead on Western-educated economists to formulate the details involving policies like controlling inflation, restoring trade balances, and creating conditions favorable for foreign and domestic investment.

Yet many army officers used their positions to secure licenses, contracts, credit, and other amenities for enterprises with which they were privately associated. The business activities of officers' wives, brothers, and cousins expanded correspondingly.[43] Any economic rationality promoted by technocrats thus typically confronted selective resistance from military officers whose power and private incomes relied on their ability to bypass formal rules and regulations. Economic policy efforts that might have been technologically rational therefore often proved politically unsustainable.[44]

Despite serious limitations in the technical skills of their administrative services and pervasive levels of petty and high-level corruption, political institutions in Malaysia, Indonesia, and Thailand enjoyed a measure of coherence and capacity at the highest level. Even in the institutionally weakest of the three, Thailand, political elites who shuttled in and out of the top ranks shared agreement on the basic directions of policy and collaborated to marginalize or suppress potential opponents, particularly popular sectors that might press for enhanced redistributive policies.

Also worth noting is that in all three countries, political elites more often used economic policy as a tool for consolidating or maintaining political authority than as a mechanism for national economic transformation. Rapid growth in GDP provided political elites with ready access to cash with which to fund both development schemes (generating performance legitimacy) and crony enterprises (generating elite compliance).[45] Dense webs linked political and business elites in an ongoing exchange of favors, bribes, and inducements. Political elites in turn used this combination to encourage favored capitalists to invest in the economy while using kickbacks to shore up political support and win elections.[46] In short, certain socioeconomic forces cooperated with segments of state institutions; however, those cooperative socioeconomic forces enjoyed limited societal sweep and consequently only compromised influence.

Socioeconomic Forces

The developmental regimes all benefited from minimal levels of ethnic, religious, linguistic, or other ascriptive criteria, as well as from the relative absence of powerful rural property owners. No such conditions existed in Malaysia, Indonesia, or Thailand. All faced far deeper and more fragmenting socioeconomic conditions.

Indonesia, for example, confronted extensive geographical and linguistic fragmentation. The country is comprised of some 13,500 islands in an archipelago stretching across five time zones. The country has over 700 living languages. Although the Indonesian/Malay and Javanese ethnolinguistic groups are by far the largest, with 240 million and 84 million citizens respectively, another twenty groups have 1 million or more speakers. Indeed, only in 1945 did Indonesia adopt Bahasa as its national language. Local loyalties frequently surpassed nation identity.

An additional socioeconomic division arose with the sizable significance of the rural agricultural sector. None of the MIT regimes faced a substantial segment of large landowners opposed to economic development or the wrenching process of land reform; however, all three had substantial agricultural sectors that contributed greatly to the national economies and thus deflected any single-minded focus on urban industrialization. Within Indonesia and Malaysia, this took the form of heavy investments in the modernization of small-holder rice agriculture. Although Thailand was a major exporter of rice, ironically the governments did little to modernize rice agriculture outside the Central Plain. Yet a low land/individual ratio and plenty of uncultivated land induced Thailand as well to invest government resources in massive rural programs and smallholder advances.[47] Such an extensive agricultural focus deflected movement in all three countries away from industrialization.

Interlaced with urban–rural divisions has been cleavages over ethnicity. All three countries have substantial minority populations of ethnic Chinese, most of whom are descendants of nineteenth-century immigrants. In Indonesia and Malaysia, Chinese migrants retained a high degree of separateness from the rest of society, continuing to display distinctive cultural, language, marriage, and culinary predispositions. The pervasiveness of Islam in both countries added to that ethnic division.

Large numbers of the early Chinese arrivals were petty traders and merchants who provided a resource for British and Dutch economic policies of exploitation and export of natural resources. Ethnically distinct and trade-oriented Chinese proved convenient intermediaries, willing to collaborate with the colonial overlords at the expense of the exploited indigenous populations. Ethnic Chinese took full advantage of colonial divide-and-conquer tactics, leaving them in postcolonial Indonesia and Malaysia with disproportionately greater riches, albeit also with the stigma of having been colonial-era exploiters. As political power shifted to the indigenous majority, the ethnic Chinese faced systematic patterns of exclusion and discrimination, becoming what Sidel calls "pariah capitalists"[48]

Thailand had its own wave of Chinese migrants, but having evaded colonial rule it avoided the legacy of ethnic Chinese as exploitative intermediaries. Indeed, the children of Chinese immigrant men and Thai women enjoyed broad freedom to choose between identifying themselves as Chinese (by wearing a queue and paying a head tax) or as Thai (by cutting their hair and performing labor services at the behest of a Thai patron). Given the essentially cultural as opposed to racial definition of ethnicity that prevailed in fin de siècle Siam, "anyone who used a Thai name, spoke the language, and behaved as a Thai was accepted as a Thai regardless of ancestry." Thus, "the movement from Chinese society into the Thai elite consequently became a veritable flood in the 19th century, and by 1900 Chinese ancestry was common among Thai bureaucratic nobles."[49]

These numerical minorities account for disproportionately outsized shares of total national wealth (see table 2.1), resulting, particularly in Malaysia and Indonesia, in an overlap between ethnic and class cleavages. Equally problematic, in both Indonesia and Malaysia the indigenous majority controlled state institutions even as a Chinese minority dominated in business. This posed a serious impediment to fusing political power and socioeconomic power in the service of a shared economic paradigm aimed at rapid industrialization.

From 1945 in Indonesia and from 1971 in Malaysia, ethnic considerations and ethnic-biased policies constrained the ability of state policymakers to mobilize domestic sources of private capital from the source of its greatest concentration, namely, ethnic Chinese executives. Golkar's state-led corporatist dominance meant that socioeconomic forces in Indonesia could gain or exercise power only to the extent that they comported with state goals. As a small numerical minority, the Indonesian Chinese were especially vulnerable. In 1965, mobs killed thousands, as the military looked on (and often participated), while in 1997 a similar wave of anti-Chinese marauding left many dead and others fleeing the country.

Table 2.1 Share of population and share of private capital for ethnic Chinese in Malaysia, Thailand, and Indonesia

	% population	Share of private capital
Malaysia	35	65
Thailand	10	80
Indonesia	3	80

Source: Walter Hatch and Kozo Yamamura, *Asia in Japan's Embrace: Building a Regional Production Alliance* (Cambridge: Cambridge University Press, 1996), 82.

Normally, however, the Suharto regime protected the Chinese business elite in exchange for financial support for his interests. Under his New Order, most successful businesspeople owed their riches to personal links to Suharto and his immediate family and personal circle. The government used its patronage powers to foster an indigenous "crony capitalist" elite dependent on the state.[50] Originally, the bulk of these were ethnic Chinese, although with time many ethnic Indonesians, a large number of them immediate relatives of Suharto, also accumulated extensive wealth. Similarly, an embryonic middle class emerged, but it was always much weaker than in Thailand or Malaysia, and it never developed a significant independent voice. In short, most powerful business interests lacked substantial independence from state institutions; instead, they were intimately, but subordinately, blended with them.[51] Those not so connected to state institutions lacked the interest or capacity to advance major industrial projects on their own,

Such pervasive ethnic divisions militated against the creation of a unified national business sector that could collaborate with state institutions in a pro-growth alliance. Instead, the ethnic logic of accumulation in the MIT regimes contrasted with the national logic of accumulation in the developmental regimes. The former privileged state-owned enterprises and then doled out their surpluses along ethnic lines. Meanwhile, foreign multinationals provided state policymakers with an alternative to economic partnership with wealthy ethnic Chinese. As a result, numerous ethnic Chinese businesses opted either to remain small and out of the political crosshairs or else to move into finance and real estate, both of which promised attractive and rapid returns, along with quick exit possibilities in emergencies. None of those riches promised a substantial contribution to rapid national development.[52] Ethnic divisions in turn restricted the capacity of state institutions to target selected industrial sectors or firms by providing below-market credit or generous subsidies. Thailand, however, with a less restrictive ethnic blockage against such efforts, achieved greater economic inclusion of indigenous Thai capital, even that dominated by ethnic Chinese.[53]

In contrast to the complex industrial conglomerates that dominated the economies of the developmental regime, family-controlled firms have been key economic drivers in all three regimes, at 40.7 percent in Indonesia, 32.2 percent in Thailand, and a lower 17.3 percent in Malaysia. Pyramid organizational arrangements predominated, with larger firms controlling smaller firms in a potentially endless chain. Most deviated too from the one-share-one-vote rules, with a prevalence of cross-holdings and the appointment of managers and directors related to the controlling family.[54] The result was a small number of very large conglomerates—Indonesia's *cukong* entrepreneurs, Malaysia's trust agencies and large Bumiputera conglomerates, and Thailand's Sino–Thai corporations dominating industry in all three economies.[55]

Further impeding rapid technological upgrading was the limited emphasis on human development and enhanced skills training for substantial portions of the population. The abundance of natural resources and vast labor pools reduced state and business incentives to invest heavy sums to enhance human skill levels. Ample exports of agricultural products or natural resources could generate needed foreign reserves, thereby reducing state or business incentives to bolster the human talent needed to create advanced products for export.

In contrast, as noted in chapter 1, the developmental regimes in Japan, Korea, and Taiwan invested heavily in education, including tertiary education with a strong emphasis on engineering, science, and technology. Public education and corporate training steadily enhanced national human resources. In contrast, Indonesia, Malaysia, and Thailand fell far short. All had low proportions of scientists and engineers, and even lower levels of national investment in research and development, a combination that made it difficult to expand horizontally or vertically and thereby connect cognate industries and move up the technology curve.[56] In the 1980s, for example, Japan had 49.6 scientists per 10,000 and Korea had 24.4. By contrast, there were only 7.3 in Indonesia and 4.8 in Thailand. The gap widened further when one considers the numbers of *potential* scientists and engineers because Malaysia, Indonesia, and Thailand have few institutions capable of supplying talent to the science and technical pipeline.[57] Education levels in all three remained well below those of Taiwan and South Korea a decade earlier, even though the MIT regimes then stood at higher levels of per capita GDP.[58] The failure to invest in such human skill improvement limited the long-term ability of indigenous firms to scramble quickly up the technological ladder.

The greatest socioeconomic congruence between Japan, Korea, and Taiwan (JKT) and MIT occurred in their mutual ability to marginalize potential challengers, especially organized labor and popular movements that could pose challenges to the regime. Labor faced an additional problem in organizing workers because of the presence of a substantial informal labor force in all three countries. In Thailand, informal workers constitute well over 60 percent of the total workforce, even capturing a significant portion of those with college educations, perhaps as much as 30 percent, many of whom work in small shops and eateries.[59] In Indonesia, an even larger 70 percent of the workforce was engaged in informal employment.[60] Malaysia's informal sector, though smaller, still stood at 8 to 9 percent. Such significant supplies of informal labor drove down wages and reduced the chances for collective labor force mobilization.

In all of these ways, socioeconomic forces in Malaysia, Indonesia, and Thailand lacked cohesion, and only a limited segment of the economic elite was predisposed to pursue an agenda of rapid industrialization. Vital socioeconomic sectors remained divorced from close ties to state institutions. Constituted differently and facing different political constraints, they defined their underlying interests as quite distinct from their counterparts in the developmental regimes. Rapid industrial transformation was less high on their agendas.[61] Consequently, each of the three MIT regimes lacked a cohesive progrowth socioeconomic coalition that could marry their resources to state institutions in a common drive toward indigenous economic upgrading. Instead, as the next section details, all three faced tempting pools of foreign investment, along with resource exports, as the drivers for their high levels of GDP growth.

External Forces

The MIT regimes were similar to those of JKT in that all were broadly pro-Western and connected to, and benefited from, a host of Western-led global institutions. The United States was also the major export destination for all six until the end of the twentieth century. Yet none of the three Southeast Asian regimes received the sustained political and economic nurturance that the United States lavished on the three developmental regimes. Nor did any other external state actors infuse themselves as deeply to shape their regimes or their economic policies.

That said, Suharto's 1965 coup enjoyed covert US support and the United States subsequently provided various military aid and training for Indonesian forces. Still, neither Malaysia nor Indonesia had extensive security relationships with the United States, nor did they reap economic largess remotely comparable to that provided to domestic power holders in Japan, South Korea, and Taiwan.

United States–Indonesia relations had been frigid under Sukarno as American Cold War calculations disdained his efforts to fuse ostensible neutrality with pro-China policies. This motivated the CIA to provide critical support to Suharto's coup and the purge of the Left, even though US officials knew that the vast majority of those purged were innocent of any antistate actions. The United States also helped to suppress media coverage of the killings.[62] Consequently, the Suharto regime began from a broadly pro-American and anti-Communist agenda and received a mix of US economic and military assistance that, between 1946 and 1980, amounted to approximately $3.2 billion ($2.7 billion in economic aid and $436 million in military assistance).[63] The United States also offered training to Indonesian military officers, but those programs ebbed and flowed. Thus, the two countries remained far from allies and the Soviet Union was Indonesia's major supplier of military equipment.

Malaysian relations with the United States were by far the coolest of the three. Ethnic and religious considerations led Malaysian leaders to prioritize the country's Muslims. Mahathir was particularly contentious in his comments about the United States and was a vociferous proponent of Asians-only regional organizations, a format that US policymakers interpreted as a direct challenge to its preponderant influence in the Asia-Pacific.

Only in Thailand was US support notably robust. Although it lacked the formal bilateral alliance with the United States that underpinned American ties with the three developmental regimes,[64] Thailand had security links to the US through the Manila Pact. Thailand received economic, military, and technological assistance from the United States starting in the 1950s and expanding in the 1960s, as the United States grew increasingly enmeshed in combating insurgencies in Indochina. From the mid-1950s until 1976, the United States spent nearly $3.5 billion in Thailand, constituting over half of all Thai defense expenditures.[65] In addition, between 1966 and 1971, US military aid combined with World Bank loans to provide roughly one-third of public capital spending.[66] American funds promoted expanded infrastructure and the initiation of import substitution that later became a platform from which Thailand endeavored to build an export-led development strategy. Ironically, US military spending in the late 1960s and early 1970s provided Thailand with sufficient foreign reserves so that business and political elites had little incentive to upgrade their exports as a means to gain foreign exchange.[67] Following the loss of the Vietnam War and the subsequent reduction in US troop levels in East Asia, US military and diplomatic engagement in Southeast Asia fell off sharply although in 2003 the US designated Thailand a Major non-NATO ally (MNNA).

Nevertheless, if the US relationship with the Southeast Asian three was less fulsome than its backing of Japan, Korea, and Taiwan, all three benefited from sustained economic engagement by Japan. The United States, starting in spring 1947 and accelerating in the aftermath of the Communist takeover in China, had pressed Japan to shift its geoeconomic focus southward and away from its historical links across Northeast Asia (Manchukuo-Korea-China). Meanwhile, Southeast Asia was rich in natural resources and offered a logical market for low cost Japanese consumer and manufactured goods, including relatively cheap Japanese machinery.[68]

Japan thus shifted its emphasis away from China and toward Southeast Asia, comporting well with postcolonial thinking across that region, especially in Malaysia and Indonesia. For these two countries, engagement with the West connoted a return to colonialism or dependency. Japan, in contrast, appeared less predatory and more reflective of so-called Asian values, while still being a potential source of technological and economic assistance. As Mark Beeson wrote, "The unprecedented success of Japan's post- war developmental project" gave it—for a while, at least—a talismanic status for other would-be developers."[69]

Japanese trade with Southeast Asia mounted quickly. In 1938, Japanese exports to Southeast Asia totaled a scant 8.4 percent of its national total; by 1978, that figure had risen to 24.6 percent.[70] Japan soon became the number-one trading partner for all three regimes. Japan bought substantial portions of the raw materials exported from all three, especially from Malaysia and Indonesia. In turn, Japanese capital goods, technology, and manufactured components became essential imports. Japanese companies also began investing heavily in Southeast Asia, and by the first half of the 1970s, Japanese investment there had risen ninefold over the latter half of the 1960s.[71] In addition, ODA provided substantial infrastructure support across all three countries with an emphasis on ports, roads, dams, bridges, and power plants.

Indonesia, in particular, welcomed such relations with Japan, not least because toward the end of World War II, Japan officially acknowledged Indonesian independence.[72] Indeed, some three thousand Imperial Japanese Army troops joined Indonesian nationalist forces in the fight against Dutch efforts to recolonize the islands. A reparations agreement between the two countries delivered $223 million to Indonesia, with a substantial portion involving the provision of infrastructure projects and technology transfers by Japanese companies that established a powerful beachhead for subsequent private investments.[73]

Thai leaders also welcomed a Japanese economic partnership with the result that US economic involvement in Thailand soon gave way to that of Japan. Initially allies during World War II, the two reached a postwar reparations agreement of ¥5.4 billion ($15 million), much smaller than went to many other victims of Japanese military actions but one that nonetheless reenergized bilateral relations. Japan soon flooded Thailand with aid and foreign investment. As Stubbs argued, "it was essentially Japanese foreign direct investment in the 1980s that led to the export boom that swept the Thai economy to prosperity."[74]

Japanese government aid complemented the economic engagement of its private companies. ODA to the ASEAN-4 (the MIT economies plus the Philippines) rose from $1.14 billion in 1975 to $3.3 billion in 1980, and to $8.9 billion in 1989. Between 1987 and 1991, Japan provided 57 percent of the bilateral aid received by Indonesia and a full 81 percent of that received by Malaysia.[75] Technical assistance from the Japan International Cooperation Agency (JICA) supported things like seed development, agricultural crop improvement, and water resources.

Japan also played a leading role through the Asian Development Bank (ADB), contributing one-fifth of the bank's total capital ($200 million), with the United States pledging an equal amount. Asian participants reciprocated by agreeing to situate the ADB headquarters in Manila rather than in the United States. Japan also won Southeast Asian plaudits with the 1977 articulation of the so-called Fukuda Doctrine. Prime Minister Fukuda pledged that Japan would never again become a military power and instead would create a relationship of mutual confidence and trust in a diversity of fields, while cooperating as an equal partner with the ASEAN member countries in their own efforts.[76]

The Plaza Accord of 1985 triggered an even greater onrush of monetary and investment shifts in East Asia. Indonesia, Malaysia, and Thailand all saw currency devaluations post-Plaza, while the Japanese yen, the Korean won, and the currencies of Singapore, Taiwan, and Hong Kong all soared. Furthermore, in February 1988 the United States withdrew prior privileges under the generalized system of preferences (GSP) for Japan, Korea and Taiwan, and erected punitive trade measures against products originating from these economies.

The combination triggered the outsourcing of many labor-intensive production facilities away from the home markets of East Asia's sophisticated economies into countries such as Indonesia, Malaysia, and Thailand. Japanese FDI alone jumped fivefold in Malaysia between 1985 and 1989, while that in Thailand grew an astonishing twenty-five-fold. Large jumps in investment from the other rich economies of East Asia added to the investment infusion, so that by

1994 nearly 60 percent of the new FDI entering Indonesia was coming from Korea, Taiwan, Hong Kong, and Singapore.[77] Taiwan also became a significant investor in Malaysia, while Korea made substantial investments in Indonesia.

In addition, the emergence of the Growth Triangle linking Singapore with the Malaysian state of Johor and the Indonesian province of Riau exemplified Singaporean investment in its surrounding region.[78] These injections of foreign capital, technology, and management skills were integral to the expansion of the regional production networks noted in chapter 1. Such investments from their richer East Asian neighbors helped all three Southeast Asian countries to boost their manufacturing exports and exports in higher value-added sectors.

These production networks underscore another decisive difference between the developmental regimes and those in Malaysia, Indonesia, and Thailand, namely, how the regimes in these respective groups dealt in contrastive ways with potential incoming technology transfers and capital investments. As chapter 1 showed, the developmental regimes resisted most foreign investment in principle and when FDI did materialize, state institutions vetted potential licensing agreements or foreign partnerships in advance, and then monitored them rigorously. In this way, state institutions explicitly sided with local licensees or investors, helping them to strike favorable bargains with their foreign partners. Powerful state institutions ensured the best possible terms and guaranteed the rapid dispersal and absorption of all incoming resources for national companies.

Such state institutions and scale-tipping were lacking in Indonesia, Malaysia, and Thailand, and even when state officials sought to tip contractual balances to favor local firms, they often lacked the technical skills essential for effective bargaining, monitoring, or implementation.[79] Thus, the impressive growth rates the three rang up remained far more dependent on incoming monies than on indigenous capital and far more reliant on the local contribution of cheap labor for low-value assembly and packaging supportive of subsequent export by multinationals. Domestic innovation was minimal, resulting in less national control and less indigenous benefit from rapid national economic successes.

Consequently, integral as Japanese and other foreign investments were to the economic paradigms of Malaysia, Indonesia, and Thailand, these monies most often reinforced rather than altered preexisting factor endowments. FDI did little to change *comparative* endowments by enhancing the *competitive* advantages of these ersatz developmental regimes. Japanese firms in particular set strict limits on the technologies they would transfer and the prices they would demand; tight strings enveloped most technology transfers. Overseas investors could justifiably argue that given the workforces' low levels of education, especially in engineering, science, and technology in all three of the ersatz developmental regimes, such restrictions were logical. Yet the consequence was that even though many Malaysian, Indonesian, and Thai firms became profitable and gained new markets, neither they nor the national economies received substantial boosts toward technological breakthroughs, self-sustaining growth, or national economic transformation.[80] Consequently, all remained vulnerable to the possibility of rapid FDI outflows in search of potentially even lower cost locations.

Economic Policy Paradigm

Chapter 1 contended that embedded mercantilism in the developmental regimes revolved heavily around protecting and advancing domestic firms, exporting their increasingly sophisticated manufactured goods globally, all the while keeping foreign investments and competition at bay. The result was that indigenous businesses and workers reaped the lion's share of national economic growth. The policy paradigm of the ersatz developmental regimes provides a striking contrast.

Those regimes delivered high economic growth rates and export success; however, they did so through a very different route that relied far more on the export of raw materials and agricultural goods, followed by selective import substitution industrialization, a heavier dependence on state-owned enterprises, far greater openness to FDI, and exporting industrial components rather than fully finished products.

Such policies were logical given their configurations of state institutions, domestic socioeconomic alignments, and the scarcity of domestic capital. Specifically, absent political, socioeconomic, or international pressures to do so, each of the ersatz developmental regimes pursued economic paradigms that differed materially from those of the developmental regimes. None created the kind of nationally accepted hegemonic project aimed at radical industrial transformation in which the economic benefits would redound primarily to their own citizens. None succeeded in major enhancements of their *competitive* advantage; instead, all three continued to play to their *comparative* advantages, that is, limited capital and technology but an abundance of labor and natural resources. Globalized finance and foreign investors faced correspondingly fewer barriers to entry than was true of the developmental regimes.

In addition, unlike Japan, Korea, and Taiwan, import substitution in Malaysia, Indonesia, and Thailand never received the same boost from state institutional injections of the capital and technological enhancement of infant industries that would enable them to go toe-to-toe with international competitors.[81] The regimes privileged external investors who in turn harvested far larger shares of joint venture successes.

Critically, richness in resources differentiated Malaysia, Indonesia, and Thailand from the resource-poor regimes of Japan, Korea, and Taiwan. British and Dutch colonization of Malaysia and Indonesia pivoted on developing and exploiting raw materials and agricultural products. Like colonized Malaysia and Indonesia, Thailand's prewar economy revolved around the export of raw materials and agricultural products. Indeed, Thailand was the world's leading exporter of rice. Yet rice cultivation for export demanded little in the way of infrastructure development. As a result, none of these three regimes entered the postwar period with infrastructures comparable to those that the Japanese colonial experience bequeathed to Taiwan and Korea, and from which postwar Japan itself had benefited.

All three Southeast Asian regimes instead continued to rely on their well-established export streams in resources and agricultural products. Such exports benefited from plentiful supplies of cheap labor that kept national wage bills low while generating the reserves necessary to purchase foreign goods. In theory, agriculture might have acted as the starting point for indigenous production of industrial goods; however, in practice, agricultural products and raw materials provided such a steady stream of revenue for entrenched political and business elites that continued reliance on their export remained a compelling regime alternative in all three.

Malaysia had vast land tracts and between 80 and 90 percent of the population was rural at the time of independence. In response, the government introduced a draft plan for agricultural development in 1950 that focused, among other things, on agricultural diversification and income equalization between urban and rural areas.[82] Since the vast majority of the rural population was ethnic Malay, it is not surprising that this and subsequent plans for agricultural development bled into the NEP of 1971 designed to advance the economic fortunes of the rural Malay population.

Malaysia is also rich in oil, rubber, and tin. As late as 1989, the country was still the world's leading producer of rubber, generating 1.6 million tons, or about one-third of the world's total. It also mined 52,000 tons of tin worth $1 billion in exports, enough to make it the world's leading producer, with nearly 25 per cent of the world's total.[83] To reduce its dependence on these two commodities, state policymakers sought to diversify, but mostly by expanding exports of other commodities such as palm oil and cocoa.

Indonesia too was rich in rubber and tin, as well as cash crops such as coffee, indigo, tobacco, tea, and sugar. Oil, however, proved by far the country's most valuable resource. Indonesia earned two-thirds of its domestic revenues and about 80 percent of its total export income from oil. Thailand's riches lay in rice, rubber, tin, and sugar.

Postwar nationalism predisposed policymakers in all three regimes to opt for state-dominated enterprises, a course rarely as conducive to international competitiveness as privately owned firms subject to rigid market discipline. Immediately following independence, Malaysian state corporations bought into and then gradually took over the plantations, mines, banks, and trading enterprises that had given the British control of the commanding economic heights.[84]

Following independence, the Indonesian government nationalized many of the institutions and businesses linked to the agricultural system overseen by the Dutch. From the 1960s until the 1980s, the state made every effort to expand the agricultural sector. Suharto even launched a transmigration program designed to relocate landless farmers from the crowded island of Java to the less populated outer islands. The goal was to alleviate the landless peasant problem while expanding production in the country's outer islands, particularly through the expansion of palm oil. Such policies deepened the national reliance on the primary sector, in the process enhancing the economic and political advantages of that sector.

In Thailand, vast land tracts fostered peasant mobility while expanding lands under cultivation. As early as the 1932 coup,[85] the dominant productive activity in Thailand was export-orientated rice monoculture. Indeed, until the middle of the 1960s, agriculture remained the country's primary economic activity. In contrast, the remainder of the economy remained inwardly focused and centered on import substitution. This pattern continued until the early 1980s, when recession and a debt crisis propelled the turn toward the FDI-led export manufacturing driven by Japanese and other foreign investors noted above.[86]

Unlike the developmental regimes to the north, the three Southeast Asian regimes proved less capable of generating, mobilizing, and relying on, indigenously controlled capital. In Indonesia from 1945 and Malaysia from 1971, ethnic considerations limited political support from indigenous Chinese who controlled the bulk of domestic capital. In Thailand, however, the government had abandoned formal policies of ethnic discrimination in the late 1950s, stimulating greater participation by Thai industrial capital, largely dominated by ethnic Chinese.[87]

That said, Malaysian state institutions had in place a system that generated vastly more domestic capital for state use than was the case in Indonesia or Thailand. As early as 1951, Malaysia created an Employees Provident Fund (EPF), a system of forced citizen savings. Participation became mandatory for all employees after the riots of 1969, so that by 1994 the EPF was collecting compulsory contributions from 6.6 million employees and 210,000 employers, and generating more than M\$64 billion.[88] Its broad coverage and steep rates of mandatory contributions (23% of an employee's salary) provided the government with an ideal mechanism to mobilize domestic capital in the service of state economic projects. State coffers ballooned further with the explosion of oil prices during the 1970s, a boon enjoyed by Indonesia as well.[89] Yet during the 1980s, around 90 percent of the EPF's accumulated funds flowed not into development of industrial capacity but into safe Malaysian Government Securities (MGS) and into SOEs; the same was true for a high proportion of the enhanced oil revenues. State investment strategy rose or fell on SOE performance and was divorced from any major stimulus to private ownership. It is important to note that such safe investments meant little government money went into upgrading industrial production.

It was not that the Malaysia state ignored the capital needs for expanded industrialization. In 1958, it put in place a "Pioneer Industries Ordinance," followed by a similar program in 1967. Tax holidays, locational benefits, tariff protection, and freedom from labor unions were among the incentives proffered; however, the government gave little emphasis to infant industries, technology appraisal, or performance standards,[90] thereby immunizing most of the favored industrial projects from financial discipline, profitability, and global competitiveness. As might be expected, the key beneficiaries of such industrialization projects were either foreign firms or ethnic Chinese owners. Out of ninety-two companies enjoying pioneer status in 1963–67, ten companies (all foreign-owned), with an annual average rate of profit of over 18 percent, received 78 percent of the total tax relief granted.[91] Manufacturing's share of GDP remained a relatively feeble 9 percent.

The gaps between ethnic Chinese wealth and indigenous Malay poverty, combined with the ethnic basis behind political organization and electoral competition, exploded in the race riots of 1969. Two years later, the government introduced the NEP that sought, by 1990, to reduce the poverty level from 50 percent to 15 percent and to increase Bumiputera corporate equity ownership to 30 percent. A host of cognate programs gave ethnic Malays better access to training, capital, and land; ensured entry of Bumiputera into tertiary education; and required companies to restructure their corporate holdings in ways that would ensure the goal of 30 percent Bumiputera ownership.[92] Not surprisingly, such state efforts on behalf of UMNO's Malay constituency exacerbated tensions with Chinese business executives who feared encroachment on their well-established businesses. At the same time, the NEP provided Chinese capital holders with a strong incentive to ally with Malay politicians, a coalition that blurred the distinction between Chinese and Malay capital while solidifying the forces favoring strong state protection of the nontradable sectors.[93] These moves provided a robust boost to Bumiputera, creating a class of ethnic Malays who benefited from the program and gained substantial wealth through corporate connections.

Meanwhile, state institutions further expanded the country's public enterprises in sectors such as finance, commerce, and industry, all previously dominated by the private sector. Between 1970 and 1975, the national budget allocations for government corporations averaged more than ten times those of the previous five years.[94] Not surprisingly, the bulk of these were under the control of, and for the benefit of, UMNO's Malay constituents. The number of Malaysian public enterprises leapt from 109 to 1,014, and public sector employment jumped fourfold. Such expansion relied largely on deficit financing and oil reserves. Consequently, between 1980 and 1987, the accumulated public sector foreign debt grew from RM4.9 billion to RM28.3 billion. Loans from domestic sources brought the total from RM26.5 billion in 1980 to RM100.6 billion in 1986.[95] By 1987, public enterprises accounted for a third of public debt and 30 percent of total debt servicing.[96]

The Malaysian preference for SOEs found parallels in Indonesia's predisposition for dirigisme, mercantilist interventions, state ownership, and nationalist industrial planning, particularly after the big jump in oil prices in the 1970s. The state gained sufficient capital to reignite efforts at state-led industrialization in fields such as cement, fertilizer, textiles, glass, and auto assembly. SOEs also controlled various utilities, including ports, railroads, postal and telegraph services, and coal mines.[97]

Indonesian government investments in SOEs leapt almost tenfold between 1972 and 1976 alone.[98] New laws introduced after 1974 required all foreign investors to take on local equity partners. In many of these, the government introduced a system of import monopolies for private and public firms, thereby providing a lucrative system of rents for well-connected state enterprises, entrenching domestic cartels dominated by the sociopolitical elite, essentially the political and social coalitions surrounding the Suharto family.[99]

Not until the mid-1980s, as world oil prices fell, did Indonesia retreat from SOEs and allow a greater share of industrialization by private capital, mostly through incoming FDI or partnerships with foreign investors. Even then, state-owned enterprises dominated the manufacturing sector. In 1981, indigenous Pribumi, Chinese, and state ownership shares were 11, 22, and 62 percent, respectively.[100]

In more market-oriented Thailand, the small number of indigenous capitalists exercised outsized influence within the national economy. Although ethnicity was far less determinative of status and opportunity, most of the emerging industrial elites were first-generation Chinese and bankers were largely Sino-Thai who had nurtured close relations with leading military figures.[101] Manufacturing grew rapidly during the 1960s led by entrepreneurs who shifted from commerce to the production of textiles, automobiles, glass, electrical appliances, consumer goods and processed food for the domestic market.[102] Foreign trade became a valued engine of growth, with the state relying heavily on export taxes to finance imports. Import cartels, meanwhile, were pervasive, leaving officials to look unfavorably on any ISI policies that lowered the ratio of foreign trade to national income. As in Malaysia and Indonesia, beneficiaries of the cartelized arrangements in nontraded goods sought government protection, not help in enhancing their global competitiveness.

With domestic capital constricted from venturing into expensive and large-scale industrial development for global export, increases in industrialization across all three regimes rested far more heavily on globally mobile capital searching for productive investments. Overseas investors welcomed the combination of political stability, good infrastructure, and literate, low-cost labor, along with developed communication, transportation, and trade links.[103] The ruling political elites in both Malaysia and Indonesia had forged close links to particular socioeconomic supporters in ways that favored SOEs and continued dependence of exports of raw materials and agricultural goods. In Thailand, the strong laissez-faire orientation of most administrations and entrenched market positions of domestic business also constrained state institutions from heavy investments in projects aimed at rapid industrial transformation.

All three regimes thus attracted substantial foreign capital, as shown in table 2.2. The figures also show that Malaysia was consistently more reliant on foreign investment capital than either Thailand or Indonesia, but all three re-

Table 2.2 Foreign direct investment in gross domestic investment, 1971–93 (%)

	1971–75	1976–80	1981–85	1986–90	1991–93
South Korea	1.9	0.4	0.5	1.3	0.6
Taiwan	1.4	1.2	1.5	3.5	2.6
Malaysia	15.2	10.5	10.8	10.5	24.6
Thailand	3.0	5.9	3.2	5.9	4.7
Indonesia	4.6	2.4	1.0	2.0	4.5

Source: UNCTAD (United Nations Conference on Trade and Development) *UNCTAD Stat*, http://unctadstat.unctad.org/wds/ReportFolders/reportFolders.aspx?sCS_ChosenLang=en.

lied distinctly more on outside capital than did the developmental regimes in Taiwan or Korea.

The MIT regimes responded to these new opportunities from outside by loosening constraints on incoming investments through deregulation, privatization, and elimination of prior constraints over trade and investment.[104] Reduced controls over the operations of foreign capital and their subsidies combined with tightened laws governing industrial relations in ways that constrained workers' wages, working conditions, and mobility.[105] In the process, all three regimes moved from predominantly domestic and distributional economic paradigms to one that was more expansionist and export oriented.[106]

Unarticulated ethnic motivations behind the encouragement of FDI were not hard to discern in Malaysia. Indeed, some policymakers welcomed FDI as a way to limit ethnic Chinese influence over the economy.[107] When foreign firms balked at the quota requirements of the NEP, the government passed the 1986 Investment Promotions Act relaxing NEP rules on ethnic hiring. The consequence was the erection of a corporate empire blessed with unrestricted access to state-issued licenses and Malay preferences under the direct control of the governing party, UMNO. These could then support constituent and electoral purposes.[108]

Thailand and Malaysia were quicker to make the shift to exports than Indonesia. Indeed, in 1980 Dr. Mahathir, then minister of international trade and industry, initiated the state-owned Heavy Industries Corporation of Malaysia (HICOM) to forge joint venture firms with foreign partners in heavy and chemical industries, promote advanced exports, and lay an industrial and technological foundation for Malaysia's future growth.[109] Local businesses (particularly those under Chinese ownership) were reluctant to commit private capital, in part because of the huge amounts required, the long gestation periods before profitability, and not least because of the ethnic requirements of the NEP. As a result, the bulk of Malaysia's heavy industry projects involved Japanese partners (notably in the national car project, the Proton).

By the late 1980s, Indonesia also began to de-emphasize import substitution and to prioritize internationally competitive export industries, especially in labor-intensive industries.[110] This effort found willing partners as companies like Nike and Reebok relocated their production facilities from Korea and Taiwan into Indonesia. The resulting production networks wove the MIT economies into globally competitive industries, the export revenues from which could feed back to finance politically important and protected business interests.[111] Producers in Malaysia, Indonesia, and Thailand eagerly coupled their fortunes to incoming global and regional production networks.

In the 1970s and 1980s, export-oriented manufacturing began to overtake the export of agriculture and commodities in all three countries. Exports as a whole gained even greater significance from the second half of the 1980s. Indonesia's exports to GDP ratio rose to over 24 percent in 1987, and that of Thailand to over 34 percent in 1988. In Malaysia, rapid expansion in manufacturing pushed up the exports to GDP ratio to 89.9 percent in 1994.[112] Yet it is noteworthy that falling commodity prices did not lead to a reduction in such exports, due to balance of payments concerns.

High-tech products constituted a growing share of the exports by the ersatz developmental regimes as shown in table 2.3. A triangular pattern of trade prevailed. Firms headquartered in richer countries such as the United States, Japan, Korea, Taiwan, and Singapore shipped high-value-added components and intermediate products to Malaysia, Indonesia, and Thailand. There, assemblers turned them into final goods for export to those richer countries as well as to Europe.[113]

All participants profited from such networks but to dramatically differing degrees. Thus, Malaysia became the second largest exporter of semiconductors to the United States, but the industry remained relatively stuck at the same downstream stages of production; it continued to do assembly, testing, and packaging for multinational corporations (MNCs).[114] Since most of the components and technology were imported, few forward and backward linkages stimulated other segments of the indigenous economy. Nor were new jobs so numerous as to make a serious dent in unemployment; nor were they so bountiful as to stimulate the domestic consumer economy. Similarly, Thailand became one of the world's largest exporters of hard disk drives in the 1980s and 1990s, but there are still no significant Thai suppliers of parts or services to the foreign-owned disk driver producers.[115]

Table 2.3 High-tech exports as a percentage of manufactured exports

	1995	1996	1997	1998
Indonesia	6.92	8.54	10.73	9.74
Malaysia	45.64	43.94	48.51	54.49
Thailand	24.62	29.06	30.62	34.42

Source: World Bank Development Indicators, https://data.worldbank.org/indicator/TX.VAL.TECH.MF.ZS?locations=TH&name_desc=false.

As both a contributor and a consequence of the nature of their regimes, workers in Malaysia, Indonesia, and Thailand also failed to benefit from any sweeping upgrades in human capital improvement, unlike their Japanese, Korean, and Taiwanese counterparts. In the MIT regimes, few workers gained enhanced education or skill sets, leaving them less well positioned to contribute to, or to benefit from, the kinds of comprehensive technological upgrading that marked the economic transformations in the developmental regimes.

The industrial paradigms of the ersatz regimes were thus characterized by bifurcation. One component involved the burgeoning export-orientated international segment, and the other, the highly cartelized domestic segment.[116] As Jayasuriya has demonstrated, early industrialization efforts focused largely on import substitution in nontradable sectors. Such ventures redounded to the benefit of a limited number of participants with close links to the politically powerful. In the case of Indonesia, for example, politically connected entrepreneurs from both the Chinese Indonesian and the indigenous Pribumi business community were able to capitalize on the new economic opportunities afforded by deregulation and privatization. Politically connected figures nurtured large and diversified business empires with tentacles reaching into nearly all sectors of the Indonesian economy.[117]

In contrast, export-oriented activities in tradable sectors involved unions between foreign investors and local producers that were less protectionist and far more internationally oriented but with the bulk of the profits going to the foreign investor.[118] Numerous firms in the ersatz developmental regimes found themselves consigned to the production of low value-added components and low-wage jobs involving assembly, finishing, and packing of imported components. All drew on their large supplies of low-wage and irregular labor. All three regimes failed to deepen their production profiles by either integrating vertically or lowering unit costs for assembly and processing activities. Thus, manufacturing expanded only by widening the reliance on cheap, unskilled labor.[119] In turn, those large and unskilled labor pools reduced the pressures on governments to enhance the educational or technical skills of their workforce, creating a vicious cycle of low-wage/low-skill industrialization.[120]

These regimes' vulnerability to foreign capital showed in the economic and political buffeting each took during the AFC. In all three countries, investment capital, currency values, and GDP growth rates plummeted while unemployment soared. Even though GDP growth returned within two to three years, the collective vulnerability of the economic paradigms to the whims of foreign investors was unmistakable. The crisis also catalyzed major regime changes. In Indonesia, the Suharto regime lost power, secessionist movements broke out in several provinces, and a democratic system emerged. In Thailand, the economic crisis triggered constitutional changes, greater business engagement in politics, and populist electoral successes that in turn triggered a series of military coups. In Malaysia, repression kept the regime largely intact but scarred by an intra-UMNO split, a newly empowered opposition, and the firing and arrest of Deputy Minister Anwar Ibrahim.

This chapter analyzed how the prevailing policy paradigms in Malaysia, Indonesia, and Thailand bore certain similarities to the developmental regimes, particularly in export success and in rapidly rising GDPs. At the same time, the underlying economic paradigms were far less capable of generating continual industrial upgrading and enhanced sophistication. Those paradigms, in turn, were logical corollaries of the key regime configuration among state institutions, socioeconomic forces, and external forces. These too were far less cohesive than forces in the developmental regimes.

As a result, although the MIT regimes oversaw undeniable improvements in their national economies, extensive reliance on foreign investment combined with low investments in enhanced skills for their citizens left all three vulnerable to the priorities of external forces and far less capable of retaining substantial proportions of the riches generated within their countries. It also left them perpetually vulnerable to the next ersatz developmental regime able to undercut their labor costs and present itself as more appealing to foreign investors and the hot capital they can mobilize.

Chapter 3

Rapacious Regimes

Plunder over Prosperity: Philippines, North Korea, and Myanmar

In June 2018, DPRK leader Kim Jong-un arrived in Singapore for a summit meeting with President Donald Trump. His entourage, made up of relatives and associate overseers of a country whose per capita GDP ranked in the lowest dozen in the world, caravanned through the city in Mercedes-Maybach S600 Pullman Guard limousines, each costing $500,000, despite UN sanctions that banned the purchase of such luxury items. Ironically, impoverished North Korea, in the 1970s, had been richer than the now flourishing Republic of Korea to its south.

Consider also deposed Philippine president Ferdinand Marcos, who in February 1986, arrived in Hawaii with control of secret bank accounts holding between $5 and $10 billion that he had salted away over his twenty-one-year rule. In addition to his wife's repeatedly photographed two thousand pairs of luxury shoes in the presidential palace, the couple abandoned a citizenry riven by huge income inequality and extensive poverty. As with the DPRK, the contrast with earlier economic riches is confounding. During the early 1960s, manufacturing output in the Philippines exceeded that of both Taiwan and Korea, and the Philippine economy was the second most successful in Asia.

Economic improvement might seem a self-evident goal for any country and its leaders. After all, enhanced productivity and technological advances correlate robustly with higher profits for producers, healthier and better-paying jobs for workers, and enhanced citizen well-being. Certainly, the rapid economic transformations of East Asia's developmental regimes dramatized such sweeping enhancements; so did the more modest performances of their ersatz cousins. National upsides in all six dwarfed accompanying shortcomings. The presumption that countries should pursue economic improvement has its individual parallel in the oft-cited aphorism: "I've been poor and I've been rich. Believe me, rich is better!"[1]

To be sure, numerous structural impediments can hamper development. Far more puzzling are cases where regimes themselves erect steep barriers against material improvement. This chapter analyzes three such instances. Despite enormous resources that once gave them vast economic advantages over their once poorer neighbors, many of those prior laggards quickly went on to surpass them with stunning successes. Meanwhile, those countries that once held such promise remained lethargic bystanders before the national advances parading across the region.

This chapter follows the same format as the last two and examines three regimes with incredible potential for economic advancement that instead blended state institutions, socioeconomic forces, and external linkages into a witch's brew that fabricated an economic paradigm favoring rejection rather than pursuit of national economic transformation. The aggrandizement of a small circle of the politically and/or socioeconomically powerful took priority as personal predation eclipsed national prosperity. Widespread citizen impoverishment and macroeconomic stagnation was the result. I label these "rapacious regimes."

That those controlling state institutions or enjoying disproportionate socioeconomic influence should prioritize their own well-being is scarcely puzzling. Selflessness is hardly a pervasive by-product of power. Nevertheless, as the regional merry-go-round of economic improvement gained momentum, more and more regimes jumped aboard and reached for the golden ring that would guarantee them a continuing ride. In doing so, most regimes converged around policy paradigms that while invariably enriching a few also raised citizen living standards more broadly. This chapter analyzes why three East Asian regimes stood apart from regional trends and resisted their neighbors' compelling lessons.

Many excellent works have demonstrated that institutional patterns once established are difficult to replace; instead, they channel future options.[2] That logic sheds light on why, despite the promising possibilities of transformative economic paradigms, several regimes instead pursued policies contrary to those fostering successes across large swaths of the Asia-Pacific. Well-entrenched political and socioeconomic elites forged regimes that served their unilateral interests rather than opting for objectively better alternatives that might undermine the prevailing regimes. Whereas components of the developmental regimes formed protection pacts against existential threats by actions that advanced national economic improvement, the rapacious regimes saw an existential threat in radical industrialization that might topple them from their advantageous positions. Consequently, they opted for predatory pacts and economic paradigms to protect and enhance their powers of plunder.

This chapter contends that such regimes were radically different from those in the developmental or ersatz developmental regimes. The rapacious regimes embraced extractive and predatory institutions and economic paradigms that fed back in the form of disproportionate booty to core elements of the regimes. For the DPRK, protection of its antidevelopmental regime continued virtually unchallenged during the period since World War II. A similar pattern prevailed in the Philippines under Marcos (with residues well after), as did that of the military regime in Myanmar from roughly 1962 into at least the second decade of the twenty-first century.

These three rapacious regimes, despite similarly predatory behaviors, show far greater variations from one another than the earlier triads of developmental and ersatz regimes. To paraphrase the opening line from Leo Tolstoy's Anna Karenina, "Successful countries are all alike; every unsuccessful country is unsuccessful in its own way."[3] Consequently, I analyze them separately, rather than as a cohesive cluster.

The Philippines under Marcos

During the 1950s and 1960s, the Philippines had one of the fastest-growing and most industrialized economies in Southeast Asia. Its colonial legacy had bequeathed a comparatively well-educated, English-speaking citizenry, plus a civil service with numerous pockets of expertise.[4] The country had a substantial salaried middle class, high levels of education, and a parliamentary democracy. Into the early 1960s, its manufacturing output exceeded that of both Taiwan and Korea, and was among the most advanced in East Asia, ranking behind only that of Japan. The Philippines seemed poised for continued advances. Yet by the 1990s, it registered as one of East Asia's most abject economic failures. Where once its citizens enjoyed per capita incomes well in excess of Indonesia and Thailand, it had become the country with the highest level of poverty among the six original ASEAN countries.[5]

This dismal trajectory took its sharpest downward arc during the regime headed by Fernand Marcos from the mid-1960s until his toppling in 1986. The early Philippine economic promise vanished under a rapacious regime devoted to bolstering the bank accounts of the few at the expense of actions that might benefit the many. Although some of that rapaciousness faded after 1986, the Philippines as late as 2019 continued to rank among the most pervasively corrupt countries in East Asia, barely ahead of Indonesia and well behind Thailand or Malaysia.

Like the three developmental regimes, the Philippines provided an integral link in the United States' East Asian alliance structure. In conjunction with the IMF, the United States provided the country with substantial economic assistance. Subsequently, Japanese reparations and ODA injected additional foreign capital. Such monies were less fulsome than those provided by the United States to Japan, Korea, and Taiwan; however, the Philippines nonetheless enjoyed substantial external support while confronting minimal external security challenges. Yet unlike US support for the industrializing paradigms of the developmental regimes, in the Philippines, US policy provided a powerful prop supporting a regime of predation.

Thus, the regime configurations under Marcos proved far less conducive to economic transformation. Instead, all three regime elements cohered around resistance to expanded industrialization in favor of systematic pilfering of the state treasury. It was a regime that Paul Hutchcroft aptly labeled "Booty Capitalism."[6]

State Institutions

Three centuries under Spain, followed by five decades of US colonial rule, left the newly independent Philippines with local elites and state institutions that competed for power while jointly lacking an orientation toward developing a well-lubricated hegemonic agenda of growth.

This was particularly true regarding the relative autonomy of its multiple geographic regions. While the majority of local areas lacked budgetary autonomy and remained dependent on appropriations from Manila, several localities enjoyed greater self-reliance. There, local strongmen substituted personal muscle for official authority, with violence as their main tool of control. These regions prevented the central government from approximating Max Weber's most elemental state task: monopolizing violence over its assigned territory.[7] Instead, numerous powerful caciques commanded formidable private militias, exerting virtually unchecked control over their respective territorial empires.[8]

National political power in Manila from 1945 until 1972 rested largely with the legislature. Two large political parties with colonial forebears, the Nationalists and the Liberals, continued their legislative dominance after the war. The core constituents of both were deeply entrenched precolonial elites, most particularly locally rooted and phenomenally wealthy property owners. Intra-elite rivalries played out in legislative politics, with party loyalty being mercurially fluid. Legislators switched parties frequently, bringing with them their loyal lieutenants and core electoral supporters. Ideology and programmatic consistency exerted little hold. The prize for electoral success was the ability to dole out patronage and to extract benefits from state actions. Surface-level competition masked the reciprocity that united the two parties around mutual predation rather than national economic transformation.

In many respects, the Philippine civil service had the potential to be an efficient component of state institutions. Yet the colonial legacy of bureaucratic patrimonialism and exploitation of institutional positions deprived most agencies of the technocratic and professional traditions that pervaded the civil services of Japan, Korea, and Taiwan. Legislative patronage predilections further impeded coherent and meritocratic administration.

Technically, all civil servants in the Philippines must pass qualifying examinations. In reality, patronage appointees who never took such exams soon dominated administrative offices. For decades, the National and Liberal parties competed with one another, and both competed with the president, to control civil service appointments. In 1959, a three-way bargain divided patronage appointments in the civil service 50/50 between the president and the legislature.[9] As president, Marcos exploited such patronage to plunder the treasury. By the mid-1970s, those who had not passed the qualifying exams held 65 percent of civil service positions.[10] The result was state institutions neither sufficiently competent technically nor structurally motivated to target or implement any progrowth agenda.

Under Marcos, patronage merged with repression. First elected in 1965, and reelected in 1969 in a contest marked by corruption, violence, and voter intimidation, Marcos confronted the dual challenge of regional insurgency, most explicitly on the island of Mindanao, and a nationwide leftist and Communist insurgency. In 1972, citing civil unrest as his justification, Marcos suspended the constitution and declared martial law. His rule drew critical support from the army, but, as Hunt noted at the time, in the strictest sense of the word, what resulted was not a military regime.[11]

The president's commands drove military action and were viciously effective. State security forces mounted an ongoing persecution of individuals, mainly from the Left, who opposed government policies. The military arrested and detained some 30,000 opposition figures, including journalists, students, and labor activists. In addition, the army and the Philippine constabulary seized weapons and disbanded many of the private armies controlled by prominent politicians and other influential figures. Three thousand two hundred and fifty-seven extrajudicial killings and 737 enforced disappearances were registered, and approximately 35,000 were tortured and 70,000 incarcerated. Marcos also took control of the legislature and banned or exerted tight rein over numerous media operations. State institutions became tools to implement presidential dictates to crush criticism of both martial law and executive actions.

Benedict Anderson notes that Marcos also managed to arrogate power from the localities to the presidential palace. Doing so transformed the previously localized cacique system:

> Don Ferdinand [was] the Master Cacique or Master Warlord, in that he pushed the destructive logic of the old order to its natural conclusion. In place of dozens of privatized "security guards," a single privatized National Constabulary; in place of personal armies, a personal Army; instead of pliable local judges, a client Supreme Court; instead of a myriad pocket and rotten boroughs, a pocket or rotten country, managed by cronies, hitmen, and flunkies. . . . almost from the beginning of his presidency in 1965, Marcos had moved mentally out of the nineteenth century, and understood that in our time wealth serves power, and that the key card is the state.[12]

Until his ouster in 1986, Marcos and his presidency benefited from an extensive concentration of state institutional powers. Under martial law, the state expanded its controls over economic activity and Marcos manipulated state instruments in ways analogous to Park Chung-hee in Korea and Chiang Kai-shek or Chiang Ching-kuo in Taiwan.

Yet even under military rule and the strong concentration of executive power, private business continued to control important economic activities and most of them happily welcomed the congenial stability ensured by martial law. The state was never able to exert sustained dominance over the socioeconomic elite. Instead, political and socioeconomic elites converged in a de facto alliance that shared little with the comparable alliances in Japan, Korea, or Taiwan and their collective commitment to rapid industrialization. Instead, state institutions responded in preferential, partisan fashion to demands from socioeconomic allies.[13]

Where the political and socioeconomic elites found greatest common cause was in mobilizing the state machinery to extract treasury resources. As Paul Hutchcroft said of Marcos, "He believed he could have a vision for society . . . and still loot it." In this, he was almost without peer. According to Transparency International, Marcos ranks as the second most successful kleptocrat in modern history, having stolen roughly $5 to $10 billion during his two decades in the presidential palace.[14] As president, Marcos had multiple sources of highly discretionary revenues that underpinned a multipronged network of patronage from the country's timber, media, and utility sectors. Marcos added to his resources by expropriating the assets of political enemies.[15] Such domestic extractions were supplemented by kickbacks from foreign business leaders. Thus, in one instance, six Japanese companies operating under ODA auspices paid more than $50 million in bribes to Marcos and his associates in the late 1970s and early 1980s.[16]

In hindsight, the Marcos-led regime overreached its almost unlimited power when it authorized the assassination of opposition leader Benito Aquino in 1983 (similar to the KCIA's failed attempt to assassinate Kim Dae-jung). As civil unrest expanded, Marcos sought to quell it via a snap election in 1986 in which he faced an opposition spearheaded by Aquino's widow, Cory Aquino. Although he declared himself the winner, Marcos confronted widespread allegations of intimidation and vote tampering, including the walkout of thirty-five computer technicians handling the election results who testified to widespread official fraud. A cobbled-together opposition of parliamentarians, religious groups, students, civil servants, and some segments of the military, dubbed People's Power, rejected the results and ultimately drove Marcos from office, ending twenty-one years of one-man political rule as Corazon Aquino ascended to the presidency.

Socioeconomic Forces

Socioeconomic forces in the Philippines are fragmented and predisposed to resist mobilization, especially behind economic transformation. The Philippines is a multiracial, culturally diverse society. As such, it is distinctly dissimilar from societies in the developmental regimes and more similar to its Southeast Asian neighbors in the ersatz developmental regimes. The country has more than 7,600 islands, 2,000 of which have inhabitants. Distinct local identities predominate and social forces are hardly cohesive.

Offsetting such centrifugal forces is the powerful Catholic Church. Over 80 percent of the population is Catholic, providing church authorities with considerable sway over social policies such as birth control and educational textbooks. Rarely mobilized beyond such policy specifics, the church retains nascent sociopolitical influence such as that exerted in toppling Marcos in 1986. It has not, however, been a force for social and economic transformation.

As noted above, a small group of extremely wealthy land-based families long dominated local regions, the legislature, and the economy. They presented the most fundamental socioeconomic impediment to any national project of industrialization and economic transformation. In contrast to Japan, Korea, and Taiwan, where comprehensive land reform programs removed large landowners as potential opponents to sweeping industrialization, postwar Philippine inaction on land reform permitted such land-based families to continue their prewar, colonial, socioeconomic dominance.[17] Such outsized influence by Philippine landowners was more analogous to the long-standing predominance of the rural latifundia across much of Latin America. In particular, the Philippine sugar bloc survived as an agrarian elite intimately linked to US firms and the US market equally analogous to Latin America.[18]

Despite gaining independence from the United States in 1946, the Philippine pattern of land tenure and social structure remained semifeudal. Powerful landowners dominated their geographies through a pattern of clientelistic politics that afforded them a local power base independent of, and often antagonistic to, the central state institutions in Manila.[19] Instead, they transposed their local influence to the national level through their influence within the two major parties. The national legislature remained more an arena within which the locally powerful could flex their economic muscles than an independent political institution exerting control over society.

In contrast to business interests in the developmental regimes, the urban business community in the Philippines lacked any capacity to harmonize from a common hymnal. Philippine industrial entrepreneurs never developed into a distinct socioeconomic force with a collective interest in industrial transformation. A main reason for this fragmentation was the split between landowning families dabbling in industrialization and the prominent Chinese business class. Many businesspeople from the families of the older agrarian and commercial elites diversified family wealth by investing in a variety of low-risk traditional enterprises rather than in potentially high-growth industries with extensive global potential.[20] Meanwhile, until 1974, a stringent naturalization process and citizenship requirements banned most ethnic Chinese from multiple professions that left them subject to exploitation by the politically powerful. The one area open to the Chinese minority was business. Many took that route, complicating the otherwise predominant socioeconomic influence of the landowning class. Indeed, in the Philippines, even though ethnic Chinese comprise just 1 percent of the population, they control 60 percent of its wealth.[21]

Inequality remained pervasive as other countries in East Asia were enhancing social equality. Throughout the postwar era, the Philippines has had an exceptionally wide gulf between the wealth and income levels of the numerically small elite and the millions of workers, urban poor, and peasants.[22] For almost three decades, from 1961 to 1991, income inequality remained consistently high, with a gini index of 0.503 in 1961, 0.505 in 1965, 0.490 in 1971, 0.452 in 1985, 0.447 in 1988, and 0.477 in 1991.[23] One official survey of incomes in the late 1970s showed that the richest 10 percent of the population received 56 percent of the national income, while the poorest 30 percent received a mere 4 percent. In the urban areas where the rich were concentrated, the figures were 81 percent and 7 percent, respectively.[24]

As the World Bank noted, this pattern continued well into the twenty-first century, even after the Marcos dictatorship had been overthrown: "Millions of Filipinos wallow in poverty as the elite few control much of the country's wealth. Notwithstanding the country's relatively high gross domestic product (GDP) growth in recent years, those living in poverty increased from 30 per cent of the population in 2003 to 32.95 per cent in 2006."[25]

Rather than serving as a tinderbox of radical opposition to the regime and to rural oligarchic dominance, widespread inequality persisted due to the impediments preventing the poor from uniting in a collective voice. Labor unions were one potential source of opposition, and even the Philippines' low-level industrialization generated trade union expansion. In 1956, with manufacturing accounting for about 13 percent of the employed labor force, 500,000 workers, or about a quarter of nonagricultural wage and salary workers, were union members, well up from the 151,000 in 1951. By 1970, union membership had grown to about 1.2 million, or 10 percent of the total workforce. Yet this figure still represented only about 30 percent of all wage and salary workers.[26] Furthermore, unionized workers were concentrated in urban areas, mostly Manila, further weakening labor's political and economic reach.

Further dissipating labor's collective voice was the country's substantial worker migration. In 1974, the state institutionalized and supported the practice, and thus between 1979 and 1985, the number of overseas Filipino workers was roughly 380,000; by 1995, that had multiplied tenfold, reaching 3.8 million. The Philippines became a prototype for labor-exporting countries and a major contribution to the workforces of numerous countries across the globe. Between the years 1975 and 1995, about 8 million Filipinos had at one time or another found employment in more than 100 countries.[27] Originally, the bulk of these overseas workers were men, but by the early 2000s, the gender balance was largely female. Foreign earnings transferred back by overseas workers reduced poverty and improved life styles. Yet the system simultaneously reduces the potential for concentrated labor opposition to the regime and its pervasive economic inequality.

Nor does education provide any broadly accessible ladder out of poverty, nor an asset to potentially sophisticated corporate development. The country hosts numerous private for-profit diploma mills that service large numbers of the city's youths from lower- and lower-middle class backgrounds, including many part-time working students. A world apart from the country's limited number of laudable public and private institutions of higher education, these diploma mills expanded in number and enrollment beginning in the 1960s. As the demand for formal credentialing increased within the urban job market, these institutions packed unprecedented numbers of fee-paying students into overcrowded and often dilapidated or condemned buildings in downtown Manila. Rarely do they provide the actual skills training that would catapult their students up the economic ladder.[28] In turn, the lack of a technocratic and educated workforce mitigates against national moves into more technologically demanding industries, thus raising further the barriers to national economic transformation.

This is not to negate opposition forces. Yet it has been outside the party and electoral system that the bulk of socioeconomic opposition has played out. Both Communists and Islamists have carried out persistent armed insurrections against the regime. The ebbs and flows of the national economy correspond in large measure to the strength or suppression of these movements.[29] The country's abundance of unemployed and unemployable intellectuals— lawyers without clients, poets without readers, authors without an audience, cinematographers without studios, historians without classrooms, and journalists without employment—provided ample staff for the Communist Party. Such people serve as the organizing and instructional cadre of the party's semilegal propaganda teams, organizing groups, and committees.[30] The Communists have been particularly effective as an organized political party in exploiting rural discontents.

Furthermore, a Muslim minority in the southern part of the country, most prominently on Mindanao, has spawned an often-violent secessionist movement. Toward the end of the 1960s, restiveness rose due to long festering frustration over land grabbing, religious discrimination, and government neglect.[31] The agent for mobilizing Islamic discontent was the Moro National Liberation Front (MNLF). MNLF enjoyed widespread support within the surrounding area, particularly when Marcos cracked down on the region and failed to honor past agreements between his government and Mindanao's Muslims.

Only with the democratic movement that overthrew Marcos in 1986 did the Philippines display a temporary cohesiveness among previously diffuse groups—human rights lawyers, nuns and priests, writers, journalists, academics, and students. It is important to note that Filipino businesspeople who had acquiesced in the martial law regime through the 1970s recognized that by the mid-1980s their economic interests and social positions were at risk if they did not break with Marcos.[32] They thus swung their economic weight behind the populist forces. Their opposition was sufficient to alter the entrenched regime, and in the process to provide at least a temporary conduit for the expression and mobilization of peasant and working-class discontent that challenged both the regime and the entrenched class system.[33] Although sufficiently cohesive to topple an unpopular and corrupt president, People Power remained far too disparate to sustain itself and thus to generate subsequent socioeconomic or policy cohesiveness.

In summary, for decades, particularly during the Marcos period, a limited socioeconomic elite aligned with an oligarchic political class faced little effective political, social, or economic opposition. Together, they exploited state institutions and the national treasury both to plunder the state and to fend off antiregime challenges.[34] In the process, they bypassed any major industrial program, perpetuating instead an economic paradigm that perpetuated vast economic inequality.

External Forces

The Philippines had no shortage of external support, particularly in the form of its membership in an array of global and regional institutions. It was a charter member of the United Nations, a member of ESCAP (Economic and Social Commission for Asia and the Pacific) and several nonregional specialized agencies, such as the World Bank, IAEA (International Atomic Energy Agency), and the WHO (World Health Organization). The nation also joined APEC (Asia-Pacific Economic Cooperation), the Colombo Plan, G-24, G-77, and the WTO. It was also one of the five original members of ASEAN; in 1966, it played a leading role in the formation of the Asian Development Bank, whose headquarters went to Manila. Engagement with this host of global and regional institutions, however, presented few sustained challenges to the dominant political and economic elites, nor did they contribute to the advancement of any project of industrialization.

Beyond such generic institutional forces, however, the most important external influences on the Philippines by no means favored modernizing and industrializing. A colony of the United States from 1898 until the end of World War II, the Philippines provided the first case of voluntary decolonization, achieving independence on July 4, 1946. Yet Cold War calculations dictated that independence be followed by a 1947 bases agreement allowing the United States to retain sixteen bases (including major facilities such as Clark Field and Subic Bay), along with seven others in cases of "military necessity." All came rent free for a period of ninety-nine years.[35] On August 30, 1951, the two signed a Mutual Defense Treaty.[36] The Philippines thus gained nominal sovereignty by becoming another link in the chain of the United States' hub and spoke alliances across the Asia-Pacific. In all of these ways, the Philippines shared the experiences of Korea, Japan, and Taiwan. At the height of US military deployment in the 1980s, the Philippines hosted between thirteen and fifteen thousand military personnel and twelve thousand Department of Defense civilians.[37]

In exchange, the Philippines received significant American largess. Between 1946 and 1980, the United States provided the Philippines with some $2.8 billion in total foreign assistance. Hardly insignificant, this amount still paled next to the $12.7 billion to South Korea and the $5.8 billion to Taiwan.[38] Nor did US ties generate any cornucopia of one-sided blessings. Colonial political institutions and the predominance of the oligarchy of rich families continued into the postwar regime. Of particular importance to US policymakers was continuation of the monopolistic positions that a number of US companies had acquired under colonialism.

In this regard, Washington insisted on a continuation of special rights for US investors and entrepreneurs as a condition for Philippine independence. In addition, a free trade agreement allowed US firms, many with deep roots developed during the prewar years, to extend their already powerful economic positions within the country. The United States also retained ultimate control over national exchange rates and monetary policy, thereby constricting Philippine monetary autonomy.[39]

The interests of US businesses in the Philippines overlapped with fears of Manila politicians that their new republic would not survive without special access to the US market, continued US investment, and Washington's payment of extensive war claims. They thus accepted the skewed arrangements.[40] American investments provided the Philippines with jobs, capital, management skills, and technology. The privileged, often oligopolistic, position of such US firms, along with their dominance over scarce capital, however, were concentrated in agriculture, raw materials, and low-tech industries; they rarely created US–Philippine partnerships around industrial upgrading, even such as took place in the ersatz developmental regimes by foreign investors.[41] Although the United States' external support provided certain undeniable benefits, it also thus disproportionately reinforced an unjust, inefficient, and graft-ridden regime.[42]

Japan also provided support. The brutality of Japanese military actions during World War II led to some 1.1 million Philippine deaths, a history that soured Japanese–Philippine relations for many years after independence. Eventually, however, in May 1956, following hard negotiations, Japan agreed to provide the Philippines with $550 million in labor and products, along with a $250 million loan. Reparations focused on infrastructure, including such things as the creation of a cement factory, the purchase of cargo ships, and other infrastructure enhancements.[43] Japanese money continued to flow in through overseas development assistance; in 1989, for example, Japan provided 48 percent of the Philippines' overseas aid.[44] As with US assistance, aid from Japan ensured numerous Japanese companies would have favorable entry points and start-up advantages in the Philippine market.

Thus, despite a variety of external supports, the quid for such support was the quo of a continuation of entrenched state institutions and social forces.

The resultant regime blended the disproportionate influence of depredatious state institutions and the power of landed elites with protected market positions for US and Japanese investors. The resultant regime militated against jettisoning the disproportionate economic and political benefits redounding to a predatory domestic oligarchy, mitigating social inequalities, or loosening the stranglehold of powerful agricultural interests. Firmly entrenched in protected oligopolies with deep roots in rural land ownership, those with the economic resources to do so demonstrated neither the motivation nor the capacity to advance an economic paradigm of nationally driven and indigenously beneficial economic transformation. Nor did the Philippine regime, particularly under Marcos, prove even as capable as the ersatz developmental regimes in garnering a measure of inclusion in the regional production networks that enabled those countries to gain beneficial shares of global industrial exports. Instead, the cooperation between external and domestic components proved an exemplary rapacious combination.[45]

Economic Paradigm

The economic policy paradigm of the Philippines was a logical corollary to the regime. Economic policies, indeed, functioned as the cohesive agent binding the predacious constellation together, fortifying regime arrangements, and extending its persistence.

The economic paradigm in the Philippine regime pivoted on four fundamentals: (1) deep dependence on foreign loans, (2) import substitution, (3) component production for global networks, and (4) a black economy and widespread corruption.

The Philippines, like Japan and Korea in particular, emerged from World War II (and in the case of both North and South Korea, the Korean War as well), with a devastated infrastructure, particularly in Manilla. The early Garcia administration (1957–61) tried to advance a developmental Filipino First economy that would guarantee that its dominant beneficiaries were Filipino citizens. Yet, as noted, the US government and entrenched US businesses exploited their economic and security advantages to block such moves. From the early postwar years, US preeminence fostered a continued Philippine dependency that constricted the policy options available to Philippine officials and business leaders.

The small number of exceedingly rich families had few incentives to surrender the steady and sustained profits from their massive landholdings and agricultural monopolies in exchange for the uncertainties of industrializing. With domestic capital for investments in infrastructure and industry so constrained, "debt for development" became a watchword for early Philippine efforts at economic improvement. Foreign borrowing became a core necessity, a cycle that began with the Macapagal administration in the early 1960s. Elected in November 1961, Diosdado Pangan Macapagal Sr had promised a liberalization of the economy along with protection of US interests. In exchange, the US government supported a $300 million IMF loan. Although tariffs cushioned the impact of decontrol on the Philippine manufacturing sector, the tight IMF credit restrictions drove hundreds of Filipino enterprises to the brink of collapse. Many ultimately accepted the vice-like embrace of joint venture arrangements with foreign interests.[46]

Official government plans reverberated with developmental rhetoric, particularly in the proposals of the Marcos government. Yet the rhetoric was most often a fig leaf covering hand-in-the-till realities. Without question, foreign investors impeded rapid economic transformation; however, rapacious domestic extractions from the treasury proved to be the greatest impediment to a more transformative economic paradigm. Developmental eloquence masked Marcos's unrelenting commitment to treating development as a tactical means to enhance the economic fortunes of his family and friends. In the ongoing bait-and-switch between the promises in Philippine development proposals and the realities of corruption, the civil service played a supportive role. Philippine technocrats proved adroit at formulating the appealing proposals, but once the funds arrived, "the political leadership then allowed the unconstrained introduction of exceptions that made a complete mockery of the spirit and letter of the plans."[47]

Borrowing from abroad was noticeably heavy during the Marcos regime. Although he continued to encourage the promotion of exports, Marcos simultaneously protected ISI firms. Manufactured exports posted gains in the late 1970s and 1980s, but the technocrats and multilateral agencies supporting exports were unable to do little more than create additional avenues of diversification for the major family conglomerates. As long as external funds were readily available, it was expedient to let debt drive growth.[48] Money that flowed in from abroad in response to well-crafted promises flowed out through the sieve of official corruption. The result was a spiraling demand for ever more borrowing. Between 1962 and 1986, the Philippines' external debt grew from $355 million to $28.3 billion. By the end of the Marcos years, in absolute terms the Philippines was the ninth most indebted nation across Asia, Africa, and Latin America.[49] Borrowing received the support of successive US governments, to whom the issue of US military bases and security, along with the profitability of the Philippine operations of US firms, took priority over green eyeshade monitoring. The result was a succession of Philippine bailouts from its multiple balance-of-payment crises.

Access to foreign funds typically carried demands for enhanced access by foreign investors to the Philippine economy. At the same time, openings to foreign capital provided an important tool by which Marcos sought to legitimize his regime's "constitutional authoritarianism" before both local and foreign audiences. It was on this basis that his government succeeded in appealing to foreign lending agencies and investors, their support in turn being vital to the maintenance of his, and the regime's, predominance.[50]

As noted, the Philippines began an ISI strategy with the promise that it would provide the basis for expansion into exports (EOI). Yet, not surprisingly, political realities quickly trumped economic assurances. Powerful interests prevented the cohesive state planning required for EOI or any form of rapid industrialization.[51] Protected firms and industries became sinkholes for political patronage. Favored firms in turn demanded extended protection as they garnered gigantic profits. In return, state officeholders harvested lavish kickbacks and patronage privileges from the firm's managers. US partners in these industries often added their influence by opposing all changes to long-standing laws protecting them. As a result, tariff protection for local industries remained constant and high from the mid-1960s to the late 1970s. In 1983, home market production still accounted for 86 percent of value-added in national manufacturing.[52]

Thus, except for a limited number of cases, Philippine ISI rarely escaped the grip of the rent-seeking rurally rooted elites. By the late 1990s, the country had abandoned earlier plans for a national car, steel plants, and an aircraft industry. Even when the Philippines did attract FDI, like many other countries in Southeast Asia, its attractiveness lay in offering inexpensive component manufacturing or rapid and cheap assembly. In such roles within the electronics and semiconductor areas, numerous Philippine subcontractors gained profitability. Yet the transition from ISI to export-led growth and deepening industrial transformation, and from protection to self-sustenance made by numerous firms in Japan, Korea, and Taiwan, or even the connections to industrial regional production networks of the ersatz developers, proved a chimera in the Philippines, always vanishing around a sequence of ever-recurring corners.

Furthermore, as neighboring countries improved their infrastructures and advanced up the technology gradient, they presented more attractive targets for foreign investors and regional production networks. The Philippines, as a result, failed to attract the levels of foreign direct investment that flowed into Indonesia, Malaysia, Thailand, China, and Vietnam. Japanese and Taiwanese capital, for example, which assumed great importance in the region, largely bypassed the Philippines for decades due to perceived political instability, corruption, and antiforeign sentiment.

Services came to prevail over industrial production: the industrial sector contributed just over 30 percent of the country's GDP, while the service sector commanded 60 percent. Tourism became an important engine of job creation and income generation. So did global call centers for everything from travel agencies to medical record maintenance. Welcome as the growth in such call center jobs was, engineering and business graduates were often the ones queueing to take them. One International Labor Organization (ILO) study noted that the country's average annual productivity growth between 2000 and 2005 was just 0.9 percent, compared with 10.3 percent in China and 4.9 percent in India. Many new job entrants remain underemployed.[53]

Finally, despite many promises by a succession of political leaders, including most notably the valiant efforts of the Ramos administration (1993–98) to end corruption, cartels, and monopolies, rapaciousness favoring the same fusion of powers that held sway during the Marcos years hardly vanished. Indeed, it made a comeback in the governments of President Joseph Estrada and Gloria Macapagal Arroyo (1998–2010).[54] Even under the allegedly anticorruption regime of Rodrigo Duterte, in 2018 Transparency International ranked the Philippines as 99th out of 180 countries for corruption.[55]

It was during the Marcos dictatorship that the Philippine regime was at its most rapacious. External and domestic forces converged to advance an economic paradigm supporting disproportionate privileges for a few wealthy families and entrenched US firms, along with a heavy dose of political corruption. Regime forces converged in ways that profited by bypassing industrialization, widespread skills development, poverty alleviation, or state regulation. The result was a continuation of high levels of corruption, the retention of a socioeconomic elite concentrated in a powerful landowning class, widespread socioeconomic inequality, and a noninclusive and minimally industrialized economy.

The Democratic People's Republic of Korea

Since the end of World War II, the DPRK has pivoted around a combination of despotic state institutions, a cohesive party apparatus, and a well-ordered military. Top state officials have enjoyed virtually unchallenged ability to control the entire country in ways that far transcend the reach of political machinery in most other countries. On the other hand, DPRK state institutions lack a deep reservoir of functional technocrats able to engineer the kind of transformative economic policy paradigm central to far less authoritarian regimes. Nor does the DPRK regime include any independent socioeconomic forces capable either of challenging state institutions or of initiating, advocating, or assisting, any meaningful economic transformation.

Indispensable external support for the regime came initially from the USSR and the PRC. Yet, until the 1979 economic shift in China and the USSR's collapse in 1991, both promoted economic policies that relied on the same kind of top-down state planning that proved such a dismal recipe for them both. Offsetting positive external support from the PRC and the USSR, for long periods the DPRK confronted counterpressures from the United States, and to a lesser extent, South Korea and Japan. Such opposition was particularly limiting on DPRK economic options as Soviet and Chinese assistance slackened and the DPRK regime increased its indigenous missile and nuclear weapons programs.

This mixture has triggered metronomic predictions that the DPRK regime was inherently unstable and on the brink of collapse.[56] As of this writing, however, and with the full awareness that limited access to information can render domestic actions opaque, the North Korean regime shows persistent signs of being well entrenched. What is the nature of that regime? Why has it pursued

economic policies so unpromising for national transformation and so preda-
torily beneficial to the profit and control of its narrow ruling elite?

State Institutions

DPRK state structures owe much to the tutelage of the Soviet Union under
Stalin. Indeed, the language originally used to draft the DPRK constitution
was Russian; only later did a Korean translation ensue. Not surprisingly, the
state apparatus bears strong resemblances to its totalitarian forebear. At the
center is the Korean Workers' Party (KWP). Officially, the party is superior to
and provides guidance for, both the civilian and military agencies of government. The totalitarian template further ensures the prevalence of a single all-
encompassing ideology. State-run media deliver nothing but the messages of
the leadership. Arbitrary terror atomizes individuals, particularly potential regime challengers. The party and the state apparatus in turn operate with full
authority over a comprehensive command economy.[57]

Totalitarian rigidity has fluctuated over time, noticeably softening following the transition from founder and committed Stalinist, Kim Il-sung, to his
son, the periodically more pragmatic Kim Jong-il, and subsequently with the
"third Kim," Kim Jong-un. Spanning the rule of these three, however, state
institutions and resource allocation have revolved around four central components. Despite the notionally centralized power of the KWP, the Kim dynasty
supersedes all formal institutions, even as the Kim family exerts its control
through those institutions.

The Kim dynasty has held office by initial investiture and subsequent he-
redity since 1945. A 1974 proclamation by Kim Jong-il institutionalized the dynastic leadership. All three Kims have ruled in sultanic fashion. Yet despite
media caricatures, none has been an unchecked dictator. Each of the supreme
leaders relied on support from a cadre of close relatives and longtime personal
loyalists, a "selectorate" numbering between two and five thousand individuals, depending on how widely one draws the inclusionary circle.[58] That selectorate monopolizes political as well as economic resources. Three key elements
reinforce dynastic control: (1) the personality cult surrounding the Kim dynasty, (2) the Supreme Leader's direct control of the KWP and the Korean
People's Army, and (3) the family loyalties of an inner circle connected by
blood or marriage to the Supreme Leader.[59]

A substantial number of the North Korean political elite are either members of the extended Kim family or descendants of the guerilla fighters who
served under Kim Il-sung in 1930s Manchuria. These individuals monopolize
top party, government, and military positions chiefly, if not exclusively, as the
outgrowth of their personal connections with the Great Leader and his family.[60]
Nepotism and a cult of personality have ensured each of the three Kim's dominance over the party. The absence of administrative or judicial checks, inde-

pendent social organizations, or independent information sources ensures the party's dominance over the entire country.[61]

The military, the KWP and the cabinet and state bureaucracy provide the main institutions implementing the leader's decisions. Not surprisingly, each of these three institutions has somewhat different priorities and uses discrete tools to sway decision making. Strict ideological adherence drives the KWP. The military, like its counterparts in most countries, prioritizes hard security along with protection of the borders and the personal well-being of the ruling elite. State bureaucratic institutions gravitate toward technical expertise and pragmatism in their respective areas of responsibility, even at the expense of ideological purity or the unchecked prioritization of hard security.

Ongoing contestation recurs regularly among these three. Notably, under Kim Il-sung, the KWP enjoyed unquestioned primacy. His son, worried about party corruption and external security challenges, reduced party predominance in favor of a military first orientation. In addition, by the end of the 1990s, the notion of a complex national economy completely subservient to state control had become a fiction as market mechanisms gained in significance, often with the indirect support of state bureaucrats and despite the hand wringing of ideologically rigid party and military leaders.

Since taking office, Kim Jong-un has returned the KWP to the top slot as a check on the military, but he has also been more tolerant than were either of his forbearers of ideologically impure marketization and increased rent seeking across all three institutions provided they deliver governing funds to him. This in turn has further accelerated marketization.[62] The differing institutional predispositions of the KWP, the military, and the state bureaucracy, however, should not be overemphasized; by no means does politics in the DPRK approximate institutional pluralism. Any give-and-take plays out within an unwavering authoritarianism; the top leader retains preeminent control over the levers shaping societal behavior and economic direction. Institutional shadings pale compared to the tight guiderails ensuring that the selectorate remains in singular conformity to decisions by the top leader.[63]

State institutions wield multiple tools of control, the main target of which is the citizenry at large. Restrictive social policies, manipulation of ideas, overt force, co-optation, and informational deprivation are among the most noteworthy.[64] Within a relatively short period after its establishment, the DPRK installed a dense web of social control mechanisms, capped most brutally by a network of prison camps. The Secret Service, the Secret Police, the Ministry for Public Security, the Ministry of State Security, and the Ministry of Defense coordinate to ensure collective social oversight and to ensure that repression is all but self-reinforcing.[65]

Citizens, however, are not the sole targets of surveillance. Members of the political elite themselves are subject to relentless scrutiny. A complex monitoring system enhances unquestioned loyalty and reduces fissures within the political elite.

Multiple overlapping conduits of information guarantee that the top leader remains apprised of any hint of antiregime stirrings within the KWP, civilian state institutions, or the military. The leader also benefits from a separate military force devoted exclusively to his personal protection. This personal force, the Guard Command, consists of three brigades, heavily equipped with tanks, artillery, and aircraft. Its mission is to defend the dynastic head in the event of any attempted coup. Parallel military forces, the Pyongyang Defense Command and the Pyongyang Antiaircraft Artillery Command, share the responsibility for countercoup defense and protection of the capital.[66] All function to coup-proof the regime.

Proximity to the leader has obvious advantages, yet carries with it a pinch of precariousness, as seen by the massive personnel purges that followed the ascent of Kim Jong-un. Anxious to surround himself with individuals whose personal loyalty is unquestioned, he purged most of his father's leadership team. In the first five years after assuming power, according to a 2016 report by the Institute for National Security Strategy, Kim ordered the execution of at least 340 people.[67] The methods of execution were remarkably grizzly, with relatives of the condemned often required to witness the death. Most prominent were Kim's uncle and putative regent, Jang Song-taek, publicly executed in 2013, as well as the high profile biological assassination of Kim's half-brother, Kim Jong-nam, in a Malaysian airport, designed to eliminate a possible dynastic challenger.

State institutions are thus efficient and controlling, but not in the service of economic upgrading and citizen improvement but precisely the opposite. State institutions ensure the continuity and security of a narrow and self-rewarding selectorate, none incentivized to risk their benefits under the current regime to promote radical departures from existing arrangements under the command economy.

Socioeconomic Power

Independent socioeconomic forces are all but negligible. State institutions devote considerable effort and resources to preventing citizens from developing even minimal relationships of intra-personal trust that might become the basis for independent collective action, let alone mobilization in service of bottom-up regime dismantling.[68]

In its early days of the regime, the KWP was composed primarily of members identified as poor peasants (50%) and laborers (20%). As the party expanded, the absolute number of workers doubled and that of peasants tripled, offering such individuals some upward status mobility.[69] At the same time, Article 65 of North Korea's constitution claims that the country's citizens "enjoy equal rights in all spheres of state and public activities"[70] In reality, the regime formally divides North Korean society into elaborate categories based on perceived political loyalty and family background, akin to castes (*songbun*). The *songbun* system developed between 1957 and 1960 as Kim Il-sung consolidated power. It continues to facilitate the isolation and purging of enemies of the Kim dynasty, real and imagined, while rewarding Kim family loyalists.

Three major categories of sociopolitical status ("core," "wavering," and "hostile") are refined into some fifty-one subcategories, all based on the family's history of supposed loyalty to the state and the leader. "Core" members enjoy a cornucopia of privileges: pay through an exclusive system, access to foreign currency, shopping at stores with higher-quality products, and the best housing. Conversely, if one is in a "wavering or "hostile" *songbun*, the reverse is true—limited schooling, dismal rations, and decrepit housing in rural backwaters.[71]

In addition, each household must belong to a group of thirty to forty families, each of which is responsible for surveillance of the others. A single individual responsible to party officials and local police oversees the collectivity. All workers must attend one to two hours a day of ideological indoctrination. The country's numerous newspapers are all subject to strict government supervision. Censorship of written work is widespread, and radio and television channels are state run and all receive only official government stations, usually broadcasting official speeches or propaganda.

Internet access is restricted to top party and government officials along with scientists and researchers working under constant government oversight. Cell phones were not even minimally available until November 2002 and these remain under state control. Eventually cell phone service expanded beyond the capital, and as of 2017, roughly four million subscribers, or one-sixth of the population, had access. However, nearly all North Korean phones, tablets, laptops, and computers run on locally developed operating systems laced with censorship and surveillance tools that prevent users from accessing the information-laden outside world.[72]

As former British diplomat David Everard declared, "The principal form of political control [is] an attempt to enclose all citizens within a mental world created by the regime."[73] Orwellian manipulation of ideas and information increases the regime's de facto legitimacy while weakening that of potential opponents

Buttressing such limitations on information are mandatory displays of regime loyalty: bows before widespread official monuments and memorials, mass rallies in stadiums, mandatory lapel pins bearing the image of one or another Kim, tediously lengthy and compulsory daily study groups, and strict internal travel restrictions.[74] Young men perform eight to ten years of strictly disciplined military service as but one dimension of the highly militarized nature of the regime. Although it boosts the ranks of the military, lengthy military service deprives the country of the strength and energy of large numbers of young men who might otherwise contribute to the civilian economy.[75]

Every organized social organization has KWP involvement, further tightening social control. For example, the Kim Il-sung Socialist Youth League (KSYL), created, operated, and monitored by the KWP, organizes students. The KSYL is then responsible for coordinating between state institutions and all youth across the country aged eighteen to twenty-eight, ensuring collective political indoctrination and active participation in state activities.[76] By injecting the party into every organized social interaction, the political machinery ensures a regime devoid of truly independent social organizations, reducing the likelihood of counterregime activities.

Work life is also subject to strict controls. Already tedious labor in factories or fields intensifies regularly with endless declarations of "100-day battles," and even "200-day battles," that necessitate twelve- to fourteen-hour days, seven days a week. Often factory or construction site workers find it impossible to return home even at night.[77]

Until the turn of the century, these restrictions were all-inclusive. Only in the early to mid-2000s did a modicum of loosening occur. Tunable radios, DVDs, and CD players trickled into the country, often smuggled in by South Korean NGOs. In addition, North Korean traffickers, contract workers, and entertainers enjoy greater contact with foreigners and thus become channels for information about life beyond the borders. The Sunshine Policy of South Korean President Kim Dae-jung (1998–2003) and continued by his successor, Roh Moo-hyun (2003–8), allowed more businesspeople from the South to enter the North and vice versa. In all, the effect was an expanded portion of the North Korean population developing a slight expansion in awareness of the vast chasm between their lives and those of counterparts in South Korea or China. Authorities had little choice but to accept such changes, and their attempted crackdowns have been uneven and only partially effective.[78]

The gradual opening of markets and the deterioration of the state-run segments of the economy have reduced but hardly eradicated the salience of *songbun* status. Yet individuals who can generate cash by marketing garden vegetables, owning a truck, lending money, or being a successful smuggler, for example, might acquire sufficient resources to bribe their way to greater perquisites than might arise from their designated *songbun*. This results in a reinforcing spiral in which market-generated cash contributes to, and takes advantage of, the rise in official corruption and the exploitation of official office for private gain.

The most draconian component of control in the DPRK is its extensive network of gulags and prison camps. Estimates are that some 80,000 to 120,000 people are currently in prison for a wide variety of mostly political crimes. Satellite photographs reveal that at least one such camp is three times the size of Washington, DC.[79] Punishment usually extends beyond the arrested individual; also deemed culpable are immediate family members. Often such imprisonments concentrate on multiyear doses of ideological reeducation until the imprisoned can convince authorities of their unwavering loyalty to the regime and its supreme leader. Until then, the prisoner undergoes a backbreaking work schedule and a meager diet with no outside visitations.[80]

State institutions thus are independent from meaningful social or economic partners or counterpressures. The DPRK lacks a meaningful basis for independent socioeconomic action. Rigid control mechanisms prevent the emergence of social or economic forces with significant autonomy from the state machinery. The combination also obviates any beneficial fusion between politics and socioeconomics aimed at the joint advancement of a policy paradigm targeting substantial industrial upgrading.

External Forces

The DPRK long owed its very survival to support from China and the Soviet Union. During the Korean War, China provided the regime with critical military assistance—including soldiers and matériel. From then until the early 1990s, these two external powers were the DPRK's most important markets and its major suppliers of oil and other basic necessities, typically through substantially discounted friendship prices. The collapse of the Soviet Union and its Eastern European satellites, along with the demise of bipolar rigidities in East Asia, frayed those welcoming lifelines. Consequently, DPRK leaders struggled to reorient the country's foreign policy toward improved relations with the United States, Japan, and even with its archrival to the south, the ROK. Regime leaders hoped that a more favorable external environment might provide tangible security and economic assistance that might improve the country's dismal lot. This attempted shift never acquired sufficient traction to offset foreign opposition to the North's unstinting pursuit of nuclear weapons and sophisticated missile systems, its repressive human rights abuses, and its steady stream of conventional military provocations.

As bipolar tensions eased in the early 1990s, the George H. W. Bush administration removed some one hundred tactical nuclear weapons from South Korea. In January 1992, the two Koreas signed a Joint Declaration on the Denuclearization of the Korean Peninsula. Several days later, the North concluded an agreement for nuclear inspections with the IAEA; however just over a year later, the IAEA declared that the North was not complying with the agreement. The North responded by announcing its intention to withdraw from the Nuclear Non-Proliferation Treaty (NPT).

The North's leadership claimed that its nuclear program was designed to meet critical civilian energy needs and not to produce weapons. The Clinton administration, however, threatened military attacks to prevent continuation of the program, insisting on the regime's return to the NPT. Following the 1994 Agreed Framework, tensions again abated with both the United States and eventually with South Korea.[81]

In 1998, South Korea elected its first nonconservative president, Kim Daejung, who introduced his so-called sunshine policy promising economic aid for the struggling North Korean regime in an effort to improve bilateral relations and reduce security tensions. In October 2000, following positive signs in Pyongyang's talks with South Korea, Vice Marshall Jo Myong-rok, a senior North Korean military leader, visited Washington and met President Clinton. Secretary of

State Madeleine Albright reciprocated three weeks later with a visit to Pyong-yang and a meeting with Kim Jong Il. The visits sought to lay the groundwork for an expanded Agreed Framework and a potential visit to the DPRK by President Clinton.[82] As the DPRK's relations with the ROK and the United States were improving so were DPRK links to Japan. Years of behind-the-scenes negotiations set the stage for a Pyongyang visit by Japanese prime minister Koizumi in September 2002, portending their improved bilateral ties as well.

The improving external situation for the DPRK came asunder with the presidency of George W. Bush. Citing alleged secret information showing violations of the Agreed Framework, Bush ended that agreement, lambasted the "sunshine policy," and declared that North Korea was part of an "axis of evil."[83] Several years of US confrontation followed, along with dithering developments in the multilateral Six Party Talks, until a successful DPRK nuclear test in 2006. Several promising breakthroughs in Six Party negotiations soon surfaced, but external relations deteriorated further with the failing health of North Korean leader Kim Jong-il and the reinvigoration of US predictions of DPRK regime collapse.[84]

After that, the DPRK's only semireliable external assistance came from China, whose leaders continually pressed the DPRK regime to devote greater attention to economic improvements and less to single-minded security enhancements, essentially arguing that the DPRK should emulate China's post-1979 economic experiences.[85] China has continued to be the regime's major source of food and energy assistance. Thus, in 2006–7 the DPRK was the recipient of roughly half of China's annual development assistance.[86] In the mid-2010s, Chinese investments accounted for as much as 85 percent of total incoming FDI to the DPRK as Chinese investors expanded beyond their original investments in restaurants and tourism to concentrate on resource extraction and infrastructure projects such as roads, bridges, and railways.

As with its support during the Korean War, a key Chinese goal has been to avert DPRK regime collapse, which could have potentially devastating consequences for Chinese border security. In the process, the DPRK has become ever more dependent on China. That showed no signs of changing simply in response to the sequence of high-profile photo ops between Donald Trump and Kim Jong-un even as those meetings enhanced the international visibility and normalization of both Kim and the DPRK regime.

The DPRK's external relationships have always fixated on a limited number of countries, they have rarely involved multilateral linkages, and they have seldom been conducive to domestic economic transformation. The political leadership in Pyongyang has remained dubious about Chinese contentions that greater economic openness would not undermine continued party control. Circles around the leadership remain convinced that any such DPRK opening would in fact introduce disruptive investment, trade, information, and diplomacy, all likely to trigger the kinds of regime collapse that took place across Eastern Europe. The fates of Romania and Ceaușescu, in particular, haunted both Kim Il-sung and his son. The chaotic consequences of regime protection are manifest in the North Korean economic paradigm.

Economic Paradigm

As was noted with regard to South Korea, postwar North Korea was a legatee of a far more sophisticated industrial infrastructure than was the South. When World War II ended, the North, particularly the areas around Pyongyang, housed the most substantial concentrations of sophisticated Japanese industrial facilities.[87] Following the destruction of the 1950–53 war, Kim Il-sung set about rebuilding the national economy, following the Soviet model of mobilizing labor to construct heavy industry. That kept the North far more economically successful than its southern half into the early 1970s. Yet the regime and its associated economic policies squandered that initial advantage.

The DPRK economic paradigm rests on three discrete economic systems. The numerically limited elite operates within what one analyst labeled the "Royal Court economy." That economy revolves around the country's core businesses; it can earn and traffic in foreign currency. It operates various affiliated agencies, banks, and enterprises, and is responsible for securing governing funds for the Kim family and its supportive selectorate. It does this through a variety of domestic and overseas economic activities—both licit and illicit.[88] A second and largely separate economy involves the military, with its generous government funding and access to foreign military equipment and exchanges. These two components constitute almost half of North Korea's total economic activity. Finally, the remainder, the people's economy, falls under the control of the cabinet and state institutions.

Guaranteed a relatively well-heeled lifestyle by these first two economies, the politically and militarily privileged have few incentives to surrender such benefits to press for policies of economic transformation within the public economy. Thus, the regime lacks, for example, the internal motivations that drove the Taiwanese or South Korean militaries and party leaders to advocate widespread industrialization and techno-nationalism.

Three major periods in DPRK economic policies followed. First came roughly forty years of state planning under a command economy, bolstered by the Japanese legacy and massive injections of Soviet, along with some Chinese, aid. A second period of recurring economic failures followed, exposing the inherent limitations of state planning absent massive foreign assistance. Finally, and third, the regime began a balancing act between the command economy and tolerance for the emergence of numerous bottom-up market mechanisms. None of these periods saw any serious moves toward policy paradigms replicative of those that propelled any of the regimes discussed in the prior two chapters.

Aside from the separate "royal economy" rewarding the narrow political elite, state planning and the command economy were all-inclusive. During the

1960s, North Korea was unique in being the only nation in the world where markets disappeared almost completely. Few other Communist countries were as successful as the DPRK in limiting market activities.[89] Nonetheless, on several occasions in the 1950s and 1960s, the leadership in Pyongyang embarked on modifications, tinkering with agricultural policy, increasing investment in light industry, and easing restrictions on the possession of private land or the operations of markets. "These measures could not be classed as major reforms, but in the context of trying to develop a socialist society, the leadership found even these decisions ideologically sensitive and difficult to make."[90]

During this period, DPRK economic policies underwent virulent criticisms from East European Communists resident in Pyongyang. Most assessed the efforts as badly conceived and poorly executed. Yet official secrecy prevented even those diplomats from gaining much detailed knowledge. Their embassies had only slightly better information than did any outsider, and even most Communist observers sneered at North Korean economic decisions.[91]

The collapse of the Soviet Union snatched away vital export markets and aid for the DPRK. Despite the regime's constant solipsistic paeans to its self-reliance, the DPRK economy had survived on the back of Soviet subsidies, and those vanished as Moscow discontinued its aid in 1990. The crisis that followed cut industrial output by 50 percent within a few years.[92]

Never economically self-sufficient, the DPRK consequently had an even stronger need for hard currency to sustain the regime and to gain foreign capital. DPRK embassies and overseas personnel lack central government funding and instead must raise their own funds, often through criminal activities, to sustain their missions and to contribute income back home to sustain the royal economy. In addition, the regime dispatches hundreds of thousands of laborers to foreign countries to earn needed revenues. The vast majority of that labor goes to China and Russia in construction, agriculture, logging, garment work, and traditional medicine.

Under these new conditions, economic "realists" at home enjoyed more freedom to propose fresh ideas. The first came in the mid-1980s, following the resolutions of the Sixth Workers' Party Congress and coinciding with the development of a more accommodating line toward South Korea. The second was in the early 1990s. During the 1993–94 nuclear crisis with the United States, many protoreformers sought to open channels to the West in hopes of counterbalancing the rigid command economy and its prioritization of security-oriented allocations for the military. In the minds of such reformers, foreign policy and security concerns had acquired a singularity that handicapped national economic growth. Both instances fell short, even though no government policy officially reversed these directions; both simply petered out when negative events overtook them.[93]

Officially, the DPRK maintains significant residues of the planning system, but the scale of the command economy began to shrink as marketization expanded.[94] The DPRK faced an economic disaster and a nationwide famine between 1991 and 1998. Under such dire conditions, nascent markets began to spring up across the country. Nearly all plants and factories ceased to operate sometime between 1995 and 1997. By early 1997, the average production of major plants was reportedly a mere 46 percent of capacity.[95] The public distribution system (PDS) largely collapsed and ration coupons guaranteed little. The United Nations Food and Agriculture Organization (FAO) found that 57 percent of the population that depended on the PDS and nearly all farmers had kitchen gardens. Furthermore, 60 to 80 percent of PDS dependents and 65 percent of co-op farmers foraged for food, and 40 percent received some support from relatives living in the countryside (either as gifts or through barter).[96]

State institutions and political leaders responded to this rising private sector with ambivalence. They generally accepted that some expanded degree of private enterprise was unavoidable, but for ideological reasons, they were not prepared to legalize it completely. Broadly speaking, the KWP interpreted any ideas surrounding words like "reform" and "opening" as equivalent to regime collapse, precisely what they saw as having followed such openings in Eastern Europe. The military in turn argued that even minimal market openings would undercut its ability to protect the country from threats.[97]

In 2002–3, the regime again attempted to conduct a number of reforms aimed at stimulating the private economy and partially extricating it from the shadows. In 2004 these reforms were rolled back, however, and then, from 2005 to 2009, the authorities actively undermined the private economy. The regime did its best to resist reform and maintain the domestic status quo, despite strong pressure from Beijing and Seoul to do otherwise. In particular, in 2005 the government attempted to revive the comprehensive rationing system; however, the shortage of funds and ineffective bureaucratic controls resulted in only partial success. The government also launched a series of intense anti-market campaigns and increased security on the border with China in a vain effort to limit smuggling and unauthorized crossings by migrant workers.

A particularly draconian antimarket measure followed on November 30, 2009, when the government replaced existing bank notes with new bills at a rate of one hundred to one, along with a cap on how much old money any citizen could exchange. Justified as a way to seize capitalist profits, the move effectively confiscated virtually all accumulated private wealth and triggered sharp price increases and social unrest. In response, Leader Kim skirted personal blame and ordered the public execution of the designer of the currency revaluation, Pak Nam-gi.[98]

Following such failed efforts to prevent conspicuous market openings and the accumulation of private wealth, the government slowed its crackdown on the country's nouveau riche, limiting itself to administrative restrictions over private sector activities, most of which lacked consistent enforcement.[99] This policy of benign neglect became even more extensive once Kim Jong-un took power in December 2011. He demonstrated more tolerance of private enterprise than his father or grandfather, in some instances allowing designated government-sanctioned markets. While the opacity of DPRK data makes it difficult to be sure, estimates are that private markets by 2016 accounted for 30 to 50 percent of the GDP.[100]

In spring 2013, Kim Jong-un took another step toward even greater tolerance of markets and an enhanced focus on economic growth by announcing the so-called *byungjin* policy of parallel development of the economy and nuclear weapons, effectively lessening the regime's long-standing military first status.[101] Then in his New Year speech in January 2018, and more explicitly in April 2018, Kim declared that his country had achieved a credible nuclear deterrent and would be able to suspend future testing. The "new strategic line" for the ruling KWP would be "socialist economic construction."[102]

As a relatively young man facing the possibility of future decades in power, Kim is freer than his father was to focus on the long term. Looking to the successful economies of Communist Vietnam and China, while not acknowledging any debt or imitation, Kim Jong-un expanded the national economic playbook to include special economic zones and experimentation and selective rule bending within a limited geography. The initial results were encouraging. In 2016, according to the Bank of Korea the national economy recorded its fastest expansion in seventeen years, although such economic growth faces longer-term challenges due to UN Security Council sanctions.

Kim's new policy was in fact an official acknowledgment of the rising significance of markets throughout the country. Ruediger Frank summarized the situation in 2018: "consumerism has taken a firm hold in the country. Cars, smartphones, electric bicycles, flat screen TVs, fashion and fancy food and cafes are all available. The over 400 markets and even state-run shops and stores of North Korea are full with a great variety of top-quality products. A society that for a long time was economically largely homogeneous and where differences between individuals existed because of political merits such as Party membership, or political shortcomings such as family ties to South Korea, is getting more diversified."[103] The DPRK is witnessing the emergence of a new middle class. At the same time, the regime remains far from developing and sustaining a sophisticated industrial economy; its powerful undertows designed to protect structural and policy legacies of the past make it likely that such development is at best a distant target.

As in the other cases examined, the DPRK economic paradigm resonated with the dominant regime. Yet as policy changes include more marketization, components of the regime may respond differently to the shifting incentives. Of particular note, the military's political and economic significance look to be weakening as the party gains in strength. Furthermore, markets are gaining increased salience, as is the growing advantage of those who can make money within them. How such socioeconomic shifts might affect (or constrain) the current regime is a dynamic that continues to unfold and is likely to be a key national driver going forward.

Myanmar

From Myanmar's January 4, 1948 independence into the first decades of the twenty-first century, the single most powerful regime component was the military.[104] Yet military control confronted severe geographic constriction because of the numerous quasi-autonomous regions where non-Burman ethnic groups have dominated since independence, often powering guerilla campaigns against national military forces. These have prevented the emergence of any truly inclusive national regime, let alone a forward-looking economic paradigm. Instead, military officers have monopolized control over state institutions to dominate a substantial portion of the country, enrich themselves, and prevent the emergence of independent socioeconomic forces, all the while impeding the emergence of even minimal technical competence in economic planning or national development.

External relations further entrenched the military while handicapping industrialization. Powerful foreign governments have pushed and pulled the country's leadership in competing directions, ever since the early postwar years. Fearful of such foreign influences and swept up by nationalistic anxieties about neocolonial influences, political and military leaders opted to isolate the country from global engagement. The results were a geographically limited but authoritarian regime that delivered decades of economic disaster for most citizens but privilege and profit for the officer corps.

State Institutions

The Myanmar military (*tatmadaw*) in a variety of guises has been the drive shaft within postcolonial Myanmar's creaking state institutions. Military officers have held a virtual monopoly over state institutions, along with sociopolitical influence, since soon after the country gained independence in 1948. Military preeminence stems from the country's constant enmeshment in violence and internal warfare that in turn valorized the particular skill set of the army.

As the British colonial state disintegrated, a dizzying array of indigenous non-state organizations of violence emerged, guns were everywhere, power was fragmented, and coercion was the key political currency. The weakened central state was only one of the numerous entities with claims over violence, territory, resources, and people. Postcolonial Burma suffered decades of civil war, the result of which was that the national military, trained and honed as a war-fighting machine, emerged as the ultimate arbiter in the pervasive power competition.[105]

Sporadic fighting continued for decades, during which time military officers often found it difficult to distinguish between citizens and enemies of the state. Improvements in civilian bureaucratic capacities could not keep pace with the army's resources. Consequently, the military accumulated greater assets, responsibilities, and powers in traditionally nonmilitary realms.[106] All the while, officers enriched themselves.

More than a decade of unstable civilian parliamentary rule following independence convinced senior officers in the *tatmadaw* that direct military rule was essential for national cohesion and a clean break from dependence on foreign powers. The result was a 1962 coup led by Ne Win, a minimally educated general obsessed with numerology and astrology, who ruled until 1988. Following that coup, military officers became the prime overseers of state institutions under a Revolutionary Council that ruled by decree.[107] The council attempted to eradicate all forms of pluralism, leaving the military with primacy over the affairs of state. At the height of the Ne Win regime, the *tatmadaw* endeavored to regulate all aspects of social life, an ambition that continually fell short, not least because of the constant challenges posed by armed insurgencies on the peripheries. The result was what Huang labeled an "arrested-totalitarian regime."[108]

Defying predictions that "military rule is the shortest form of authoritarian regime in the developing world,"[109] Myanmar underwent the longest-running military regime in the modern world.[110] As Nick Cheesman put it, "All militaries are violence specialists, and the one in Myanmar has had more opportunities to develop its specialty through armed combat than most."[111] State coercion gained additional support from the police and the intelligence service.

Not surprisingly, expertise in warfare left most officers devoid of training in the technical specifics needed to publish the news, collect taxes, or manage import–export operations. State institutions operated with greater regard for rigid chains of command than for the give-and-take of politics and administration. For decades, most notionally civilian state institutions swirled tetherless in eddies of woeful inefficiency.

By 1971, in an attempt to create a facade that might establish some distinction between its dual role of governing and fighting, the Revolutionary Council began to civilianize itself. Twenty senior officers of the Revolutionary Council retired from their positions in the military in exchange for civilian positions in the Burmese Socialist Program Party (BSPP). From 1974 until 1978, the BSPP exercised nominal control, but in practice it was little different from the direct military rule seen in other periods. A new 1974 constitution deepened the military's political superiority and required military training and service for all citizens.[112]

The BSPP mimicked a Marxist–Leninist revolutionary party, with an ideology that reflected an idiosyncratic amalgam of communism and Buddhism. The result was a party-state, not unlike the KMT in Taiwan or the CCP in China. In an effort to mobilize broad swaths of the citizenry through a form of state corporatism, the BSPP opened its membership to ethnic minorities, peasants, youth, and local officials, among others, and soon had a membership of over one million and local branches throughout the country that extended its reach into numerous corners of the country.[113] At its height, the BSPP had more than two million members.[114] Yet the BSPP never permitted nonmilitary voices to affect core decisions.[115] The pointed tip of the military bayonet was always close at hand.

On the highly memorable date of August 8, 1988 (8/8/88), a brutal military crackdown against student protests left several thousand dead. The brutality spawned nationwide prodemocracy demonstrations that saw the BSPP government replaced by the State Law and Order Restoration Council (SLORC), an even more draconian institutional arrangement that sought to eliminate all forms of internal dissent by solidifying the already formidable role of the *tatmadaw*. SLORC abolished all state institutions, with the exception of the Ministry of Defense portfolio. In a gesture to prodemocracy demands, SLORC promised free elections that in fact proceeded as planned on May 27, 1990. Stunning the military, however, the democratic opposition, centered on the National League for Democracy (NLD), won a landslide victory after which SLORC refused to relinquish control. Another reorganization followed on November 15, 1997, with the SLORC rebranding itself as the State Peace and Development Council (SPDC).[116] It also changed the official name of the country from Burma to Myanmar and moved the capital from Rangoon (Yangon) to the newly created and heavily fortified city of Naypyidaw.

That the military junta was able to maintain control without falling prey to internal divisions offers an intriguing example of intraorganizational conflict management. The military purged itself of most ethnic minority officers soon after independence, effectively restricting the officer corps to ethnic Burmans, thereby eliminating a frequent source of internal division among military juntas elsewhere. Ne Win was generous to officers of proven loyalty, offering substantial retirement pensions, special department stores for their exclusive use, and retirement housing. It is important to note that he left officers free to supplement their official incomes by selling excess fuel allotments on the private market and receiving lavish gifts from business leaders in the territories under their command. Essentially, he provided each with discrete domains of operation, from which they could extract a variety of rents.[117] To ensure officer loyalty, Ne Win also maintained incriminating evidence against senior members of the military to use in the event that he wished to discipline them.

Tatmadaw control faded rapidly as one approached the country's outer boundaries.[118] Following independence, the central government had made no sustained effort to form a genuine federation that included the outer regions, fearing that any such federation would prove a prelude to centrifugal fragmentation. Decades of civil rebellions left many regions capable of substantial autonomy from the government in the capital.[119] Groups such as the Karen National Union, the Kachin Independence Army, the Shan State Army, the Mong Tai Army, and the United Wa State Army continuously resisted control from the capital. Many remained insulated from serious influence by central state institutions, denying the state any credible claim to a monopoly of legitimate violence across the claimed national territory.

The national military forces responded to such separatism by policies aimed at "Burmification" (later "Myanmafication") of the entire country. The goal was to use military force to bring the disparate regions under central control.[120]

Such efforts were often brutal. In 1996, for example, the army launched what it called its "four cuts" strategy, an effort to cut off rebel access to food, funds, intelligence, and recruits. The *tatmadaw* destroyed some twenty-five hundred villages, resulting in the displacement of over one million people, mostly Karen and Shan minorities.[121] Ethnic groups on the periphery, in turn, resisted federation because they deemed it likely to undercut, if not destroy, their long-standing separate identifies.

During the late 1980s and early 1990s, the governing SLORC successfully negotiated a series of ceasefire agreements with the majority of the armed ethnic groups through what Kevin Wood called "ceasefire capitalism." Groups accepting the ceasefire acquired material benefits and relative peace, generating the country's longest period of sustained amity.[122] Nonetheless, by far the largest beneficiary was the *tatmadaw*. The suspension of conflict allowed the army to tighten its control and expand its presence throughout much of the country, creating the closest thing to a unified Myanmar.[123]

Nor was the *tatmadaw* ever fully able to suppress direct nonviolent protest. Various uprisings periodically sprung up around regime challengers, most typically student groups (e.g., the previously mentioned August 8, 1988 massacre) or Buddhist monks (e.g., the Saffron Revolt of 2007). Further constraining unbridled military rule was the charismatic presence of Aung San Suu Kyi, daughter of the revolutionary leader, Aung San who had led the anti-colonial movement. Suu Kyi stood as the unquestioned leader of the only meaningful opposition political party, the NLD, and despite long periods under house arrest, Suu Kyi continually stood as a reminder that military rule lacked widespread popular support.

Cracks in the military's armor eventually began to widen. Two key events, the Saffron revolt of 2007 and Cyclone Nargis in 2008, fractured SPDC rule. The first, involving a mass protest by saffron-robed monks whose religious stature gave them widespread support among the populace (and not a little among the military), crystalized the pressures for democratization. The second, a natural disaster that killed more than one hundred forty thousand people, demonstrated state institutional ineptitude that exacerbated the damage caused by the cyclone itself. Rescue efforts by the *tatmadaw* proved feckless; however, even more damaging, as casualties mounted, the government continued to reject Western aid, fearful that such offers were but thinly disguised rationales for foreigners to force regime change.[124] When outside aid groups finally received permission to enter, the devastating impact of *tatmadaw* delay was unmistakable to all.

An important shift followed, with a new constitution in 2008 that notionally provided a road map to what acting Prime Minister General Thein Sein called "disciplined democracy."[125] Still, the military was by no means double-timing back to the barracks. The new constitution reserved a quarter of the seats in Parliament for military appointees; it required that the president be a military officer; and it guaranteed that the army would control important ministries, including defense and home affairs. In addition, the military would set its own budget, and would retain the right to declare a state of emergency and seize power whenever it deemed necessary. In an effort to transform all dissident armies operating under ceasefires into border guard forces, the constitution also stated that all armed groups in Myanmar should be under the command of the *tatmadaw*.[126] Perhaps most important to ensuring military influence, a special provision barred anyone from holding office who had been married to a foreigner or whose children held foreign passports, a restriction tailored specifically at Aung San Suu Kyi.[127]

The NLD boycotted the transparently fraudulent elections in 2010; however, in the next election, the NLD won forty-three of the forty-four contested seats. In a stunning break with past behavior, the military junta in 2011 officially dissolved, establishing a civilian Parliament, which appointed former army bureaucrat Thein Sein as president.

Upon taking office, Thein Sein began a truncated series of moves to loosen military controls and to inch the country toward greater political pluralism and citizen freedoms. He permitted the media to publish and criticize, freed thousands of political prisoners, and oversaw new and freer elections in 2015 in which the NLD won yet another powerful victory. What followed was a dramatic increase in the number of meaningfully civilian overseers of state institutions in a more diffuse multilayered system of government.[128] Thein Sein and other state officials also backed away from the long-standing policy of Myanmafication by issuing calls for religious tolerance.[129]

Dramatic as such moves were, this relaxation of military dominance reflected a strategy of institutionalizing the military's influence over state institutions without the responsibility for direct administration.[130] In turn, the NLD's septuagenarian leadership demonstrated little of the energy, imagination, or skill sets needed to circumvent the military's limitations and advance political renewal.[131] Whether the 2011 changes prove to be a pivotal inflection point marking the onset of a substantially different configuration of political power remains unclear. The military has monopolized state power since 1962; even since 2011, it has retained a commanding role. Loosening the military's mailed fist was slow to develop and the army continues to exert overwhelming influence over the state machinery. Thus, its 2021 coup merely underscored its continued primacy.

Socioeconomic Forces

Myanmar has deep chasms of social and economic fragmentation that limit any extensive nationwide socioeconomic collectivity from becoming a reliable partner to state institutions. As noted previously, ethnic, religious, and geographical fissures overlap, putting large swaths of the country beyond the control of central state institutions. Even within areas under control of the capital, socioeconomic forces remain fragmented, leaving no concentrated core capable of checking the military's muscular dominance or forcing it into accommodation or into a less narrowly rapacious agenda.

As the previous section made clear, the *tatmadaw* was the overwhelming, if pernicious, locus of control across the two-thirds of the country where it had direct jurisdiction. Yet the remaining third of the country is a thinly stitched quilt of more than one hundred separate ethnic and religious groups, including Indian and Chinese minorities, the vast majority seeking a measure of autonomy from Burman rule. Many of the largest minorities, such as the Shan, the Kahin, the Mon, the Kachin, the Wa, and the Rakhine (as well as the Muslim Rohingya within Rakhine) are concentrated geographically on the country's periphery, where they function with varying degrees of autonomy; ethnic division and economic interests heighten the pull of political separation.[132]

At the same time, as noted a plurality of Myanmar's population is Buddhist; Burman ethnicity and the Buddhist religion overlap and Buddhism occupies a sociocultural prominence in Myanmar. A 1961 law designated Buddhism as the state religion. Buddhist monks in particular enjoy a position of official respect.[133]

The overlay between religious diversity and ethnic identity exacerbates the country's centripetal tendencies. Chi, Kachin, and a large number of Karen are Christian. The Rohingya, though technically stateless under Myanmar law, are Muslim; substantial numbers of other Muslims reside throughout the country, predominantly in the cities. Sensitivities about religious identification have been so acute that the government often delays or tampers with census results, fearful that accurate numbers, particularly of Muslims, would exacerbate already tense religious and regional tensions.[134]

Many of the country's autonomous regions are rich in natural resources, allowing ethnic authorities and local warlords to operate semiautonomous economies based on exploitation of gold, precious gems, noble metals, timber, and marine resources. Localities levy fees and taxes, mobilize independent militias, create their own language schools, lionize their particular histories, and engage in economic activities independently of central state institutions. They are states within the state.

The closest to a semi-independent economic force in Burman areas has been the small class of oligarchs, closely aligned with the *tatmadaw* and themselves the beneficiaries of military concessions. For the most part, they add to regime support but hardly as the product of an independent economic base. Rather, they share the predatory spoils through concessions that afford them dominance over otherwise restricted economic activities, including petroleum imports, logging and mining rights, banking, real estate, and the arms trade.[135] These oligarchs and their officer patrons may control as much as 80 percent of the national economy, meaning that there are few independent socioeconomic forces in areas under Burman control. State institutions and socioeconomic forces collaborate in joint national predation.

External Forces

Throughout the postwar period, Myanmar opted for national isolation that left it the frequent target of geopolitical power contests. Certain neighboring countries offered support; more were regime opponents. Regional power games often reinforced one or more peripheral ethnic regions, further weakening central government authority.

Even at the time of independence, domestic options were constrained by foreign influences as large numbers of Kuomintang military forces fighting against the Chinese Communist armies flourished within Myanmar's borders. The United States, as a strong supporter of the KMT, refused Myanmar's requests to cease its military and financial assistance and force the KMT to leave. This proved a foretaste of what was to come.

Amidst Cold War bipolarity, Myanmar's leaders, fearful of plunging the country back into dependency or neocolonial victimization, resisted choosing between friend and foe, opting instead for rigid foreign policy neutrality. Unlike most former British colonies, Myanmar did not join the British Common Market. It rejected Soviet aid and insisted on paying for any incoming assistance with rice. It recognized the post-1949 government in China but supported UN actions in the Korean War while at the same time forcing out the US aid program because of its support for KMT insurgents. Indeed, Myanmar proved such a model of neutrality that one of its diplomats, U Thant, was chosen to head the United Nations, less because he was the single most qualified individual and more because he was from a truly neutral nation.[136]

Following the 1962 coup, Ne Win transformed neutrality into isolation; however, isolation failed to inoculate the country from outside influence. Numerous separatist regions in Myanmar conspired with foreign governments, thereby turning the country's borders into sieves that left Myanmar open to influences from Chinese traders and arms dealers, Thai black marketers, Indian supporters of nonviolent democratic opponents, and Muslim majority countries such as Indonesia and Malaysia backing the country's Muslims. Nor did most foreign countries remain consistently pro- or antigovernment. Far more typical were cases such as Thailand, which supported the military government in principle while simultaneously cooperating in various regions with arms dealers and opium traders against state interests and overtly supporting ethnic insurgents, including the Mon, Kayin, Kayah, and Shan.[137]

Not all external relations were unwelcome. Following years of failing economics, Myanmar's political leaders agreed to accept aid. In 1976, the Aid Group on Burma formed under World Bank auspices and the regime began attracting foreign economic support, which jumped some twenty times over about six years, rising from about $20 million annually to over $400 million.[138] Because foreign assistance funneled through state institutions, however, as was true in the Philippines under Marcos, such assistance reinforced rather than disrupted prevailing predacious arrangements.

Japanese money and infrastructural assistance were among the earliest to flow in, with Japanese companies having already established a toehold as part of a 1954 war reparations agreement. Like reparations to other Southeast Asian countries, these monies provided infusions of scarce capital and technical assistance. Japan paid reparations of $20 million annually over ten years, as well as $5 million in annual loans for technical assistance. By March 1988, Japanese economic aid totaled $2.2 billion. Yet, as was true with such aid to the ersatz developers, Myanmar found that incoming assistance usually necessitated Japanese procurement, affording many Japanese companies first mover access to rich natural resources and commercial markets. The first project paid for by Japanese reparation funds, for example, was the Baluchaung hydroelectric plant at a cost of ¥19 billion ($52.7 million), with the research, design, and construction supervision all undertaken by Nippon Koei Co. Ltd.[139]

Moreover, Japanese aid often came with stern advice. Appalled at Myanmar's economic management, Japan quietly but officially declared that significant (but unspecified) economic policy reforms were necessary or it would reconsider its relationship.[140] Such criticisms joined with voices from other democracies following the brutal military crackdown on 8/8/88, leading the United States, Western Europe, and a number of NGOs to introduce strict economic sanctions. Most Western companies pulled out, but a few, especially in oil exploration, exploited loopholes in the sanctions to remain.

One of the more nuanced external pressures on the regime came from the awarding of the Nobel Peace Prize to Aung San Suu Kyi for her long-term nonviolent campaign advocating for democracy and human rights in her country. A behind-the-scenes campaign orchestrated by her husband, Michael Aris, an Oxford professor of Tibetan studies, played a large part in convincing the committee that the award could shine a valuable light on the small country's problems and magnify pressures for changes within the military regime.[141]

Even as the West tightened sanctions, regional actors expanded trade, aid, and diplomatic engagement. In 1989, Japanese companies began pressing their government to loosen sanctions so they could begin or continue projects in Myanmar lest companies from other countries rush to fill the void.[142] China, anxious to expand its own trade, worked with military officials to clear and hold the various trade routes linking their two countries, freezing out the Kachin and other ethnic groups that had previously dominated much of the China–Myanmar trade. Chinese consumer goods flowed in, displacing both local and Japanese products, and China came to dominate the economy in northern Myanmar.[143] China also developed multiple ties through arms sales and narcotics, for example, to several of the dissident regions, most notably those areas bordering China's Yunnan Province.[144]

China also became the main provider of military assistance, development aid, and external infrastructure funding to the central government, and both countries' leaders frequently visited one another's capitals and commercial centers.[145] By the mid-2010s, the aggregate value of Chinese investment in

Myanmar had reached about $18.4 billion (31% of all foreign investments), with an additional $7.5 billion in investments arriving through Hong Kong (12.5%). Most of the investment was in energy and natural resources, with some diversifications in real estate, hotels, and banking.[146]

Big power politics has also involved India. Hostile to the regime from its early days, during the 1990s the Indian government under the Congress Party was a strong ally of the NLD because of its nonviolent commitment to democratic change. As the Chinese influence in Myanmar grew, however, the Indian government began to shift its allegiance to the central government to counter its longtime adversary.

Further complicating external influences is the DPRK. Western intelligence officials long suspected that in the early years of the twenty-first century, the *tatmadaw* had developed an interest in following the DPRK toward military autarky behind an arsenal of ballistic missiles and nuclear weapons. In spring, 2006, Myanmar's junta normalized relations with the DPRK and initiated conventional weapons trade in violation of UN sanctions against Pyongyang.[147] In addition, despite the country's ample reserves of oil and gas, it signed an agreement with Russia to develop what it said would be peaceful nuclear capabilities.

In turn, the rising Chinese presence drew the attention of ASEAN, whose leaders made counterefforts to attract Myanmar to membership. Concerns were especially strong over Chinese access to the Andaman Sea, creation of infrastructure projects, acquisition of naval bases, and $1 billion in arms sales.[148] ASEAN leaders also sought to reduce the negative regional effects of Myanmar's involvement with the narcotics trade, drugs, human trafficking, HIV/aids, and human rights abuses. By some assessments, Myanmar accounts for 80 percent of all heroin produced in Southeast Asia.[149] Ultimately, on July 23, 1997, Myanmar joined ASEAN, following an especially important concession by Muslim Indonesia (which was previously opposed due to Myanmar's military repression of the Muslim minority).[150]

ASEAN provided a dollop of socializing influence, not least of which occurred on many regional golf courses. The ASEAN goal was not so much to replace Myanmar's military leaders as to reduce the junta's paranoia about the dangers of dissent and the potential loss of influence through economic openness. ASEAN leaders delivered reaffirming messages about the potential advantages of greater openness and economic reform, as shown in neighboring countries such as Malaysia, Thailand, and Indonesia, none of whose military and political elites surrendered their political power or economic perquisites following economic development.

ASEAN sticks accompanied such reassuring carrots. ASEAN leaders prevailed on Myanmar's junta to skip the country's turn as chair of ASEAN's 2006 meeting due to its negative image. Again, in 2007, ASEAN foreign ministers broke with the organization's prior precedent of noninterference by issuing a blunt criticism of the regime for its crackdown on civilians, and especially on the country's monks.[151]

Finally, the United States also turned its attention to Myanmar as part of President Obama's so-called repositioning toward the Asia-Pacific. The United States normalized diplomatic relations, appointed an ambassador, and Obama made two presidential visits to the country.[152] Improved relations with the United States triggered a diminution of projects with China, a clear instance of which was the Myitsone Dam. A Chinese state-owned corporation was to carry out construction on the hydroelectric dam, but local residents feared flooded communities and mass relocation, and bristled at the revelation that 90 percent of the electricity generated by the dam would go to China. On September 30, 2011, the government suspended the project. A similar controversy bubbled up over the Monywa Copper Mine in central Myanmar.[153]

In short, the regime in Myanmar attracted no shortage of external interest, but it has lacked any consistent patron. Instead, virtually all regional powers have pressed for the regime to shift in competing directions. Myanmar's geographic location, resources, and overall economic vulnerability make it an object of affection to larger geopolitical neighbors, leaving it unclear whether domestic political and economic elites will ever be able to avoid competing tugs at its autonomy or to ally with certain external forces in ways that will foster a coherent and positive economic policy paradigm.

Economic Policy Paradigm

A close analysis of Myanmar's economy is difficult because national accounting data has been unreliable for decades. The World Bank, for example, does not even attempt to provide a figure as basic as annual growth in GDP for years prior to 2000.[154] Nevertheless, several facts about the economic paradigm are clear. Fifty years of economic mismanagement under the military-led regime upended the fortunes of what, prior to World War II, was the most successful economy in Southeast Asia. Myanmar had been a major exporter of rice (although roughly 80% of the most productive land was owned by absentee landlords, most of whom were foreign).[155] By 1987, Myanmar stood among the United Nations' catalogue of least developed countries. Moreover, corruption was rampant. External evaluators rank Myanmar among the least free economies in Asia (below Cambodia, Laos, and Vietnam, for example, although still ahead of the DPRK);[156] and in 2007, Transparency International ranked Myanmar close to the worst in its world rankings for corruption.[157]

Such a dismal record is congruent with the military-dominated regime. It has control over only part of the country and lacks powerful socioeconomic partners with the incentives and resources to improve the national economy, state institutions suffer from technocratic ineptness, and self-aggrandizing outside forces buffet domestic arrangements. The result is a regime rife with predation, all reflected in a failing economic paradigm.

Following independence, the Myanmar government, like most postcolonial governments, sought national economic independence as a corollary to its newfound political autonomy. State institutions endeavored to insulate the national economy from the world beyond its borders. The military policy labeled "the Burmese Way to Socialism" hinged on self-reliance and industrialization from within. Yet investment capital was lacking, with the result that it proved fruitless.[158]

A policy of strict nationalization of private enterprises was equally unsuccessful. Nationalization began with commercial banks in 1963 and soon encompassed private commercial businesses. Between 1962 and 1988, the state made ongoing attempts to eradicate the profit motivation from companies, leading to the creation of a number of state-owned manufacturing enterprises (SOEs).[159] As noted, few former military officers who became managers of these SOEs had any professional expertise in business management. Limited domestic sources of investment capital and inept SOE leadership proved a recipe for failure. In addition, strict government production and pricing schedules made it difficult to squeeze capital from farmers who had few incentives to increase their efficiency.[160]

Nor was capital available for the replacement or renovation of foreign machinery, partly because of the shortage of foreign exchange, but more because of the abiding conviction that industrial production should reject reliance on foreigners. Not surprisingly, the SOEs proved to be a major failure and their economic losses between 1989 and 1998 ranged between a low of 30 percent and a high of 68 percent of the total government deficit.[161]

Between 1963 and 1965, the government nationalized all banks, industries, and large shops. In 1985, and again in 1987, it also removed a number of currency notes from redemption, purportedly to confiscate foreign wealth and to curb black marketers and smugglers. In fact, numerologists had convinced Ne Win of the power of number nine, so decimal-based notes gave way to forty-five and ninety-kyat notes (the total of both denominations being nine). However, the sudden demonetization restricted cash holdings across the nation, triggering among other things the student protests that led to the 8/8/88 protests and crackdown. The crippled economy prompted state officials to begin ignoring smuggling since a vast proportion of commercial activity and consumer satisfaction depended on it. As early as the late 1970s, more than 90 percent of the population relied on illegal trade for about 80 percent of their basic needs.[162]

In the hope of acquiring as much foreign exchange as possible, the military government did just what its counterpart in the Philippines did, namely, it encouraged its citizens to work outside the country. The vast bulk of such overseas workers went to neighboring Malaysia and Thailand and returned monies home, thus providing a small substitute for foreign capital. Again, however, this tactic lacked any broader integration with a strategy of economic transformation.

The national treasury, meanwhile, gained no benefit from the 20 percent of the economy tied to the smuggling of rice, rubber, teak, gems, and antiques. The same was true of illegal drug production. Such illicit activities benefited only a cluster of marginal farmers, local warlords, ethnic separatists, and a number of high military officials but provided little help to the national budget or broader economic development.

Eventually, as awareness of the downside of national economic policies began to pervade officialdom, state leaders moved to enhance private sector liberalization and internationalization. In 1988–89, SLORC officially ended the ban on international economic transactions and dropped its commitment to the dubious "Burmese Way to Socialism." Nationalization of industry formally ended except for twelve designated sectors. A measure of privatization took place; the banking sector, for example, saw foreign holdings rise to 30 percent of the total. In addition, new laws and institutions in the early 1990s permitted FDI, creating what David Steinberg called "the most liberal foreign investment law in Burma's history."[163] Openings occurred in trade, finance, and investment; however, most of the incoming FDI went into the service sector, particularly into hotels, real estate, and mining, along with gas and oil. Very little flowed into manufacturing; until the late 2000s, any green shoots of industrialization remained minimal.[164]

Reform of the SOEs remained incomplete. The privatization of only small factories and retail shops left the bulk of the SOEs intact. In addition, the monetary sector and the foreign exchange system underwent only minimal alteration while a rigid foreign exchange system perpetuated an unrealistic official exchange rate, rendering any strategy of export-oriented industrialization unfeasible and instead facilitating a large-scale black currency market.[165]

Paying for the import of vital raw materials and components essential to the functioning of Myanmar's embryonic industrial production was problematic. External debt that was only $106 million in 1970 rose to $1.6 billion in 1980, and then, exacerbated by the revaluations of the Japanese yen and the German mark in 1985, it ballooned to $4.4 billion in 1986 and $5.3 billion in 1989. The government's internal debt continued to rise as SOEs borrowed consistently from the national treasury.[166]

Since the mid-2000s, the Myanmar economic paradigm became increasingly dependent on natural gas exports, with the country taking on the characteristics of a natural resource exporter. Given its newfound energy riches, one might expect the country's public finances to be rather flush, allowing for an elimination of public sector debt or investments in industrialization, infrastructure, or human resource enhancements. Instead, almost none of Myanmar's gas revenues actually made its way into the national budget as the result of a rather ingenious system employed by the *tatmadaw*. Relying on a dual exchange rate system, the military found it easy to record earnings at the official exchange rate and to skim off the real profits to presumably private and overseas accounts under their control. Hugely profitable gas reserves show up as less than 1 percent of the regime's official public spending.[167]

In all of these ways, the rapacious Myanmar regime sustained a nationally ruinous economic paradigm even as military leaders and their cohorts extracted as many resources as possible. Foreign influences rarely made much difference in remedying that paradigm and it remains unclear whether the limited democratization and enhanced foreign interest of the 2010s will move the regime onto a more fruitful economic trajectory.

These three regimes resemble one another in their predatory character and their resistance to participation in the surrounding East Asian economic transformation. Yet each plundered in its own way. All three had concentrated state powers, but unlike such concentrations in the developmental regimes, all three rapacious regimes were characterized by deep wells of technical ineptitude. Neither the DPRK nor Myanmar manifested significant independent socioeconomic power; in the Philippines, the anti-industrializing sector of rich property owners collaborated with political elites to resist industrialization and continue an antidevelopmental pilfering of the treasury.

Notably, in contrast to the DPRK and Myanmar, the Philippines enjoyed extended external support from the United States. That affinity, however, was contingent on continued access to bases and protection of the oligopolistic positions of US corporations in the local economy, the latter seriously impeding national industrialization. In addition, and not surprisingly, important inflows of aid from Japan focused on benefits to Japanese, not Philippine, corporations. Much the same arrangement dominated Chinese investment and aid into the DPRK and Myanmar. Myanmar's regime zigzagged between incomplete efforts at isolation and buffeting by foreign neighbors.

Regimes of predation left all three without significant traction to move toward economic paradigms advancing the national well-being. All three were rich in natural resources or agricultural capacity. Yet despite such assets, for decades none of the three regimes advanced far from the bottom on most lists of economic underdevelopment and poverty. Reliance on natural resources and cash crops further reduced regime incentives to industrialize. Consequently, investments in human skills remained commonly minimal; inequality and poverty were similarly pervasive. The developmental and ersatz developmental regimes demonstrate that there is more than one path to economic advancement. Similarly, these three rapacious regimes show there are numerous routes to immiseration.

PART TWO

PART TWO

Chapter 4

Developmental Regimes Reconstructed

Regimes, like aging buildings, more often undergo remodeling than total demolition. To be sure, exceptions exist. Revolutions, civil wars, or foreign invasions are but a few of the notable events that can shatter even deeply entrenched regimes. More commonly, longtime regime beneficiaries facing challenges to regime cohesion have strong incentives to instigate some mixture of resistance, adjustment, and innovation in an effort to retain as many advantageous arrangements as possible. Such was the case when Japan, Korea, and Taiwan faced an escalating salvo of challenges to developmental regime cohesion and embedded mercantilism. Yet none of the regimes collapsed completely; instead, all three underwent substantial alterations. Rather than *destruction*, these regimes and embedded mercantilism went through *reconstruction*.[1]

Dominant for decades, all three regimes, starting most conspicuously in the 1980s, began to confront challenges that diminished the incentives for intraregime cooperation while simultaneously threatening economic paradigms. Three external challenges were particularly disruptive. First, unstinting US support for domestic arrangements and the paradigm of embedded mercantilism wavered. Second, global finance strengthened parabolically. Third, global and regional production networks took root. Domestically, meanwhile, the very successes of regime stability and embedded mercantilism reconfigured the incentives facing both regime components and regime opponents. In combination, these disruptive forces weakened the centripetal energies essential to regime cohesion.

This chapter analyzes those challenges and the reconfigurations that followed. It examines the erosion of prior regime unity and embedded mercantilism as well as the myriad adjustments that followed. In all three cases, adjustments involved complex dramas pitting entrenched regime beneficiaries against contenders brandishing new resources as they challenged the status quo. Even as regime bonds loosened, however, they did not dissolve.[2] Deeply institutionalized relationships and entrenched advantages proved highly effective at preventing total regime collapse.

The three regimes met their respective challenges with varying degrees of speed, direction, and substance.[3] Adjustments came more quickly and comprehensively in both Taiwan and Korea than in Japan as key regime figures in the prior two retained substantial long-term influence by demonstrating what Slater and Wong label "the strength to concede."[4] Yet in all three, state institutions surrendered considerable cohesion and control, socioeconomic alliances frayed, and previously unflagging external support became inconsistent. Critically, the paradigm of embedded mercantilism also lost much of its embeddedness. In these ways, rather than a sudden shattering, as of a crystal goblet crashing to the ground, the developmental regimes resembled riverbanks subjected to incremental erosion. Yet as reconstruction progressed, it became undeniable that the developmental regimes and their corresponding policy paradigms had been the unusual products of a fortuitous confluence of conditions not easily reproduced elsewhere.[5]

External Support Became External Challenge

As chapter 1 demonstrated, for decades all three developmental regimes benefited from the postwar global financial, trade, and monetary order, as well as the United States' region-wide security engagement. More specifically, the United States, motivated predominantly by security considerations, provided extensive economic and political backing to the conservative coalitions formed by state institutions and progrowth socioeconomic forces. American policymakers lavished covert funds on Japan's LDP and shaded their eyes when viewing authoritarian abuses in Korea and Taiwan. As the global economic hegemon, the United States was able to dole out lavish assistance and asymmetrical trade benefits. Simultaneously, global economic arrangements facilitated all three regimes' export strategies. Yet, starting in the 1970s for Japan, and with accelerating speed for all three during the 1980s, Cold War frigidities thawed and economic globalization expanded. The consequence was a less benign external environment for the three regimes.

Well before the collapse of the Soviet Union and its Eastern European partners in 1989–91, Cold War temperatures began warming in East Asia. After its defeat in Vietnam, the United States jettisoned its domino theory and its corresponding containment policy. In 1971, China and the United States moderated decades of hostility as each acknowledged their common security anxieties about the USSR. In addition, in 1972, Japan, a previous stalwart in maintaining strict economic and ideological separation from China, normalized diplomatic relationships with the PRC, quickly expanding the economic options of both countries. In turn, the PRC reduced its "lips and teeth" closeness to the DPRK and normalized diplomatic relations with South Korea.

As chapter 5 will analyze in detail, a critical inflection point for the region came in 1978–79 when the Chinese political leadership followed the diplomatic shattering of the previous security order by welcoming heavy doses of economic internationalization. Closer economic engagement with China became both feasible and tempting for all three developmental regimes, including even Taiwan. Trade and investment interactions advanced. Previously negligible foreign aid, along with Western economic doctrines, flooded into China with investments, technology, and corporate infusions from Western and Asian-based firms.

Economic engagement was complicated for Taiwan. In 1971, its government lost its de jure status as the legitimate representative of "China," along with the "China seat" on the United Nations Security Council and other international bodies. Terminated too were Taiwan's official diplomatic relations with the United States, Japan, and South Korea. Consequently, US support for Taiwan's conservative domestic arrangements lost much of its prior dynamism. It took far longer for Taiwan–PRC economic and cultural exchanges to gain momentum.[6]

Positive as these changes were in easing security tensions, they also weakened a critical stanchion of the developmental regimes. Under bipolarity, the concept of "national security" had cemented military protection and economic growth together in an interdependent unity. That adhesion loosened within the developmental regimes as "security" took on far more nuance. The term morphed into new and multifaceted understandings. Economic security, food security, environmental security, and security from pandemics and international crime, to mention only a few conspicuous challenges, gained salience in debates about external threats and national protection. Of particular relevance to the developmental regimes' overarching project of embedded mercantilism, it became increasingly feasible for each of the three to treat military security interests and economic interests as traveling along distinct tracks.[7] At the most basic level, the prospect of profits through trade and investment with China expanded, complicating the longstanding regime claims that tightly constrictive state institutions were the only barrier to the menacing threats of communism and China. As economic engagement with China flourished, prior constrictions over the boundaries of legitimate political debate blurred.[8]

Simultaneously, the United States began delivering the message that economic forbearance of developmental trade and monetary policies would no longer be the codependent twin of hard military relations. Firms and products from Japan, Korea, and Taiwan had been gobbling up larger shares of world manufacturing markets, leaving many once preeminent US manufacturing sectors facing devastation and decline. In response, US policymakers pulled up the one-way welcome mat for its Asian allies' exports. Unshackled from the straitjacket of Cold War bipolarity, a succession of US administrations from the 1970s into the 1990s began responding more robustly to internal political demands from industrial sectors such as textiles, steel, and automobiles, as well as semiconductors and finance, by aggressive pushbacks against imports from the developmental regimes. Rather than continuing to reiterate the iconic slogan of "free trade," the US mantra became "fair trade."[9]

Altered American priorities unleashed a range of actions aimed at reducing bilateral trade imbalances. Among the most powerful was the demand for sweeping currency revaluations, the presumption being that exports from the United States' Asian allies were thriving in US markets because of their undervalued currencies. Japan was the initial target in 1971 when President Nixon withdrew US support for the Bretton Woods monetary order, devalued the US dollar, and triggered a major escalation in the value of the Japanese yen. Nearly fifteen years later, the 1985 Plaza Accord brought about an even more wholesale currency revaluation that included not just Japan, but Taiwan and Korea as well.

Even though currency revaluations reduced the price competitiveness of numerous exports from the developmental regimes, they failed to assuage US industrial and political concerns. Washington escalated its pressure with subsequent demands for what it labeled "voluntary" export restraints (VERs), taking sequential aim at specific sectors, including steel, aluminum, machine tools, televisions, and computer chips.[10] US policymakers simultaneously pressed state institutions in the developmental regimes to open larger segments of their domestic markets for US investments and products, particularly in sectors where US firms enjoyed technological advantages such as finance and insurance. Other politically influential sectors, including beef, oranges, and autos also enlisted US government pressures to facilitate their market entry.[11] In extreme cases, US negotiators even demanded implicitly guaranteed shares of the local market for US exporters.[12] Such multipronged and heavy-handed efforts demonstrated that US priorities had changed and there would no longer be unilateral tolerance for embedded mercantilist arrangements in all three developmental regimes.

As the United States increased its pressures for particularistic market access, a more generic external challenge materialized with the parabolic rise in the power and reach of international capital. That story is complex, with its modern intellectual roots in the writings of Friedrich Hayek and Ludwig von Mises and their neoliberal followers. All advocated freeing capital from the controls of both governments and mass democracy.[13]

The deregulatory revolution crystallized during the Reagan and Thatcher administrations, both of which adapted Hayekian logic and the ideological conviction that self-regulating financial markets were possible as the ideological justification for weakening domestic regulations and unshackling capital. Deregulation, innovation, and internationalization followed.[14]

The deregulatory revolution overlapped with an expansion in innovative financial products such as derivatives, futures, forwards, swaps, and options. Computers brought about a similar revolution in information technology that expanded the possibilities and profitability of speed in financial interactions. Mathematical wizardry rather than steady and conservative banking calculations became the new jet fuel propelling financial success.

In the search for previously untapped sources of profit, finance expanded quickly in overseas markets. A quantum jump occurred in the sensitivity and interconnectedness of the pricing for financial instruments across the world. Market actors big and small leaped at the opportunity to pursue maximum paper profits with little constriction by national boundaries."[15] Gross sales and purchases of securities between residents and nonresidents rose from 9 percent of US GDP in 1980 to 89 percent in 1990. According to Bank of International Settlements (BIS) estimates, at the end of 1996 the total dollar value of outstanding derivative instruments totalled over $34 trillion, a fourfold escalation from the $7.9 trillion of five years earlier. Such private capital surges soon surpassed the reserves of big banks, ultimately gaining a 4:1 advantage in their share of daily trading activity. Cross-border capital flows exploded, outstripping trade in goods by a 70:1 margin.

As a result, finance catapulted to unquestioned dominance of the commanding heights of the US economy. Between 1973 and 1985, finance never accounted for more than 16 percent of domestic corporate profits. In 1986, that figure rose to 19 percent; during the 1990s, it oscillated between 21 percent and 30 percent; and by the 2000s, it reached 41 percent. In 2016, some $5.1 trillion per day was moving across national borders with the stroke of a few computer keys, a figure 25 percent higher than five years earlier and astronomically greater than in the 1970s or 1980s.

As the power of finance grew within the United States, it expanded as well in countries such as the United Kingdom and Germany, affirming William Greider's claim: "In the history of capitalism's long expansionary cycles, it is finance capital that usually rules in the final stage, displacing the inventors and industrialists who launched the era."[16]

Such displacement occurred in all three of the developmental regimes, as ever more powerful and less regulated financial institutions eyed the dynamic markets of Japan, Korea, and Taiwan. Enhanced political muscle in Washington fused with that of the IMF in pressing for the liberalization of capital accounts and the reduction of government oversight within the previously cosseted financial markets of Japan, Korea, and Taiwan.[17] The rising wave of fluid foreign capital began lapping over the monetary and financial breakwaters integral to the developmental regimes and their policies of embedded mercantilism.

A cognate challenge from fluid finance was the increased modularization of industrial production. Modularization allowed companies to diversify discrete corporate functions such as design, manufacturing, packaging, wholesaling, and retailing, moving them from a single location into multiple locations selected to maximize efficiency, boost market access, and bolster bottom-line profitability with little restriction by national boundaries. The mantra became "move the product, not the factory." The result was the widespread proliferation of truly multinational production networks.[18]

Western-based companies were hardly the sole adopters of such production models. Spurred by suddenly strengthened national currencies as well as the quest for reduced production costs and proximity to final markets, numerous companies in Japan, Korea, and Taiwan used the enhanced opportunities of financial globalization and stronger currencies to make their own outward investments and to take advantage of the expanding regional production networks, either as originators or participants. .[19] Japanese companies, as early as the 1970s, followed by Korean and Taiwanese companies by the mid-1980s, began relocating many low-wage production facilities overseas.

This result was a spurt of Schumpeterian creative destruction that birthed new and mutually beneficial linkages between these regimes and other East Asian countries (as detailed in chapters 2 and 5). Domestically, however, such corporate exit undercut relations between corporations and domestic stakeholders such as banks, subcontractors, workers, local communities, and state institutions. In combination, therefore, the altered external security order and the rising pressures of global capital weakened the supportive external pillar integral to the developmental regimes and their policies of embedded mercantilism. The result was a scrambling of the incentive structures that confronted key domestic actors. Certain groups in Japan, Korea, and Taiwan, to be sure, benefited from the new external conditions; however, others did not.[20] As subsequent sections will demonstrate, domestic state institutions and socioeconomic coalitions in the developmental regimes responded differently to these altered international incentives, but few were unaffected. The next section examines how that reconstruction played out for the dominant socioeconomic coalitions.

Fragmentation of the Socioeconomic Coalitions

Cohesive socioeconomic coalitions able to meld with state institutional control were integral to all three developmental regimes. Centered on big corporations plus small- and medium-sized businesses, a variety of professional groups, and small-scale farmers, these progrowth coalitions underpinned decades of developmental regime durability. Potential socioeconomic challengers, on the other hand, such as organized labor, NGOs, and consumer groups remained economically subordinate and politically marginalized. Holding the coalition together was collective support for the economic paradigm amalgamating rapid economic transformation, protectionist domestic regulations, and minimal economic redistribution. Steady national economic advances and multiple side payments, in turn, benefited coalition partners and refurbished their commitments to one another.

Those dominant socioeconomic coalitions, however, faced challenges from two major directions. The external challenges, noted in the previous section, provided the first, while domestic socioeconomic transformations provided the second. In tandem, the two scrambled many of the incentives and resources available to key socioeconomic actors.

Constant social improvements were integral to regime continuity and the advancement of its economic paradigm. At the same time, the flowers of success contained the seeds of socioeconomic disruption. Expanded education, skill development, and long-term employment, along with decreased poverty levels and the incubation of vibrant middle classes all militated against regime continuity. Individual mobility and enhanced skill levels advanced together with technological upgrading and improved corporate productivity. All of these eroded demands for redividing the economic pie while they enhanced regime legitimacy and the collective march to the technological cutting edge.

Yet as corporations neared that cutting edge, the challenges to their continued growth expanded. Corporate advances through copying or technology purchases became increasingly problematic while individual corporate options and incentives shifted with the increases in globalization and liberalization, and the soaring value of domestic currencies. Home market competition intensified and retained corporate profits increased. As noted in the previous section, many corporations that were previously integral contributors to the developmental regimes responded by shifting portions of their domestic production to overseas locations. Doing so loosened their ties to former socioeconomic allies and decreased their intimate interdependence with state institutions.

Japanese corporations were the first to make significant moves in that direction. The first surge of outgoing FDI came as the yen soared 30 percent after the breakdown of Bretton Woods. Corporations had new incentives to invest both in sophisticated target markets (such as the United States) as well as in countries offering lower production costs (initially Taiwan and Korea but later Southeast Asia and China). The subsequent revaluation of the yen following the 1985 Plaza Accord catalyzed an even more robust second outflow. In the period from 1985 to 1989, Japanese investments in Taiwan jumped fourfold; in Malaysia and South Korea, fivefold; in Singapore, sixfold; and in Thailand, an explosive twenty-five-fold.

The New Taiwan dollar rose by roughly 41 percent in the three years following Plaza, just as Taiwan was running out of underemployed rural laborers and facing consequent increases in wages and other production costs. In response, Taiwanese producers followed the Japanese example, transferring a considerable portion of their labor-intensive operations to more cost-efficient locations. What had been a trickle of Taiwanese investment into China through Hong Kong in the early 1980s became a cascade in the ten years that followed. The twenty-seven years 1959–1986 saw only 80 Taiwanese investments in China totaling a paltry $220 million. In 1988, this jumped to 335 cases totaling $420 million, and in 1989 an additional 540 cases worth $500 million occurred.[21] Between 1986 and 1991, between 2,500 and 4,000 Taiwanese companies invested approximately $3 billion in China. By the end of 1992, some 10,000 Taiwanese investments in China were worth $9 billion, making Taiwan the second largest foreign investor in China after Hong Kong (itself often a through-station for Taiwanese firms).

Taiwanese companies also boosted their investments in Malaysia, Thailand, and Indonesia by three- to twenty-fold in the two years 1988–89 over the five prior years.[22] Cross-border ethnic, linguistic, and family ties facilitated such moves.[23] The result was what Barry Naughton identified as an expansion of "China circles" enveloping large swaths of Southeast Asia.[24]

Korean firms had been investing overseas since 1968, but like Taiwan, and further inhibited by strict governmental controls over foreign exchange outflows, the annual Korean outflow remained small (less than $200 million) until the mid-1980s. In 1987, the South Korean government, responding to IMF, global capital, and US political pressures, liberalized its outward FDI regulations,[25] a liberalization that coincided with the rapid rise in the Korean won. Over the next decade, like Japan and Taiwan, outgoing Korean FDI increased exponentially, totaling $4.2 billion in 1996.[26]

At the same time, continuing domestic protectionist barriers against incoming FDI reduced the pressures to go multinational. Up until 1994, outgoing Korean FDI largely involved small firms in labor-intensive industries looking for cheaper foreign labor. Yet following the Asian financial crisis (AFC), the IMF, as part of its bailout conditions, demanded even more extensive liberalization than in the previous decade. The targets included finance, but also sectors totally disconnected from the currency crisis.[27] The result was a rupturing of many internal alliances within the extensive chaebol and a spur to greater investment by Korean corporations abroad. By 2007, Korean outward FDI as a percent of GDP had caught up to that of Taiwan.[28]

Overseas operations weakened the incentives for corporations in all three regimes to remain as committed to arrangements previously integral to the developmental coalition. The socioeconomic nexus connecting multiple businesses, a cooperative and skilled domestic labor market, domestic suppliers and subsidiaries, and dominant state institutions, lost its collective interdependence. Corporate loyalties to a complex array of previously privileged stakeholders such as employees, communities, or subcontractors, dissipated, as did corporate receptiveness to state institutions and government blandishments. In contrast, less globally competitive firms tightened their ties to one another and to political protectors in a defensive crouch against foreboding changes. Significantly, in all three countries, economic inequality began to widen as companies shifted to increased reliance on part-time and irregular employment at home.[29]

External challenges coincided with domestic challenges that were reshaping these societies more broadly. Many were straightforward manifestations of "the dilemmas of success."[30] Decades of explosive economic transformation led to Japanese, Korean, and Taiwanese populations that were larger, richer, healthier, older, more urbanized, and more educated and skilled compared with the generations that preceded them. Large swaths of the national workforces moved from farming and fishing into manufacturing and services. Economic success lessened the power of formerly regime-critical sectors and enhanced the influence of formerly peripheral sectors that gained new influence on decisions by state institutions. The cumulative result was a diluting of prior coalitional cohesion.

The most noteworthy example of this shift was the reduced socioeconomic influence of farmers and small businesses and the corresponding rise in the number and influence of urban service workers. In addition, older citizens and those with more education became larger and more demanding segments of the population. Rising income levels brought enhanced numbers and influence to the middle-class.

In Japan, the population nearly doubled from 72 million at the end of World War II to 120 million in the mid-1980s, during which the proportion of families living on farms dropped from 50 percent to below 10 percent. In 1947, 40 percent of Japanese workers held jobs in small- or medium-sized firms, while an additional 20 percent were self-employed. By 1985, 80 percent of Japanese worked in larger firms, about 60 percent in the services sector. Birthrates fell and life expectancy rose; the proportion of people older than sixty-five grew, as did health-care and retirement costs. In 1950, only 17 percent of the national population had more than the nine years of compulsory education; by the mid-1980s, that figure had risen to over 50 percent, and nearly 40 percent of the relevant age cohort was attending an institute of higher education. Per capita income rose from around $3,500 in 1950 to over $30,000 in 1990, creating what Murakami called "Japan's new middle mass."[31] Rural Japan, farming cooperatives, and the politicians linked to them saw their comparative influence decline.

The population of South Korea rose similarly, from 25 million in 1960 to 45 million in 1995, with the capital, Seoul, experiencing a tenfold expansion of its population. The proportion of urban residents increased steadily, passing the 50 percent mark in the late 1970s, and reaching 80 percent in 2000. Whereas the primary sector accounted for 82 percent of the labor force in 1958, by 1985 that was down to 25 percent, roughly the same as the number in the secondary sector. Manufacturing's share of GDP was 14 percent in 1960, but by 1983 it was 30 percent. Light manufacturing declined from a share of 61.8 percent to 43.2 percent, while heavy industry rose from 28.2 percent to 56.8 percent.[32] Tertiary workers meanwhile leaped to 51 percent of the workforce.[33] Over the same period, life expectancy rose by 14 years (from 55.8 to 69.7).[34] Concomitantly, the average household size decreased from 5.5 to 3.3 between 1960 and 1995. Primary and secondary education coverage reached nearly 100 percent in the 1990s, with tertiary education comparable to that of most industrial democracies. GDP per capita leaped nearly twelvefold between 1962 and 1995.[35]

The Taiwan story is similar. Between 1956 and 1980, the island's population nearly doubled from 9.4 million to 18 million. Infant mortality fell while life expectancy rose to seventy-two years. GDP per capita rose from $3,463 in 1980 to $17,807 in 1997.[36] Employment in the primary sector dropped from 56 percent in 1952 to 18.9 percent in 1982, with many of these being part-time farmers. Employment in manufacturing rose from 12.4 percent to 31.6 percent over the same period.[37] The ratio of privately owned enterprises in Taiwan's economy surged from 43.4 percent to 82 percent.

Nine years of education was made compulsory in 1968, and by 1990, 95 percent of the population went on to complete academic or vocational high school; higher educational enrollments more than tripled.[38] Manufacturing accounted for 22 percent of Taiwan's GDP in 1960, but it rose to 29 percent in 1983. Between 1965 and 1984, the share of light manufacturing declined from 51.2 percent to 41.5 percent, while heavy industry rose from 49.8 percent to 58.5 percent.[39] As Taiwan's economy advanced, a substantial portion of the workforce moved from agriculture to white-collar jobs and into small- and medium-manufacturing enterprises. In this way, new employment freed many Taiwanese from the enveloping KMT corporatist networks that had previously tethered them to the ruling party and the state.[40] It also boosted the numbers ripe for organizing around their roles as workers.

Meanwhile, economic advances and the deicing of bipolar frigidities contributed to reductions in the sustained regime emphasis on military survival and personal sacrifice. It is a truism of political science that in addition to fostering a more diverse pallet of socioeconomic forces, sweeping socioeconomic improvements often generate increased demands for a loosening of the manacled fist of authoritarianism.[41] Previously suppressed demands, especially in Korea and Taiwan, gained a new prominence.[42] The protectionist pact so integral to a concentrated focus on economic development forfeited its powers of conviction and coherence,[43] making it more difficult for prevailing socioeconomic elites and state institutions to agree on priorities, stick together, and marginalize regime challengers.

Antiauthoritarian movements gained momentum in both Korea and Taiwan, fueled in large part by the better-educated, more middle-class, and urban citizenry (the front lines of which were often students). Similar demographic trends in Japan lessened previous electoral loyalties while boosting electoral support for opposition parties and triggering preemptive moves by conservative elites to preempt and mitigate the chances for more radical changes.

In Taiwan prior to 1975, strict authoritarian controls and pervasive corporatist networks minimized the opportunities for viable socioeconomic challengers to the regime. Yet domestic growth and the variety of accompanying socioeconomic changes combined with outside pressures from the United States to challenge domestic repression. A major inflection point came with the violent suppressions of democracy advocates in the Kaohsiung Incident of 1979. Kaohsiung was the opening salvo in a steady escalation of popular protests on a wide array of issues, including a consumers' movement, a women's movement, an antinuclear movement, an aboriginal human rights movement, and a disabled citizens' movement.[44] As Michael Hsiao summarized it: "One objective of Taiwan's protest movements of the 1980s [was] to acquire autonomy from the domination of the authoritarian state. Reform has been sought not only of a specific public policy or a specific function of the state apparatus but also to transform the power between the authoritarian state and the mobilizing civil society."[45] The beating hearts of such movements were often ethnic Taiwanese with regime-challenging demands for greater collective inclusion and national attention to issues other than maximizing economic growth; eventually, they sought enhanced democratization of state institutions and eventually the sovereignty of Taiwan.[46]

As these forces gathered strength, KMT leaders moved to shore up the ruling party-state and the regime itself by reducing socioeconomic favoritism for mainlanders and their descendants as well as that minority's vice-like grip over socioeconomics institutions. During 1988–89, the KMT enacted a number of measures to reduce existing rules on political associations, moderate media restrictions, legalize opposition parties, and broaden secondary group autonomy. The goal was to convince regime opponents that they could gain significant improvements without toppling the KMT and its supporters entirely.[47]

A transformative overhaul of existing socioeconomic arrangements came with a process of Taiwanization. Realizing that reliance exclusively on mainlanders might trigger social violence that could completely topple the regime's power holders, President Chiang Ching-kuo opted to dilute the power of aging mainlanders while widening the channels for upward mobility and political influence for native-born Taiwanese. Indigenous groups began to compete on a more equal and legitimate footing with mainlanders and their offspring, both within the KMT and from outside party ranks. Of particular importance, in 1984, Chiang selected Taiwan-born and longtime KMT stalwart Lee Teng-hui as his vice president and heir-apparent to the presidency, an office to which Lee rose in 1988.

Such KMT efforts diluted prior regime strength and cohesion, and in the end, proved only partly successful. Not all ambitious Taiwanese sought to join the KMT; many opted instead to mobilize outside the party-state. With the KMT and mainlanders dominating the state apparatus, many indigenous Taiwanese turned to business as an alternative channel of upward mobility. In the process, this enhanced the economic resources of potential regime opponents.[48] In addition, a substantial sector often linked to Taiwanese small- and medium-sized business owners through educational, family, or locational relations took advantage of more open media outlets to criticize the ruling authorities. This conglomeration of socioeconomic regime challengers ultimately joined forces in the Democratic Progressive Party (DPP), the major opposition party challenging the KMT's control over state institutions.

In Korea, like Taiwan, socioeconomic changes fueled an increasingly broad coalition of middle-class activists, urban professionals, workers, church leaders, and students in the Minjung movement. The movement was explicitly antiauthoritarian, framed in the context of state repression and heroic resistance.[49] Its key demands centered on a new democratic constitution and the direct election of the president. As such, like the DPP opposition in Taiwan, the Minjung challenged the regime's core affinity between authoritarian state institutions and socioeconomics.

Starting around 1984, these new Korean social forces gathered momentum. Taking advantage of a decline in state repression, they forged cooperative linkages among student groups, labor, and the farmers' movement, gaining increased support as well from the urban middle class. Throughout the 1960s and 1970s, labor unrest in Korea had remained low—an average of one hundred labor disputes each year, most of them unorganized, spontaneous, and short lived.[50] During the mid-1980s, the country witnessed an unprecedented outburst of strikes, all in pursuit of a larger share of the benefits of economic growth but also aimed at political democratization.[51]

The rise in opposition merged with intensifying US pressure for greater democratization along with the impending start to the 1988 Seoul Olympics, as state and business leaders sought to present the Olympics as a capstone achievement.[52] Antiregime forces led massive demonstrations against the military leader Chun Doo-hwan in May through June 1987, with Chun eventually stepping down for a favored successor, Roh Tae-woo. Domestic social pressures, however, were enough to shift Roh's calculations, and in June 1987 he promised direct presidential elections and constitutional reform.

In both Korea and Taiwan, the predominant challenges to the fusion of socioeconomic forces and state institutions came via the mobilization of antiregime forces focused principally on achieving political democratization from outside the regime. In Japan, the pattern was different. The dominant coalition began to fray from within long before it confronted meaningful challenges from without.

As noted in chapter 1, the socioeconomic coalition underpinning the developmental regime in Japan was an oil-and-water blending of groups seeking pork benefits from the trough of public spending with forces focused on enhancing national productivity. The former included agricultural cooperatives incorporating the vast majority of independent farmers, along with small businesses, while productive forces were concentrated in big business, numerous state institutions, and urban professionals. The fortunes of both segments advanced in conjunction with the rapid economic transformation achieved via embedded mercantilism. High growth and burgeoning state budgets permitted the relatively low side payments of subsides, protection, and price supports to agriculture and small businesses.[53]

By the late 1980s, foreign pressures mounted for Japan to liberalize selected agricultural imports and to reduce the stringent protections for small stores. In addition, the country's most successful exporters found that continued domestic protectionism risked impeding their own access to overseas markets. They used their intraregime influence to press for reduced regime protections for agriculture and small business, risking the severance of socioeconomic elements whose prior cooperation had been vital to the developmental regime. A series of state-led liberalizations followed, reducing the incentives for both sectors to continue supporting the LDP. As coalitional coherence between pork and productivity fragmented, the electoral support of many pork beneficiaries shifted to opposition parties.[54]

Not until after the turn of the century, by which time the socioeconomic coalition had frayed considerably and state institutions were losing their prior singularity of purpose and strict control, however, was a quasi-coherent opposition able to overturn longtime LDP political control.[55] Consequently, state institutions in Japan remained under the formal if weakened control of the LDP, retaining the party's semblance of quasi-dominance. Even though LDP superiority continued, from the mid-1980s onward, it was never as dominant as it had been during its developmental heyday. Nonetheless, the LDP continued to retain cabinet control and parliamentary majorities long after the KMT and the Korean DJP (Democratic Justice Party) surrendered the reins of government to regime opponents.

Alternating Drivers Steering Weaker State Institutions

Reduced external support and fragmenting socioeconomics exacerbated and joined with new frictions in the once smooth-running machinery of state institutions. Prior coherence, competence, and control by state institutions contracted.

At the heart of this contraction of state institutions in the three developmental regimes were two changes. First, once dominant conservative political forces no longer enjoyed their previously unchallenged control over the levers of state institutions. Second, state institutions themselves surrendered much of their former cohesions and control.

To the first point, within Japan, Korea, and Taiwan, previously marginalized regime opponents gained control over state institutions for sustained periods. The Korean military and its conservative successors loosened their authoritarian control with democratization in 1987. Conservatives continued to control the presidency until 1997, yet after that the country underwent sustained periods where progressive hands maneuvered the wheels of state institutions. Progressives and conservatives sought to steer the machinery of state in radically different directions and the subsequent twists and turns also meant alternative policy paradigms. Much the same was true of the LDP in Japan and the KMT in Taiwan.

Still, neither the LDP nor the KMT disintegrated or permanently surrendered their direction of state institutions. Nor did Korean conservative political forces lose all electoral appeal. Such postdevelopmental continuities provide a striking contrast to the total collapse of many once-formidable Eastern European Communist machines in the late 1980s or early 1990s, or several high-profile military dictatorships in Latin America between 1982 and 1989.

Second, alternating hands on the steering wheels of state institutions presented continuity problems for state agencies and senior officials, long integral to the smooth operation and unidirectionality of state institutions. Senior administrators frequently found themselves taking orders from new political overseers to implement radically divergent policy agendas.

Japan provides the clearest case of internal fragmentation within the ranks of the long dominant LDP and the national civil service. As noted in chapter 1, for nearly forty years following its 1955 formation, the LDP won overwhelming parliamentary pluralities, if not outright majorities that allowed it to commandeer virtually all cabinet positions for decades.[56] Long-term LDP dominance eviscerated the organization, talent base, and public confidence in potential electoral challengers.[57] Nonetheless, the conservative machinery began to sputter and cough long before the LDP actually surrendered cabinet control to a multiparty coalition in 1993 (and subsequently in 2009–2012 to the more internally cohesive DPJ).

As external challenges and domestic demographic changes mounted, the LDP's electoral base weakened. By the middle of the 1980s, voter de-alignment had created a vast trove of voters with weakened party loyalties.[58] Nonetheless, the LDP and most Japanese state institutions resisted severing regime arrangements in which they had high stakes. Congruent with the findings of neoinstitutionalist analysis in multiple other cases, the Japanese forces of resistance proved highly sticky.[59]

An anemic prime minister's office contributed to this stickiness. Compared with the rather strong presidential offices in Korea and Taiwan that afforded incumbents sweeping personal discretion, the Japanese Prime Minister's Office (PMO) had limited staff and prime ministers were largely artifacts of internal party maneuverings that allowed party bigwigs to circumscribe any prime ministerial initiatives that threatened their interests. Short-term electoral fortunes prevailed over long-term adjustments in the party's electoral base or in public policy.[60] Holding on to long-standing supporters prevailed over appeals to new socioeconomic groups. As was noted in the previous section, in the late 1980s the LDP opted for partial liberalization of various agricultural imports and reduced protection to small stores, without replacing the loss of such electoral blocs with successful appeals to new (largely urban) constituencies.[61] The electoral result was the inability to attract sufficient electoral support in the 1989 Upper House election. The LDP lost its majority, leaving the two houses of Parliament under competing majorities that in turn deprived the party of a critical institutional lever essential to passing any new national policies. More critically, the developmental regime surrendered the prior bond between state institutions and a supportive socioeconomic coalition.

In addition, prime ministerial weakness allowed bureaucratic agency autonomy in interpreting and often circumventing top-down prime ministerial or cabinet direction. Numerous veto points ensured sustained resistance against socioeconomic, institutional, or policy changes. As a consequence, formal democracy or not, of the three countries, it was state institutions in Japan's developmental regime that proved the most resistant to internal adjustment and most instrumental in maintaining regime and policy paradigm continuity.[62]

Not until the beginning of the twenty-first century did substantial changes to state institutions begin in earnest. In January 2001, Prime Minister Hashimoto oversaw a major restructuring that consolidated ministries, weakened links between agency and constituent interest groups, and beefed up staffing of the Cabinet Office, the Cabinet Secretariat, and the PMO. Combined, these changes expanded prime ministerial powers to initiate and coordinate new policies while reducing the abilities of LDP higher-ups or the miscellany of state agencies or interest groups to stymie executive initiatives.[63]

In contrast to Japan, state institutions in Taiwan and Korea underwent far greater transmutations as the consequence of earlier electoral takeovers by regime opponents and the ending of authoritarian structures. As security tensions eased across the region, political leaders in both Taiwan and Korea made tentative moves toward democratization in hopes of preventing opposition forces from linking antiauthoritarian demands to the complete purge of regime leaders and the upending of the regime itself.[64] Such a loosening of repression, however, advanced the opportunities, credibility, and organizational successes of opposition forces and legitimated previously illegal democratic forces.

In 1987, both Korea and Taiwan saw opposition forces gain enhanced control within the legislature and in local governments. Eventually, reform-minded regime opponents went on to gain executive control over state institutions. Although Korean and Taiwanese democratization took place at about the same time and in response to analogous socioeconomic and international pressures, an important difference influenced their subsequent adjustments. As noted in chapter 1, both countries had efficient and effective civil bureaucracies; however, in Korea political parties functioned largely as fragile personal support groups for political strongmen. Thus, as democratization pressures gained momentum in Korea, the nominally ruling party, the DJP, enjoyed only minimal institutionalization and little geographical reach. Whoever controlled Korean state institutions lacked the pervasive and deep-rooted party and socioeconomic support found in Taiwan. As a powerful and well-entrenched Leninist party with strong corporatist tentacles controlling most social groups, the KMT consequently exerted longer dominance in electoral contests,[65] whereas conservative power holders in Korea went down to quicker defeat after the introduction of democratic elections.

Still, as Shelly Rigger notes for Taiwan, "Elections offered the opposition a chance to demonstrate its commitment to peaceful reform, build a grassroots following, and beat the KMT at its own game."[66] Yet before formal democratization of elections, the KMT had already spent nearly two decades recruiting indigenous Taiwanese into the party and the state apparatus, reconstituting the KMT as a more inclusive organization and mitigating the long-running tensions between Taiwanese and mainlanders associated with the émigré ruling party.[67] As such, the KMT's electoral reach allowed it to retain substantial influence over politics and policy for far longer, and with greater effect, than was true in Korea.

Thus, in Taiwan's first fully contested legislative elections in 1992, the KMT won 59 percent of the legislative seats and in the first democratic presidential election in 1996, it also won handily, with the KMT's Lee taking 54 percent of the vote. Under Lee's presidency, the KMT carried out parliamentary reforms that included the retirement of aging mainland members of Legislative Yuan and Control Yuan, most of whom represented mainland constituencies they had not visited since 1949, if ever. Thus reinvigorated, the KMT did not lose a presidential election until 2000, and then by the slimmest of margins. After losing again in 2004, it proved sufficiently adept to recapture the office in 2008 and 2012 (only to lose again in 2016 and 2020).[68]

Korea's developmental regime confronted a more formidable opposition both at the ballot box and in the streets. A major inflection point came with the elections of 1985. Opposition forces unified as the New Korea Democratic Party (NKDP), an alliance of convenience between "the two Kims," namely, Kim Dae-jung and Kim Young-sam. The NKDP did not win control of the National Assembly, but it succeeded in rendering the issue of regime legitimacy the central electoral question.[69]

In February 1986, Korean opposition forces launched a petition campaign to push for the immediate introduction of a new constitution ensuring direct elections to the presidency.[70] As noted above, despite the rising tide of democratic forces, President Chun succeeded in nominating his successor, Roh Tae-woo. Yet even though Roh had been a leader of the coup that brought Chun to power, he moved Korea away from its military-based authoritarianism. Roh's strategy paid off, though with less resounding success than Taiwan's KMT. Facing a divided opposition, he won the presidency in 1987, albeit by the slimmest of margins.

A three-party merger of conservative electoral forces in 1990 created the Democratic Liberal Party (DLP). The DLP controlled nearly three-quarters of the seats in the National Assembly during the early 1990s,[71] and proved to be a vital tool in the 1992 presidential electoral victory of Kim Young-sam, another conservative regime stalwart. Nevertheless, Kim broke with the ruling military, compromised with the opposition forces to allow direct presidential elections, and went on to win, making him the first civilian president in over thirty years. Once in power, Kim established firm civilian control over the military and endeavored to make state institutions more responsive to the electorate.[72]

In this regard, much as South Korea and Taiwan had emulated Japan's state-led approach to rapid economic development, both showed evidence of pursuing a Japanese-style strong party-state path that could embrace democracy in principle while simultaneously ensuring conservative control through a dominant party.[73] Yet Taiwan's KMT proved far more successful than did any

Korean political party, remaining a potent political force for at least three decades following democratization. In Korea, the DLP's roots were thin, and Roh's extended forms of democratic participation ironically undercut many of the political and parapolitical tools long used to mobilize mass opinion.

The opposition took control of the Korean presidency, first with the victory of longtime democratic advocate, Kim Dae-jung, in 1997 and then his progressive successor, Roh Moo-hun. Over the ten years of their two presidencies, Korean progressives transformed or dismantled numerous instruments of the developmental regime, many of them economic. It took the conservative political elite that same decade to create an electoral vehicle capable of ousting the progressives and regaining the levers of state power.[74] Ironically, the democratization of 1988 boosted chaebol influence as both politicians and parties across the ideological spectrum turned to big corporations for the huge financial contributions the latter could provide.

Democratization in Taiwan and Korea meant that electoral contests ceased being foregone ratifications of the ruling political elite; rather, they became sufficiently contested as to keep bookmakers and pollsters thriving. Korea and Taiwan underwent radical shifts in state institutions as opposition forces and residues of the old regime alternated in their exertion of legislative and executive control, all the while advancing contradictory policy agendas. Yet in none of the three former developmental regimes were state institutions totally upended. Instead, shards of consistency continued as all three conservative political forces retained viability, however weakened.

A final point to note is that bureaucratic agencies in all three regimes surrendered much of their prior influence over the creation and direction of policy. Career officials, once the loyal implementers of an unchallenged developmental project, and often the singular architects of critical policy details, found themselves subject to vastly more intrusive political oversight, particularly when nonconservative governments came into office. This was definitely true in Taiwan, where democratization, in addition to weakening the KMT's dominance of the executive and legislative branches, eroded the consistent assurance that the bureaucracy would steer the economy in the same direction.[75] At the same time, certain developmental regime agencies such as the Bank of China frequently proved effective in withstanding political pressures, even during the ten years of DPP rule.[76] The common result was that state institutions in all three regimes no longer functioned with their prior degree of low friction efficiency. Institutional gears ground more slowly as opposition forces compelled developmental regime components to share control of the levers of power as electoral fortunes vacillated. None of the developmental regime's state institutions remained capable of ensuring unswerving service to advancing the prior economic paradigm. The regimes became rearranged in ways that made a continuation of embedded mercantilism politically, socioeconomically, and internationally unfeasible.

The Fragmentation of Embedded Mercantilism

Embedded mercantilism was the common policy paradigm pursued by all three developmental regimes. As analyzed in chapter 1, four key elements were critical: (1) targeted industrial upgrading; (2) mobilization and selective directing of capital; (3) domestic market protection; and (4) expanding exports, of which a particularly large proportion went to the United States. Continuation of that paradigm would surely have been difficult regardless of the changes noted in the prior three sections. Obviously, geometric increases in GDP have built-in limitations. The closer a national economy, or a company, gets to the cutting edge of technology, the more difficult it becomes to continue at the pace maintained during catch-up. Importing, copying, pilfering, or adapting the technology of others is easier than fresh innovation. Similarly, ever-escalating exports face market saturation limits; at the extreme, no country can produce all of the world's goods. In addition, as economies and markets grow larger, they attract more competitive attention than when they were smaller and weaker.

Nonetheless, in addition to these and other natural limits, the weakening or erosion of key regime props accelerated the disintegration of embedded mercantilism. As the developmental regimes splintered, unwavering support for the policy mix essential to embedded mercantilism faded as well. Major changes followed.

Increased FDI, both incoming and outgoing, was among the most potent forces damaging embedded mercantilism. By moving parts of their operations abroad, companies eliminated, or took with them, many of the better-paying jobs their domestic production workers held and removed the guaranteed purchases their many subcontractors enjoyed. Even as the process might increase quality jobs in management, marketing, R&D, and the like, midlevel manufacturing jobs gave way to part-time or lower-level service jobs, or both.[77] Outsourcing firms became less dependent on state largesse, capital infusions, and market protection, in turn loosening their receptiveness to administrative directives and their tolerance of large government outlays to prop up or protect less efficient sectors of the economy. Instead, they pressed for further liberalization of the home market along with the national embrace of various free trade agreements. In short, firms investing heavily abroad no longer continued their previous contributions to the positive spiral linking national economic success with the developmental regime.

Consumers, workers, and subcontractors lost some of their prior trust in both large corporations and state institutions since neither continued to buffer them from the disorienting chills of globalization. In addition, workforce training, widespread education, and other forms of human resource development, along with broadly shared citizen prosperity, no longer flowed as generously and singularly from corporations. Propelled by changes in the employment structure and demographic shifts, inequality levels rose in all three countries.

As investments *flowed out* from all three countries, pressures increased from external global financial forces and corporations anxious *to move in*, both through FDI and competitive imports. Liberalization of domestic financial systems lowered many of the protective walls behind which domestic corporations flourished. Previously insulated national greenhouses suddenly had to contend with numerous open doors and far more chilling winds. In turn, Japanese, Korean, and Taiwanese consumers, aided by strengthened currencies, suddenly found themselves with enhanced purchasing power enabling them to take advantage of a broader array of global products.

All three countries underwent enhanced levels of foreign ownership of corporate shares, which in turn challenged existing economic monopolies and oligopolies. Foreign stock holdings in Taiwan rose from 16 percent in 2000 to 37 percent in 2007; in Korea, the increase was from 5 percent in 1992 to 40 percent in 2004; and in Japan, from 5 percent in 1990 to 30 percent in 2010. The cumulative effect was to weaken the intimate links connecting domestic firms, firms and banks, and firms and their labor forces.

In Korea, combined pressures from the United States, the IMF, and global capital had been stimulating financial liberalization since Park Chung-hee's death in 1979. The result was a reduction of government deficits, tight monetary policy, privatization of commercial banks, relaxation of controls over foreign investment, and the phasing out of government subsidies. In the early 1980s, the government went further, privatizing banks, reducing policy loans, and deregulating bank entry and interest rates.[78]

An even more extensive liberalization program began in the early 1990s under Kim Young-sam's government. Anxious to meet the requirements for OECD membership, Kim introduced a five-year liberalization plan that included interest rate deregulation, abolition of policy loans, enhanced managerial autonomy to banks, reduction of entry barriers to financial activities, and most important, capital account liberalization. The government moved away from its long-standing coordinated investment policy, in the process dismantling key political tools the developmental regime used to coordinate investment.[79] The Economic Planning Board (EPB) merged with the Ministry of Finance (MOF), creating the super Ministry of Finance and Economy (MOFE), symbolizing the demise of formal planning in Korea. The government also abandoned its traditional approach to exchange rate management.[80] Promarket ideology advanced and centralized coordination lost legitimacy.[81]

These moves undercut long-standing oligopolies and ties among government, business, and banking. Despite pushback from numerous business and governmental interests, the overall effect was severe erosion of prior policies. Between 1991 and 1996, Korea's cumulative inward portfolio investment increased from $2.3 billion to $21.2 billion, vastly greater than longer term FDI activities such as plant development or retail sales outlets.[82]

These early policy shifts in response to globalized finance paled in comparison with those that followed the lambasting blow delivered by the Asian financial crisis (1997–98). Rapidly expanding Korean firms searching for global markets and cheaper sources of capital had found welcoming partners in international capital scouring the world for profitable and promising investments. The chaebol gained new abilities to finance their business ventures by direct overseas borrowing, thereby reducing their dependence on domestic capital and government regulation. Private borrowing surged, as did that of the government that borrowed from abroad to offset growing budget deficits. Domestic borrowing of foreign capital worked well until exchange rates reversed direction, leaving Korean firms, as well as the government, weaponless in the face of a collapsing Korean currency, sudden demands for repayment to lenders, and capital flight by short-term investors.[83]

Capturing the consequent quandary, Meredith Woo-Cumings argues that the regime showed "an inability to resolve the long-standing and widely recognized dilemma of its developmentalism. Twenty years of 'financial liberalization' notwithstanding, the Korean state was unable to sever the Gordian knot between the state and the banking sector on the one hand and the highly leveraged corporate sector on the other."[84]

The AFC represented an economic tsunami that swamped most remnants of the Korean developmental regime's policy paradigm. At the same time, as noted in the prior section, the regime suffered the political earthquake embodied in the stunning election of longtime regime opponent Kim Dae-jung as president in December 1997. Kim, a formidable critic of the old regime and its policy priorities, took office at the height of the AFC and concluded that an IMF bailout, despite its strict demands, was inevitable.[85]

IMF conditionality left numerous Korean firms vulnerable to foreign purchase at fire sale prices. Rather than engineering a nationalist resistance to foreign takeovers, however, Kim's left-of-center administration embraced IMF demands as a handy foreign truncheon with which to bludgeon long-targeted elements of the developmental regime that had consistently benefited his conservative political opponents and their chaebol allies. Kim introduced measures to break up and reorganize the chaebol by forcing through substantial corporate reorganizations (the Big Deal and the Workout), nationalizing or closing several banks, and providing 100 percent opening of the financial sector to foreign investors. By the turn of the century, six of the seven nationwide commercial banks were under foreign shareholder majorities, and three were under complete foreign control. Family-owned shares of the largest firms also shrunk. Kim's government further advanced the deregulation and liberalization of the capital and foreign exchange markets, reforms aimed at shifting Korea from a bank-centered to a market-based financial system.[86] In addition, at the behest of labor and lower-class supporters, his administration wove thicker strands for the nation's relatively thin safety net, shifting government funds away from corporate largesse and toward redistribution.[87]

Kim's successor, Roh Moo-hyun (2003–8), forced through additional changes in entrenched economic patterns with an expanded agenda of income redistribution and governmental decentralization.[88] At the same time, in defiance of many of his labor supporters and economic nationalists, he initiated a bilateral free trade pact with the United States (KORUS) (United States-Korea Free Trade Agreement) that sought to bolster the bilateral relationship through improved trade ties in exchange for acceptance of many US demands for expanded liberalization of the domestic Korean economy and greater access for US corporations. Collectively, such moves shattered the embedded mercantilist greenhouse, and opened the door for extensive two-way movement by globalization forces.

What had once been a cohesive political approach supporting embedded mercantilism subsequently vacillated between liberal and conservative presidents. If the progressive presidencies of Kim and Roh swung left, successive conservative presidents Lee Myung-bak (2008–13) and Park Geun-hye (2013–18) labored to resuscitate or retain key elements of the earlier paradigm, including efforts to return to a friendlier governmental climate for business, large investments, and public works projects. By the time conservatives returned to power, however, neoliberalism had supplanted vital elements of embedded mercantilism.[89] The old regime and Korean conservatives had little alternative but to embrace greater economic internationalization and forego national economic insularity.

Ironically, one area of the developmental regime that remained largely intact was the country's extensive level of exports. Rising steadily, Korea's share of global exports reached 0.56 percent of the global total in 1975 and continued to increase even after the currency revaluations of the 1980s. Korea's total share in 1990 was 1.86 percent, and by 2010 it was over 3 percent.[90] Those exports, however, shifted in their ultimate destination. The United States had long been the major terminus, taking 38 percent of Korea's total exports in 1985. The second most popular destination, Japan, was purchasing 15 percent. By 2000, the US figure had dropped to 24 percent and Japan's to 6 percent, while China's rose to 13 percent. By 2010, the changes had become even more dramatic, with the United States taking a paltry 10 percent, Japan taking 6 percent, and China receiving the largest share at 29 percent.[91]

In the case of Taiwan, as chapter 1 noted, as early as the 1960s, economic policy had encouraged certain types of incoming long term foreign investments, mostly from the United States and Japan, but only as confined to exclusive export zones devoted to domestic assembly with no domestic sales. These attracted technology and managerial expertise while also encouraging domestic businesses to focus on exporting. While Taiwan's incoming FDI quadrupled from 2 percent to 8 percent of total investment between 1962 and 1973, it remained marginal as a portion of overall business expansion.[92] Indeed, foreign investment actually declined slightly as a percent of total investment between 1973 and 1987 (from 8 to 7 percent), and in 2000 it had risen only to 10 percent.[93]

Beginning in the mid-1980s, and continuing stepwise into the early 2000s, Taiwan's trade and financial systems underwent extensive liberalization.[94]

Party-state enterprises lost their prior protection as the government reluctantly privatized many. Anxious to retain competitiveness for Taiwanese exports, the government gradually phased out long-established trade policies such as mandatory export requirements, domestic content requirements, and export subsidies.[95] Market-opening measures allowed foreign, mostly Japanese, capital to join forces with local capital in capturing the domestic automobile and retail markets. Foreign-owned department stores, mass merchandizers, and convenience stores started to pervade Taiwan's streets and many previously independent retail shops chose to affiliate with these foreign retail chains.[96]

Nevertheless, of the three developmental regimes, Taiwan's was the most resistant to the pressures for financial globalization, with opposition centered in the Central Bank of China, a stalwart opponent of measures that might leave the country vulnerable to foreign political interference via currency manipulation, especially from neighboring China. Thus, although Taiwan's economy fared far better than did many others in the region during the Asian financial crisis, the BOC (Bank of China) and the Financial Supervisory Commission (FSC) were convinced that premature liberalization of domestic finance had been the root cause of the region-wide financial meltdown.

The BOC consequently adopted measures designed to slow the growth of foreign businesses.[97] Even as the cumulative amount of inward portfolio investment rose steadily from 1980 onward, going from $800 million to $3.2 billion between 1991 and 1996,[98] Taiwanese banking and financial officials resisted liberalizing capital markets and reducing government oversight over monetary policy. Even the progressive and independence-minded DPP found that the powerful Bank of China retained effective tools that enabled it to resist the party's decade-long efforts to become more responsive to short-term political considerations favoring greater reregulation.[99]

Selective investments, particularly in high tech, were nevertheless encouraged. There, state institutions retained substantial political control, primarily by channeling investments into government created science parks. Hsinchu Science Park developed an intensive semiconductor connection with Silicon Valley in California; Tainan Science Park transferred the thin-film transistor-liquid crystal display (TFT-LCD) technology from Japan to forge another high-technology industrial cluster in southern Taiwan.[100] Such moves aligned local manufacturers' interests with those of their international partners while undermining prior links with domestic partners. Yet the parks' success created strong cluster effects that gave both local and foreign firms a stronger stake in Taiwan and ensured that a substantial amount of the total gains from such ventures flowed to domestic companies and business partners.

Reorienting away from embedded mercantilism posed a particular problem for Taiwan with regard to its economic engagement with China. Taiwan's share of global exports continued to expand for fifteen years after Plaza. In 2000, it ranked fourteenth in the world for exports, accounting for 2.3 percent of total world exports, but this export significance then began to slide. By 2015, it had fallen to seventeenth place and its share of total exports to 1.75 percent.[101] Although China presented an asymmetrically attractive destination that had the potential to invigorate exports and engage Taiwan more fully in the rapidly expanding nexus of regional production networks, Taiwanese policymakers remained anxious about the possible security damage that might result.

Nonetheless, with time and changes in government, Taiwan's cross-straits linkages soared. China became a major destination for outgoing Taiwanese FDI and exports, eventually replacing the United States as the nation's number-one export destination. In 1990, the United States was Taiwan's largest export market, taking 32 percent of the total and its second-largest source of imports at 23 percent. By 2015, Taiwan's total US-bound exports were down to just 12.2 percent, while US imports had fallen to 11.5 percent. Meanwhile, China (including Hong Kong) saw its share of Taiwanese exports rise from 12.7 percent in 1990 to 41.8 percent in 2010, a stunning jump.[102] In the process, the underlying capability of state institutions to steer components integral to embedded mercantilism gave way to expanded and uncoordinated corporate autonomy.

Security considerations meant continued restrictions on investment in certain critical sectors in both Korea and Taiwan. Korean officials, for example, retained restrictions on foreign investment in sectors such as railroads, natural gas, and cable television. Taiwan similarly kept a list of industries closed to foreign investment for reasons related to security and environmental protection. These sectors, however, constitute less than 1 percent of manufacturing in Taiwan and less than 5 percent of the island's service sector.[103]

In contrast to the relative speed with which regime dismantling triggered paradigm adjustments in Taiwan and Korea, Japan retained key elements of the developmental regime and embedded mercantilism for much longer. Consequently, Japan's four decades of hypergrowth (~1950–90) gave way to more than two lost decades of slow to no growth as the country's economic paradigm remained tightly in the grip of regime power holders, all the while failing to deliver its earlier rewards. This was most notable in the context of financial liberalization. The subtitle of Jennifer Amyx's masterful study aptly summarized the situation: *Japan's Financial Crisis: Institutional Rigidity and Reluctant Change.*[104]

Regime resistance was glaring in the aftermath of the potentially upending 1985 Plaza Accord. Prime Minister Nakasone Yasuhiro established a commission to investigate how best to deal with the suddenly stronger yen. The consequent 1986 Maekawa Report argued that Japan should transition from its export orientation and domestic protection to a policy paradigm focused on expanded domestic consumption, dramatic deregulation, a stronger yen, and an opening of domestic markets to foreign corporate and product penetration. In effect, Japan should abandon embedded mercantilism. Yet such a shift would challenge numerous beneficiaries of the existing system.

The government and the LDP rejected the report, opting instead to slow the rising yen and to bolster Japan's exporters by driving down interest rates.

Low interest rates in turn set off a surge of speculative borrowing, the oft-told consequence of which was Japan's five-year economic bubble (1985–90) and its subsequent bursting in 1990–91.[105] Elite presumptions that the economic slowdown was but a temporary blip and that past institutions and practices would quickly regain their vaunted vitality proved illusory. Meaningful structural economic adjustments were slow to take place.

During the 1990s, Japan did privatize several of its major state-owned entities such as the Japan National Railways, Nippon Telephone and Telegraph, and the Tobacco and Salt Monopoly. Other sectors, including airlines, energy, finance, and pensions underwent varying degrees of deregulation. Yet it was only in November 1996 that substantial deregulation began in the financial sector, dubbed, as was Britain's earlier project, the big bang. The goal was to make the Japanese financial system more efficient, transparent, and globally competitive. Among other things, the big bang erased the strict separation among the banking, insurance, and stock sectors, thereby injecting new competitiveness into once hermetically insulated financial oligopolies.[106] Simultaneously, incoming portfolio investments meant a rising share of foreign ownership of Japanese corporations, much as happened in Korea and Taiwan.

As noted above, Japanese companies responded to the rising yen by expanding their overseas investments. By 1995, Japanese-owned companies were manufacturing more overseas (¥41.2 trillion) than they were exporting from the home islands (¥39.6 trillion).[107] Nevertheless, reflective of the stickiness of regime components and embedded mercantilism, incoming FDI remained low. Although Japan liberalized its capital and financial markets in the late 1990s, the country rejected even the tepid openings undertaken by the other two developmental regimes. Japan retained numerous barriers against incoming FDI. As late as 2014, FDI stock in Japan was only 3.7 percent of GDP, whereas in Korea it constituted 12.8 percent and in Taiwan, 13.0 percent. (See figure 4.1.) Japan remained one of the OECD countries least receptive to FDI and all three countries received far less FDI than the OECD or G-20 averages.[108]

On the final area of exports, Japan, like Taiwan and Korea, shifted destinations. After sending 30 to 35 percent of its exports to the United States over most of the postwar period, the expansion of regional production networks and more welcoming Chinese investment conditions incentivized Japanese firms, like those in Taiwan and Korea, to invest heavily in China. The result was that the US share of Japanese exports fell to 19 percent, a figure roughly equal to that of Japanese goods going to China.

In contrast to the long bout of policy floundering in Japan, both Korea and Taiwan, despite vigorous political and electoral competition and economic policy zigzags, made sharper breaks with their prevailing developmental policy paradigm. This proved to be one of the greater economic benefits of the radical democratization in both Taiwan and South Korea. Since democratization, governments in both countries have consistently pursued broadly parallel economic policies toward these similar ends, despite DPP efforts to undercut

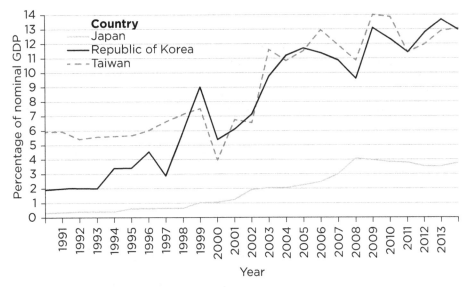

Figure 4.1 Accumulated FDI (foreign direct investment): Japan, Korea, Taiwan.
Source: https://en.santandertrade.com.

Taiwan's monetary rectitude,[109] or the continued centrality of chaebol shares of Korea's GDP.[110] Newly enfranchised voters became the beneficiaries of government policies that by design or coincidence generated larger and more sophisticated middle classes and workforces. In addition, both advanced public sector investment in human skill development, welfare reforms, education, and health insurance, all of which positioned both countries for greater competitiveness at the cutting edges of technology.

Both Taiwan and South Korea consequently saw their economic policy profiles change considerably since the 1990s, but in ways that proved far more beneficial to their national economic well-being than Japanese efforts to protect huge components of embedded mercantilism. Both underwent substantial global integration, becoming more internally diversified than they had been during their developmental phases. The two reconfigured their political economies and continued to retain global competitiveness, positive annual growth rates, and expansions in the size of their middle classes. Yet such benefits are now the products of substantially transformed economic paradigms.

The previous analysis makes it clear that the three developmental regimes underwent substantial disentanglement in response to new internal and external conditions. Key regime components saw their prior reinforcing linkages weaken. During the late 1980s and early 1990s, all three countries experienced greater plasticity. What had worked before, no matter how cleverly constructed or how cohesive, could no longer guarantee future successes. As these regimes saw their prior cohesion and control fragment, their affinitive policy paradigms of embedded mercantilism underwent correlative fragmentation.

At the same time, new conditions did not generate wholesale regime collapse or paradigm crumbling. Decades of ingrained linkages, entrenched powers, and memories of past successes fertilized resistance to quick alterations, even when they were promising. As Ulrike Schaede observed concerning corporations, "The stronger the alignment between critical tasks, formal organization, people and culture, the more successful is the organization, yet the more difficult it is to change."[111] Her observation is equally valid for regimes and their accompanying economic arrangements, particularly when those have long generated reinforcing cycles between both.

Despite many obvious continuities with the past, all three regimes confronted loosened bonds of regime cohesion and the singular embrace of embedded mercantilism. In all three countries, the bonds that once united impregnable state institutions, cohesive socioeconomic coalitions, and implacable international support suffered major challenges. Following democratization in Taiwan and South Korea, state institutional control and economic policies vacillated widely under strong presidents representing competing socioeconomic coalitions. The result in both instances was greater economic and financial liberalization, but also expansion of their already strong commitments to human development. Annual GDP growth rates over the period 2004 to 2017, while well below the steaming levels of 1970–90 developmentalism, were solid, with Korea's rate at 3.4 percent and Taiwan's at 3.7 percent. Levels of social inequality, while not as impressively low as in the past, remain low by comparison with other industrialized countries.

Japan, long topped by a much weaker executive branch and stronger conservative sociopolitical control over state institutions, preserved more regime components for much longer. Breaks with the prevailing economic paradigm were also slower and delivered less positive economic results. Annual Japanese GDP growth for all but one year between 2004 and 2017 was below 2 percent, and was often negative. Despite his long tenure heading a more concentrated prime minister's office, Abe Shinzo's promise of structural economic reform met blockages and resistance by powerful veto groups that retained long-standing regime influence. Meanwhile, opening the doors on the Japanese greenhouse for outbound investments, increasingly to China, has not seen corresponding investments moving in. Consequently, Japan remains far less welcoming of foreign capital and investment than have its developmental counterparts.

How these dynamics will play out in the future is, of course, unclear. What is evident is that both the international economic conditions and the domestic political economies of Japan, Taiwan, and South Korea underwent transformative changes during the late 1980s and 1990s that undercut their previous economic juggernaut performances. Yet even as they faced formidable changes, all three countries confronted them with substantially higher levels of GNP, vastly more sophisticated economies, and far deeper levels of political coherence and stability than virtually anyone would have predicted as recently as the 1960s. Unlike in Malaysia, Thailand, and Indonesia, the benefits of economic growth have remained largely in the hands of indigenous citizens. Even as firms in all three countries have increased their overseas investment and entered into a host of important cross-national alliances, doing so has left all three with economic and political futures substantially more advantageous than those of two or three decades earlier. To be sure, even if developmental regimes were a historical anomaly, they succeeded in achieving their most important raisons d'être.

Chapter 5

China

Composite Regime?

China embarked on an extensive economic reform program in the late 1970s. Over the next four decades, the previously agricultural economy became a manufacturing powerhouse. Vast numbers of peasants left the hinterlands to take up employment in the secondary and tertiary sectors. Moreover, manufacturing, initially reliant on FDI and simple assembly and packaging of components for exports, gained a multifaceted capacity for forward-and-backward linkages, domestic innovation, and cutting-edge technologies. T-shirts and toys gave way to computers, consumer electronics, steel, automobiles, pharmaceuticals, and solar power. Once dependent on foreign capital, China became transformed into a global financier. Throughout the process, the economy delivered quantum leaps in GDP.

From 1979 to 2018, China's annual real GDP averaged 9.5 percent. China has thus doubled the size of its economy in real terms every eight years. Between 1978 and 2020, the country's share of global GDP expanded from 3 percent to 20 percent, making China the second largest economy in the world. The country accounted for nearly 30 percent of the world's global growth and was the world's largest repository for foreign reserves. Per capita GDP rose from under $200 in 1979 to nearly $10,000 in 2020, generating an extensive middle class. The World Bank declared the Chinese experience to be "the fastest sustained expansion by a major economy in history."[1]

Beyond such statistics, the country's stunning transformation was unmistakable to even the casual observer: gleaming glass towers in Shanghai, numerous swishing fashionistas on the streets of major cities, and awesome displays of sophisticated technology and organization at the 2008 Beijing Olympics. The IMF's 2011 decision to award China a vice presidency further testified to its enhanced global status, as did President Xi Jinping's announcement that the country would use its treasure chest of foreign reserves to support massive regional and global infrastructure improvements through the Asia Infrastructure Investment Bank (AIIB), its Belt and Road initiative (BRI), and the New Development Bank (NDB).

The regime driving this transformation diverged sharply from its prereform predecessor. Despite fulsome efforts at socialist transformation in the aftermath of the 1949 Communist Party takeover, Maoist China remained one of the poorest countries in the world thirty years later, as the regime stuck loyally to the twin pillars of Leninist authoritarianism and economic autarky. Ideological factionalism endangered domestic stability, while from outside both the Soviet Union and the United States loomed as military challengers. From 1949 until at least 1971, the Communist Party retained power through ideological intolerance and brutal force superimposed on a claim of legitimacy linked to its long and successful revolutionary struggle. During the Maoist period, ideological dogma drove economics; pragmatism lagged far behind.

To be sure, the legacies of colonial voracity, contentious warlords, triad gangs, a devastating war with Japan, and a decades-long civil war had bequeathed far more daunting challenges than promising panaceas to the incoming Communist leaders. Still, the politically driven turmoil of the Great Leap Forward and the Cultural Revolution manacled the national economic paradigm. China was ripe for foreign caricature, and until the early 1970s showed little that foreshadowed the country's eventual economic dynamism.

Initially, under Hua Guofeng and then, starting in December 1978, under Deng Xiaoping, the Communist Party engineered a sequence of breaks from past policies, injecting a dollop of capitalist spice into the country's Marxist-Maoist gruel, a process euphemistically marketed as "socialism with Chinese characteristics." Puritanical self-sacrifice and permanent revolution gave way to Deng's Gordon Gekko-esque aphorism that "to get rich is glorious" and Deng's[2] pithy pragmatic observation that "it doesn't matter whether a cat is black or white so long as it catches the mice." What followed was forty years of meteoric economic transformation at least as impressive as that achieved by Japan, Korea, and Taiwan.

To paraphrase Mark Twain, regimes do not repeat themselves, but they may occasionally rhyme. In this regard, the Chinese regime, for much of the period from 1978 to 2020, bore some resemblances to those in Japan, Korea, and Taiwan at the height of their respective developmental successes.[3] Certainly, all four shared the goal of catch-up industrialization. Strong state institutions and the marginalization of potential regime opponents were similar. With several important exceptions discussed below, the Chinese regime embraced an economic paradigm of deep industrialization, capital targeting to selected sectors, an undervalued currency, human skill enhancement, and export successes of manufactured products, all redolent of embedded mercantilism.

Similar to the ersatz developmental regimes, however, for decades China relied heavily on foreign direct investment for capital and technology, while it provided vast injections of indigenous low-wage labor. Also dissimilar from the developmental regimes but like the rapacious regimes analyzed in chapter 4, a powerful and cohesive Communist Party controlled the most influential levers of state power with little worry about checks by cohesive and independent socioeconomic forces. In addition, senior-level corruption was widespread in both. Unlike the rapacious regimes, however, the Chinese party-state did not restrict economic gains to the pockets of the ruling few, instead overseeing a dispersal of benefits to vast numbers of the Chinese citizenry. Some 600 million Chinese escaped from abject privation, with the national poverty rate falling from 85 percent to roughly 5 percent between 1981 and 2015.[4] To what extent China has replicated the traits of the other regime clusters, and to what extent it differed, presents the primary question addressed in this chapter.[5]

State Institutions

China's party-state machinery commanded uninterrupted authority and power. If the developmental regimes enjoyed cohesive, technically competent, and controlling state structures, none wielded the sweeping powers of the Chinese Communist Party (CCP)—under Mao unquestionably—but with protracted continuities into Xi Jinping's presidency.

Party structures mirror those in other Communist countries. Central is the institutionalized fusion of the Communist Party, on the one hand, and state administrative organs on the other, that is, the party-state. As Franz Schurmann, in his masterful analysis put it, the state involves the bureaucracy, the army, the law, the "body of organized formal instruments from which command flows." The party on the other hand, "is the organized expression of the will of society; it actualizes the control of society over the state."[6] In principle, the state apparatus controls society, while the party, representing society, runs state institutions. Party cadres and cells, down to the grassroots level, extend the authoritative reach of the party-state through microcontrol of all social organizations of substantial size or significance, such as factories, schools, hospitals, army units, and local communities.

This system of double control is fundamental to the regime's institutional composition.[7] As Ringen phrased it: "If it were not for a determination to control, there would be no rationale for the double system. And once there is a party-state, the determination to control is a given."[8] The combined forces of party and state knit together an extensive network of mechanisms directing politics, society, and policy. Party-state authorities wield a variety of institutional tools enabling resistance to any challenges to that dominance.[9]

Anxieties about party control reached fever pitch following the collapse of the Soviet Union and its Eastern European Communist satellites. Chinese party-state leaders internalized a singular lesson from Mikhail Gorbachev's pursuit of political reforms as the prelude to economic reforms: the combination was disastrous and was responsible for the loss of party control and the collapse of the Soviet empire. Equally worrisome were the color revolutions that burst forth in several countries of the former Soviet Union and the Balkans during the early 2000s.[10] In defensive response, Chinese leaders labored to retain strict political control, even as they embraced an economic paradigm designed to move away from state ownership, collectivization, and state planning

The CCP constitution grants its Central Committee the power to choose top party leaders and gives the party the legal authority to appoint government officials. In the immediate aftermath of the military victory in 1949, however, formal lines of authority were blurry due to the de facto capacity of individual revolutionary personalities, some retired or holding no formal position, to manipulate the choice of top party officials. With time, however, and spurred by a landmark 1980s speech by Deng Xiaoping, the party's and the Central Committee's powers became institutionalized through formal rules, clear lines of authority, and collective decision-making.[11]

Many analyses of China bifurcate the Maoist period from the post-Mao period.[12] Valid as this may be for economics and living conditions, the developmental miracle of China owes much to the historical heritage of the Maoist era. Most critically, the Maoist legacy provided China with a strong Leninist party-state and a concentration of power in the Communist Party.[13]

Nonetheless, the Chinese Communist Party was less fully centralized than was its Soviet counterpart.[14] China's massive population and geographical diversity and sheer vastness favored a measure of decentralization. As of 2017, China had 33 provincial level units (22 provinces, plus 5 autonomous regions, 4 municipalities, and 2 special regions). Below these were 334 prefecture-level divisions, 2,862 county-level divisions, 41,034 township-level administrations, and 704,382 village-level subdivisions. The ruling CCP assigned extensive power to mayors and party secretaries at such lower levels, where most functions of local governance take place.

At the center, a complex of party-state institutions directed and implemented policy. Most important were the Ministry of Foreign Trade and Economic Cooperation (MOFTEC), the Industrial and Commercial Management Bureau, the Committee for Reform of the Economic System, along with several other bureaucratic agencies that collectively constitute the "brain trust" in charge of functionally differentiated reforms. Recruitment of economic bureaucrats became increasingly meritocratic.[15]

Strict organization was vital to party-state supremacy. Certainly, Deng Xiaoping, the primary architect of China's initial reform program, was a consummate believer that the party needed deep institutional roots to retain long-term power. As Lucian Pye observed: "Whereas Mao and many other Chinese leaders thought Communism's greatest strength was in its ideology and its world view . . . Deng [believed] that the supreme imperative was the preservation of the Party's organizational identity and monopoly on power."[16] Fused interactions between state and party were essential to ensuring high levels of social compliance with political priorities.

Party-state control benefits from an extensive network of state corporatist organizations that burrow deeply into society and facilitate mobilization in compliance with the political agenda. Such organizations take the form of state-created and state-led corporatist bodies that are hierarchical, exclusive, and noncompetitive.[17] During the 1980s, the CCP created numerous such associations, and by the early 1990s, the government had approved tens of thousands of such bodies at all levels of government. Included were science and technology associations, organizations for specific economic sectors, cultural groups, as well as health, sports, social welfare, and public affairs associations.[18] The government subsequently supplemented these with a new type of organization, anomalously labeled, government-organized NGOs, designed to fuse private firms into bodies such as the Private Enterprises Association and the Federation of Industry and Commerce.

Communist Party officials lead all such organizations. Their appointments and directions come from party committees. While such corporatist bodies afford an element of political space to societal actors, they do so only within tightly confined limits subject to party-state authority. Their primary function is less to aggregate interests from the bottom up, and more to disseminate downward centrally controlled propaganda and dictates.

A particularly effective cudgel is domination over information, where Orwellian powers enhance party-state control. Virtually all media outlets are state run and state organs retain tight reins over both new and traditional media. In print, Xinhua serves as the nodal driver of party-state print propaganda; it is vast, strong, and officially sanctioned. Meanwhile, one billion citizens have television access and China Central Television (CCTV), with its twenty-two program channels, is the country's only national network.[19] Like Xinhua, it is huge, operating under the direct supervision of the Propaganda Department for content and the State Administration of Radio, Film and Television for operations. The CCTV's main news broadcast at 7 p.m. must be broadcast by all local stations and nearly 500 million people countrywide regularly tune in.[20]

Internet use is also extensive and strictly monitored. Top party and government officials enjoy open access; yet most citizens confront myriad limitations, particularly in locating information the government deems problematic. A 2010 articulation of Internet sovereignty requires all Internet users in China, including foreign organizations and individuals, to abide by Chinese laws and regulations. Many international social media sites face complete bans, while search engines must accede to government restrictions preventing unwanted links or sites. Vague regulations and some two million Internet monitors facilitate state crackdowns, often triggering self-censorship.[21]

Equally instrumental in restricting the flow of politically unwanted information is control over journalistic access along with selective lifting or denial of press credentials to foreign journalists deemed less than friendly. The Committee to Protect Journalists thus claims that China "continues to be the world's leading jailer of journalists."[22] Reporters without Borders ranked China at very near the bottom of its World Press Freedom Index.[23]

Party-state institutions thus wield multiple levers that ensure cohesive control. In summer 1975, for example, Muslim villagers in a remote area of Yunnan Province refused to pay a grain tax until authorities met their demands for greater religious freedom. Deng dispatched military forces to suppress the dissident movement, resulting in an estimated sixteen hundred deaths.[24] Similarly, following the funeral of Zhou Enlai on April 5, 1976, large numbers of Beijing citizens mobilized in Tiananmen Square to mourn, a move that violated the ban on all citizen demonstrations in the Square. The PLA (People's Liberation Army), militias, and other security forces violently cleared the mourners. Similarly, on April 25, 1999, over ten thousand followers of the meditation and exercise cult Falun Gong appeared with no apparent warning outside the party's leadership compound to meditate in protest against what they claimed was harassment by police officials. Three months later, the party announced that the demonstration had laid siege to the central government compound, after which President Jiang initiated a systematic decades-long crackdown on the group.

The most notorious example of government suppression of popular protest, of course, was the 1989 crackdown on demonstrators in Tiananmen Square. As with the 1976 response to the death of Zhou Enlai, students began clustering in Tiananmen Square on April 15, 1989, to honor the memory of recently departed Hu Yaobang, whom many considered to have been a sympathetic party leader.[25] The numbers in the square swelled over the next month as tens of thousands of students and local residents crowded in, displaying a dimension of citizen activism not seen since the Maoist period.

The Tiananmen demonstrations were almost coterminous with the collapse of communism across Eastern Europe and the first Gulf War (1989–92), telegraphing even more dramatically to CCP leaders the likelihood that China was at a critical inflection point. Politburo leadership cohered around responding with overwhelming force. On May 20, the government declared martial law, and on the night of June 3–4, PLA troops poured in to clear the square. Some estimates contend that as many as ten thousand died.[26] Efforts to express social demands outside those integrated with the party-state political machinery proved evanescent.

In the aftermath of Tiananmen, the CCP forged a model of collective leadership, term limits, and mandatory retirement ages, all designed to mitigate internal leadership disagreements and counterbalance one-man rule. Neither Jiang Zemin, general secretary from 1989 to 2002, nor Hu Jintao, 2002–2012, ever gained singular control or became the "core" leader capable of ensuring discipline among other party bigwigs. Only with Xi Jinping did collective leadership surrender to the reconcentration of power in a singular dominant leader.[27]

Xi Jinping, like Deng, gained singular individual authority as head of the party, the military, and the government. He used his presidency to return leadership to what Schell and Shirk labeled "personalistic dictatorship, Leninist party rule, and enforced ideological conformity."[28] Rules tightened, Internet censorship increased, cyberspace policing expanded. By 2019, the government was also creating facial recognition techniques, along with a social credit system designed to monitor and assess the conduct of every Chinese citizen. Xi also incarcerated vast numbers of Uighur Muslims in internment camps notionally designed to ensure what was euphemistically labelled "reeducation."

Among other things, such measures aim to reduce the chances that the Chinese Communist Party will suffer the fate of such parties in the USSR and Eastern Europe, all of whom surrendered substantial portions of their prior dominance to regime opponents. Beyond self-protection of the party-state domestically, President Xi has portrayed the Chinese regime as offering "a completely new option for countries and peoples who want to speed up their development while preserving their independence."[29]

At the same time, powerful as the Chinese party-state apparatus has been, state power alone was insufficient to advance a successful economic paradigm. Critical as well were two additional regime components: first, the animal spirits of socioeconomic creativity, and second, a supportive international environment. Their fused symbiosis with state institutions was essential for the regime to function effectively in conjunction with the transformative economic paradigm

Socioeconomic Forces

From its origins in 1949, the Communist Party and the governmental institutions under its control have been the most dominant components of the Chinese regime. Socioeconomic forces reflect that preeminence. As rapid growth led to improved socioeconomic conditions, however, new forces emerged that the party-state sought to absorb and regulate rather than allowing them sufficient autonomy to in any way serve as an independent check.

The party has long treated economic class as the defining structural underpinning of political power. Class was the initial determinant of eligibility for party membership. Peasants and workers basked in official valorization as the forces from which the party hypothetically drew its legitimacy and in whose collective interests party leaders purportedly toiled. Powerful landowners vanished as a force with the brutal reforms following the Communist takeover. The elimination of large landholders solidified peasants as a pillar of CCP support, even if peasants enjoyed none of the economic powers accruing to private ownership.

Private property owners or businesses, in contrast, faced waves of nationalization of such private assets. Well into the late 1970s, Chinese society was devoid of independent socioeconomic forces capable of presenting any meaningful counterweight to the party-state. Top-down central direction faced minimal challenge or feedback from autonomous social entities. Nonetheless, the combination of the Great Leap Forward and the Cultural Revolution advanced the fiction that party leaders were continually following the masses.

Traditionally, the CCP claimed to represent the interests of five major groups: workers, peasants, intellectuals, members of the PLA, and government officials and cadres. The majority of the party's original rank and file were those who could demonstrate a proletariat background. Private entrepreneurs— actually an official euphemism for capitalists or private businesspeople— were barred from the party. This changed with the economic shifts.

Starting in 1979, a household responsibility system became the key instrument in rural reform, replacing collective peasant groups. Nor was such enhanced influence restricted to farmers, minor shopkeepers, and small factories. As the economy expanded, private enterprises of considerable scale began to replace the previously dominant collective enterprises. By the 1990s, the private sector, entrepreneurs, and numerous citizens had acquired substantial economic muscularity. Rather than allowing these newly enriched forces to fester as a potential regime threat, however, the party-state advanced a sequence of slow adjustments to clasp the newly enriched within a constrictive embrace.

Extolling the progress made by privatized ventures, the Fourteenth Party Congress in 1992 consecrated the expression "socialist market economy" as an integral party objective.[30] In 1997, it went further, acknowledging that private enterprise was an integral component of the Chinese economy. It moved preemptively to remove its ban preventing party cadres from entering private businesses, thereby opening the way for political elites to leverage their official positions to gain economic advantage.[31] Finally, in 2001, Premier Jiang Zemin, celebrating the eightieth birthday of the Party, dismayed the ghosts of Marx, Lenin, and Mao by announcing that private entrepreneurs, business owners, self-employed artists, as well as white-collar professionals employed by foreign companies and joint ventures, were welcome to join the party. According to Jiang, such people could make a positive contribution to the rebuilding of China's socialism and should not face party exclusion. He argued that simply being a property owner should not determine whether individuals are politically progressive (*xianjin*) or backward (*luohou*).

Following Jiang's speech, more than 100,000 "private entrepreneurs" applied to join the party. The party then sought to recruit an additional 200,000 such entrepreneurs before the Sixteenth Congress in September 2002. In championing the inclusion of such protocapitalists, Jiang's supporters hailed the move as a theoretical breakthrough shedding withered party dogmas, including the shackle of class. This change brought newly rich business executives into the party, lashing political resources and economic resources together for their mutual benefit and the advancement of the transformative national economic project.[32]

The move ensured that those newly enriched by the economic reforms would remain dependent on party forbearance and would neither impede continued party control nor challenge the regime more broadly. Consequently, most individuals and groups who gain wealth or social power in China seek not autonomy but intimacy with the state. Autonomy is akin to powerlessness. Those who want to best pursue their interests and maximize their influence search out ways of connecting to the state.[33]

CCP membership evolved to reflect the party's adaptation. In 1978, the party consisted of 46 percent peasants, 19 percent workers, 7 percent military, and only 26 percent white-collar workers, professionals, and students. By 2013, the percentage of peasants had fallen to 30 percent and workers had dropped to 9 percent. The CCP instead brought larger numbers of what it deemed intellectuals, that is, those with college educations into its ranks. At the Sixteenth Party Congress in 2002, college-educated party members accounted for 24 percent of the total. This rose to 40 percent at the Eighteenth Party Congress five years later, and by the end of 2013, 42 percent of CCP members were college educated, a striking contrast to 1978, when less than 3 percent of the party membership had college experience.[34]

In a relentless effort to rebuild its grassroots organizations, and even to push for their expansion into the new social spaces created by marketization, the party also loosened its previously rigid control over workplaces, schools, communities, and the day-to-day life experiences of most citizens.[35] It reduced microcontrols so that workplaces in particular, from agricultural cooperatives to the SOEs, came increasingly to operate in conjunction with market rather than political forces. As a result, most individuals no longer needed to depend on the party for jobs, living quarters, or essential supplies such as food, clothing, health care, or education. These needs could instead be readily satisfied by the market.[36]

Considerable state effort went into enhancing the breadth and depth of education and skill development. Before 1949, only 20 percent of Chinese children attended primary school; by 1986, that figure was 96 percent. In 2017, China had 2,631 colleges and universities producing more than 7 million graduates per year, with nearly 20 percent of the age cohort in attendance.[37] Over one-third of students were in programs of engineering, with figures even higher for STEM subjects. An equally critical component of reform was the funding of tens of thousands of students sent for study abroad. The returns were high, with vast improvements in the quality of Chinese universities and the skill levels of graduates.

Technology spending was equally robust. China's R&D spending surged by an annual average of 20.3 percent between 1992 and 2017, reaching about $257 billion, or 123 times higher than in 1991. By the end of 2017, the country had 6.2 million employees in R&D, spending for which accounted for 2.12 percent of China's GDP.[38] By then, China accounted for about 23 percent of scientific publications in international journals.[39] In all of these ways, the skill levels of the workforce expanded, providing both upward mobility options to many individuals and an enriched talent pool for the economy.

Yet such changes heightened rather than diminished income inequalities. In contrast to the developmental regimes that maintained low inequality throughout their major growth spurts, China experienced a rapid widening of income differentials.[40] The country's Gini index climbed steeply, from 0.3 in 1978 to 0.45 in 2016.

At the heart of this increasing inequality was the fusion of economic and political interests. In particular, greater marketization offered enhanced opportunities for political officials to use their offices to pursue personal profit. Businesspeople sought regulatory exemptions and other competitive advantages from state officials, who in turn were free to exercise their discretionary powers in service of petitioners likely to manifest their gratitude in fiduciary ways.

Military commanders too acquired controlling interests in rent-generating enterprises within areas under their geographic command.[41] Politico-bureaucratic corruption and abuse of public office increased substantially with market reforms. More people became involved, those involved were more senior, and the scale of abuse was more extensive.[42] A 2012 *New York Times* investigation focused on Prime Minister Wen Jiabao revealed the extent to which official corruption permeated the regime at the very top. After tracing the impoverished conditions of Wen's family and his early life, the investigation reported, "the prime minister's relatives—some of whom, including his wife, have a knack for aggressive deal making—have controlled assets worth at least $2.7 billion."[43]

The rise in China's inequality and the escalation in official corruption made for a more active and periodically contentious citizenry.[44] As Ming Wan noted, this fusion between the politically and economically powerful shared a common interest in repressing any societal discontent from the "losers."[45] Citizen protests expanded as a result. The Chinese Academy of Social Sciences estimated the number of annual mass incidents to exceed 90,000 in 2006. Sociology professor Sun Liping estimated 180,000 incidents in 2010.[46] Such incidents range from relatively low key and nationally unproblematic local disputes over land use or petitioning of local officials up to massive and more destabilizing ethnic protests such as those in Xinjiang or Tibet.

As part of his overall effort to tamp down such dissent, reduce corruption, and consolidate his singular control, President Xi Jinping, after his ascent in 2012, began a massive corruption crackdown (which, not at all coincidentally, enveloped many of his political enemies as well). Between 2012 and 2017, the Central Commission for Discipline Inspection (CCDI) carried out an unprecedented crackdown, subjecting more than 1.5 million officials to disciplinary actions that ranged from party expulsion to prosecution and imprisonment.[47] The anticorruption campaign became a defining element of Xi's presidency while contributing substantially to his quick consolidation of power. There is no evidence, however, that the campaign contributed in any meaningful way to dislodging the profitable symbiosis between self-aggrandizing officials and the already well off.[48] Xi's campaign did, however, reassert the authority of the party-state while reminding private profiteers, whether government or party officials or private businesspeople, that their wealth was incapable of inoculating them from its overweening power.

External Forces

As it began its developmental trek, China encountered external conditions that closed off certain paths but rendered others more tempting.[49] The United States certainly provided none of the unilateral support it had rendered to the developmental regimes. In 1949, China, like all Communist countries at the time, faced an international environment structured by hostile US-led sanctions. By the 1979 reforms, such constraints had loosened, but Chinese leaders nevertheless had to make major domestic adjustments to meet daunting international demands and to reckon with the enhanced influence of global finance, much as was true of the ersatz developmental regimes.

Thus, following the Communist takeover in 1949, the United States, in tandem with its Western allies, endeavored to isolate China from the multilateral economic system it was forging. The CCP had no part in establishing, nor any interest in joining, GATT, the World Bank, or the IMF. Nor was China integrated into global transportation, communication and trade networks, corporate joint ventures, and the like. The United States sought to deny China access to Western technology, foreign aid, trade, foreign direct investment, and other forms of economic engagement, and through such sanctions, to force regime change or collapse.

US-led efforts found a mirror in the Chinese party-state's own predisposition to avoid entanglements with what it viewed as imperialist powers. In addition to prioritizing state planning at home, the party embraced anticolonialism, anti-imperialism, and the promotion of revolutionary movements abroad. China sought to position itself as the leader and model for countries that had recently shucked off their colonial shackles. Zhou Enlai, for example, took a commanding presence at the 1955 Bandung Conference, the precursor of the so-called nonaligned movement. In addition, China maintained a network of political and economic ties to the other Communist regimes in Asia and Europe. For over two decades, China entrenched itself on one side of the bipolar chasm cleaving the Asia-Pacific.

Well before the collapse of the Soviet Union and its East European satellites, Cold War rigidities blurred in East Asia as tensions between the PRC and the USSR expanded and the United States and China found overlapping geostrategic reasons to form closer ties.[50] Both the United States and China tiptoed toward ad hoc cooperation accompanied by a number of well-catalogued accommodations. The PRC replaced Taiwan in the China seat at the United Nations and its component bodies. Formal diplomatic normalization of US–China relations occurred in 1979 under President Carter. A nine-day visit by Deng and a huge Chinese entourage in February 1979 followed, highlighted by the famous photo of Deng in a ten-gallon hat at a Texas rodeo, a public relations coup that led many in the United States to conclude that the Chinese leadership was coming over to the United States' side. Thus began what proved to be decades of increased economic interdependence between the two prior enemies.

Although security tensions hardly vanished, the improving external conditions paved the way for China's internal economic moves. Until the collapse of the Soviet Union, China, the United States, and the USSR engaged in a three-way balancing act of calculated oscillations between cooperation and confrontation. On the economic front, however, US leaders encouraged China's domestic transformation as an additional counterweight against the USSR. Given the abysmal condition of the Chinese economy at the time, US policymakers exhibited little anxiety that an economically more vigorous China would pose any short- to medium-term risk to the United States' own economic or security preeminence.

Japanese leaders also hurried to improve relations with China. In 1972, Prime Minister Tanaka made a visit to Beijing that normalized their bilateral relations while terminating Japan's official relations with Taiwan. Japan went on to become China's most generous donor of economic assistance and a strong proponent of bilateral economic interdependence. The Nixon and Tanaka visits were vital first steps in improving China's external environment.

Japanese assistance was of particular value.[51] Following diplomatic normalization and the signing of the Treaty of Peace and Friendship between the two countries, Japan became China's closest capitalist collaborator. From 1979 to early 2016, Japan sent China approximately ¥3.3164 trillion in loan aid, ¥57.2 billion in grant aid, and ¥181.7 billion in technical cooperation.[52] Private sector investments from Japan were equally extensive. For the period 2005 to 2012 alone, Japanese FDI to China ranged between $5 billion and $15 billion per year.[53] By 2007, China and Hong Kong in combination accounted for 9.1 percent of Japan's total FDI overseas stock. Only the United States (31.9 percent) and the Netherlands (11.7 percent) garnered larger proportions of Japanese money.

As China began its economic transition, global manufacturing processes were becoming modularized, fostering the expansion of regional and global production networks. Meanwhile, international capital and foreign companies were impatient to penetrate the enormous Chinese market. Even though American domestic political and business forces were resisting intense competition from foreign imports, free trade principles remained broadly pervasive. China's desperate need for capital, technology, and managerial skills further constrained policymakers who had few alternatives but to work within existing trade and financial constrictions.[54] Rather more positive for China, once the Soviet Union had collapsed and the United States was out of Vietnam,

China could operate within low levels of geostrategic competition and fewer demands to expend scarce resources on the military.

Chinese leaders took full advantage of existing global institutions, joining the IMF and the World Bank in 1980, the Asian Development Bank in 1986, and the WTO in 2001. China's senior leaders saw membership in the first three as entailing few costs. IMF borrowing was minimal and domestic capital controls were sufficiently extensive to ensure that China's financial system remained almost completely insulated from global markets.[55] Furthermore, rather than challenging the CCP's power, such incoming investments reinforced the strength of the party-state, which retained ultimate authority to approve or reject such deals. At the same time, joining the WTO would prove to entail serious costs by constricting SOEs, encouraging foreign competition on Chinese soil, and necessitating far greater transparency in state subsidies and purchases.

Yet even as China won foreign favor by advancing its domestic economic transformation and improving its foreign relations, the brutal crackdown at Tiananmen met international revulsion. As the demonstrators' spellbinding cacophony gained momentum, so did global media coverage, creating an ominous challenge for CCP leaders. The brutality of the suppression unleashed an onslaught of economic sanctions that threatened China's access to foreign markets as well as the inflow of foreign capital and technology. The previously positive international environment shifted 180 degrees, demonstrating to China's leaders the country's ambivalent standing among foreign powers. Tiananmen did less to damage Japan–China relations, however, and Japan became the first democracy to end economic sanctions against the regime and to resume normal economic relations, a move for which Chinese leaders were at the time quite grateful.

The Chinese leadership sought ways to portray Tiananmen as an unfortunate parenthesis in a more positive trajectory rather than as some logical manifestation of authoritarian party-state rule. To deal with Tiananmen sanctions, China pursued a "blunting" strategy toward the United States, seeking renewed US ties, keeping a low profile diplomatically, and attempting to demonstrate the peaceful and positive nature of China's rise.[56] The operative doctrine was Deng's admonition that China should hide its strengths and bide its time.

Chinese leaders also shored up the country's diplomatic architecture by improving relations with Taiwan and India as well as normalizing relations with Vietnam and South Korea. Furthermore, it managed to settle more than a dozen previously unresolved land boundaries with its fourteen neighboring states.[57] In addition, a series of Chinese economic decisions following the Asian financial crisis of 1997–98 enhanced the regime's overseas image, because China resisted the economic and political temptations to devalue its currency. Doing so would have aligned the yuan with the falling currencies elsewhere in East Asia; however, China kept its currency stable, thereby winning foreign appreciation from its Asian neighbors for not using its temporary advantage to cut into their export markets.

Foreign financial opportunity soon trumped moral hesitations about authoritarianism and human rights, leading to a resumption of favorable external conditions. As memories of Tiananmen faded and liberalizing reforms in China gained traction, the United States, along with other capital-rich countries, sought to integrate China into the broader global trade and investment order. George H. W. Bush, an enthusiastic US envoy to China in the 1970s, had resisted calls to sever ties with the Chinese regime after Tiananmen. Then, despite decrying the "butchers of Beijing" as a candidate, President Clinton negotiated a series of Chinese structural reforms that led first to Permanent Normal Trading Relations (NTR) status and then to US sponsorship of China's membership in the WTO in 2001.[58]

China's entry into the WTO required costly accommodations. As Mark Beeson notes: "Not only had greater trans-border economic integration become the norm in the intervening decades, the international regulatory architecture had become more influential and intrusive as well. Nowhere was this more apparent than in the conditions required for China's accession to the World Trade Organization (WTO). China agreed to 'open to the outside world.' In joining, China was required to agree to terms that 'far surpassed those made by founding members.'"[59] Of particular note, the TRIPS (Trade-Related Aspects of Intellectual Property Rights) and TRIMS (Trade-Related Investment Measures) requirements of the WTO made it far more difficult for the Chinese regime, as compared with earlier entrants, to engage in free riding by continued technology, trade, and domestic market protection.

Chinese policymakers were convinced that opening the domestic economy to the outside world would best serve China's (and the party's) long-term interests.[60] They thus welcomed the newfound financial opportunities and China's global economic ties expanded rapidly. In addition, WTO accession became a lever by which the national leadership could force through domestic structural changes over resistance from SOEs, prefectural governments, and others.

In all of these ways, the global environment came to provide a number of formidable supports for the existing Chinese regime and the corresponding economic developmental project, even as those supports forced harsh regime and policy adjustments. Yet despite the expectations of many Western policymakers and academics that a richer China would become a more democratic China, accommodation to the global liberal order did not generate political loosening. If foreign investment and global engagement may ultimately improve the environment for future democratization through the promotion of the rule of law, transparency, and the freer flow of information, in the short term the openness of foreign markets and the tolerance of foreign policymakers afforded the regime more time and political space to pursue economic reform without political liberalization.[61] As the analysis above made clear, democratization and constraints on party-state supremacy were not on the CCP's agenda.

Economic Policy Paradigm

The transformative economic strategy of the Chinese regime shared the goal of the developmental regimes in its fulsome commitment to catch-up industrialization. As Tsai and Naughton have argued, "China's highly interventionist form of state capitalism certainly accords with the general spirit of a Gerschenkronian world, in which massive investment in modern infrastructure, mobilized through a state-run banking system, serve to catapult a formerly poor country into the ranks of modern developed economies."[62] The regime in post-1979 China resonated as well with the developmental regimes in their common emphasis on garnering large shares of global exports through enhanced global competitiveness of domestic production. Yet if Chinese policymakers aspired to follow in the path of the developmental regimes in those respects, the external conditions they confronted were less favorable. Therefore, China's successful economic paradigm rested on a delicate balance between state direction and the quest for private profit. It is important to note that this balance shifted with time—broadly speaking, toward foreign investment, local control, and private ownership, but then back to greater centralization and reduced foreign control.

Limited domestic sources of capital, managerial skills, and technology combined with the radically enhanced mobility of capital meant that, reluctantly or not, the initial Chinese policy paradigm faced strong incentives to permit foreign penetration. Limited domestic capital reduced the opportunities to protect domestic markets, instead favoring a turn toward foreign capital and technology. Chinese leaders opted for state policies to bring in what they needed from outside. Thus, the percentage of total foreign fixed investment reached 7 percent in China during 1980–2005, whereas, during periods of comparable economic development, it ranged from only 0.2 percent in Japan (1950–72) to 2.4 and 2.6 percent in Taiwan (1960–85) and Korea (1965–90).[63] Greater domestic openness left China in its early industrialization efforts resembling the ersatz developmental regimes and the more globally penetrated dismantling years in South Korea, Taiwan, and Japan.

Despite accepting imports and FDI, the party-state sought to circumvent the risks of permanent dependence and economic inferiority. This required it to navigate a treacherous path between the Scylla of constricted access to essential capital and technology and the Charybdis of permanent dependence and inferiority. The Chinese economic paradigm pivoted around a complicated juggling of state-owned enterprises, private domestic firms, and foreign corporations. Policy began with heavy doses of domestic liberalization and infusions from abroad, but gradually shifted to a reduction of foreign dependence and enhanced national control over the nature and profitability of sophisticated industrial and financial sectors.

Throughout the process, the party-state rarely released its grip on the national economic steering wheel, even as it shared the economic front seat with local government officials and private entrepreneurs in search of their own profits. China's sheer size made face-to-face coordination among central state officials, local cadres, and enterprises complicated. It was both difficult and inefficient to impose uniform national plans for entire industries or the country as a whole; thus, national leaders relied more heavily on local experimentation and trial and error. A famous Chinese saying captures the dynamic: "the mountains are high and the emperor is far away."

The major economic changes introduced by Deng in 1978 advanced that mixture. Chinese economic policies had long rested on state planning, collectivized agriculture, and state-owned enterprises. Deng laid down the ideological tracks along which sweeping economic reforms could advance. His powerful speech at the Third Plenum in 1978 declared, "From this day forward, we renounce class struggle as the central focus, and instead take up economic development as our central focus." As Schell and Delury note, "With that single sentence, Deng summarily canceled two decades of Maoist policy."[64]

In the search for appropriate direction, Deng drew numerous lessons from abroad. As he declared in his youth, he felt it necessary to "study the West in order to save China."[65] Among his most important foreign influences were those of overseas economists. Some of the most influential had grown up in socialist systems, thus gaining firsthand knowledge about transitions away from centralized planning. These included the Hungarian Harvard professor Janos Kornai, the Czech émigré Ota Sik, and the Polish-born Oxford don Wlodzimierz Brus. However, Deng simultaneously encouraged the study of the successful experiences of capitalist countries. To that end, China invited economists such as Nobel laureates James Tobin and Milton Friedman for high-level consultations. Both Chinese leaders and economic technocrats absorbed numerous lessons from such foreigners, even as they resisted the temptation simply to gulp down any single foreign diet.[66]

Many of the most important lessons came from the successful transformations of neighboring regimes. Deng constantly peppered visitors from such countries for information about the economic, technological, and industrial lessons they might afford for China. Thus, in Lee Kuan Yew's Singapore, Chinese leaders found an example they could advance, namely, economic reforms under political authoritarianism.[67] Deng also studied Japan's success, and apparently jokingly asked Okita Saburo whether the latter could continue to advise China even after he became Japan's foreign minister.[68] In 1994, China released a new industrial policy that officially acknowledged the government's attention to the industrial policies of Japan's Ministry of International Trade and Industry (MITI).[69]

In December 1978, two years after Mao's death, the new party leadership committed itself to a modernization program in four key areas: industry, agriculture, science and technology, and national defense—the so-called four modernizations. Government officials signed contracts with Coca-Cola and Boeing, welcoming these two icons of capitalism into the Chinese market.

A few days later, Deng and his entourage embarked on their journey to the United States. The new policy paradigm had begun in earnest.

The reforms started in the rural areas with the transition from communes and production brigades into household responsibility, while devolution of greater authority to villages and townships meant a major compromise of top-down control. From 1949 until the reforms of the late 1970s, all peasants had been required to meet strict quotas for production and then to turn over each morsel of grain to state authorities for subsequent redistribution. China's economic reforms began by decollectivizing agriculture and loosening state reins in selective regions of the country.

An early example began in response to peasant demands in Anhui to take back their farms. The process allowed peasants to keep, and to sell on the open market, any grain they could produce that exceeded the official required quota. Massive jumps in total agricultural production followed, as swelling numbers of peasants embraced the animal spirits of profitability. Eventually, such additional production surpassed state quotas, with private profitability crops accounting for the bulk of the production. As agricultural production soared, ideological skeptics had to acknowledge that the reforms were producing positive results. At that point, acquiescence gave way to promulgation.[70]

A complete end to the commune system occurred in 1982 and the family became the primary unit of agricultural production. This proved compatible with the broader economic goals. As market reforms put more money into peasants' pockets, they bought more manufactured products and delivered more tax revenues to the state.[71] Even as growth and industrialization sped forward, agriculture remained a defining characteristic of the Chinese economic paradigm. As late as 2010, half of the Chinese population was rural; farming continued to account for 40 percent of rural employment.[72] Agricultural reforms, however, were extensive and included extensive modernization that transformed China into one of the world's largest producers of cereals, meat, and vegetables. In the late 2010s, the country was providing food for 22 percent of the world's population from 7 percent of its arable land.[73]

The central government also permitted the provincial governments to make and retain money. Thirty years under Mao had bequeathed an economic paradigm in which party-state institutions in Beijing retained top-down oversight of economic development. That component evaporated in the face of an array of far-reaching deviations from the actual policies advanced by the center to match more smoothly with local-level conditions. The result was the dramatic transformation of the political and economic machinery away from the centralized Maoist model, even as economic policy retained China's authoritarian bureaucratic political institutions and oversight. The combination of central authority and local flexibility became indispensable to both state governance and economic reform.[74]

Local officials worked from a centrally created list of quantifiable political and revenue deliverables. As long as local officials met these goals, they remained free to experiment. Other localities could then emulate any successes, while the risk of damage at the national level remained minimal. Local party officials could, in turn, become entrepreneurs or collaborate with such individuals to reap portions of any local economic successes.[75] As the national economic pie expanded, individual slices grew larger, successes that fed back to enhance national political stability and to legitimate and strengthen CCP control.

Low levels of domestic savings, however, limited domestic capital. Chinese savings rates were only around 10 percent of GDP when the economic reforms began. As a result, FDI proved the most attractive option for essential funding. To induce foreign investment, the government, long reliant on SOEs for most industrial production, eased regulations on incoming foreign monies and made SOEs responsible for their own profits and losses.[76] In addition, in 1980 a new policy apportioned revenues and expenditures between the national and local authorities, with the latter responsible for their own profits and losses as long as they met five-year revenue quotas.

Foreign monies accounted for as much as one-third of all national investment. This brought access to new technology, in large part because government requirements in key sectors required incoming foreign firms to take domestic partners and to transfer technology to them.[77] Concentrated as it was in export industries, this incoming FDI further advanced the overarching goal of economic catch-up. Official efforts to restrict the overweening force of global capital and FDI continually conflicted with the need for steady infusions of technology and capital. The result was far more penetration of China's economy by foreign capital and overseas firms than had been true in Japan, Korea, or Taiwan, rendering China's FDI levels more akin to those of Malaysia, Indonesia, and Thailand.

FDI streamed in from two different directions. The first came primarily from industrialized countries anxious to obtain access to the huge Chinese market; the second came largely from Taiwan and Hong Kong, typically initiated by ethnic Chinese. The latter aimed to utilize low-cost land and labor, and focused on assembly and final-stage manufacturing of goods designed for global export. During the period 1994–2002, Hong Kong was the largest such investor (41.9 percent), with Taiwan a distant fourth at 7 percent. Japan and the United States held places in between, with 9 percent and 8 percent, respectively.[78]

The mid- to late 1990s saw a series of huge public offerings by Chinese multinationals that raised billions, despite what Edith Terry called "murky accounting and majority government control of virtually all such entities."[79] Growth was prodigious and integrated with global markets. During the 1990s, China quadrupled its exports; however, foreign companies accounted for 46 percent of the nation's exports and 52 percent of its imports.[80] Meanwhile, the weight of the long-dominant SOEs in total industrial production in China plummeted from 80 to 15 percent in the twenty-five years to 2000.[81] Simon Pritchard accurately analyzed the wave of incoming investment: "The magnet of cheap labor, strong domestic demand and a pro-reform government created a compounding effect of expanding inward investment, supplier networks, and trading channels. Growth creates its own dynamic and Beijing is reaping the benefits of the shape of regional diplomatic muscle."[82]

To encourage greater inward investment, the Wholly Foreign Owned Enterprise (WFOE) Law of April 1986 freed foreign investors from the need to set up joint ventures with domestic Chinese companies. To be sure, the range and freedom of such activities remained heavily monitored by the state and at this stage they were still relatively small in number. Nonetheless, WFOEs were accepted as legitimate privately owned organizations and the law noted that there could be no interference in their operation and management activities.

The number and scale of FDI from other Asian countries grew rapidly. By 1993, Hong Kong, Singapore, Korea, and Taiwan collectively were investing $21.2 billion in China. Japan was investing an additional $1.3 billion. A year later, those numbers had risen to $24.9 billion and $2 billion, respectively.[83] Then in 1994, President Jiang Zemin made a triumphal visit to several Southeast Asian countries, after which the regime rolled out the welcome mat for investments for that region as well. As noted, much of the incoming money came from ethnic Chinese, often channeled through Hong Kong and Taiwan. In 1996, about one-fifth of ASEAN's investment in East Asia, accounting for $31.2 billion, went to China.[84] In all of these ways, continued Chinese upgrading depended increasingly on foreign companies and foreign money. Like many other industrializing countries, China's economic paradigm saw huge numbers of rural residents flood into urban areas, away from agriculture and toward industry. Figure 5.1 captures the rapid rise in the number of Chinese employed in industry. Tertiary industries also saw a steep, though time-lagged, leap, as show in figure 5.2.

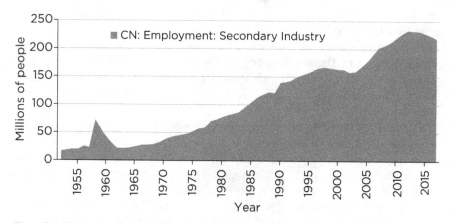

Figure 5.1 Chinese industrial employment (unit: million persons).
Source: Chinese Ministry of Human Resources and Social Security, http://english.www.gov.cn /state_council/2014/09/09/content_281474986284102.htm.

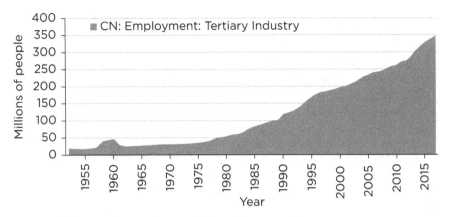

Figure 5.2 Chinese tertiary employment (unit: million persons).
Source: Chinese Ministry of Human Resources and Social Security, http://english.www.gov.cn/state_council/2014/09/09/content_281474986284102.htm.

As Boltho and Weber point out, "Using the trading skills of the Chinese diaspora in Hong Kong and Taiwan and the cheap labor and other facilities available in many of China's coastal provinces, foreign enterprises invested massively in the country."[85] Both types of investors liked the potential of the market, the centrality of China within a rapidly expanding region, and the opportunity to avoid the difficulties associated with gaining similar access in countries such as Japan.

By the first few years of the twenty-first century, the country's economic paradigm had catapulted China into a position as the world's second largest destination for foreign direct investment. The central government erected few formal barriers to such investment, however, a valuable magnet for the inflow was the autonomy given to localities over their own industrial development. Regions competed vigorously to attract foreign capital.[86] Furthermore, local politicians and bureaucrats used their official positions to become entrepreneurs, triggering a process that Nee and Opper label "capitalism from below."[87] These new local entrepreneurs had an unambiguous stake in sustaining the overall political structures from which they so demonstrably benefited, while at the same time national officials effectively injected market incentives into the economy as a whole. State and market advanced together.[88]

Membership in the WTO had required a substantial liberalization of domestic policies affecting foreign imports. In 1982, tariff rates had averaged a quite high 56 percent. A host of less visible but countervailing nontariff barriers (NTBs) reinforced these tariffs. The latter included explicit quotas, import licenses, registration requirements, import substitution lists, restricted trading rights, tendering requirements, and the like. All tipped the scales in favor of domestic producers over foreign competitors. By 2001, just before China's entry into the WTO officials slashed tariff rates to one-quarter that level, or about 15 percent.[89] By early 2004, these were down to 11 percent. In addition, only about 10 percent of total tariff lines remained subject to NTBs and the share of imported goods subject to such restrictions fell from 90 percent in 1980 to 11 percent in 1998.[90] Exports subject to licensing and quotas fell from a peak of 235 in 1991 to 50 products in 2000.[91]

Central to the local dynamism thus created were so-called township and village enterprises (TVEs). Most began between 1984 and 1997; it was through these TVEs that China's initial growth spurt in manufacturing began. As noted, local authorities competed to attract foreign investment, while both private firms and SOEs vied for start-up capital from local authorities. The shared goal was the upgrading and diversification of production to generate more domestically and globally competitive manufacturing. Spurred by the combination of agricultural reforms and the generation of local industry, including the TVEs, peasants moved off the land, affording firms vast pools of low-cost labor, a combined process that Susan Shirk labeled "playing to the provinces."[92] By the end of the 1980s, the TVEs accounted for a quarter of industrial production, and brought in around a third of China's foreign exchange earnings.[93]

Important as the TVEs were to jump-starting China's industrial modernization, most of them remained small, undercapitalized, and localized. Their contribution to the upgrading of China's strategic industries was limited.[94] Far greater contributions came with the creation of Special Economic Zones (SEZs) initially situated along the southern coast of China and proximate to ethnic Chinese investors from Hong Kong, Taiwan, and Southeast Asia. These zones offered tax relief and other incentives designed to attract FDI. The goal was to produce goods for export that could earn foreign exchange. Like the processes that propelled improvements in agriculture, the SEZs afforded similar testing and transitional examples of industrial production.[95]

The earliest SEZs were those created in 1979 in Guangdong and Fujian; these eventually expanded to include fourteen coastal cities and the island of Hainan in 1984, and then to three coastal river deltas in 1985. Local economies flourished, while the country as a whole gained access to valuable foreign technology and managerial know-how.[96] During the 1980s and 1990s, policymakers allowed private domestic and foreign businesses to enter the majority of Chinese economic sectors. Where there were no barriers to entry, private businesses quickly outcompeted SOEs and became the largest component of the Chinese economy, most notably in manufacturing. State firms nonetheless remained important in sectors protected by rigid entry barriers.[97]

The combination of localization, profit seeking, and pragmatism was central to China's economic paradigm. State planning by no means evaporated; however, instead of state plans aimed at comprehensive inclusion of all facets of the national economy, diverse shoots of market competitiveness gradually blossomed within limited geographical areas. These complemented central planning rather than challenging the principle of top-down control, in which numerous state and party officials remained politically and ideologically invested.[98] Local experiments advanced in parallel with state plans; state planning coexisted with greater marketization. The combination ensured an acceptance of ideological compatibility and party-state control, assuredly reducing the likelihood of sharp political pushback.

Private entrepreneurship was an increasingly important component in the paradigm. Indeed, Nicholas Lardy demonstrates that real profits and growth in China increasingly come from the introduction of market mechanisms and the reduction of the centrality of SOEs. The most important source of investment capital eventually became the retained earnings of firms, followed only then by bank credit. Market competitiveness had delivered larger retained earnings to China's most productive firms and these were therefore able to grow even more quickly using their own rather than state or foreign capital. Yet rather than functioning independently of state institutions, private entrepreneurs fused with them through membership in the CCP. To be sure, the importance of private business in the economic paradigm did not reflect any prominence for laissez-faire economic liberalization or complete privatization.[99]

The dominant economic paradigm always retained heavy doses of state direction, even as it underwent reforms. Thus, following Deng's spring 1992 southern tour where he visited a number of the more successful SEZs, the state role in enhancing such zones increased. Further acceleration followed in the late 1990s when Zhu Rongji, sought to rectify what had become a "landscape filled with a wild assortment of disconnected provincial and local projects without any central nervous system to guide the process."[100] He led a cast of technocrats in reestablishing stronger state direction by centralizing the fiscal and financial systems while streamlining and strengthening the state sector.[101]

Zhu worked continually to boost the strength and authority of government institutions.[102] Reflecting on the Asian financial crisis, he concluded that the main problem in the countries most damaged was their weak banking systems and highly leveraged industrial investment. Their failure to respond effectively to global financial swings reinforced his instincts that state institutions needed to speed up financial reforms so that the Chinese banking system, at the time quite similar to those of the most devastated countries, would avoid comparable vulnerabilities.[103] His financial reform included draconian measures aimed at eliminating irregularities and preventing the emergence of speculative bubbles.[104] Included were reforms of the People's Bank of China that inserted politically powerful but technically competent lieutenants into key posts. In this, they had the advantage of formal institutions that retained the highly authoritarian organizational principles of the Communist Party and its dominance in state institutions.[105]

Recentralization of the fiscal and financial systems strengthened state control. So did a revised tax system requiring all local taxes to flow first through Beijing and only then to return to the localities—not surprisingly after the central government had taken its cut. National government revenue increased by 20 percent and local authorities scrambled to find more proximate sources of investment and industrial dynamism. Fiscal policies continued to ensure balanced or overbalanced national budgets that eschewed what was portrayed as reckless public spending or even systematic deficits. Monetary policies and exchange rates remained state controlled rather than market determined, with exchange rates manipulated to favor exporters over importers.

In keeping with the moves toward privatization and reduced state reliance on SOEs, the latter underwent a major transformation involving nearly eighty thousand SOEs. Operational autonomy was granted to SOEs from 1979 to 1986, followed by delegation of authority to managers from 1987 to 1992. The basic principle driving these SOE reforms was *zhuada fangxiao*—"grasp the big, let go of the small."[106] Smaller and less efficient SOEs merged, shed excess workers, and either became more efficient and competitive or vanished. In the process, the survivors reduced their dependence on state ownership and support.

These smaller SOEs had to perform more in accord with market rather than political logic, operating on hard budgets and strict top-down accountability. Not until 1997, nearly two decades after reforms began, were the bulk of them sold off, merged, or closed.[107] The SOEs ultimately shed 45 million jobs, shattering the long-revered employee protection of the iron rice bowl., i.e. lifetime economic security. Between 1978 and 1993, the SOE share of industrial output had dropped from 78 percent to 43 percent; however, reflecting their role in job retention, their share of employment had only fallen from 75 percent to around 60 percent.[108]

In 2003, following admission to the WTO, the party-state nonetheless established institutions that moved in opposition to the presumed WTO liberalization and gave it tighter and more efficient control over the management of giant SOEs, allocation of subsidies, enforcement of regulations, and approval of investments. Variously dubbed "state capitalism," "techno-nationalism," and "China Inc.,"[109] the shifts allowed the private sector to remain vibrant but expanded the pervasiveness of party-state interventions. Foreign firms that had once been welcomed increasingly fell victim to a bewildering array of obstacles and industrial policies designed to promote and protect indigenous competitors favored by the party-state.[110]

Initially, the ownership structure in China had moved from state or collective firms producing most economic output to private firms accounting for roughly two-thirds of total output.[111] As FDI flowed into many smaller SOEs and private firms, the larger SOEs consolidated, creating even bigger, more capital-intensive and internationally competitive enterprise groups (*qiye jituan*) as the bedrock of the economy. Most gained increasingly political roles, playing enhanced roles in advancing Chinese competitiveness in innovative technologies, becoming national champions, and serving as macroeconomic stabilizers—able to increase investment when growth slows.[112]

These SOEs continued to dominate "strategically important sectors," defined as "the vital arteries of the national economy . . . essential to national security."[113] These included armaments, electrical power and distribution, oil and chemicals, telecommunications, coal, aviation, and shipping, which accounted for three-quarters of SOE assets and 79 percent of their profits.[114] State ownership conversely is minuscule in retail, restaurants, and lodging. Yet many of these large SOEs remained unprofitable, with the result that a considerable portion of Chinese state capital continued to flow disproportionately to loss-making, often obsolete firms; unviable agricultural enterprises; and regions left disadvantaged by market-oriented reforms.[115]

The large conglomerates became the major recipients of state capital and are essential instruments in ensuring that integral and high value–added sectors of the economy avoid capture by foreign investors. In addition, the state retains a dominant position in the banking sector and equity markets. The result is an economic paradigm increasingly anchored in a complex amalgam of state ownership and control in certain sectors functioning next to numerous sectors where marketization and enmeshment in globalized networks of production and finance prevail.[116] Yet by the mid-2010s, the mixture allowed the party-state–dominated regime to retain control over the economy's key pillars.[117]

This was clear in the aftermath of the global financial crisis of 2008–2009. Responding to G-20 efforts to keep global markets afloat, Chinese officials injected vast sums into the economy as the nation's contributory stimulus to global growth and recovery, gaining China foreign plaudits for its support of the global commons.[118] Yet such domestic expansion rested heavily on a further infusion of state monies into the large, state-favored SOEs in critical industrial sectors, and a corresponding decline in the official emphasis on privatization, liberalization, and market-led reforms, all at odds with the global liberal order.[119]

In sum, the economic paradigm moved China from being a closed economy in the mid-1970s to the world's largest trading nation. Its share of the global export market ballooned from about 2 percent in the early 1980s to 20 percent in 2020. China also complimented its earlier policy of "bringing in" FDI to being sufficiently flush with capital to allow for a "going out" through its own overseas investments, starting in the mid-1990s.[120] It became one of the world's primary sources of investment capital. At the microlevel, numerous Chinese companies also became globally successful. In late 2018, China had nine of the twenty largest companies in the world—Alibaba, Tencent, Ant Financial, Baidu, Xiaomi, Didi, JD.com, Meituan, and Toutiao— while the United States had eleven. Twenty years earlier, China had none.[121]

An important point in this successful transformation, however, is the extent to which the Chinese regime has fostered an economic paradigm aimed at ensuring regime continuity and endeavoring to ensure that Chinese firms, both public and private, retain substantial portions of the expanding array of more advanced technologies and hence a larger share of the benefits of national GDP growth. State controls thus remain dominant in the banking sector and equity markets. Equally, the party-state has injected vast sums of public money into next-generation technologies, from artificial intelligence to solar power to electric cars, while government financial injections into SOEs have led to their resurgence in key sectors of the economy. Foreign firms, consequently, have often faced rising barriers against equal treatment with domestic firms. Two 2015 national programs are indicative of that thrust: "Made in China, 2025,"[122] and Internet Plus. The long-term goal is to ensure that Chinese-owned entities, most with close ties to the party-state, gain dominance in the technology and manufacture of pivotal sectors and high value–added products in the global marketplace.

China has thus managed to incorporate significant elements of truly multinational production while carrying out an extensive economic transition.[123] The successful economic paradigm has fed back to bolster the Chinese regime, and especially the party-state, at times enhancing authoritarian political controls.[124] Indeed, the party-state has retained, and in fact clawed back, substantial shares of the rapidly expanding national growth. This combination reduces the likelihood that China will become stuck in the middle-income trap, instead positioning it for continued growth and steady climbs within the global production hierarchy.

Chapter 6

Regimes and the Regional Order

The previous chapters examined the interplay between external and domestic alignments in an array of East Asian regimes. The first three chapters analyzed distinct clusters of regimes sharing key similarities in their configurations of state institutions, socioeconomic forces, and external influences. They underscored as well how the regimes in each cluster also shared analogous economic policy paradigms.

Central were the ways external power configurations reinforced or challenged domestic sociopolitical arrangements, an approach congruent with studies of the "second image reversed,"[1] that is, analyses of external influences on domestic political economies. Left unaddressed were the ways the Asia-Pacific region has reflected changing mixtures of domestic regime types, and their shifting interplay over time. The goal of this final chapter is to reverse the regime mirror to analyze the ways regimes and their policy paradigms have shaped variations in the regional order of the Asia-Pacific.

The central argument is that as varying combinations of regimes strengthened or weakened, the regional order fluctuated synchronistically.[2] Three discrete, albeit overlapping, phases of regional order stand out. The first was the regional order prevailing during Cold War bipolarity; its defining characteristic was sharp-edged security and economic confrontation between two hardened blocs. The regimes and policies identified in chapters 1, 2, 3, and 5 were all in their embryonic stages of consolidation. As such, they predominantly focused inward, and superpower rivalries were the principal shapers of regional relations. Even though many regimes, particularly in Southeast Asia, endeavored to remain neutral in the bipolar clash, the domestic components of most of the East Asian regimes nonetheless reflected large swaths of the bipolar order.

A second order subsequently took shape, characterized by a reduction in the centrality of hard security clashes and an amplification of economic interdependence. The developmental and ersatz regimes, along with a reforming

China, enhanced their economic robustness, in turn increasing their combined regional agency. Simultaneously, even as superpower influences waned, that of financial globalization rose, triggering the reordering of the developmental regimes analyzed in chapter 4, and contributing to the character of the ersatz developmental regimes. Meanwhile the rapacious regimes remained marginal to regional reshaping and the United States adopted a largely supportive rather than a defining position of the shifting order. Though lauded as the new global hegemon, in the Asia-Pacific, any such US hegemony was at best incomplete.[3] As security tensions ebbed and interdependent economic development gained priority for numerous regimes, the regional order experienced its highest levels of peace and prosperity in at least a century.

The third and most recent regional order reveals an undeniable resurgence of geopolitics, nationalism, and heightened state-to-state tensions, marked most conspicuously, but not exclusively, by acrimonious relations between the United States and China on both economics and security. Yet attachment to the second order of peace and prosperity, and the focus on regional economic advancement, remains compelling among many of the region's less muscular regimes. These have been collaborating fitfully to the retention of much of the order of peace and prosperity and to preventing the regional order from devolving into a twenty-first-century variant of the first bipolar order, that is, Cold War 2.0.

Bipolarity: A Region Divided

From the end of World War II, with diminishing rigidity until the collapse of the Soviet Union in 1989–91, the East Asian regional order resonated with the tense geostrategic bipolarity led by the United States and the USSR. The power of these two Titans left few East Asian regimes with only limited agency beyond their national borders. Domestic arrangements between state institutions and socioeconomic forces typically sought partnership with one or the other of the two superpowers or, as in most of the ersatz developmental regimes, sought to avoid constrictive enmeshment with either. In those ways, the global geopolitical clash was critical in the shaping of the regional order. Nevertheless, hindsight makes it clear that the United States played a far greater shaping role in the East Asian order than did the USSR or China.

Pervasive binary differences surrounding both security and economics undergirded decades of intraregional confrontations between the capitalist and Communist blocs, and the Asia-Pacific was a core component in the global conflict.[4] Even regimes that began to demonstrate economic robustness remained domestically focused, often reinforced in that internal orientation by their external linkages. This was most evident in the embedded mercantilist paradigms of the developmental regimes. Those three regimes, together with the rapacious regime in the Philippines as well as the South Vietnamese dictatorship not examined here, all depended existentially on extensive US support, which they reciprocated by close adherence to US anti-Communist policies. The DPRK and China, along with North Vietnam and later a unified Vietnam, aligned with the USSR and were stalwart mainstays of the competing bloc. Within both blocs, domestic regime arrangements gained dominance as the result of the reinforcing contributions from their respective alignments.

Domestic political and socioeconomic elites in the former regimes advanced security and economic policies that reflected the fusion of their policy predispositions with their reliance on US money, munitions, and markets. Across the chasm, regimes in the DPRK, China, and other Communist states supported Communist insurrections in diverse locations across the region while advancing their internal commitments to state planning, large military budgets, authoritarian politics, and mutual economic interdependence. Clusters of regimes on both sides mobilized their resources to repress domestic challengers as treasonous loyalists of the opposing camp. Regimes on both sides resisted efforts to bridge the ideological chasm; rarely did individual regimes stray far from their bipolar comfort zones.

Devastating security clashes, most notably the Korean and Vietnam Wars, solidified Cold War battle lines, reflecting the predominant parameters for the Asia-Pacific order. Echoing the overarching bipolarity, numerous guerilla wars following Cold War battle lines burst forth within the Philippines, Indonesia, Malaysia, and Thailand, shaping each of those regimes. In addition, the regimes in North and South Korea dispatched numerous military teams on mutual assassination missions. Missiles and mortars arced across the Taiwan Straits on a recurring basis. Brutal domestic repression was unleashed against real or alleged indigenous traitors in regimes on both sides of the divide.

Analogous in that it was advancing at gunpoint as analyzed in chapter 3, the military regime in Myanmar engaged in decades of ethnic and regional conflicts. Military clashes over unresolved national boundaries and national identity also played out in the fighting between Indonesia and Malaysia from 1963 until 1966, in Indonesia's anti-Sukarno coup, and in the decade-long war in French Indochina.

A partial exception to the rigidities of the bipolar order came with the collective effort by a number of newly independent ex-colonies to sidestep the competing pulls of the two camps. Leery of superpower threats to their sovereignty, they labored to consolidate domestic borders and inculcate a sense of nationalist loyalty among previously fragmented subregions and ethnicities. In Southeast Asia, for instance, Myanmar, Indonesia, Thailand, and Cambodia, along with twenty-five other countries, joined the seminal Bandung Conference (1955), and its heir, the nonaligned movement (NAM), whose primary message was that all states had the inherent right to maintain neutrality.[5] Such efforts, though globally significant, exerted far less influence on the regional order as a whole until the formation of ASEAN in 1967.

The vast majority of domestic regimes, including all of those in Northeast Asia, however, accepted—indeed fostered—the underlying regional bipolarity, even if, as with ASEAN, they were also trying to avoid its negative undertow. Economic interactions mirrored the bifurcated security-driven framework and regional economics, like security relations, involved two largely isolated economic blocs.[6]

Bipolarity in the Asia-Pacific reflected the broader global architecture set up by the United States in the aftermath of World War II. Each of the superpowers focused on relative gains—each presumably benefiting from any losses or denial of gains suffered by the other side. As is well detailed, the United States took the lead in forging a dense web of institutions to foster the global international order that has largely prevailed until today. To this end, the United States treated military and economic powers as intimate partners.[7] In service of that goal the United States initiated a multilateral effort to forge the array of security alliances and neoliberal institutions aimed at containing conflict by fostering global trade, stable exchange rates, convertible currencies, and economic assistance to developing countries. Charles Meier categorized this economic orientation as the "politics of productivity."[8] In 1950, the United States also initiated an anti-Communist trade embargo that the Communist regimes matched by restricting most of their economic links to one another. Intrabloc economic and security interests were thus mutually reinforcing; security partners traded preponderantly with one another; economic bridges across the security divide were narrow, shaky, and far apart.[9] A mutual commitment to not trading with the enemy prevailed.[10]

The three developmental regimes proved fulsome contributors to the American-led order. Regional security hostilities generated outsized US beneficence to all three. Meanwhile, as long as the regimes adhered closely to US priorities, their economic paradigms of embedded mercantilism gained traction at home and welcoming markets abroad. US support allowed them to maintain undervalued currencies, expand their export markets, inject large amounts of capital into research and development, and expand domestic skills training, all in service of the upgrading of their civilian manufacturing capabilities.[11] Furthermore, American procurement expenditures during the Korean War catalyzed the economic takeoff of Japan, while a similar push from procurement spending during US military actions in Vietnam benefited all three developmental regimes, along with selective regimes in Southeast Asia.[12]

Japan, by joining virtually all of the US-initiated institutions, rehabilitated its international reputation, advancing its regional image as a peaceful and collaborative international participant. Correspondingly, once conservative regime forces consolidated sociopolitical control in South Korea and Taiwan, and their countries delivered solid levels of economic dynamism, they emerged as the more successful halves of divided Korea and China. Political stability and economic advances in all three fed back as validation of the regime's fusion of domestic sociopolitical forces with US foreign policies while simultaneously bolstering anti-Communist appeals across the rest of East Asia.

The economic costs of no trading with the enemy, meanwhile, caused less damage than might otherwise have occurred because of the offsetting openness of the United States and Southeast Asia as export markets. For Japan in particular, access to Southeast Asian raw materials was a strong incentive spurring its war reparations to the Philippines, Thailand, Indonesia, South Vietnam, and Burma. In addition, export-led growth by Japan, Korea, and Taiwan found receptive buyers in the US market. Exports from all three markets received preferential treatment as US policymakers turned a security-blinkered eye away from discriminatory trade practices favoring indigenous firms in their home markets. Ensuring the domestic stability and economic success of allies outweighed any temptation for sustained government intervention on behalf of US firms or communities bruised by the inflow of Asian products. Such domestic costs were mere penny ante in the high stakes geopolitical poker game.

The United States' anticommunism and desire for military bases played out in the Philippines as well, but with dramatically different consequences. In the Philippines, US assistance reinforced the domestic stranglehold of large landowners and their political allies, contributing to its rapaciousness while impeding comprehensive development.[13] This linkage was at its most mendacious in US support for the plundering Marcos regime. Bilateral ties were close when Marcos was in power; once he was ousted, however, new democratic forces ended the base leases, in large part because of prior US enmeshment with Marcos's predatory authoritarianism.[14]

Thus, for most of the early postwar period, domestic regimes embraced structural bipolarity while armed conflicts, Cold War tensions, and bloc-to-bloc emphasis on relative gains were the overriding shapers of the Asia-Pacific regional order, even as the budding nonalignment movement, in reaction to bipolarity, reflected the opt-out efforts of many of the regimes in Southeast Asia. National regimes and their economic paradigms replicated that broader framework. Industrial transformations, such as those taking place in the developmental regimes, remained congruent with that bipolarity, serving as little more than a tangential regional subplot until the region's icy bipolarity warmed, the United States' preeminence faded, and the economic robustness of many of the regional regimes took on greater salience.

Bipolarity, as noted in earlier chapters, started to shed its rigidity with the Nixon-Kissinger visits to China (1970–71), the reunification of Vietnam (1975), the diminished US security presence articulated in the Guam Doctrine,[15] the suppression of multiple guerilla conflicts, and the transformative improvement of political and economic ties between China and numerous of its neighbors. As the US shadow faded, individual regimes, especially those in Northeast Asia with their combinations of domestic sociopolitical stability and rapid economic growth, began to exert greater autonomy over the regional order and to concentrate on the possibility for collectively beneficial absolute gains by multiple countries, many of which had previously been on opposite sides of the bipolar divide. The result was to structure relationships that were more complex and that stretched beyond the rigid constrictions of bipolarity. This occurred most particularly through expanded intraregional trade and investment.

In the process, the ersatz developmental regimes in Malaysia, Indonesia, and Thailand succeeded in suppressing their internal uprisings and in establishing internal coherence and domestic control. The same was true of the Philippines. Such regime consolidations dampened, at least temporarily, the divisive inter- and intrastate conflicts that had been characterizing the region since the end of World War II. They opened up the possibility for greater opportunities for both sets of regimes and their economic paradigms to help in reshaping regional relations.

One of their most determinative influences came with the expansion of the concept of national security. Bipolarity had favored bonding military protection and economic growth into a unified alloy. Such solidity diminished as military confrontations eased and national security came to acquire greater nuance. Of particular salience, individual regimes found it increasingly feasible to treat military security and economic security as potentially advancing along distinct tracks.[16] Even more liberating from their prior straitjackets, many regimes began to demonstrate that hard security might advance best as the result of reduced emphasis on guns and greater prioritization of butter. Prior calculations stressing relative gains by the competing blocs gave way to a more positive sum emphasis on absolute gains that could be achieved by former competitors if they expanded their economic cooperation.

That was most true of the three developmental regimes. By the 1980s, all three had generated decades of sustained GDP and export growth, along with rapidly rising incomes per citizen. Japan was the first country whose economic buds began to flower. In a cascading sequence, however, South Korea, Taiwan, Singapore, Hong Kong, China, and a number of Southeast Asia countries began learning from, and emulating, one another's successes as they, too, launched their own paradigms aimed at economic transformation and less ideologically driven relations with one another.

More and more domestic regimes began fostering economics as their top priority. At the same time, as noted in chapter 4, many of those successes triggered pushback, particularly against the developmental regimes, by a more domestically focused US that undercut the ability of regimes to count on untrammeled access to the US market. At the same time, the escalating power of global capital also fragmented the embedded mercantilist policy paradigms. Yet as the currencies of the developmental regime exploded in value and their corporations became increasingly sophisticated, the developmental regimes unleashed a wave of outgoing FDI, large portions of which flowed into Malaysia, Indonesia, Thailand, Vietnam, and China. The developmental regimes, the ersatz developmental regimes, and China collectively reprioritized economic development, the concept of regional production networks, and intraregional economic linkages.

Without glossing over the many security frictions that continued to mitigate against the kind of East Asian security community in which war is unthinkable, relations among numerous states improved for the better part of the three decades from 1980 to 2010. Numerous warnings claimed that the region was "ripe for rivalry,"[17] the "cockpit of battles,"[18] and a region "moving forward to an unhappy future."[19] Yet such predictions proved hollow as Northeast Asia continued to avoid state-to-state wars as they had since the 1953 Korean Armistice and peace prevailed in Southeast Asia following the defeat of Chinese armies in Vietnam in 1979. Consequently, regimes across the region gained the flexibility to explore alternative foreign and economic paths unburdened by the pressures to camouflage domestic choices as capitalist or communist, or to worry constantly about existential foreign security challenges. The seeds of economic development spread their transformative roots across the region, hybridizing previously nationally distinctive economies.

During the late 1970s and early 1980s, as military tensions faded and cross-border economic interdependence blossomed, a new dynamic marked by a deepened degree of mutual gains through peace and prosperity achieved pre-eminence in the Asia-Pacific. The developmental regimes in both their original and their reordered manifestations, the ersatz developmental regimes, and the Chinese regime, to credit the most prominent actors, through their enhanced emphasis on interdependent economic connections exerted greater agency in forging a distinctive regional order. National economic asymmetries blended into a region-wide interdependence that advanced their collective fortunes and prioritized economic development as a region-wide goal.

For roughly three decades between 1980 and 2008, a large number of regimes, and the region as a whole, experienced rapid rises in GDP and global exports. Regional economic interdependence rose and cross-border production networks proliferated. In addition, a spiraling number of new regional organizations and trade agreements harnessed state institutions and national economies into deepened commitments to an interdependence that, in turn, fostered a regional order focused on more inclusive and wide-ranging economic growth and state-to-state security accommodation. With notable exceptions discussed below, those regional arrangements fused compatibly with the broader global trading and financial systems.

Enhancing Regional Peace and Prosperity

The deepening linkages that enveloped the Asia-Pacific during roughly thirty years between 1980 and 2010 are familiar. As I have suggested elsewhere, two rather distinct processes reinforced one another in forging a more connected and less contentious region. One was the process of *regionalization* that involved bottom-up, corporate, and society-driven linkages, largely independent of official state actions as a host of socioeconomic forces within East Asian regimes rode the rising wave of globalization. Multiple socioeconomic actors within the developmental regimes, the ersatz developmental regimes, and China expanded their cross-border interactions through regional production networks, enhanced transportation links, cross-border communications, tourism, and NGO projects, among others. The result was an explosion of intraregional trade, foreign direct investment, multinational production chains, export-free zones, multicountry citizen movements, track II dialogues,[20] and the like. Although official state actions were hardly irrelevant to such ties, the key agents advancing them were private, even as they emerged logically from domestic regimes.

This was particularly visible as the developmental regimes in Japan, Korea, and Taiwan experienced the dismantling analyzed in chapter 4. All adjusted their previous economic paradigms toward enhanced liberalization of domestic markets and greater FDI. Waves of outgoing foreign direct investment took advantage of regional economic asymmetries, dovetailing with regime priorities and policy paradigms in the ersatz developmental regimes and in China.[21] With time, investors and component manufacturers from those latter four regimes also began to move significant amounts of capital and product into regional (and global) projects. The result was ever more complex supply chains, investment corridors, growth triangles, and export-processing zones crisscrossing national borders.

Nonetheless, other regimes, most notably those in Myanmar and North Korea, concluded that regime protection demanded resistance to extranational, let alone panregional, economic interdependence. In addition, even as many businesses in Taiwan rushed to invest in China, state policymakers took painstaking efforts to prevent cross-strait ties that risked hollowing out the island economy, constraining political freedoms, or threatening Taiwan's de facto autonomy. Thus, certain regimes took official actions to prevent anything like complete and open movement of goods and services to all parts of the region. In addition, at the microlevel, and countering the integrative trend, multiple protected industries, from South Korean film and Malaysian finance to agriculture and forestry in most East Asian countries, resisted unvarnished globalization and pressed state institutions for protection from more open markets.

A process of *regionalism* complemented such socioeconomic and bottom-up linkages. State institutions were the drivers of regionalism as they forged an expanding phalanx of formal institutions designed to address an array of transnational problems beyond the authoritative scope of any single state, ranging from financial cooperation to pandemics to transborder crime. Regimes in Malaysia, Indonesia, Thailand, and the Philippines were early movers toward such regionalism in forging ASEAN and other bodies such as the Asian Development Bank, the ASEAN Regional Forum (ARF), the ASEAN plus Three (APT), the Chiang Mai Initiative Multilateralization (CMIM), and the East Asia Summit (EAS).[22] In such processes, the United States was more the follower than the leader. In fact, Asian governments labored hard to convince an initially reluctant Clinton administration to embrace regional multi-lateralism through APEC and the ARF.

Regionalism expanded exponentially in the wake of the AFC and the devastating consequences delivered by financial globalization to the numerous regimes that had moved to embrace market-based and internationally open financial systems without comparably robust regulatory shock absorbers.[23] As chapter 2 revealed, these regimes proved vulnerable to the rapid exodus of the hot money that had previously flowed in so liberally. The devastating effects on their currencies and real economies triggered a collective pan-Asian response aimed at providing regional insulation against the negative effects of global capital. In particular, thirteen regimes, unevenly affected by the crisis but linked under the umbrella of the APT, created a series of currency swap arrangements, substantially independent from IMF regulations, in the Chiang Mai Initiative (CMI) and its multilateral successor CMIM.[24] The willingness of the regimes in Korea, China, and Japan to compromise with one another played a pivotal role in CMIM's establishment.[25]

At roughly the same time, virtually all East Asian regimes began to participate in a flurry of bilateral and minilateral trade agreements. As with the independence of CMIM from the IMF, these free trade agreements (FTAs) proved vastly easier to conclude as they bypassed the lumbering efforts at global-level agreements undertaken by the WTO. The most aggressive proponents of such FTAs were regimes having economic paradigms most fully enmeshed in regional production networks. Many viewed such FTAs as stepping-stones toward enhanced regional interdependence while remaining congruent with broader global liberalization.[26]

Although most of these bodies lacked strong institutionalization, they nonetheless fostered collective problem solving and mutual socialization. As regionalization and regionalism advanced, more and more elites operated from the conviction that economic growth could enhance their respective regimes and protect their particular economic paradigms. The developmental regimes, the ersatz developmental regimes, and the Chinese regime, for their diverse purposes, all promoted and participated actively in such government-led regional efforts. The result was more dense networks of regional integration and cohesion. It is worth noting that the United States, while focused on maintenance of its alliance structures in the region, remained fundamentally tangential to these deepening Asia-centric financial and economic developments.

In the process, large segments of the regional population adopted increasingly common middle-class and urban lifestyles that, in turn, further tempered the divisiveness of hitherto self-defining cultural, social, and religious differences while bolstering greater cross-border cooperation.[27] Shiraishi sums this up well: "Successive waves of regional economic development . . . nurtured sizeable middle classes that have a lot in common in their professional lives and their lifestyles, in fashion, leisure, and entertainment, in their aspirations and dreams. They are the main engine of hybridization. . . . [In turn] the regional market of which the middle classes are the main consumers mediates new forms of national and regional identities that can potentially advance regional integration."[28]

Enhanced cross-border linkages, intermeshed economic paradigms, and collective economic improvements buffed down some of the spikey and bristle-ridden regional tensions lingering from a century of Western empire, Japanese expansion, civil wars, Cold War divisions, and the domestically focused demands of nation building. Historical obstacles receded in salience as regional interactions grew and the promise of win-win collaborations gained widespread acceptance. Thus, in 1990 Indonesia and Singapore normalized relations with China; in 1992, South Korea did the same. China settled land disputes with fourteen of its neighbors.[29] ASEAN also expanded its membership from six to ten, overcoming long-standing animosities between the newcomers and the original six. This included the regime in Myanmar as noted in chapter 4, which discarded prior isolationist predispositions in the process.

The changing Taiwanese regime softened tensions with the PRC. Korea's regime transformation helped to improve Japan–Korea ties as seen in President Kim Dae-jung's historic October 1998 visit to Japan, the joint 2002 ROK–Japan hosting of the World Cup, and the subsequent explosion in cultural exchanges between the two regimes. In like manner, a series of trilateral summits among the state leaders of Japan, Korea, and China contributed to a reduction in numerous long-standing tensions and fostered trilateral cooperation on a host of cross-border problems, including pollution mitigation. Significantly, the DPRK's acceptance of the Agreed Framework of 1994 brought the regime back under monitoring by the IAEA and the NPT, thereby reducing regional anxieties over previous DPRK expansion of its nuclear weapons capabilities. Even the autarkic regime in Myanmar loosened its authoritarian controls, entered into numerous intrastate ceasefires, and embraced greater engagement with both its ASEAN neighbors and global investors.

The Chinese regime contributed monumentally to the region's more tranquil climate and perceptions of mutually beneficial gains. China became the number-one trading partner of most other countries in East Asia, as well as the United States, as it adopted the role of factory to the world. All the while, as noted in chapter 5, Chinese policymakers telegraphed the message that the regime would rise peacefully and its economic paradigm would be collaborative with existing global and regional institutions.[30] Not at all coincidentally, the vast speedup in China's economic transformation, along with its improved geopolitical relations and economic interdependence with numerous prior adversaries, confirmed for many within the party-state the wisdom of concentrating national resources on economic transformation and downplaying extant military and security concerns. Indeed, the first Iraq War, carried live on CNN, convinced most Chinese security analysts that the technological superiority of US weaponry vastly surpassed anything China could defend against at a global level, thereby reinforcing domestic voices advocating a single-minded focus on domestic economic improvements and the avoidance of any direct foreign confrontations with the United States.[31]

Security tensions by no means vanished before the tide of economic interdependence and new regional institutions. At most, state-to-state cooperation reflected what Miles Kahler once called "the peace of the prudent."[32] Swords, though sheathed, had hardly become plowshares. Yet such limitations should not obscure the extent to which the majority of regimes across the region were commonly pursuing congruent economic paradigms and region-wide institutional arrangements that, in turn, facilitated cross-border cooperation and reduced the temptations of military confrontation.[33]

Overholt captures this transformation well: "For centuries, the principal route to wealth and power had been conquest of neighboring territory. Wealth came from seizing neighbors' golden temples and taxing their peasants. The dawn of the Asian miracle transformed this ancient reality. Now wealth and power accrued to whoever grew the faster by reforming the domestic economy. Conversely, the arrival of modern military technology put the quest for power through war at risk of achieving Pyrrhic victories."[34]

In sum, a large number of East Asian regimes found it increasingly in their interest to forge and facilitate a region-wide order marked by peace and prosperity. Earlier prioritizations of fissiparous zero-sum security tensions and military prowess dwindled in the face of a common redirection toward compatible and positive sum economic paradigms. The result was a noteworthy combination of regional peace and prosperity.[35]

The Resurgence of Competitive Geopolitics

Regional cooperation and mutual accommodation have, particularly since the global financial crisis of 2008–2009 (GFC), faced at least three major challenges. First was the changing character of the Chinese regime. Second was the shifting character of a number of other East Asian regimes. Third was the spasmodic inconsistency of US engagement with both China and the region as a whole. These three have been combining in ways that threaten cross-border cooperation and with it, regional peace and prosperity. Compared with a decade or two earlier, intrastate relations within the Asia-Pacific by the early 2020s had become an increasingly toxic cocktail of resurgent geopolitics, reenergized nationalism, the weaponization of national wealth, and an amplification of armed assertiveness. As international conditions shifted the domestic regime components scrambled to find the most beneficial ways to adjust to them.

As noted in chapter 5, as numerous Chinese firms climbed to the top tiers of global sophistication, party-state leaders reconfigured the national policy paradigm to reverse the earlier tilt toward marketization and privatization. Mammoth SOEs expanded their domestic and global significance while foreign firms and overseas investors confronted ever stricter barriers and the party-state's scale-tipping powers in favor of indigenous firms and state control. The regime's Internet Plus plan and its Made in China 2025 plan put state muscle behind the promotion of China's most sophisticated production processes in an all agency effort to gain global dominance for indigenous firms over the technology and manufacture of a dozen twenty-first-century sectors. Simultaneously, the CCP increased its controls over party members, state institutions, and the general citizenry, tightening party-state authoritarianism and dramatizing that political liberalization would not be the conjoined twin of economic progress.

The Chinese regime also mobilized the country's ballooning foreign reserves in service of the investment aspirations of less wealthy, infrastructure-hungry countries by initiating new financial institutions such as the Asian Infrastructure Investment Bank (AIIB) and the BRI. These new bodies offered borrowing alternatives to US- and Japan-dominated institutions such as the World Bank or the ADB. Hardly coincidentally, state officials anticipated that such extensive efforts would weaponize Chinese wealth and enhance the regime's influence across the region.[36]

In addition, the Chinese regime poured larger amounts of the bourgeoning state riches into enhancing national military and quasi-military capabilities, expanding its maritime security perimeter and challenging the sovereignty claims of numerous maritime neighbors. In a separate security advance, China took the lead in forming the Shanghai Cooperation Organization (SCO), a Central Asian security body that critics labeled an "anti-NATO."[37]

Such security shifts broke with decades of party-state behavior. Then Chinese leaders, concluding that regional instability and threats to the status quo were counterproductive to regime efforts at attracting FDI, technology, component imports, and international acceptability, made dramatic cutbacks in the share of state resources devoted to the PLA and conspicuously downplayed national military prowess. Doing so reflected Deng's hide and bide admonition. Nonetheless, even though the absolute *amounts* devoted to military spending spiraled upward (see figure 6.1), the balance between total government spending and the *proportion* devoted to military matters declined annually (see figure 6.2).

Enhanced military capabilities dovetailed with mounting military assertiveness. Resurrecting historical claims to ancient fishing grounds and other uses of the waters, the Chinese regime laid claim to virtually the entire South China Sea. To solidify those claims while defying multiple contradictory sovereignty assertions, starting in 2013 the regime began converting barely visible rocks and islets into militarized islands. Nothing was more emblematic of China's rejection of its earlier embrace of peaceful rise and charm offensive than its rejection of the UNCLOS (United Nations Convention for the Law of the Sea) decision that such enhanced maritime claims had no legal standing. Equally telling of the newfound bravado was Chinese foreign minister Yang Jiechi's provocative proclamation at the ARF meeting in Hanoi in 2010. Fuming at the temerity of countries that had raised the contentious South China Sea dispute,

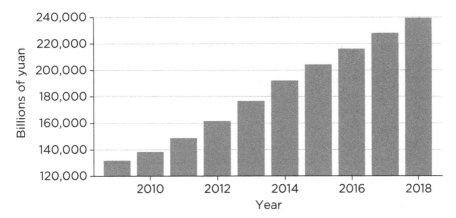

Figure 6.1 Annual Chinese military spending.
Source: Stockholm International Peace Research Institute (SIPRI); database, https://www.sipri.org
/sites/default/files/Data%20for%20all%20countries%20from%201988%E2%80%932019%20
in%20constant%20%282018%29%20USD.pdf.

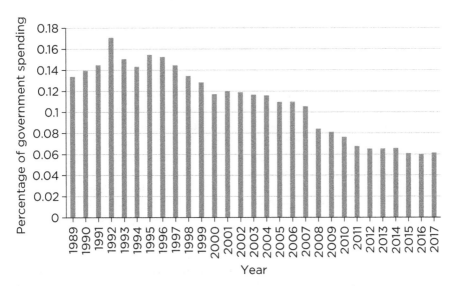

Figure 6.2 China's military spending as a percentage of government spending.
Swedish International Peace Research Institute (SIPRI) https://www.sipri.org/sites/default
/files/Data%20for%20all%20countries%20from%201988%E2%80%932019%20as%20a%20
share%20of%20GDP.pdf.

Yang stared at his Singaporean counterpart and thundered, "China is a big country and other countries are small countries and that is just a fact."[38]

By the mid-2010s, the regime had become more authoritarian, state-centric, and self-assertive. China had joined and long benefited from the liberal global order, and numerous regional institutions; however its new assertiveness made it obvious that the regime was ready to challenge the regional order, and in the process, to throw down a gauntlet to neighboring regimes while reducing its commitment to Asia-Pacific peace and prosperity, unless both advanced on China's terms.

A regionally erratic and less muscular United States complemented, and often spurred, China's greater regional imperiousness. Since at least the mid-1990s, the United States has experienced polarizing sociopolitical divisions across a host of domestic valence issues. The two major political parties have moved further apart ideologically while becoming more homogeneous internally; demographic and residential patterns increasingly divide the daily lives of most Americans into alternative social and occupational experiences, with public media dominated by echo chambers purveying conflicting narratives. Economic and foreign policies have consequently swung in radically opposite directions according to which of the two antagonistic camps controls state institutions, particularly the presidency.

It was always an oversimplification to suggest that US politics stopped at the water's edge[39] during the Cold War, however, Congress and most administrations agreed on broadly congruent foreign and economic policies for the Asia-Pacific. In contrast, since at least the early 1990s, successive administrations have moved in divergent directions.[40] In East Asia, these generated regionally destabilizing uncertainty.

Thus, President George H. W. Bush after Tiananmen labored to overcome strong popular opposition to his economic engagement with China. Yet dealing with the collapse of the Soviet Union took top priority in his foreign policy agenda, leaving East Asia to receive far less emphasis. His successor, President Bill Clinton, despite castigating the "butchers of Beijing" during his campaign, reversed course to enfold China into a broader strategy of multilateral geoeconomic engagement with East Asia. His administration negotiated terms for China's entry into the WTO and provided enthusiastic support for APEC and the ARF as conducive to pan-Pacific cooperation, especially in economics. Clinton's Asia-Pacific engagement was hardly limited to economics, however, and included the threat of massive bombing against the DPRK regime's nuclear program. The result was to spur the DRPK, as noted in chapter 4, to pursue more bilaterally and regionally cooperative arrangements that resulted in the 1994 Agreed Framework, the shuttering of DPRK plutonium facilities, and the DPRK's return to the Nuclear Non-Proliferation Treaty and IAEA inspections. Indeed, toward the end of the Clinton administration in 2000, US–DPRK diplomatic relations were hovering near normalization.[41]

The George W. Bush administration, powered by a committed cadre of hardcore neoconservatives with radically different policy preferences broke sharply from most of Clinton's regional moves. Skeptical in principle about multilateralism, the Bush administration reduced the United States' participation in multiple Asia-Pacific institutions in favor of bilateral engagement and a heavier reliance on US military muscle. It also scrapped the Agreed Framework, not only ending any prospect for diplomatic normalization with the DPRK but also triggering a resumption in the DPRK's production of weapons-grade nuclear material and a succession of increasingly efficacious nuclear tests.[42]

Although the Bush administration had a confrontational start to relations with China, the two sides resumed positive relations not least because of China's cooperation in the Global War on Terror. Yet the Bush administration broke with many long-standing policies toward the region, shunned multilateralism, and devoted most of its foreign policy attention to the wars in Iraq and Afghanistan, thereby triggering a precipitous drop in US popularity and trust in its policies across Asia. Numerous East Asia regimes began to hedge against the less engaged and accommodating United States.[43]

For the most part, however, these three administrations, while differing in the centrality they attributed to the East Asian region and to multilateral engagement, welcomed China's economic potential and promises of peaceful development while simultaneously anticipating its gradual accommodation to the existing global economic order. All broadly accepted the view that China could become what former deputy secretary of state Robert Zoelick called "a responsible stakeholder," and that benign behavior and economic liberalization would continue, in turn fostering increased Chinese contributions to the global commons and the prevailing US-dominated global and regional order.[44]

Nonetheless, and of perhaps the most monumental import, the Bush administration was in office at the time of the GFC. The crisis delivered a sharp blow to the global prestige of the United States, as well as to confidence in neoliberal economics and deregulated financial markets. The GFC and its devastating impact on the US economy and global prestige gave ammunition to Chinese hardliners convinced that the United States was past its prime and on the same downward slope as had been followed by history's previous declining global hegemons.[45] Chinese policymakers had ample evidence to conclude that any government that could not govern itself would surely find it impossible to lead the world. Further boosting the self-confidence of leaders in the Chinese party-state, in 2012 China's GDP surpassed that of longtime regional economic leader, Japan.

Further complicating the regional mix and challenging peace and prosperity, regime protection spurred the DPRK to become a de facto nuclear power, while, as analyzed in chapter 4, the key developmental regimes, Japan, Korea, and Taiwan, were undergoing a dismantling of their previously impregnable regimes and their economically adrenalized policy paradigms. Sharp shifts in the parties controlling the executive branches in Taiwan, Korea, and Japan between 2000 and 2020 meant less cohesive regimes and inconsistent policies. Once stable economic and foreign policies gave way to extreme zigzags in foreign policy and bouts of xenophobic nationalism, less economic control, and greater interdependence with China.

Geopolitical tensions and security concerns advanced to the foreground of the regional order as fears of regional abandonment by the United States rose. Numerous regimes began distancing themselves from, rather than reaching out toward, one another. Coercive mechanisms and nationalistic competition began to outstrip compromise and cooperation. Numerous geopolitical flash points erupted episodically, often driven by domestic regime demands.

Sovereignty contests in the East China Seas, between China and Taiwan on the one hand and Japan on the other, arose in no small part due to inept diplomatic actions by a novice DPJ government in 2010. ASEAN's ability to provide a common front splintered over a succession of issues, including South China Sea disputes, the Myanmar regime's ethnic cleansing campaign against Rohingya, the military coup in Thailand, and the brutal authoritarianism of Duterte in the Philippines. Simultaneously, a rising Islamic fundamentalism threatened prior regime coherence in Malaysia, the Philippines, and Indonesia, all adding to security anxieties across large swaths of Southeast Asia.

The DPRK regime was particularly flamboyant in its challenges to regional peace and prosperity. Convinced that nuclear weapons were providing the regime with a fail-safe guarantee against externally induced regime change, the DPRK by 2020 had conducted at least six nuclear tests, built up an arsenal of perhaps thirty to fifty nuclear bombs, and launched a series of increasingly sophisticated ICBMs (intercontinental ballistic missiles). These actions came on top of a resurgence of its more conventional security disruptions. Such actions reinforce the argument in chapter 3, demonstrating that the DPRK regime was detached from and hostile to prevailing regional economic and institutional linkages. How to deal with DPRK actions became a regional wedge issue triggering strong sanctions from the United Nations, the United States, and neighboring countries such as Japan, while the Chinese regime consistently and the Korean regime when under progressive presidents, leaned toward diplomatic and economic engagement.

Additionally disruptive of regional peace and prosperity, the Japanese and Korean regimes began to lock nationalistic horns over long-simmering historical issues. Progressive presidents in Korea began stressing North–South integration, advancing shared anti-Japanese nationalism as a first step toward binding the two Koreas together. The Japanese regime, in turn, when under conservative rule, emphasized the perceived threat from a rising China, minimized the brutality of Japan's prewar history, and disdained progressive regimes in Korea as overtly antagonistic.

The CCP also advanced historical issues to the forefront. Anxious to bolster its domestic legitimacy as the essential repository of Chinese sovereignty and national security, the party expanded anti-Japanese museum exhibits and encouraged xenophobic netizen outbursts and populist Chinese boycotts of both Korean and Japanese products. The once-promising Trilateral Dialogue among those three regimes saw multiple cancellations or postponements of top-level meetings over alleged misbehaviors by one or another party.[46]

In short, particularly since the GFC, a number of national regimes backed away from earlier prioritization of collective regional cooperation and national and regional economic development in favor of nationalism, security claims, and binary tensions. Such moves threatened to reverse the earlier order of deepening cooperation, peace, and prosperity. Regimes once favoring positive sum gains through regional cooperation and mutual economic development began to emphasize the purported zero-sum threats to national sovereignty posed by foreign adversaries.

President Barack Obama took office in the midst of this stew of declining US engagement, an erosion of US prestige, challenges to regional multilateralism, a global financial crisis, and disjointed policies among US allies and friends. His administration sought to engineer US policies toward the region that would reverse deteriorating regional relations, check an increasingly assertive China, and reestablish US regional leadership through its repositioning or pivoting toward East Asia. The strategy involved a tactical flurry of activities. Senior-level visits and multilateral engagement increased substantially.[47] The United States and China created the bilateral Strategic and Economic Dialogue that brought together the top military and financial officials from each government in a regularized process of tension reduction and cooperation enhancement. The United States also cooperated with China on an array of extraregional issues such as the Paris Climate Accord, the Iran nuclear deal and Somali piracy. It also embraced East Asian expansion of FTAs with the passage of the Korea–US free trade pact (KORUS) and then, more significantly, taking a leading role in fashioning the twelve-nation Trans-Pacific Partnership (TPP), the most comprehensive regional trade agreement the United States had ever entered.

TPP demanded monumental shifts in both the policy paradigms and state institutions of several Asian regimes. Long resisted liberalization measures would replace numerous domestic protections. Counterbalancing the multiple moves for US–China cooperation, TPP explicitly excluded China, demonstrating that both the United States and many of the other eleven partners viewed TPP as having not just commercial, but also geopolitical, ramifications. If successfully implemented, TPP would, they anticipated, exert multilateral pressure on the Chinese regime to scale back its resistance to equal treatment of foreign high-tech firms and to check aspects of its military assertiveness and unilateralism. Only by doing so, TPP implied, could China join the regional body and continue to benefit fully from economic relations with a dozen or more key neighbors.[48] In these ways, TPP sought to both nurture regional cooperation and to shore up the long-standing global liberal order and US regional leadership.

Asking whether a continuation of the Obama administration's policies could have refocused the regional order back toward peace and prosperity and renewed US leadership is a futile venture into counterfactuals. To be sure, the GFC damaged US prestige and faith in neoliberal markets and freewheeling capital in ways unlikely to vanish during a single administration. Increasing Chinese assertiveness hardly abated after Obama took office.

Still, any such possibilities were shattered with Donald Trump's "America First" nationalism, his disdain for past pillars of US policy, and his radical challenge to a peaceful Asia-Pacific order.[49] Decades-long alliances lost priority, diplomatic offices and top policy positions went unfilled, and multilateral engagement evaporated. Oval Office tweets and foreign photo ops replaced diplomatic expertise; dictators became presidential soul mates; human rights and democratization disappeared from the White House agenda; and the global liberal order, so beneficial for decades to economic development on both sides of the Asia-Pacific, gave way to trade wars.

In defiance of all economic evidence and debilitating to cross-national economic interdependence, President Trump prioritized the United States' bilateral trade deficits with regimes throughout East Asia as the administration's primary target. Such deficits became starkly Manichean: American was "winning" when its exports to any single country were greater than its imports from that country; the reverse meant that the United States was "losing." More broadly, the global trading system as organized under the WTO, along with most multilateral trade agreements such as NAFTA (North American Free Trade Agreement), KORUS, and the TPP, were collectively characterized as "taking advantage of the United States." Allies and adversaries came in for equal castigation, as the administration demanded "a better deal for America." Particularly damaging was the decision, made within days of Trump's inauguration, to pull the United States out of the TPP. Then, contending, "Trade wars are good and easy to win,"[50] in March 2018, the administration imposed unilateral tariffs on steel and aluminum imports under the guise of national security. These fell disproportionately on many of the United States' long-standing allies; however, they proved but a prologue to the even more sweeping and escalating tariffs specifically aimed at Chinese imports.

The Trump administration also began to portray China as an existential threat to US security. The Pentagon has long pursued a grand strategy aimed at preventing the emergence of any "peer competitor" in the Asia Pacific.[51] That strategy, at first, was generic rather than country specific; however, the 2017 National Security Strategy explicitly characterized China as a security competitor and a revisionist power poised to "challenge American power, influence, and interests [and] attempting to erode American security and prosperity."[52] In the same vein, Vice President Pence leveled a more broadly gauged and withering case against China, explicitly branding China an existential threat to the United States. In keeping with the effort to castigate China, top Trump officials, including the president, sought to relabel the WHO designation of COVID-19 as "the China virus" while seeking to elevate opposition to China into the main issue of the 2020 presidential campaign. In short, the administration engaged in an "all of government" confrontation with China.[53]

Not surprisingly, US soft power in the Asia-Pacific crashed under Trump as it had under George W. Bush. Three-fifths to three-quarters of those surveyed in multiple East Asian countries identified Trump as intolerant, dangerous, and arrogant. Respondents castigated his signature policy proposals; confidence in the US president to do the right thing in world affairs fell 55 points in Australia, 54 points in Japan, and a stunning 71 points in South Korea.[54]

The upsurge in US xenophobia added fuel to the already bubbling cauldron of geopolitical tensions in the Asia-Pacific. Consequently, there are growing assertions among international relations specialists and policymakers in both the United States and China that the most accurate prism through which to assess contemporary US-China relations involves "power transition theory."[55]

Popularized as the "Thucydides Trap," power transition theory contends that almost every declining regional or world hegemon, apprehensive about its impending declining influence, is structurally "trapped" into military conflict against the rising power using its enhanced might to press for new rules and norms governing regional or global interactions. One power tries to prevent erosion of its preeminence, whereas the other seeks to gain a deserved preeminence denied; both consequently move inexorably toward confrontation.[56]

Applied to the Asia-Pacific today, the logic envisions China as the ascendant young chest beater challenging the aging US silverback long past its prime and incapable of retaining its prior dominance over food and females. Military conflict and a dramatic power shift between them is thus but an inevitable matter of time.[57]

Certainly, China's rise has been astonishing and its influence within the Asia-Pacific is impressive. The United States, in turn, no longer occupies the singular hegemonic economic and military superiority it held following World War II, or even at the end of the Cold War. The GFC, along with the draining military conflicts in the Middle East and Central Asia, present dramatic evidence to those envisioning a United States in decline. Meanwhile, domestic political and socioeconomic polarization has paralyzed Washington's ability to reach policy agreement on a host of issues such as budgets, infrastructure, and confirmation of government officials, let alone on support for advanced technologies, the science of climate change, or how best to deal with a global pandemic.

Nevertheless, most regimes in East Asia remain anxious to avoid any bifurcated choice between the United States and China that might replicate the United States versus the USSR choices of the early postwar period. Numerous regimes have entwined their military security policies with those of the United States. Many who have not would still prefer a strong US engagement with the region. Simultaneously, however, virtually all East Asian regimes now have deep and interdependent economic entanglements with China. The trade war between the United States and China inflicted lacerating wounds on the supply chains of most East Asian regimes while devastating regional prosperity. Even minor military confrontations between the two would inflict far greater damage.[58]

Most regimes across the region have consequently resisted an either/or choice between their economic and security interests. Simultaneous retention of a militarily and economically strong United States and a correspondingly economic engagement with a dynamic China would stand as a minimal goal for most East Asian regimes; cooperative engagement between the US and China would be far better. Furthermore, a large number of East Asian regimes depend on a continuation of the liberal global trade order and regional supply chains. As such, they are anxious to avoid trade wars and to offset American protectionism and unilateralism.

Thus, even as security tensions have built, several of the region's lesser powers have endeavored to retain and enhance the infrastructure integral to region-wide economic interdependence in the hope of both prosperity and peace. Consequently, even as President Trump announced that he was pulling the United States out of the TPP, the eleven remaining members collaborated to advance a second best alternative, namely, a revised pact that recommitted the signees to the agreed-upon trade and investment relations with one another. The newly named Comprehensive and Progressive Trans-Pacific Partnership (CPTPP) went into effect on December 30, 2018, with expectations that other countries might ultimately join.[59]

In addition to CPTPP, many countries began advancing their own respective free trade pacts at the bilateral and minilateral level, including agreements between several East Asian regimes and the European Union. The coverage ratio of such pacts continues to expand.[60] Likewise, a number of Southeast Asian countries, with Indonesia in the lead, succeeded in advancing China's favored free trade arrangement, the Regional Cooperation and Economic Partnership (RCEP), which when signed on November 15, 2020, made it arguably the world's largest single regional free trade pact, and one that is more congruent with the liberal trading order than China might have preferred.

Several regimes, furthermore, have invested vast sums to expand regional infrastructure projects. Japan formulated the multibillion-dollar "Connectivity Initiative" that emphasizes sustainable infrastructure construction projects across Asia. India forged ahead with the International North–South Transport Corridor (INSTC) railway and port projects that aim at strengthening regional integration. Korea introduced the "New Southern Policy" to focus on infrastructure development in certain Southeast Asian countries, while Australia signed an investment agreement with the Association of Southeast Asian Nations (ASEAN) to develop a pipeline of high-quality infrastructure projects that would attract private and public investment.[61]

Domestic actors in many regimes in East Asia also began to recalibrate their relationships with China to offset the double-barreled challenge of US tariffs and disengagement. Japan and China, for example, backed away from prior confrontational rhetoric and the downturn in their normal diplomatic exchanges over tensions concerning the Senkaku/Daoyu Islands, conservative domestic politics in Japan, and chauvinistic netizens in China. Leaders in each regime recognized that as the world's second- and third-largest economies, they benefited from continuing their already-deep economic relations. With improved political relations, Japanese FDI in China leapt in the second half of 2018, the first major surge in FDI since 2005.[62]

Such actions are no substitute for the kind of regional leadership that the United States exercised during most of the postwar period. Yet East Asian regimes have resisted the challenges to their economic paradigms and the painfully constructed networks of supply chains. Deep institutionalization of regional production networks and multilateral institutions have fueled past successes and contributed to regional peace and prosperity. The Trump administration's efforts did not obliterate the value placed on those experiences and the Biden administration entered office committed to rectifying much of the damage done to such institutions under the Trump presidency. To what extent that will happen remains uncertain, but it portends at a minimum, one more radical turn in the US approach to the region. Yet, it was a turn designed to minimize xenophobia and foster the earlier positive sum order of peace and prosperity.

Nor has China's assertiveness destroyed the commitments of many regimes throughout the region to retain free trade, multilateral cooperation, and continued, if hedged, engagement with China. A familiar adage across Asia notes, "China will always be here; America has the freedom to leave."

If the end of the Cold War in 1991 launched a golden age of Asia-Pacific economic integration, the threat that the region is again icing over in a new cold war 2.0 looms ominously. Unchecked, it will undoubtedly spawn division, fragmentation, and zero-sum choices, enhancing the likely reemergence of the insular trade blocs that divided Communist from capitalist economic engagement in the aftermath of World War II. Yet a number of regimes across East Asia that have benefited from reduced regional fragmentation and several decades of peace and prosperity have sought to prevent that outcome.

How devastating and long lasting are current regional trends likely to be? Three decades of peace and prosperity across the Asia-Pacific make it tempting to downplay subsequent security tensions as unfortunate, but temporary, deviations from a more intensely entrenched set of structural trends marked by multilateral engagement, minimal state-to-state conflicts, and rising economic globalization, all integral components of the liberal world order. They certainly provide powerful incentives for most regimes to retain such positive sum cooperation. Such sanguinity, however, requires a conviction that recent trends are reversible rather than structural and that actions by a number of regimes can defend the regionally beneficial barricades until less confrontational relations can return between the United States and China.

Human agency remains. Yet as of this writing, policymakers in the United States and China show few moves toward accommodation. The longer their actions continue to shred the liberal and regional economic order, the more likely it is that such actions will continue to poison the Asia-Pacific order.

Nevertheless, many other regimes still exert varying degrees of regional influence. The developmental regimes, despite their dismantlement, maintain robust economic influence. The ersatz developmental regimes retain their own sway, especially across Southeast Asia and when advanced collectively though ASEAN. Singapore, Hong Kong, and Vietnam, to name several prominent regimes not examined in this book, also have the potential to play influential regional roles. Finally, geopolitical relations still face the pressures and priorities of global finance that rarely favors state conflict. In short, even if the saber rattling by the United State and China provide the noisiest activities on the regional stage, a number of other regimes and global forces will also exert essential influences in the evolving drama of the Asia-Pacific region.

Notes

Introduction

1. Angus Maddison, *The World Economy* (Paris: OECD [Organisation for Economic Co-operation and Development], 2006), 127, https://www.stat.berkeley.edu/~aldous/157/Papers/world_economy.pdf.

2. World Bank, *The East Asian Miracle: Economic Growth and Economic Policy* (Oxford: Oxford University Press, 1993), 2.

3. A useful summary of these efforts is that of Richard Stubbs, *Rethinking Asia's Economic Miracle* (London: Palgrave MacMillan, 2018), chap. 1.

4. Susan Strange, for instance, argues that the notion of regime "is yet one more woolly concept that is a fertile source of discussion simply because people mean different things when they use it." Susan Strange, "Cave! Hic Dragones: A Critique of Regime Analysis," *International Organization* 36, no. 2 (1982): 479–96.

5. Gosta Esping-Andersen, *The Three Worlds of Welfare Capitalism* (Princeton, NJ: Princeton University Press, 1990).

6. Ruth Berins Collier and David Collier, *Shaping the Political Arena: Critical Junctures, the Labor Movement and Regime Dynamics in Latin America* (Princeton, NJ: Princeton University Press, 1991).

7. James Mahoney, *The Legacies of Liberalism: Path Dependence and Political Regimes in Central America* (Baltimore, MD: Johns Hopkins University Press, 2001).

8. Nathan Jensen and Leonard Wantchekon, "Resource Wealth and Political Regimes in Africa," *Comparative Political Studies* 37, no. 7 (2004): 816–41.

9. Juan J. Linz, "Totalitarian and Authoritarian Regimes," *Handbook of Political Science* 3 (1975): 175–411.

10. T. J. Pempel, ed., *Uncommon Democracies: The One-Party Dominant Regimes* (Ithaca, NY: Cornell University Press, 1990).

11. The literature on this is extensive. An excellent overview of the concept's evolution is found in Stephan Haggard's *Developmental States* (Cambridge: Cambridge University Press, 2018).

12. Atul Kohli, *State-Directed Development: Political Power and Industrialization in the Global Periphery* (Cambridge: Cambridge University Press, 2004); Daron Acemoglu and James A. Robinson, *Economic Origins of Dictatorship and Democracy* (Cambridge: Cambridge University Press, 2005).

13. Linda Weiss, "Developmental States in Transition: Adapting, Dismantling, Innovating, Not 'Normalizing,'" *Pacific Review* 13, no. 1 (2000): 23.

14. Ben Fine, introduction to *Beyond the Developmental State: Industrial Policy into the 21st Century*, ed. Ben Fine, Jyoti Saraswati, and Daniela Tavasic (London: Pluto Press, 2013), 1–32.

15. Kohli, *State-Directed Development*.

16. Stephen D. Krasner, *Structural Conflict: The Third World against Global Liberalism* (Berkeley: University of California Press, 1985), 28; Samuel P. Huntington, *Political Order in Changing Societies* (New Haven, CT: Yale University Press, 1968), 2. Both as cited in Joel S. Migdal, *Strong Societies and Weak States: State-Society Relations and State Capabilities in the Third World* (Princeton, NJ: Princeton University Press, 1988), 7.

17. Theda Skocpol, "A Critical Review of Barrington Moore's Social Origins of Dictatorship and Democracy," *Politics and Society* 4, no. 1 (1973): 16.

18. As Haggard phrased it, "the success of the East Asian NICs rested not only on certain discrete *policies* but on the particular political and institutional context that allowed [them] to adopt those policies in the first place." Stephan Haggard, *Pathways from the Periphery: The Politics of Growth in the Newly Industrializing Countries* (Ithaca, NY: Cornell University Press, 1990), 21.

19. Meredith Woo-Cumings, "Introduction: Chalmers Johnson and the Politics of Nationalism and Development," in Meredith Woo-Cumings (ed.), *The Developmental State*. Ithaca, NY: Cornell University Press): 19.

20. Peter B. Evans, *Embedded Autonomy: States and Industrial Transformation* (Princeton, NJ: Princeton University Press, 2012), esp. chapter 1.

21. Barrington Moore, *Social Origins of Dictatorship and Democracy: Lord and Peasant in the Making of the Modern World* (Boston: Beacon Press, 1993).

22. Krasner, *Structural Conflict*, 28; Huntington, *Political Order in Changing Societies*, 2. Both as cited in Migdal, *Strong Societies and Weak States*, 7.

23. Stephan Haggard and Robert R. Kaufman, *The Political Economy of Democratic Transitions* (Princeton, NJ: Princeton University Press, 2018), 6. Kohli, *State-Directed Development*, inter alia.

24. Oran R. Young, "International Regimes: Toward a New Theory of Institutions," *World Politics* 39, no. 1 (1986): 115. See also John Gerard Ruggie, ed., *The Antinomies of Interdependence* (New York: Columbia University Press, 1983).

25. John G. Ruggie, "International Regimes, Transactions, and Change: Embedded Liberalism in the Postwar Economic Order," *International Organization* 36, no. 2 (1982): 379–415.

26. Oran R. Young, ed., *The Effectiveness of International Environmental Regimes: Causal Connections and Behavioral Mechanisms* (Cambridge, MA: MIT Press, 1999).

27. Joseph S. Nye, "Nuclear Learning and US–Soviet Security Regimes," *International Organization* 41, no. 3 (1987): 371–402.

28. Peter J. Katzenstein, ed., *The Culture of National Security: Norms and Identity in World Politics* (New York: Columbia University Press, 1996).

29. Matthew J. S. Windle et al., "Fishing Occupational Health and Safety: A Comparison of Regulatory Regimes and Safety Outcomes in Six Countries," *Marine Policy* 32, no. 4 (2008): 701–10.

30. Andreas Hasenclever, Peter Mayer, and Volker Rittberger, *Theories of International Regimes*, vol. 55 (Cambridge: Cambridge University Press, 1997).

31. Esping-Andersen, *The Three Worlds of Welfare Capitalism*.

32. Peter J. Katzenstein, *Small States in World Markets: Industrial Policy in Europe* (Ithaca, NY: Cornell University Press, 1985).

33. Sven Steinmo, *Taxation and Democracy: Swedish, British, and American Approaches to Financing the Modern State* (New Haven, CT: Yale University Press, 1993).

34. Peter A. Hall and David Soskice, eds., *Varieties of Capitalism: The Institutional Foundations of Comparative Advantage* (Oxford: Oxford University Press, 2001).

35. Kathleen Thelen, *Varieties of Liberalization and the New Politics of Social Solidarity* (New York: Cambridge University Press, 2014).

36. Robert D. Putnam, "Diplomacy and Domestic Politics: The Logic of Two-Level Games," *International Organization* 42, no. 3 (1988): 427–60. See also Peter B. Evans, Harold K. Jacobson, and Robert D. Putnam, *Double-Edged Diplomacy: International Bargaining and Domestic Politics* (Berkeley: University of California Press, 1993).

37. Theda Skocpol, "Bringing the State Back In: Current Research," in *Bringing the State Back In*, ed. Peter Evans, Dietrich Rueschemeyer, and Theda Skocpol (Cambridge: Cambridge University Press, 1985), 8.

38. George Tsebelis, *Nested Games: Rational Choice in Comparative Politics* (Berkeley: University of California Press, 1990).

39. See Alexander Gerschenkron, *Bread and Democracy in Germany* (Ithaca, NY: Cornell University Press, 1989), and *Economic Backwardness in Historical Perspective: A Book of Essays* (Cambridge, MA: Belknap Press of Harvard University Press, 1962).

40. Ha-Joon Chang, *Kicking Away the Ladder* (London: Anthem Press, 2002).

41. On bureaucratic authoritarianism, see Fernando H. Cardoso and Enzo Faletto, *Dependency and Development in Latin America* (Berkeley: University of California Press, 1979); David Collier, "Overview of the Bureaucratic-Authoritarian Model," in *The New Authoritarianism in Latin America*, ed. David Collier (Princeton, NJ: Princeton University Press, 1979): 1–4.

42. Examples include Peter Gourevitch, *Politics in Hard Times: Comparative Responses to International Economic Crises* (Ithaca, NY: Cornell University Press, 1986); Peter J. Katzenstein, ed., *Between Power and Plenty* (Madison: University of Wisconsin Press, 1977); Duane Swank, "Globalization, Domestic Politics, and Welfare State Retrenchment in Capitalist Democracies," *Social Policy and Society* 4, no. 2 (2005): 183–195; Stephan Haggard, *The Political Economy of the Asian Financial Crisis* (Washington, D.C.: Peterson Institute, 2000); Miles Kahler and David A. Lake, eds., *Politics in the New Hard Times: The Great Recession in Comparative Perspective* (Ithaca, NY: Cornell University Press, 2013).

43. A rather conspicuous external contribution came from prewar Japanese colonialization that prepared local officials in Korea and Taiwan for postcolonial governance by fostering advanced educational systems, modern civil services, railways, roads, rice mills, smelters, oil refineries, shipyards, and modern cities undreamt of in either country decades earlier. Moreover, following World War II and in accord with US Cold War alliance policies, all three regimes became the beneficiaries of American economic largess in the form of direct foreign aid, military support and purchases, and technology transfer, as well as open markets for their exports. See Bruce Cumings, "The Origins and Development of the Northeast Asian Political Economy: Industrial Sectors, Product Cycles, and Political Consequences," *International Organization* 38, no. 1 (1984): 1–40.

44. Jeffrey A. Winters, "The Determinants of Financial Crisis in Asia," in *The Politics of the Asian Financial Crisis*, ed. T. J. Pempel (Ithaca, NY: Cornell University Press, 1999), 79–97; Gregory W. Noble and John Ravenhill, eds., *The Asian Financial Crisis and the Architecture of Global Finance* (Cambridge: Cambridge University Press, 2000).

45. Wolfgang Streeck, *Buying Time: The Delayed Crisis of Democratic Capitalism* (London: Verso Books, 2014); Lucio Baccaro and Jonas Pontusson, "Rethinking Comparative Political Economy: The Growth Model Perspective," *Politics and Society* 44, no. 2 (2016): 175–207.

46. John Ravenhill, "Production Networks in Asia," in *The Oxford Handbook of the International Relations of Asia*, ed. Saadia Pekkanen, John Ravenhill, and Rosemary Foot (Oxford: Oxford University Press, 2014), 348–68; Richard Stubbs, *Rethinking Asia's Economic Miracle: The Political Economy of War, Prosperity, and Crisis* (London: Macmillan International Higher Education, 2017); Henry Wai-chung Yeung, *Strategic Coupling: East Asian Industrial Transformation in the New Global Economy* (Ithaca, NY: Cornell University Press, 2016).

47. Haggard, *Pathways from the Periphery*.

48. David Easton, *A Systems Analysis of Political Life* (New York: John Wiley, 1965), 190–221; E. E. Schattschneider, *The Semi-Sovereign People* (New York: Holt, Rinehart and Winston, 1960), 71. In an early treatment of the notion of regime, John G. Ruggie gave the following definition: regimes were "sets of mutual expectations, generally agreed-to rules, regulations and plans, in accordance with which organizational energies and financial commitments are allocated." See John G. Ruggie, "International Responses to Technology: Concepts and Trends," *International Organization* 29 (Summer 1975): 569.

49. See, e.g., Albert Hirschman, *The Strategy of Economic Development* (New Haven, CT: Yale University Press, 1958).

50. T. J. Pempel, introduction to *Uncommon Democracies: The One-Party Dominant Regimes*, ed. T. J. Pempel (Ithaca, NY: Cornell University Press, 1990), 16.

51. These ten cases are far from comprehensive, but most excluded economies closely resemble the patterns of those chosen. Singapore resembles the developmental regimes of Japan, Korea, and Taiwan. The regime in Vietnam since the economic reforms known as Đổi

Mới resembles China but with far less regional weight. Laos and Cambodia present further examples of rapacious and nondevelopmental regimes. The largest outlier in my thinking is Hong Kong, which as a city-state is similar to Singapore but which lacked the strong state institutions of the developmental regimes while driven by a far more independent business sector than most other Asian countries and whose external influences remained heavily British colonial until the 1997 turnover.

52. David Waldner, *State Building and Late Development* (Ithaca, NY: Cornell University Press, 1999), 160.

53. Waldner, *State Building and Late Development*, 159. The economic changes made in Japan, South Korea, and Taiwan also dovetail with Michael Porter's notion that a country's long-term economic success necessitates a high and rising standard of living for its citizens. See Michael E. Porter, *Competitive Advantage of Nations: Creating and Sustaining Superior Performance* (New York: Free Press, 1990).

54. I originally use this term in T. J. Pempel, *Regime Shift: Comparative Dynamics of the Japanese Political Economy* (Ithaca, NY: Cornell University Press, 1998). This definition is also resonant with analyses presented in Investopia by Andrew Bloomenthal, "Mercantilism," 2020. https://www.investopedia.com/terms/m/mercantilism.asp. For an elaboration of its applicability, see Kanishka Jayasuriya, "Embedded Mercantilism and Open Regionalism: The Crisis of a Regional Political Project," *Third World Quarterly* 24, no. 2, (2003): 339–55.

55. This concept first gained credence with Indermit Gill and Homi Kharas, *An East Asian Renaissance: Ideas for Economic Growth* (Washington, DC: World Bank, 2007), https://openknowledge.worldbank.org/handle/10986/6798. See also Richard F. Doner and Ben Ross Schneider, "The Middle-Income Trap: More Politics Than Economics," *World Politics* 68, no. 4 (2016): 608–44, and Veerayooth Kanchoochat and Patarapong Intarakumnerd, "Tigers Trapped: Tracing the Middle-Income Trap through the East and Southeast Asian Experience," *Southeast Asian Experience*. Working Paper 04/2014. Berlin: Berlin Working Papers on Money, Finance, Trade and Development.

56. Evans, *Embedded Autonomy*, 43.

57. Charles Tilly, "War Making and State Making as Organized Crime," in *Bringing the State Back In*, ed. Peter Evans, Dietrich Rueschmeier, and Theda Skocpol (Cambridge: Cambridge University Press, 2005), 169–91.

58. On the predatory state, see inter alia, Peter B. Evans, "Predatory, Developmental, and Other Apparatuses: A Comparative Political Economy Perspective on the Third World State," *Sociological Forum* 4, no. 4 (1989): 561–87; Douglas Marcouiller and Leslie Young, "The Black Hole of Graft: The Predatory State and the Informal Economy," *American Economic Review* 85, no. 3 (1995): 630–46; James A. Robinson, "When Is a State Predatory?" (CESifo Working Paper No. 1k78, 1999).

1. Developmental Regimes

1. The dates I would assign would be roughly 1955–91 for Japan; 1965–89 for Korea, and 1960–89 for Taiwan. These represent the high points of regimes that had important antecedents and unquestioned follow-ons. Yet for analytic purposes, these periods were the ones during which the highlighted traits were most conspicuous.

2. Dan Slater, *Ordering Power: Contentious Politics and Authoritarian Leviathans in Southeast Asia* (Cambridge: Cambridge University Press, 2010), 5. See also Richard F. Doner, Bryan K. Ritchie, and Dan Slater, "Systemic Vulnerability and the Origins of Developmental States: Northeast and Southeast Asia in Comparative Perspective," *International Organization* 59, no. 2 (2005): 327–61. They argue that political elites will only build such institutional arrangements when simultaneously staring at three major challenges. These are (1) the credible threat that any deterioration in the living standards of popular sectors could trigger unmanageable mass unrest, (2) the heightened need for foreign exchange and war materiel induced by national insecurity, and (3) the hard budget constraints imposed by a scarcity of easy revenue sources. They label this interactive condition "systemic vulnerability."

3. William Shakespeare, *Henry IV,* Part 1, Act 3, Scene 1, page 3. http://find.gale.com.libproxy .berkeley.edu/ecco/quickSearch.do?now=1606691094529&inPS=true&prodId =ECCO&userGroupName=ucberkeley.

4. See, e.g., Francis Fukuyama, *Political Order and Political Decay: From the Industrial Revolution to the Globalization of Democracy* (New York: Farrar, Straus and Giroux, 2014), 225, 337–38.

5. Linda Weiss, "Developmental States in Transition: Adapting, Dismantling, Innovating, Not 'Normalizing,'" *Pacific Review* 13, no. 1 (2000): 23.

6. Bob Jessop, "A Neo-Gramscian Approach to the Regulation of Urban Regimes: Accumulation Strategies, Hegemonic Projects, and Governance," *Reconstructing Urban Regime Theory: Regulating Urban Politics in a Global Economy* 5 (1997): 1–74.

7. On the notion of strong versus weak states, see inter alia, Peter Evans, Dietrich Rueschemeyer, and Theda Skocpol, eds., *Bringing the State Back In* (Cambridge: Cambridge University Press, 2005); Peter J. Katzenstein, ed., *Between Power and Plenty* (Madison: University of Wisconsin Press, 1977); Eun Mee Kim and Ŭn-mi Kim, *Big Business, Strong State: Collusion and Conflict in South Korean Development, 1960–1990* (Albany: SUNY Press, 1997); Joel S. Migdal, *Strong Societies and Weak States: State-Society Relations and State Capabilities in the Third World* (Princeton, NJ: Princeton University Press, 1988).

8. George Akita, *Foundations of Constitutional Government in Modern Japan, 1868–1900* (Cambridge, MA: Harvard University Press, 1967); E. Herbert Norman, *Japan's Emergence as a Modern State: Political and Economic Problems of the Meiji Period* (Vancouver: Institute of Pacific Relations, 1940).

9. In addition to having strong administrative structures, both Korea and Taiwan emerged from their years under Japanese rule with extensive educational systems, modern civil services, railways, roads, rice mills, smelters, oil refineries, shipyards, and modern cities undreamt of in either country in 1900. Consequently, the two former colonies achieved independence with assets rarely enjoyed by other late developers, assets that, without a doubt, facilitated their postwar economic transformations. See Bruce Cumings, "The Origins and Development of the Northeast Asian Political Economy: Industrial Sectors, Product Cycles, and Political Consequences," *International Organization* 38, no. 1 (1984): 1–40."

10. The term gained its initial credibility in Chalmers Johnson's *MITI and the Japanese Miracle: The Growth of Industrial Policy: 1925–1975* (Stanford, CA: Stanford University Press, 1982). See also Meredith Woo-Cumings, *The Developmental State* (Ithaca, NY: Cornell University Press, 1999). An excellent overview of the concept's evolution is Stephan Haggard's *Developmental States* (Cambridge: Cambridge University Press, 2018).

11. This phrase is Philippe C. Schmitter and Guilermo O'Donnell's, from "Transitions from Authoritarian Rule," in *Transitions from Authoritarian Rule: Comparative Perspectives,* ed. Guillermo O'Donnell, Philippe C. Schmitter, and Laurence Whitehead (Baltimore, MD: Johns Hopkins University Press, 1986).

12. Yun-Han Chu, "State Structure and Economic Adjustment in the East Asian Newly Industrializing Countries," *International Organization* 43, no. 4 (1989): 658.

13. See H. H. Gerth and C. Wright Mills, eds., *From Max Weber: Essays in Sociology* (New York: Oxford University Press, 1958), chap. 8, 196–244.

14. See the essays in Takashi Ishida and Ellis Krauss, eds., *Democracy in Japan* (Pittsburgh: University of Pittsburgh Press, 1990), for a generally positive assessment of Japanese democracy. My own view is in T. J. Pempel, "Japanese Democracy: A Comparative Perspective," in *Japan: A New Kind of Superpower?,* ed. Craig Garby and Mary Brown Bullock (Baltimore, MD: Johns Hopkins University Press, 1994).

15. See, for example, Prime Minister Kishi's focus on revising the US–Japan Security Treaty and his and other conservatives' efforts to revise the so-called MacArthur constitution. Not until 1960 and the prime ministership of Ikeda Hayato was economic transformation clearly the government's hegemonic project.

16. See, for example, Richard J. Samuels, *Kishi and Corruption: An Anatomy of the 1955 System* (Washington, D.C.: Japan Policy Research Institute, 2001).

17. This is not to argue that political executives were the principals and bureaucrats their mere agents; most often, political executives and top-level civil servants worked in tandem

rather than being in two separate camps. See, for example, Mark Ramseyer and Frances Mc-Call Rosenbluth, *Japan's Political Marketplace* (Cambridge, MA: Harvard University Press, 1993); contrast their analysis with Donald P. Green and Ian Shapiro, *Pathologies of Rational Choice Theory* (New Haven, CT: Yale University Press, 1994).

18. Dan Slater and Joseph Wong, "The Strength to Concede: Ruling Parties and Democratization in Developmental Asia," *Perspectives on Politics* 11, no. 3 (2013): 725.

19. Kim and Kim, *Big Business, Strong State*, 43–44; Jung-en Woo, *Race to the Swift*: State and finance in Korean industrialization (New York: Columbia University, 1991).

20. Etel Solingen, "Pax Asiatica versus Bella Levantina: The Foundations of War and Peace in East Asia and the Middle East," *American Political Science Review* 101, no. 4 (2007): 764. See also Doner, Ritchie, and Slater, "Systemic Vulnerability and the Origins of Developmental States," 327–61.

21. See Carter J. Eckert, *Park Chung-Hee and Modern Korea: The Roots of Militarism, 1866–1945* (Cambridge, MA: Harvard University Press, 2016).

22. James Cotton, "From Authoritarianism to Democracy in South Korea," *Political Studies* 37 (1989): 250.

23. Tun-jen Cheng, "Democratizing the Quasi-Leninist Regime," *World Politics*, 41, 4 (1989): 471–99. Worth noting in this regard is that Chiang Kai-shek's son and heir to Taiwanese rule, Chiang Ching-kuo, was educated in Moscow and even applied for membership in the Communist Party. See Sung M. Pae, *Testing Democratic Theories in Korea* (Lanham, MD: University Press of America, 1986), 155.

24. Tun-jen Cheng, "Democratizing the Quasi-Leninist Regime in Taiwan," 480.

25. Slater and Wong, "The Strength to Concede," 723.

26. Richard J. Samuels, *Special Duty: A History of the Japanese Intelligence Community* (Ithaca, NY: Cornell University Press, 2019).

27. Tun-Jen Cheng, Stephan Haggard, and David Kang, "Institutions and Growth in Korea and Taiwan: The Bureaucracy," *Journal of Development Studies* 34, no. 6 (1998): 87–111.

28. Stephan Haggard, Byong-kook Kim, and Chung-in Moon, "The Transition to Export-Led Growth in South Korea, *Journal of Asian Studies* 50 (1991): 850–73; David Kang, *Crony Capitalism: Corruption and Development in South Korea and the Philippines* (Cambridge: Cambridge University Press, 2002), 63–64.

29. Chalmers Johnson, "Tanaka Kakuei, Structural Corruption, and the Advent of Machine Politics in Japan," *Journal of Japanese Studies* 12, no. 1 (1986): 1–28; T. J. Pempel, "Between Pork and Productivity: The Collapse of the Liberal Democratic Party," *Journal of Japanese Studies* 36, 2 (2010): 227–54.

30. Inoguchi Takashi and Iwai Tomoaki, *"Zoku Giin" no kenkyû* [A study of the Diet tribesmen] (Tokyo: Nihonkeizaishimbunsha, 1987).

31. Robert Wade, "East Asia's Economic Success: Conflicting Perspectives, Partial Insights, Shaky Evidence," *World Politics* 44, no. 2 (1992): 309.

32. Gerhard Lenski, *Power and Privilege: A Theory of Social Stratification* (New York: McGraw Hill, 1966), 318.

33. Chung-in Moon, "Changing Patterns of Business-Government Relations in South Korea," in *Business and Government in Industrializing Asia*, ed. Andrew MacIntyre (Ithaca, NY: Cornell University Press, 1994), 145.

34. Benedict Anderson, *Imagined Communities* (London: Verso, 1983).

35. This has to be qualified by the fact that Taiwan confronted a stark split between Han Chinese "newcomers" who arrived with the KMT in 1949 and the resident Taiwanese and aboriginal populations.

36. Thomas B. Gold, *State and Society in the Taiwan Miracle*, Armonk, N.Y. ME Sharpe, 1986). 29–30.

37. Shelly Rigger, "Mobilizational Authoritarianism and Political Opposition in Taiwan," in *Political Oppositions in Industrializing Asia*, ed. Garry Rodan (London: Routledge, 1996), 310.

38. Rigger, "Mobilizational Authoritarianism," 60.

39. Michael Donnelly, "Setting the Price of Rice: A Study in Political Decisionmaking," in *Policymaking in Postwar Japan*, ed. T. J. Pempel (Ithaca, NY: Cornell University Press, 1977),

143–200; Patricia L. Maclachlan and Kay Shimizu, "Japanese Farmers in Flux: The Domestic Sources of Agricultural Reform," *Asian Survey* 56, no. 3 (2016): 442–65.

40. Cumings, "Northeast Asian Political Economy," 22–23.

41. Gold, *State and Society in the Taiwan Miracle*, 65–67.

42. Ki Hyuk Pak, "Outcome of Land Reform in the Republic of Korea," *Journal of Farm Economics* 38, no. 4 (1956): 1015.

43. Yong-Ha Shin, "Land Reform in Korea, 1950," *Bulletin of the Population and Development Studies Center* 5 (1976): 14–31.

44. Atul Kohli, *State-Directed Development: Political Power and Industrialization in the Global Periphery* (Cambridge: Cambridge University Press, 2004), 72.

45. See Jongsung You, *Democracy, Inequality and Corruption: Korea, Taiwan and the Philippines Compared* (Cambridge: Cambridge University Press, 2015).

46. Giuseppe Gabusi, "'The Reports of My Death Have Been Greatly Exaggerated': China and the Developmental State 25 Years after Governing the Market," *Pacific Review* 30, no. 2 (2017): 238. See also Frederic C. Deyo, *The Political Economy of the New Asian Industrialization* (Ithaca, NY: Cornell University Press, 1989); T. J. Pempel and Keiichi Tsunekawa, "Corporatism without Labor? The Japanese Anomaly," in *Trends toward Corporatist Intermediation*, ed. Philippe Schmitter and Gerhard Lehmbruch (Beverley Hills, CA: Sage, 1979), 231–70; David Waldner, *State Building and Late Development* (Ithaca, NY: Cornell University Press, 1999), 138–39.

47. See, for example, Sheldon Garon, *The State and Labor in Modern Japan* (Princeton, NJ: Princeton University Press, 1987), and Andrew Gordon, *The Evolution of Labor Relations in Japan: Heavy Industry, 1853–1955* (Cambridge, MA: Harvard University Press, 1985).

48. Stephan Haggard and Chung-in Moon, "Institutions and Economic Policy: Theory and a Korean Case Study," *World Politics* 42, no. 2 (January 1990): 220.

49. Frederic C. Deyo, "State and Labor: Modes of Political Exclusion in East Asian Development," in *The Political Economy of the New Asian Industrialism*, ed. Frederic Deyo (Ithaca, NY: Cornell University Press, 1987), 184.

50. Chalmers Johnson, "Political Institutions and Economic Performance: The Government and Business Relationship in Japan, South Korea and Taiwan," in Frederik C. Deyo, (ed.), *The Political Economy of the New Asian Industrialism* (Ithaca, NY: Cornell University Press 1987): 150

51. On Japan, see Pempel and Tsunekawa, "Corporatism without Labor?," especially 283–85. On Taiwanese corporatism, see Jonathan Unger and Anita Chan, "China, Corporatism, and the East Asian Model," *China Journal* 33 (January 1995): 34.

52. Robert Wade, *Governing the Market: Economic theory and the role of government in East Asian industrialization* (Princeton: Princeton University Press, 2004). 294–95.

53. Unger and Chan, "China, Corporatism, and the East Asian Model," 36; see also Frederic C. Deyo, *Beneath the Miracle: Labor Subordination in the New Asian Industrialism* (Berkeley: University of California Press, 1989), 118.

54. David C. Kang, *Crony Capitalism: Corruption and Development in South Korea and the Philippines* (Cambridge: Cambridge University Press, 2002), 9.

55. Jose Edgardo Campos and Hilton L. Root, *The Key to the Asian Miracle: Making Shared Growth Credible* (Washington, DC: Brookings Institution Press, 2001); Hisahiro Kondoh, "Policy Networks in South Korea and Taiwan during the Democratic Era," *Pacific Review* 15, no. 2 (2002): 225–44; Frank J. Schwartz, *Advice and Consent: The Politics of Consultation in Japan* (Cambridge: Cambridge University Press, 2001).

56. Ritchie, Doner, and Slater, "Systemic Vulnerability and the Origins of Developmental States," 327–61. On the Japanese case, see Ulrike Schaede, "The 'Old Boy' Network and Government Business Relationships in Japan," *Journal of Japanese Studies* 21, no. 2 (1995): 293–317.

57. Richard Samuels, *The Business of the Japanese State: Energy Markets in Comparative and Historical Perspective* (Ithaca: Cornell University Press, 1990): 2.

58. Michael K. Young, "Judicial Review of Administrative Guidelines: Governmentally Encouraged Consensual Dispute Resolution in Japan," *Columbia Law Review*, 84 no. 4 (1984): 923–83; Frank K. Upham, *Law and Social Change in Postwar Japan* (Cambridge, MA: Harvard University Press, 2009). See also Gregory W. Noble, *Collective Action in East Asia: How Ruling*

Parties Shape Industrial Policy (Ithaca, NY: Cornell University Press, 1998); Frank J. Schwartz, *Advice and Consent: The Politics of Consultation in Japan* (Cambridge: Cambridge University Press, 2001), inter alia.

59. Jung-en Woo, *Race to the Swift*.

60. Gold, *State and Society in the Taiwan Miracle*, 77. Hsin-Huang Michael Hsiao also captures the point by noting that economic forces exchanged political loyalty to the KMT state in return for more open opportunity structures, so that any previous separation of the political and economic forces gave way to their combined powers to accelerate capitalist development. See Hsin-Huang Michael Hsiao, "Emerging Social Movements and the Rise of a Demanding Civil Society in Taiwan," *Australian Journal of Chinese Affairs*, no. 24 (July 1990): 164.

61. Hsiao, "Emerging Social Movements," 5.

62. Migdal, Joel S. Migdal, *State in society: Studying how states and societies transform and constitute one another* (Cambridge, Cambridge University Press, 2001. See also Migdal, *Strong Societies and Weak States*; and Joel Migdal, Atul Kohli, and Vivienne Shue, eds., *State Power and Social Forces: Domination and Transformation in the Third World* (Cambridge: Cambridge University Press, 1994), especially chap. 1; Linda Weiss, "Government-Business Relations in East Asia: The Changing Basis of State Capacity," *Asian Perspective* 18, no. 2 (1994): 89, 85–118; and Geoffrey R. D. Underhill and Xiaoke Zhang, "The Changing State–Market Condominium in East Asia: Rethinking the Political Underpinnings of Development," *New Political Economy* 10, no. 1 (2005): 1–24. See also Evans, *Embedded Autonomy*.

63. Wade, *Governing the Market*.

64. T. J. Pempel, "The Developmental Regime in a Changing World Economy," in *The Developmental State*, ed. Meredith Woo-Cumings (Ithaca, NY: Cornell University Press, 1999), 170.

65. Richard F. Doner, "Success as Trap? Crises and Challenges in Export-Oriented Southeast Asia," in *Two Crises, Different Outcomes: East Asia and Global Finance*, ed. T. J. Pempel and Keiichi Tsunekawa (Ithaca, NY: Cornell University Press, 2015), 167.

66. G. John Ikenberry, "Liberal Internationalism 3.0: America and the Dilemmas of Liberal World Order," *Perspectives on Politics*, Mar., 2009, Vol. 7, No. 1 (Mar., 2009), 79.

67. NSC-68 was a 1950 policy paper that laid the groundwork for the US to confront communism militarily and attempt to roll back its influence globally. It laid the groundwork for US strategy for the bulk of the Cold War period.

68. For Kennan, see X [George Kennan], "The Sources of Soviet Conduct," *Foreign Affairs* 25 (July 1947): 566–82; Campbell Craig and Fredrik Logevall, *America's Cold War: The Politics of Insecurity* (Cambridge, MA: Harvard University Press, 2009), 109.

69. Hugh Patrick and Henry Rosovsky, "Japan's Economic Performance: An Overview," in *Asia's New Giant: How the Japanese Economy Works*, ed. Hugh Patrick and Henry Rosovksy (Washington, DC: Brookings Institution, 1976).

70. Doner, Ritchie, and Slater, "Systemic Vulnerability and the Origins of Developmental States."

71. Walter LeFeber, *America, Russia, and the Cold War, 1945–2006* (New York: McMillan, 2006), chap. 3.

72. This doctrine was congruent with the earlier and influential geostrategic thinking of Alfred Mahan, Halford MacKinder, and Nicholas J. Spykman. On the manifestation of this logic in US foreign policy, see Michael J. Green, *By More Than Providence: Grand Strategy and American Power in the Asia Pacific Since 1783* (New York: Columbia University Press, 2018).

73. Tim Weiner, "CIA Spent Millions to Support Japanese Right in 50's and 60's," *New York Times*, October 9, 1994, https://www.nytimes.com/1994/10/09/world/cia-spent-millions-to -support-japanese-right-in-50-s-and-60-s.html. See also Samuels, *Kishi and Corruption*.

74. Cumings, "Northeast Asian Political Economy," 24.

75. Yutaka Kosai and Yoshitaro Ogino, *The Contemporary Japanese Economy* (Armonk, NY: M.E. Sharpe, 1984); Takafusa Nakamura, *The Postwar Japanese Economy* (Tokyo: University of Tokyo Press, 1981); Richard Stubbs, *Rethinking Asia's Economic Miracle* (London: Palgrave MacMillan, 2018), especially chaps. 3, 4, and 5.

76. Cumings, "Northeast Asian Political Economy," 24.

77. Philip Hookon Park, "A Reflection on the East Asian Development Model: Comparison of the South Korean and Taiwanese Experiences," in *The East Asian Development Model: Eco-*

nomic Growth, Institutional Failures and the Aftermath of the Crisis, ed. Frank-Jurgen Richter (New York: MacMillan, 2000), 145.

78. Meredith Woo-Cumings, introduction to *The Developmental State*, ed. Meredith Woo-Cumings (Ithaca, NY: Cornell University Press, 1999), 19.

79. Richard E. Barrett and Martin King Whyte, "Dependency Theory and Taiwan: Analysis of a Deviant Case," *American Journal of Sociology* 87, no. 5 (1982): 1075.

80. As quoted in Bruce Cumings, *Divided Korea: United Future?* (New York: Foreign Policy Association, 1985): 43.

81. Jung-en Woo, *Race to the Swift*, chap. 5.

82. Terutomo Ozawa, *Japan Economic Journal*, October 10, 1972, as cited in T. J. Pempel, "Japanese Foreign Economic Policy," *International Organization*, 31, no.4 (1977): 761–62.

83. On the Japanese experience see, inter alia, Michael Beckley, Yusaku Horiuchi, and Jennifer M. Miller, "America's Role in the Making of Japan's Economic Miracle," *Journal of East Asian Studies* 18, no. 1 (2018): 1–21.

84. Carter J. Eckert, "Korea's Economic Development in Historical Perspective, 1945–1990," in *Pacific Century: The Emergence of Modern Pacific Asia*, ed. Mark Borthwick (Boulder, CO: Westview Press, 1992), 294.

85. T. J. Pempel, "Trans-Pacific Torii: Japan and the Emerging Asian Regionalism," in *Network Power: Japan in Asia*, ed. Peter J. Katzenstein and Takashi Shiraishi (Ithaca, NY: Cornell University Press, 1997), 47–82.

86. Cumings, "Northeast Asian Political Economy," 33.

87. Details are provided in Pempel, "The Developmental Regime in a Changing World Economy," 177.

88. Philip Armstrong, Andrew Glyn, and John Harrison, *Capitalism since World War II*, vol. 20 (Oxford: Basil Blackwell, 1991); Robert Gilpin, *Political Economy of International Relations* (Princeton, NJ: Princeton University Press, 1987), chaps. 4 and 5; Robert O. Keohane, "Hegemonic Leadership and U.S. Foreign Economic Policy in the 'Long Decade,'" in *America in a Changing World Economy*, ed. William P. Avery and David P. Rapkin (New York: Longman, 1982), chap. 3.

89. Doner, Ritchie, and Slater, "Systemic Vulnerability and the Origins of Developmental States," 328. See also Waldner, *State Building and Late Development*.

90. Nancy Etlinger, "The Roots of Competitive Advantage in California and Japan," *Annals of the Association of American Geographers* 81, no. 3 (1991), 392.

91. Stephen Haggard, *Pathways from the Periphery: The Politics of Growth in the Newly Industrializing Countries* (Ithaca, NY: Cornell University Press, 1990), 12.

92. One might note as exceptions Posco in Korea and China Steel in Taiwan.

93. Ha-Joon Chang, *The Political Economy of Industrial Policy* (New York: St. Martin's Press, 1994).

94. Wade, *Governing the Market*, 98–99ff.

95. Woo-Cumings, introduction to *The Developmental State*, 10.

96. See inter alia, Masahiko Aoki and Hugh T. Patrick, eds., *The Japanese Main Bank System: Its Relevance for Developing and Transforming Economies* (Oxford: Oxford University Press, 1995); Woo, *Race to the Swift*; Peter Drucker, "Economic Realities and Enterprise Strategies," in *Modern Japanese Organization and Decision-Making*, ed. Ezra F. Vogel (Berkeley: University of California Press, 1975), 228–50.

97. Patricia L. Maclachlan, *The People's Post Office: The History and Politics of the Japanese Postal System, 1871–2010* (Cambridge, MA: Harvard University Asia Center, 2011); Gene Park, *Spending without Taxation: FILP and the Politics of Public Finance in Japan* (Stanford, CA: Stanford University Press, 2011).

98. Gold, *State and Society in the Taiwan Miracle*, 108.

99. Wade, *Governing the Market*, 61.

100. World Bank, *The East Asian Economic Miracle* (Oxford: Oxford University Press, 1993), 41.

101. Karl J. Fields, "Not of a Piece: Developmental States, Industrial Policy, and Evolving Patterns of Capitalism in Japan, Korea, and Taiwan," in *East Asian Capitalism: Diversity, Continuity and Change*, ed. Andrew Walter and Xiaoke Zhang (Oxford: Oxford University Press, 2012), 48.

102. It is possible, however, to contend that common and central to both are trading companies rather than banks.

103. Byung-Sun Choi, "Financial Policy and Big Business in Korea: The Perils of Financial Regulation," in *The Politics of Finance in Developing Countries*, ed. Stephan Haggard, Chung H. Lee, and Sylvia Maxfield (Ithaca, NY: Cornell University Press, 1993), 23–54.

104. See, for example, T. C. Smith, *Political Change and Industrial Development in Japan: Government Enterprise, 1868–1880* (Stanford, CA: Stanford University Press, 1955); Mark Mason, *United States Direct Investment in Japan* (Cambridge, MA: Harvard University Press, 1992); and Dennis J. Encarnation and Mark Mason, "Neither MITI nor America: The Political Economy of Capital Liberalization in Japan," *International Organization* 44, no. 1 (1990): 25–54.

105. Evans, "Class, State, and Dependencein East Asia: lessons for Latin Americanists." In Deyo (ed.) *The political economy of the new Asian industrialism* (1987): 206–7.

106. Encarnation and Mason point out, however, that when foreign technologies were desired by Japan's local oligopolists, these latter became important intermediaries between foreign multinationals and the Japanese government. See "Neither MITI nor America."

107. This summary is based in part on Pempel, "Japanese Foreign Economic Policy"; John Zysman, *Governments, Markets, and Growth: Financial Systems and the Politics of Industrial Change* (Ithaca, NY: Cornell University Press, 1983); and Peter Drucker, "Financial Systems: Europe, America, Japan," in *Modern Japanese Organization and Decision-Making*, ed. Ezra Vogel (Berkeley: University of California Press, 1975).

108. This was especially true after the normalization of relations between Japan and Korea in 1965. The settlement resulted in a highly conflictual contest domestically, however. See Haggard, *Pathways from the Periphery*, 197–98.

109. Haggard, 199.

110. Anne Booth, "Is the Taiwan Model of Growth, Human Resources Development, and Equity Sustainable in the Twenty-First Century?," in *Taiwan's Democracy: Economic and Political Challenges*, ed. Robert Ash, John W. Garver, and Penelope B. Prime (London: Routledge, 2011), 105.

111. Stephan Haggard and Tun-jen Cheng. "State and foreign capital in the East Asian NICs." *The Political Economy of the New Asian Industrialism*: 115–16.

112. Yano Tsuneta Kinenkai, *Nihon Kokusei Zue [Japan NationalData] 1976* (Tokyo: Yano Hisashiro Kinenkai, 1976), 180–81.

113. Alice Amsden, "Getting Relative Prices Wrong: A Summary," in *Asia's Next Giant: South Korea and late industrialization* (Oxford: Oxford University Press, 1992): chap. 6.

114. Michael Cusamano, "Manufacturing Innovation: Lessons from the Japanese Auto Industry," *Sloan Management Review* 30, no. 1 (1988). 29.

115. Pempel, "Developmental Regime," 148–49.

116. Haggard, "The Newly Industrializing Countries in the International System," 3.

117. See, for example, Simon Kuznets, "Economic Growth and Income Inequality," *American Economic Review* 45, no. 1 (1955): 1–28.

118. See, however, Nakagawa's rather stateless and apolitical argument that Japan is a "super welfare state," which rests on arguments about private citizen and family spending for health and education. Nakagawa Yatsuhiro, "Japan, the Welfare Super-Power," *Journal of Japanese Studies* 5, no. 1 (1979): 5–51.

119. Pempel and Tsunekawa, "Corporatism without Labor?," 231–70. On liberal versus social corporatism, see Peter J. Katzenstein, *Small States in World Markets: Industrial Policy in Europe* (Ithaca, NY: Cornell University Press, 1985).

2. Ersatz Developmental Regimes

1. Erik M. Kuhonta, "The Political Economy of Equitable Development in Thailand," *American Asian Review* 21, no. 4 (2003): 70.

2. Data compiled from World Bank, "World Tables," *World Development Indicators*. See https://openknowledge.worldbank.org/bitstream/handle/10986/23969/9781464806834.pdf.

3. On this issue generally, see, for example, Richard F. Doner, *The Politics of Uneven Development: Thailand's Economic Growth in Comparative Perspective* (Cambridge: Cambridge University

Press, 2009), chap. 1; David Waldner, *State Building and Late Development* (Ithaca, NY: Cornell University Press, 1999), chap. 7.

4. Dani Rodrik, "Introduction: What Do We Learn from Country Narratives?," in *In Search of Prosperity: Analytic Narratives on Economic Growth*, ed. Dani Rodrik (Princeton, NJ: Princeton University Press, 2003): 17.

5. Steven Levitsky and Lucan A. Way, *Competitive Authoritarianism: Hybrid Regimes after the Cold War* (Cambridge: Cambridge University Press, 2010), 5. It is worth noting that part of this definition hinges on "civilian" leaders. Indonesia's two presidents and several Thai prime ministers were generals. The Indonesian presidents led heavily civilian governments and held office via regular elections, however. Thai generals normally suspended elections, but they also relied heavily on civilian technocrats, particularly in forming fiscal and economic policy. See, Doner, *The Politics of Uneven Development: Thailand's Economic Growth in Comparative Perspective*; Andrew MacIntyre, "Power, Prosperity and Patrimonialism: Business and Government in Indonesia," in *Business and Government in Industrializing Asia*, ed. Andrew MacIntyre (Ithaca, NY: Cornell University Press, 1994): 244–267.

6. Richard F. Doner, Bryan K. Ritchie, and Dan Slater, "Systemic Vulnerability and the Origins of Developmental States: Northeast and Southeast Asia in Comparative Perspective," *International Organization* 59, no. 2 (2005): 327–61.

7. Transparency International ranks countries on a corruption index. Their 2018 index ranked Indonesia at 38 on a scale of 100 or 80 out of 180 countries in the world. Thailand scored 36 and ranked 99/180. Malaysia received a less corrupt ranking of 47 and 61/180. See https://www.transparency.org.

8. Harold Crouch, "Patrimonialism and Military Rule in Indonesia," *World Politics* 31, no. 4 (1979): 575.

9. Benjamin B. Smith, "Life of the Party: The Origins of Regime Breakdown and Persistence under Single-Party Rule," *World Politics* 57, no. 3 (2005): 435.

10. Smith, "Life of the Party," 436.

11. Steven Schlossstein, *Asia's New Little Dragons: The Dynamic Emergence of Indonesia, Thailand, and Malaysia* (Chicago: Contemporary Books, 1991), 97; Richard Robison, "Indonesia: Tension in State and Regime," in *Southeast Asia in the 1990s: Authoritarianism, Democracy and Capitalism*, ed. Kevin Hewison, Richard Robison, and Garry Rodan (London: Allen & Unwin, 1993), 41.

12. Smith, "Life of the Party," 436.

13. Schlossstein, *Asia's New Little Dragons*, 436.

14. Alasdair Bowie and Daniel Unger, *The Politics of Open Economies: Indonesia, Malaysia, the Philippines, and Thailand* (Cambridge: Cambridge University Press, 1997), 46. See also Robison, "Indonesia: Tension in State and Regime," 45.

15. Andrew MacIntyre, "Political Institutions and the Economic Crisis in Thailand and Indonesia," in *The Politics of the Asian Economic Crisis*, ed. T. J. Pempel (Ithaca, NY: Cornell University Press, 1999), 155; see also Andrew MacIntyre, "Institutions and Investors: The Politics of the Economic Crisis in Southeast Asia," *International Organization* 55, no. 1 (2001): 81–122.

16. Thomas B. Pepinsky, *Economic Crises and the Breakdown of Authoritarian Regimes: Indonesia and Malaysia in Comparative Perspective* (Cambridge: Cambridge University Press, 2009), 41.

17. Andrew MacIntyre, "Power, Prosperity and Patrimonialism: Business and Government in Indonesia," in *Business and Government in Industrializing Asia*, ed. Andrew MacIntyre (Ithaca, NY: Cornell University Press, 1994), 244.

18. Richard F. Doner, *Driving a Bargain: Automobile Industrialization and Japanese Firms in Southeast Asia* (Cambridge: Cambridge University Press, 1991), 253; Alasdair Bowie, "The Dynamics of Business-Government Relations in Industrializing Malaysia," in *Business and Government in Industrializing Asia*, ed. Andrew MacIntyre (Ithaca, NY: Cornell University Press, 1994), 168–70; Pepinsky, *Economic Crises and the Breakdown of Authoritarian Regimes*; Schlossstein, *Asia's New Little Dragons*; inter alia.

19. I have combined both Malays (50%) and other indigenous natives (12%), which are usually collectively labeled Bumiputera.

20. Dan Slater, *Ordering Power: Contentious Politics and Authoritarian Leviathans in Southeast Asia* (Cambridge: Cambridge University Press, 2010), 90.

21. Levitsky and Way, *Competitive Authoritarianism*, 320.

22. MacIntyre, "Institutions and Investors," 92.

23. Harold Crouch, "Malaysia: Neither Authoritarian nor Democratic," in *Southeast Asia in the 1990s: Authoritarianism, Democracy and Capitalism,* ed. Kevin Hewison, Richard Robison, and Gary Rodan (Leonard, Australia: Allen and Unwin, 1993), 133–57.

24. Levitsky and Way, *Competitive Authoritarianism,* 319.

25. Pepinsky, *Economic Crises and the Breakdown of Authoritarian Regimes,* 64.

26. Schlossstein, *Asia's New Little Dragons,* 71, 88.

27. Harold A. Crouch, *Government and Society in Malaysia* (Ithaca, NY: Cornell University Press, 1996).

28. Richard Robison, Garry Rodan, and Kevin Hewison, "Transplanting the Neoliberal State in Southeast Asia," in *Asian States: Beyond the Developmental Perspective,* ed. Richard Boyd and Tak-wing Ngo (London: Routledge, 2005), 181.

29. Slater, *Ordering Power,* 23.

30. Michael T. Rock, "The Last Fifty Years: Development Strategy and Development Performance in Southeast Asia," *Journal of Southeast Asian Economies* 35, no. 1 (2018): 45.

31. MacIntyre, "Political Institutions and the Economic Crisis in Thailand and Indonesia," 147.

32. See Dan King, "Thailand," in *Democracy, Governance and Economic Performance: East and Southeast Asia,* ed. Ian March, Jean Blondel, and Takashi Inoguchi (Tokyo: United Nations Press, 1999), 218.

33. Adam Taylor and Anup Kaphle, "Thailand's Army Just Announced a Coup. Here Are 11 Other Thai Coups since 1932," *Washington Post,* May 22, 2014, https://www.washingtonpost.com/news/worldviews/wp/2014/05/20/thailands-army-says-this-definitely-isnt-a-coup-heres-11-times-it-definitely-was/?utm_term=.1385248fc9d7.

34. Doner, Ritchie, and Slater, "Systemic Vulnerability and the Origins of Developmental States," 350.

35. Richard Stubbs, "War and Economic Development: Export-oriented industrialization in East and Southeast Asia," *Comparative Politics* (1999): 343.

36. Doner, *Politics of Uneven Development,* 101.

37. Slater, *Ordering Power,* 23.

38. David Art, "What Do We Know about Authoritarianism after Ten Years?," *Comparative Politics* 44, no. 3 (2012): 355.

39. MacIntyre, "Power, Prosperity and Patrimonialism," 261.

40. Thinapan Nakata, "Corruption in the Thai Bureaucracy: Who Gets What, How and Why in Its Public Expenditures," *Thai Journal of Development Administration* 18, no. 1 (1978): 102. See also Jon S. T. Quah, "Bureaucratic Corruption in the ASEAN Countries: A Comparative Analysis of Their Anti-Corruption Strategies," *Journal of Southeast Asian Studies* 13, no. 1 (1982): 153–77.

41. Quah, "Bureaucratic Corruption in the ASEAN Countries," 155.

42. Suchit Bunbongkarn, "Thailand: Democracy under Siege," in *Driven by Growth: Political Change in the Asia-Pacific Region,* ed. James W. Morley (Armonk, NY: M.E. Sharpe, 1999), 163; MacIntyre, "Political Institutions and the Economic Crisis," 147.

43. Harold Crouch, "Patrimonialism and Military Rule in Indonesia," *World Politics* 31, no. 4 (1979): 577.

44. Crouch, "Patrimonialism and Military Rule in Indonesia," 581; see also Schlossstein, *Asia's New Little Dragons,* 73. It is also worth noting that the Indonesian military budget provided only about half of the actual amounts needed, with army-run businesses and commercial activities supplying the remainder.

45. Thomas B. Pepinsky, "Political Business and External Vulnerability in Southeast Asia," in *Two Crises: Different Outcomes; East Asia and Global Finance,* ed. T. J. Pempel and Keiichi Tsunekawa (2015): 140. On the broader point about economic growth and regime support, see Etel Solingen, "Pax Asiatica versus Bella Levantina: The Foundations of War and Peace in East Asia and the Middle East," *American Political Science Review* 101, no. 4 (2007): 757–80.

46. Rock, "Development Strategy and Development Performance in Southeast Asia," 40.

47. Rock, 40–41.

48. John T. Sidel, "Social Origins of Dictatorship and Democracy Revisited: Colonial State and Chinese Immigrant in the Making of Modern Southeast Asia," *Comparative Politics* 40, no. 2 (2008): 127–47.

49. G. William Skinner, "Change and Persistence in Chinese Culture Overseas: A Comparison of Thailand and Java," *Journal of the South Seas Society* 16 (1960): 89, 91, as cited in Sidel, "Social Origins of Dictatorship and Democracy Revisited," 131.

50. Lee Jones, "Explaining the Failure of the ASEAN Economic Community: The Primacy of Domestic Political Economy," *Pacific Review* 29, no. 5 (2016): 653–54.

51. Jeffrey A. Winters, *Power in Motion: Capital Mobility and the Indonesian State* (Ithaca, NY: Cornell University Press, 1996).

52. Meredith Woo-Cumings, "The State, Democracy, and the Reform of the Corporate Sector in Korea," *The Politics of the Asian Economic Crisis*, ed. T. J. Pempel (Ithaca, Cornell University Press, 1999): 139–40.

53. Rajah Rasiah, "Manufacturing Export Growth in Indonesia, Malaysia, and Thailand," in *Southeast Asian Paper Tigers*, ed. K. S. Jomo (London: Routledge, 2004), 40; MacIntyre, "Power, Prosperity and Patrimonialism," 253.

54. Stijn Claessens, Simeon Djankov, and Larry H. P. Lang, "The Separation of Ownership and Control in East Asian Corporations," *Journal of Financial Economics* 58, no. 1–2 (2000): 81–112.

55. Rock, "Development Strategy and Development Performance in Southeast Asia," 41.

56. Rasiah, "Export Growth in Indonesia, Malaysia, and Thailand," 63.

57. Schlossstein, *Asia's New Little Dragons*, 163–64.

58. Anne Booth, "Initial Conditions and Miraculous Growth: Why Is Southeast Asia Different from Taiwan and Korea?," in *Southeast Asia's Industrialization: Industrial Policy, Capabilities and Sustainability*, ed. K. S. Jomo (New York: Palgrave, 2001), 47–48.

59. Sutapa Amornivat, "Firms Struggle for Staff in a Mismatched Society," *Bangkok Post*, November 20, 2013, https://www.bangkokpost.com/opinion/opinion/380712/firms-struggle-for-staff-in-a-mismatched-society, as cited in Richard F. Doner, "Success as Trap? Crises and Challenges in Export-Oriented Southeast Asia," in *Two Crises, Different Outcomes: East Asia and Global Finance*, ed. T. J. Pempel and Keiichi Tsunekawa (Ithaca, NY: Cornell University Press, 2015), 179–81.

60. C. M. Firdausy, *The Social Impact of Economic Crisis on Employment in Indonesia* (Jakarta, Center for Economic and Development Studies, Indonesian Institute of Sciences, 2000), http://www.ismea.org/asialist/firdausy.html.

61. Richard F. Doner and Ben Ross Schneider, "The Middle-Income Trap: More Politics Than Economics," *World Politics* 68, no. 4 (2016): 619.

62. See, for example, Walter Bevins, "What the United States Did in Indonesia," *Atlantic*, October 20, 2017, https://www.theatlantic.com/international/archive/2017/10/the-indonesia-documents-and-the-us-agenda/543534/.

63. Heritage Foundation, "Indonesia and the U.S.," *Backgrounder*, October 12, 1982: 1–2.

64. This included the alliance with Taiwan, that is, the Mutual Defense Treaty between the United States and the Republic of China, operative between 1955 and 1979.

65. John L. S. Girling, *Thailand: Society and Politics* (Ithaca, NY: Cornell University Press, 1981), 235–36.

66. David Elliott, *Thailand: Origins of Military Rule* (London: Zed Press, 1978), 129–33; Richard Doner and Daniel Unger, "The Politics of Finance in Thai Economic Development," in *The Politics of Finance in Developing Countries*, ed. Stephan Haggard, Chung H. Lee, and Sylvia Maxfield (Ithaca, NY: Cornell University Press, 1993), 104.

67. Bowie and Unger, *The Politics of Open Economies*, 6.

68. Akio Watanabe, "Southeast Asia in U.S.-Japanese Relations," in *The United States and Japan in the Postwar World*, ed. Akira Iriye and Warren Cohen (Lexington: University of Kentucky Press, 2015).

69. Mark Beeson, "Developmental States in East Asia: A Comparison of the Japanese and Chinese Experiences," *Asian Perspective* 33, no. 2 (2009): 9.

70. Akio Watanabe, "Southeast Asia in U.S.-Japanese Relations," in *The United States and Japan in the Postwar World*, ed. Akira Iriye and Warren Cohen (Lexington: University of Kentucky Press, 2015).

71. Taizo Miyagi, *Japan's Quest for Stability in Southeast Asia: Navigating the Turning Points in Postwar Asia* (London: Routledge, 2018), 95–96.

72. . The Dutch sought to reestablish colonial rule as the war ended and Japanese and Indonesian troops fought several major military battles against Dutch forces. A UN Security Council resolution, and an American threat to cut off Marshall Plan funds to the Netherlands ended Dutch efforts and ensured Indonesian independence.

73. Prime Minister Kishi developed close relations with Sukarno and Japan worked against US efforts to destabilize Indonesia in the late 1950s. Japan also organized a conference to reschedule Indonesian debt in February 1966. See Miyagi, *Japan's Quest for Stability*, 35–36, 94–95.

74. Stubbs, "War and Economic Development," 346.

75. Bowie and Unger, *The Politics of Open Economies*, 39–41.

76. For details, see Sueo Sudo, *The Fukuda Doctrine and ASEAN: New Dimensions in Japanese Foreign Policy* (Singapore: Institute of Southeast Asian Studies, 1992), and Peng Er Lam, ed., *Japan's Relations with Southeast Asia: The Fukuda Doctrine and Beyond* (London: Routledge, 2012).

77. Bowie and Unger, *The Politics of Open Economies*, 63.

78. Kanishka Jayasuriya, "Embedded Mercantilism and Open Regionalism: The Crisis of a Regional Political Project," in "Governing the Asia Pacific: Beyond the 'New Regionalism,'" special issue, *Third World Quarterly* 24, no. 2 (April 2003): 346; see also Richard Stubbs, "The Political Economy of the Asia-Pacific Region," in *Political Economy and the Changing Global Order*, ed. Richard Stubbs and G. B. D. Underhill (London: Macmillan, 1994), 366–77.

79. Rasiah, "Export Growth in Indonesia, Malaysia, and Thailand," 62–63.

80. Walter Hatch, *Asia's Flying Geese: How Regionalization Shapes Japan* (Ithaca, NY: Cornell University Press, 2010), 86.

81. Rasiah, "Export Growth in Indonesia, Malaysia, and Thailand," 40.

82. P. P. Courtenay, "The Diversification of Malaysian Agriculture, 1950–80: Objectives and Achievements," *Journal of Southeast Asian Studies* 15, no. 1 (1984): 166–81.

83. Schlosssstein, *Asia's New Little Dragons*, 230.

84. Crouch, "Malaysia: Neither Authoritarian nor Democratic," 145.

85. The 1932 coup involved a joint civilian-military toppling of the King of Siam and marked Thailand's transformation into a constitutional monarchy as well as the competition between civilian and military forces for political primacy.

86. Bryan K. Ritchie, "Progress through Setback or Mired in Mediocrity? Crisis and Institutional Change in Southeast Asia," *Journal of East Asian Studies* 5, no. 2 (2005): 285.

87. Rasiah, "Export Growth in Indonesia, Malaysia, and Thailand," 40.

88. Slater, *Ordering Power*, 152.

89. Bowie and Unger, *The Politics of Open Economies*, 77–85.

90. Rasiah, "Export Growth in Indonesia, Malaysia, and Thailand," 36.

91. Fong Chan Onn and Lim Kok Cheong, "Investment Incentives and Trends of Manufacturing Investments in Malaysia," *Developing Economies* 22, no. 4 (1984): 401.

92. Edmund Terence Gomex and Jomo Kwame Sundaram, "Malaysia," in *Democracy, Governance and Economic Performance: East and Southeast Asia*, ed. Ian March, Jean Blondel, and Takashi Inoguchi (Tokyo: United Nations Press, 1999), 248. See also Rasiah, "Export Growth in Indonesia, Malaysia, and Thailand," 36; Doner, Ritchie, and Slater, "Systemic Vulnerability and the Origins of Developmental States," 354; James V. Jesudason, *Ethnicity and the Economy: The State, Chinese Business and Multinationals in Malaysia* (Singapore: Oxford University Press, 1989).

93. Jayasuriya, "Embedded Mercantilism and Open Regionalism."

94. Bowie and Unger, *The Politics of Open Economies*, 79.

95. K. L. Jomo, *Growth and Structural Change in the Malaysian Economy* (London: Macmillan, 1990), 180.

96. Jomo, *Growth and Structural Change*, 186; Gomex and Sundaram, "Malaysia," 249.

97. MacIntyre, "Power, Prosperity and Patrimonialism," 247.

98. MacIntyre, 250.

99. Jayasuriya, "Embedded Mercantilism and Open Regionalism," 348–49.

100. Rasiah, "Export Growth in Indonesia, Malaysia, and Thailand," 34.

101. Doner and Unger, "The Politics of Finance in Thai Economic Development," 107.

102. Doner and Unger, 105.

103. Rasiah, "Export Growth in Indonesia, Malaysia, and Thailand," 28.

104. Bowie and Unger, *The Politics of Open Economies*, 38.
105. Rasiah, "Export Growth in Indonesia, Malaysia, and Thailand," 44.
106. Rasiah, 88.
107. K. S. Jomo, "Introduction: Southeast Asia's Ersatz Miracle," *Southeast Asian Paper Tigers*, ed. K. S. Jomo (Routledge, 2004), 8.
108. Alasdair Bowie, *Crossing the Industrial Divide: State, Society, and the Politics of Economic Transformation in Malaysia* (New York: Columbia University Press, 1991), 182.
109. Ritchie, "Progress through Setback or Mired in Mediocrity?," 282.
110. MacIntyre, "Power, Prosperity and Patrimonialism," 29.
111. Jones, "Explaining the Failure of the ASEAN Economic Community," 655.
112. Rasiah, "Export Growth in Indonesia, Malaysia, and Thailand," 25.
113. Hatch, *Asia's Flying Geese*, 76. On the broader issue of regional production networks and production, see Mitchell Bernard and John Ravenhill, "Beyond Product Cycles and Flying Geese: Regionalization, Hierarchy, and the Industrialization of East Asia," *World Politics* 47, no. 2 (1995): 171–209.
114. Gomex and Sundaram, "Malaysia," 246.
115. Doner, *Politics of Uneven Development*, 9.
116. Jayasuriya, "Embedded Mercantilism and Open Regionalism," 346.
117. Pepinsky, "Political Business and External Vulnerability in Southeast Asia," 140–41.
118. Pepinsky, 339–55.
119. Rasiah, "Export Growth in Indonesia, Malaysia, and Thailand," 61.
120. Doner, Ritchie, and Slater, "Systemic Vulnerability and the Origins of Developmental States," 351. See also Doner and Schneider, "The Middle-Income Trap," 60844; Doner, "Success as Trap?," 179–81; Erik Kuhonta, *The Institutional Imperative: The Politics of Equitable Development in Southeast Asia* (Stanford, CA: Stanford University Press, 2011).

3. Rapacious Regimes

1. This quote has been attributed to a number of individuals, among them entertainer Sophie Tucker (see https://www.greatest-quotations.com/search/search.html), and writer Beatrice Kaufman (see https://quoteinvestigator.com/2017/07/01/poor-rich/).
2. See, for example, Paul Pierson, "Increasing Returns, Path Dependence, and the Study of Politics." *American Political Science Review*, 34, 2(July 2000): 251–267. Paul Pierson, *Politics in Time: History, Institutions, and Social Analysis* (Princeton: Princeton University Press, 2011). Sven Steinmo, *The Evolution of Modern States: Sweden, Japan, and the United States* (Cambridge, Cambridge University Press, 2010); Wolfgang Streeck and Kathleen Ann Thelen, eds., *Beyond Continuity: Institutional Change in Advanced Political Economies* (Oxford: Oxford University Press, 2005); Kathleen Ann Thelen, *How Institutions Evolve: The Political Economy of Skills in Germany, Britain, the United States, and Japan* (Cambridge: Cambridge University Press, 2004), inter alia.
3. The original quote is the opening sentence in Tolstoy's, *Anna Karenina*; see Leo Tolstoy, *Anna Karenina*, translated by Constance Garnett, with an introd. by Henri Troyat (New York: Modern Library, 1950), 1.
4. Notably, South Korea sent many of its own civil servants to the Philippines for training until the 1960s. See Richard F. Doner, Bryan K. Ritchie, and Dan Slater, "Systemic Vulnerability and the Origins of Developmental States: Northeast and Southeast Asia in Comparative Perspective," *International Organization* 59, no. 2 (2005): 336, and Ha-Joon Chang, "The East Asian Model of Economic Policy," in *Models of Capitalism: Lessons for Latin America*, ed. Evelyne Huber (University Park: Pennsylvania State University Press, 2002), 197–236.
5. Michael Pinches, "The Philippines: The Regional Exception," *Pacific Review* 5, no. 4 (1992): 390–401; Stephen Rosskamm Shalom, *The United States and the Philippines: A Study of Neocolonialism* (Philadelphia: Institute for the Study of Human Issues, 1981). That changed when ASEAN expanded to included Cambodia, Laos, Vietnam, and Myanmar, since at least three of those four were less prosperous than the Philippines.
6. Paul Hutchcroft, *Booty Capitalism: The Politics of Banking in the Philippines* (Ithaca, NY: Cornell University Press, 1998).

7. *From Max Weber: Essays in Sociology.* Translated, edited, and with an introduction by H. H. Gerth and C. Wright Mills. "Politics as a Vocation," (New York: Free Press,1946): 124–25.

8. See Benedict Anderson, *Cacique Democracy in the Philippines: Origins and Dreams* (Routledge, 2010). See also Eva-Lotta Hedman and John Sidel, *Philippine Politics and Society in the Twentieth Century: Colonial Legacies, Post-Colonial Trajectories* (Abingdon, Oxfordshire: Routledge, 2005); John Thayer Sidel, *Capital, Coercion, and Crime: Bossism in the Philippines* (Stanford, CA: Stanford University Press, 1999).

9. David Kang, *Crony Capitalism: Corruption and Development in South Korea and the Philippines* (Cambridge: Cambridge University Press, 2002), 77.

10. Shalom, *The United States and the Philippines*, 9.

11. Chester L. Hunt, "Philippine Values and Martial Law," *Journal of Southeast Asian Studies* 11, no. 1 (1980): 110.

12. Anderson, *Cacique Democracy in the Philippines*, 20.

13. Gary Hawes, *The Philippine State and the Marcos Regime: The Politics of Export* (Ithaca, NY: Cornell University Press, 1987), 32.

14. Paul Hutchcroft, "Reflections on a Reverse Image: South Korea under Park Chung Hee and the Philippines under Ferdinand Marcos," in *The Park Chung Hee Era: The Transformation of South Korea*, ed. Kim Pyŏng-guk, Byung-Kook Kim, and Ezra F. Vogel (Cambridge, MA: Harvard University Press, 2011), 543. See also Nathan Gilbert Quimpo, "The Philippines: Predatory Regime, Growing Authoritarian Features," *Pacific Review* 22, no. 3 (2009): 340.

15. Benjamin B. Smith, "Life of the Party: The Origins of Regime Breakdown and Persistence under Single-Party Rule," *World Politics* 57, no. 3 (2005): 446–47.

16. Walter Hatch and Kozo Yamamura, *Asia in Japan's Embrace: Building a Regional Production Alliance* (Cambridge: Cambridge University Press, 1996), 137.

17. See, for example, Jong-sung You, *Democracy, Inequality, and Corruption: Korea, Taiwan and the Philippines Compared* (Cambridge: Cambridge University Press, 2015).

18. Peter Evans, "Class, State, and Dependence in East Asia: Lessons for Latin Americanists," in *The Political Economy of the New Asian Industrialism*, ed. Frederic C. Deyo (Ithaca, NY: Cornell University Press, 1987), 214–15.

19. Thomas C. Nowak and Kay A. Snyder, "Clientelist Politics in the Philippines: Integration or Instability?," *American Political Science Review* 68, no. 3 (1974): 1147–70.

20. Nowak and Snyder, "Clientelist Politics in the Philippines," 1147–70.

21. Amy Chua, *World on Fire: How Exporting Free Market Democracy Breeds Ethnic Hatred and Global Instability* (New York: Doubleday, 2003).

22. Paul Hutchcroft, "Neither Dynamo nor Domino: Reforms and Crises in the Philippine Political Economy," in *The Politics of the Asian Economic Crisis*, ed. T. J. Pempel (Ithaca, NY: Cornell University Press, 1999), 179.

23. Jonah P. Estadillo, "Income Inequality in the Philippines, 1961–1991," *Developing Economies* 35, no. 1 (2009): 69–70.

24. Shalom, *The United States and the Philippines*, 40

25. World Bank, "Philippines Leads Peers with 7.3% GDP Growth but Slowdown Expected for 2008," news release, April 1, 2008, as cited in Quimpo, "The Philippines," 336.

26. Amando Doronila, "The Transformation of Patron-Client Relations and Its Political Consequences in Postwar Philippines," *Journal of Southeast Asian Studies* 16, no. 1 (1985): 105–6.

27. S. P. Go, "Towards the 21st Century: Whither Philippine Labor Migration," in *Filipino Workers on the Move: Trend, Dilemmas and Policy Options*, ed. B. V. Carino (Manila: PMRN, 1998), 9–44. See also James A. Tyner, "The Global Context of Gendered Labor Migration from the Philippines to the United States," *American Behavioral Scientist* 42, no. 4 (1999): 671–89.

28. Hedman and Sidel, *Philippine Politics and Society in the Twentieth Century*, 125.

29. Jose P. Magno Jr. and A. James Gregor, "Insurgency and Counterinsurgency in the Philippines," *Asian Survey* 26, no. 5 (1986): 501–17.

30. Magno and Gregor, "Insurgency and Counterinsurgency," 506. See also Sheila S. Coronel, "The Philippines in 2006: Democracy and Its Discontents," *Asian Survey* 47, no. 1 (2007): 175–82.

31. Quimpo, "The Philippines," 340.

32. John T. Sidel, "Social Origins of Dictatorship and Democracy Revisited: Colonial State and Chinese Immigrants in the Making of Modern Southeast Asia," *Comparative Politics* 40, no. 2 (2008): 136.

33. Pinches, "The Philippines: The Regional Exception," 395.

34. Paul Hutchcroft, "Reflections on a Reverse Image," 543. See also Garry Rodan (2019) Inequality and Political Representation in the Philippines and Singapore, *Journal of Contemporary Asia*, DOI: 10.1080/00472336.2019.1607531.

35. Heritage Foundation, *The Key Role of U.S. Bases in the Philippines*, January 10, 1984, https://www.heritage.org/report/the-key-role-us-bases-the-philippines.

36. Michael J. Green, *By More Than Providence: Grand Strategy and American Power in the Asia Pacific since 1783* (New York: Columbia University Press, 2018), 281, 283.

37. Eleanor Albert, *The U.S.-Philippine Defense Alliance* (Washington, DC: Council on Foreign Relations, 2016), https://www.cfr.org/backgrounder/us-philippines-defense-alliance.

38. Data as reported in Kang, *Crony Capitalism*, 43.

39. US Occupation authorities in Japan and South Korea also supported indigenous pro-US elites, but in those countries US businesses had very few prewar investments to protect, while domestic political and business elites lacked the natural resource base to tempt them toward profitability at the expense of development.

40. Roger Dingman, "The Diplomacy of Dependency: The Philippines and Peacemaking with Japan, 1945–52," *Journal of Southeast Asian Studies* 17, no. 2 (1986): 309.

41. Kang, *Crony Capitalism*, 31.

42. Hutchcroft, "Reflections on a Reverse Image," 548.

43. Tetsuo Ito, "Japan's Settlement of the Post-World War II Reparations and Claims," *Japanese Annals of International Law* 37 (1994): 52–53.

44. Kozo Kato, ed., *Asian Regionalism* (Ithaca, NY: Cornell East Asia Series, 1999), 4.

45. My usage is compatible with that of Peter B. Evans, "Predatory, Developmental, and Other Apparatuses: A Comparative Political Economy Perspective on the Third World State," *Sociological Forum* 4, no. 4 (1989): 561–87. For its application to the Philippines, see Quimpo, "The Philippines," 340.

46. Hazel M. McFerson, ed., *Mixed Blessing: The Impact of the American Colonial Experience on Politics and Society in the Philippines* (Westport, CT: Greenwood, 2002), 227. See also Doronila, "The Transformation of Patron-Client Relations."

47. Hutchcroft, "Reflections on a Reverse Image," 564.

48. Hutchcroft, 567.

49. James K. Boyce, *The Philippines: The Political Economy of Growth and Impoverishment in the Marcos Era* (Honolulu: University of Hawaii Press, 1993), 259.

50. Pinches, "The Philippines: The Regional Exception," 393.

51. Rodan, "Inequality and Political Representation," 7.

52. Pinches, *Philippines*, 394.

53. "The Philippines' Economy: The Jeepney Economy Revs Up," *The Economist*, August 16, 2007, https://www.economist.com/asia/2007/08/16/the-jeepney-economy-revs-up.

54. Quimpo, "The Philippines," 3.

55. See https://www.transparency.org/country/PHL.

56. For examples, see Armin Rosen, "The Long History of (Wrongly) Predicting North Korea's Collapse," *Atlantic*, August 6, 2012 https://www.theatlantic.com/international/archive/2012/08/the-long-history-of-wrongly-predicting-north-koreas-collapse/260769/; Nicholas Eberstadt, "The Coming Collapse of North Korea," *Wall Street Journal*, June 25, 1990 A18; Bruce Cumings, *North Korea: Another Country* (New York: New Press, 2004), 199; Daniel Byman and Jennifer Lind, "Pyongyang's Survival Strategy: Tools of Authoritarian Control in North Korea," *International Security* 35, no. 1 (2010): 44–74; Nicholas Eberstadt, *The End of North Korea* (Washington, D.C.: American Enterprise Institute, 1999); Michael Krantz, "The White House Is Preparing for the Possibility of North Korea Collapsing on Its Own," *Business Insider*, December 13, 2017, https://www.businessinsider.com/white-house-what-if-north-korea-collapses-tillerson-2017-12; Tom Embury-Dennis, "North Korea Could Collapse within a Year, Says Former Pyongyang Official," *Independent*, October 17, 2017, https://www.independent.co.uk/news/world/asia/north-korea-collapse-economy-pyongyang-kim-jong-un-industry-sanctions-china

-a8005001.html; and Art Moore, "Kim Jong Out? Some See Signs of Collapse," WND, December 21, 2017, https://www.wnd.com/2017/12/kim-jong-out-some-see-signs-of-collapse/.

57. Patrick McEachern, *Inside the Red Box: North Korea's Post-Totalitarian Politics* (New York: Columbia University Press, 2010), 31; Kongdan Oh and Ralph C. Hassig, *North Korea through the Looking Glass* (Washington, DC: Brookings Institution Press, 2004), 1.

58. Byman and Lind, "Pyongyang's Survival Strategy," 60.

59. Jonathan T. Chow and Leif-Eric Easley, "Renegotiating Pariah State Partnerships: Why Myanmar and North Korea Respond Differently to Chinese Influence," *Contemporary Security Policy* 40, no. 4 (2019), 502–25.

60. Andrei Lankov, "Pyongyang: Rules of Engagement," *Pacific Review* 16, no. 4 (2003): 616. For extended and detailed discussion of some of the personalities involved in Kim Il-sung's closest circle, see also Bruce Cumings, *North Korea: Another Country* (New York: New Press, 2004), 169.

61. Andrei Lankov, "Staying Alive: Why North Korea Will Not Change," *Foreign Affairs* 87, no. 2 (2008): 9.

62. Hanhee Lee, "Analyzing the Political Survival Prospects of Kim Jong-un's North Korean Regime through the Framework of Selectorate Theory," *Japanese Journal of Political Science* 19, no. 3 (2018): 483.

63. Lee, "Kim Jong-un's North Korean Regime," 477–79; McEachern, *Inside the Red Box*.

64. Byman and Lind, "Pyongyang's Survival Strategy," 45.

65. Johannes Gerschewski, "The Three Pillars of Stability: Legitimation, Repression, and Co-Optation in Autocratic Regimes," *Democratization* 20, no. 1 (2013): 27. See also Stephen Haggard and Marcus Noland, *Witness to Transformation: Refugee Insights into North Korea* (Washington, DC: Peterson Institute for International Economics, 2011), 81–100.

66. Byman and Lind, "Pyongyang's Survival Strategy" :68.

67. K. J. Kwon and Ben Westcott, "Kim Jong Un Has Executed over 300 People since Coming to Power," CNN, December 29, 2016, https://www.cnn.com/2016/12/29/asia/kim-jong -un-executions/index.html.

68. Byman and Lind, "Pyongyang's Survival Strategy," 68.

69. Cumings, *North Korea: Another Country*, 131.

70. *Korea (Democratic People's Republic of)'s Constitution of 1972 with Amendments through 1998*, https://www.constituteproject.org/constitution/Peoples_Republic_of_Korea_1998.pdf

71. Phil Robertson, "North Korea's Caste System: The Trouble with *Songbun*," *Foreign Affairs*, June 30, 2016, https://www.foreignaffairs.com/articles/north-korea/2016-06-30/north-koreas -caste-system. See also Oh and Hassig, *North Korea through the Looking Glass*, 133–34.

72. Timothy W. Martin and Warangkana Chomchuen, "North Koreans Get Smartphones, and the Regime Keeps Tabs," *Wall Street Journal*, October 30, 2018.

73. David Everand, *Only Beautiful, Please: A British Diplomat in North Korea* (Stanford, CA: Asia-Pacific Research Center, Stanford University, 2012), 53.

74. Andrei Lankov, "The Natural Death of North Korean Stalinism," *Asia Policy* 1 (2006): 100.

75. Everand, *Only Beautiful, Please*, 80.

76. Charles K. Armstrong, *The North Korean Revolution, 1945–1950* (Ithaca, NY: Cornell University Press, 2004), 213. See also Bruce Cumings, "Corporatism in North Korea," *Journal of Korean Studies* 4, no. 1 (1982): 269–94, and Helen-Louise Hunter, *Kim Il-song's North Korea* (Westport, CT: Greenwood, 1999).

77. Lankov, "Natural Death of North Korean Stalinism," 99.

78. Lankov, 110.

79. See James Jones, producer, *Frontline*, season 2014, episode 6, "The Secret State of North Korea," aired January 14, 2014, http://www.pbs.org/wgbh/pages/frontline/secret-state -of-north-korea.

80. Kang Chol-hwan and Pierre Rigoulot, *Aquariums of Pyongyang: Ten Years in the North Korean Gulag*, trans. Yair Reiner (New York: Basic Books, 2005); Blaine Harden, *Escape from Camp 14* (London: Penguin, 2012).

81. Arms Control Association, "Chronology of U.S.-North Korean Nuclear and Missile Diplomacy," https://www.armscontrol.org/factsheets/dprkchron.

82. Charles L. Pritchard, *Failed Diplomacy: The Tragic Story of How North Korea Got the Bomb* (Washington, DC: Brookings Institution, 2007): 1–2.

83. The United States had discovered proof that the DPRK was producing highly enriched uranium (HEU) that, along with the banned plutonium, could produce nuclear weapons material. The Agreed Framework had, however, been limited to a freeze on plutonium and US technical worries about HEU were deemed by Clinton administration officials as too far from delivery to be beyond subsequent negotiations to close them down. The Bush administration took an alternative view, claiming that the DPRK had violated both the spirit and letter of the Agreed Framework. See T. J. Pempel, "How Bush Bungled Asia: Militarism, Economic Indifference, and Unilateralism Have Weakened the United States across Asia," *Pacific Review* 21, no. 5 (2008): 547–81.

84. Mike Chinoy, *Meltdown: The Inside Story of the North Korean Nuclear Crisis* (New York: St. Martin's Press, 2010; James A. Kelly, "George W. Bush and East Asia: An Assessment," in *George W. Bush and East Asia: A First Term Assessment*, ed. R. M. Hathaway and W. Lee (Washington, DC: Wilson Center, 2005), 14–30; Pempel, "How Bush Bungled Asia," 547–81; Pritchard, *Failed Diplomacy*.

85. To this end, China, along with Russia, backed several United Nations Resolutions introducing sanctions against the North following such tests. See, for example, "North Korea: UN Imposes Fresh Sanctions over Missile Tests," BBC News, December 29, 2017, https://www.bbc.com/news/world-asia-42459670; Carol Morello, Michelle Ya Hee Lee, and Emily Rauhala, "UN Agrees to Toughest Ever Sanctions against North Korea," *Washington Post*, September 11, 2017, https://www.washingtonpost.com/world/in-the-push-for-oil-embargo-on-north-korea-china-is-reluctant-to-sign-off/2017/09/11/3a5b56fe-96e5-11e7-a527-3573bd073e02_story.html?utm_term=.e41fed63ba80.

86. McEachern, *Inside the Red Box*, 14–15.

87. Bruce Cumings, "The Origins and Development of the Northeast Asian Political Economy: Industrial Sectors, Product Cycles, and Political Consequences," *International Organization* 38, no. 1 (1984): 1–40.

88. Lee, "Kim Jong-un's North Korean Regime," 483.

89. Lankov, "The Natural Death of North Korean Stalinism," 110.

90. Robert L. Carlin and Joel S. Wit, "The Way Things Were," *Adelphi Papers* 46, no. 382 (2006): 22.

91. Carlin and Wit, "The Way Things Were," 21–25.

92. Lankov, "Why North Korea Will Not Change," 9.

93. Carlin and Wit, "The Way Things Were," 21–25.

94. McEachern, *Inside the Red Box*, 5.

95. Lankov, "The Natural Death of North Korean Stalinism," 110.

96. Lankov, 111.

97. McEachern, *Inside the Red Box*, 5–6.

98. Choe Sang-hun, "Economic Measures by North Korea Prompt New Hardships and Unrest," *New York Times*, February 3, 2010: A4.

99. Andrei Lankov, *The Resurgence of a Market Economy in North Korea*, Carnegie Moscow Center, January 2016, https://carnegieendowment.org/files/CP_Lankov_Eng_web_final.pdf.

100. Lankov, *Resurgence of a Market Economy in North Korea*.

101. A good analysis of the 2013 and 2014 New Year's speeches and the increased emphasis on economic development is found in https://www.38north.org/2014/01/rfrank010214/.

102. Ruediger Fran, "North Korea's Economic Policy in 2018 and Beyond: Reforms Inevitable, Delays Possible," *38 North*, August 8, 2018, https://www.38north.org/2018/08/rfrank080818/.

103. Ruediger Frank, "North Korea's Economic Policy in 2018 and Beyond: Reforms Inevitable, Delays Possible," *38 North*, August 8, 2018, https://www.38north.org/2018/08/rfrank080818/.

104. I use Myanmar rather than the earlier name "Burma" because Myanmar is the name used legally by the country's government and by the regional and global organizations of which it is a member. "Burma" has loaded political connotations, particularly in its resonance with the Burmese ethnic group that has long enjoyed majority status and political control. For historical references or in direct quotes, I honor that usage.

105. Mary Patricia Callahan, *Making Enemies: War and State Building in Burma* (Ithaca, NY: Cornell University Press, 2005), 2–3.

106. Callahan, *War and State Building in Burma*, 18.

107. Roger Lee Huang, "Re-thinking Myanmar's Political Regime: Military Rule in Myanmar and Implications for Current Reforms," *Contemporary Politics* 19, no. 3 (2013): 251.

108. Huang, "Re-thinking Myanmar's Political Regime," 249.

109. Jason Brownlee, *Authoritarianism in an Age of Democratization* (New York: Cambridge University Press, 2007), 29. See also Kyaw Yin Hlaing. "Setting the Rules for Survival: Why the Burmese Military Regime Survives in an Age of Democratization," *The Pacific Review* 22, no. 3 (2009): 271–291.

110. Andrew Seith, "Myanmar's Coercive Apparatus: The Long Road to Reform," in *Myanmar: Dynamics of an Evolving Polity*, ed. David Steinberg (Boulder, CO: Lynne Rienner, 2015), 13.

111. Nick Cheesman, "Myanmar and the Promise of the Political," in *Conflict in Myanmar: War, Politics, Religion*, ed. Nick Cheesman and Nicholas Farrelly (Singapore: ISEAS, 2015), 355. See also Sean Turnell, "Myanmar's Fifty-Year Authoritarian Trap," *Journal of International Affairs* 65, no. 1 (2011): 79–92.

112. On the 1974 constitution, see Robert H. Taylor, "Burma's National Unity Problem and the 1974 Constitution," *Contemporary Southeast Asia* 1, no. 3 (1979): 232–48.

113. Kyaw Yin Hlaing, "Reconsidering the Failure of the Burma Socialist Programme Party Government to Eradicate Internal Economic Impediments," *South East Asia Research* 11, no. 1 (2003): 6.

114. Robert Taylor, *The State in Myanmar* (Honolulu: University of Hawaii Press, 2009), 319.

115. David Steinberg, "The Persistence of Military Dominance," in *Myanmar: Dynamics of an Evolving Polity*, ed. David Steinberg (Boulder, CO: Lynne Rienner, 2015), 44; Huang, "Re-thinking Myanmar's Political Regime," 252; Yoshihiro Nakanishi, *Strong Soldiers, Failed Revolution: The State and the Military in Burma, 1962–8* (Singapore: National University of Singapore Press, 2014), 112. See also Steinberg, "Persistence of Military Dominance," and Callahan, *War and State Building in Burma*.

116. Kipgin Nehginpao, *Myanmar: A Political History* (Oxford: Oxford University Press, 2016), 11.

117. Hlaing, "Setting the Rules for Survival," 271–91.

118. A. Burke, N. Williams, P. Barron, K. Joliffe, and T. Carr. "The Contested Areas of Myanmar: Subnational Conflict, Aid, and Development," Asia Foundation." (2019).

119. Konosuke Odaka, "A New Light to Shine? Historical Legacies and Prospects for Myanmar's Economy," in *The Myanmar Economy: Its Past, Present and Prospect*, ed. Konosuke Odaka (Tokyo: Springer, 2016), 15.

120. David I. Steinberg (ed.), *Myanmar: The Dynamics of an Evolving Polity* (Boulder: CO: Lynne Rienner, 2015), 6–7.

121. Michael Green and Derek Mitchell, "Asia's Forgotten Crisis: A New Approach to Burma," *Foreign Affairs* 86, no. 6 (2007): 149.

122. Kevin Woods, "Ceasefire Capitalism: Military Private Partnerships, Resource Concessions, and Military Style Building in the Burma-China Borderland," *Journal of Peasant Studies* 38, no. 4 (2011): 747–70.

123. Mary P. Callahan, *Political Authority in Burma's Ethnic Minority States: Devolution, Occupation and Coexistence* (Washington, DC: East-West Center, 2007). Huang, "Re-thinking Myanmar's Political Regime," 255–57.

124. Huang, "Re-thinking Myanmar's Political Regime," 257.

125. Bart Gaens, Political change in Myanmar: Filtering the murky waters of "disciplined democracy," FIIA Working Paper, #78 (February 2013): 9–14, https://www.fiia.fi/wp-content/uploads/2017/01/wp78.pdf.

126. Burke et al., *The Contested Areas of Myanmar*, 16.

127. "Myanmar's Constitutional Convention: A Charter for Thugocracy," *The Economist*, September 6, 2007 https://www.economist.com/asia/2007/09/06/a-charter-for-thugocracy. See also Nicholas Farrelly, "Myanmar's Conflicted Politics," in Nick Cheesman, and Nicholas Farrelly (eds.), *Conflict in Myanmar: War, Politics, Religion* (Singapore: ISEAS-Yusof Ishak Institute, 2016.), 3–24.

128. Seith, "Myanmar's Coercive Apparatus," 14.

129. Steinberg, "Contemporary Myanmar," 6–7. The military's vicious ethnic cleansing campaign against the Muslim Rohingya in Rahkine state soon put the lie to any notion of true religious tolerance.

130. Huang, "Re-thinking Myanmar's Political Regime," 248.

131. Zoltan Barany, "Where Myanmar Went Wrong: From Democratic Awakening to Ethnic Cleansing," *Foreign Affairs*, May/June 2018, https://www.foreignaffairs.com/articles/burma -myanmar/2018-04-16/where-myanmar-went-wrong.

132. The Rakhine state is home to a substantial minority of Muslim Rohingya. Although many residents trace their ancestry to the early nineteenth century, they are technically stateless as the result of a 1982 citizen law, limiting citizenship to membership in one of the national races, namely, those the state considers to have settled in Myanmar prior to 1824, the date of first occupation by the British. The British subsequently moved a large number of Muslims from what is now Bangladesh to work in Burma.

133. Odaka, "A New Light to Shine?," 15.

134. Farrelly, "Myanmar's Conflicted Politics," 14.

135. Turnell, "Myanmar's Fifty-Year Authoritarian Trap," 85.

136. David I. Steinberg, "International Rivalries in Burma: The Rise of Economic Competition," *Asian Survey* 30, no. 6 (1990): 588.

137. Farrelly, "Myanmar's Conflicted Politics," 10–11.

138. Steinberg, "International Rivalries in Burma," 589.

139. Odaka, "A New Light to Shine?," 16.

140. Steinberg, "International Rivalries in Burma," 589. On the broader issue of Japanese reparations and overseas development assistance, see Robert M. Orr, *The Emergence of Japan's Foreign Aid Power* (New York: Columbia University Press, 1990), and Alan Rix, *Japan's Foreign Aid Challenge* (London: Routledge, 2010).

141. See the 2011 movie *The Lady*. Directed by Luc Besson. Paris: EuropaCorp, 2011.

142. Steinberg, "International Rivalries in Burma," 589.

143. Steinberg, 594.

144. See, for example, Thant Myint-U, *Where China Meets India: Burma and the New Crossroads of Asia* (New York: Farrar, Strauss and Giroux, 2011), 180–201, and Farrelly, "Myanmar's Conflicted Politics," 10.

145. Min Zin, "China-Burma Relations: China's Risk, Burma's Dilemma," in *Burma or Myanmar? The Struggle for National Identity*, ed. Lowell Dittmer (Singapore: World Scientific, 2010). See also Turnell, "Myanmar's Fifty-Year Authoritarian Trap," 87.

146. Andrze Bolesta, "Myanmar-China Peculiar Relationship: Trade, Investment and the Model of Development," *Journal of International Studies* 11, no. 2 (2018): 25.

147. Chico Harlan, "WikiLeaks Suggests N. Korean, Burmese Nuclear Cooperation," https://www.washingtonpost.com/newssearch/?query=WikiLeaks%20suggests%20N.%20Korean,%20Burmese%20nuclear%20cooperation%20&sort=Relevance&datefilter=All%20 Since%202005; Green and Mitchell, "Asia's Forgotten Crisis," 147–58.

148. Alice D. Ba, *(Re) negotiating East and Southeast Asia: Region, Regionalism, and the Association of Southeast Asian Nations* (Stanford, CA: Stanford University Press, 2009), 117.

149. Green and Mitchell, "Asia's Forgotten Crisis," 149.

150. Ba, *(Re) negotiating East and Southeast Asia*, 125.

151. Donald K. Emmerson, "ASEAN's 'Black Swans,'" *Journal of Democracy* 19, no. 3 (2008): 70–84.

152. For details, see Kurt Campbell and Brian Andrews, "Explaining the US 'Pivot' to Asia," (London: Chatham House, 2013): 6–8. https://kritisches-netzwerk.de/sites/default/files /explaining_the_us_pivot_to_asia_-_kurt_campbell_and_brian_andrews_-_the_asia_group _-_august_2013_-_9_pages_0.pdf), and Robert Sutter, "The Obama Administration and US Policy in Asia," *Contemporary Southeast Asia: A Journal of International and Strategic Affairs* 31, no. 2 (2009): 189–216, inter alia.

153. Jonathan T. Chow and Leif-Eric Easley, "No Hope without Change: Myanmar's Reforms and Lessons for North Korea," Asian Institute for Policy Studies, *Issue Brief*, no. 36 (November 30, 2012): 8–9.

154. See https://data.worldbank.org/country/myanmar.

155. Toshihiro Kudo and Konosuke Odaka, "Post-colonial Industrialization in Myanmar," in *The Myanmar Economy: Its Past, Present, and Prospects*, ed. Konosuke Odaka (New York : Springer, 2016), 156.

156. See, for example, http://www.heritage.org/index/country/Burma.

157. See https://www.transparency.org.

158. Hal Hill and Sisira Jayasuriya, *An Inward-Looking Economy in Transition: Economic Development in Burma since the 1960s* (Singapore: Institute of Southeast Asian Studies 1986), 1.

159. Kudo and Odaka, "Post-colonial Industrialization in Myanmar," 156.

160. Kudo and Odaka, 157.

161. Kudo and Odaka, 171.

162. Hlaing, "Reconsidering the Failure of the Burma Socialist Programme Party Government," 24.

163. This involved the Foreign Investment Law (1988), the Myanmar Citizen Investment Law (1994), and the Myanmar Industry Development Council (1995). See Steinberg, "International Rivalries in Burma," 587–88, and Fumiharu Mieno and Koji Kubo, "Growth Structure and Macroeconomy under Twenty Years of Junta Regime in Myanmar," in *The Myanmar Economy: Its Past, Present, and Prospects*, ed. Konosuke Odaka (New York: Springer, 2016), 55.

164. Mieno and Kubo, "Macroeconomy under Twenty Years of Junta Regime in Myanmar," 52.

165. Mieno and Kubo, 55–58.

166. Steinberg, "International Rivalries in Burma," 591.

167. Sean Turnell, "The Rape of Burma: Where Did the Wealth Go?," *Japan Times*, May 2, 2008, https://www.japantimes.co.jp/opinion/2008/05/02/commentary/world-commentary/the-rape-of-burma-where-did-the-wealth-go/.

4. Developmental Regimes Reconstructed

1. This logic finds resonance in a number of works stressing the importance of path dependency. See, for example, James Mahoney, *The Legacies of Liberalism: Path Dependence and Political Regimes in Central America* (Baltimore, MD: Johns Hopkins Press, 2001); Paul Pierson, *Politics in Time: History, Institutions, and Social Analysis* (Princeton, NJ: Princeton University Press, 2011); Wolfgang Streeck and Kathleen Thelen, "Introduction: Institutional Change in Advanced Political Economies," in *Beyond Continuity: Institutional Change in Advanced Political Economies,* ed. Wolfgang Streeck and Kathleen Thelen (Oxford: Oxford University Press, 2005); Linda Weiss, "Developmental States in Transition: Adapting, Dismantling, Innovating, Not 'Normalizing,'" *Pacific Review* 13, no. 1 (2000): 21–55; Steven K. Vogel, *Freer Markets; More Rules: Regulatory Reform in Advanced Industrial Countries* (Ithaca, NY: Cornell University Press, 1996).

2. For a US example of policymakers' difficulties in adjusting to new conditions, see Walter Russell Mead, "The Big Shift: How American Democracy Fails Its Way to Success," *Foreign Affairs,* May/June 2018, https://www.foreignaffairs.com/articles/united-states/2018-04-16/big-shift.

3. For theoretically rich analyses of different responses to similar challenges, see David R. Cameron, "The Expansion of the Public Economy: A Comparative Analysis," *American Political Science Review* 72, no. 4 (1978): 1243–61; Peter Gourevitch, *Politics in Hard Times: Comparative Responses to International Economic Crises* (Ithaca, NY: Cornell University Press, 1986); Peter J. Katzenstein, ed., *Between Power and Plenty* (Madison: University of Wisconsin Press, 1977); James Mahoney, *The Legacies of Liberalism: Path Dependence and Political Regimes in Central America* (Baltimore, MD: Johns Hopkins University Press, 2001); Beth A. Simmons, *Who Adjusts? Domestic Sources of Foreign Economic Policy during the Interwar Years* (Princeton, NJ: Princeton University Press, 1997).

4. Dan Slater and Joseph Wong, "The Strength to Concede: Ruling Parties and Democratization in Developmental Asia," *Perspectives on Politics* 11, no. 3 (2013): 717–33.

5. This analysis parts company with those focused on continuities in "developmental states," such as Ben Fine's "The Developmental State Is Dead—Long Live Social Capital?," *Development and Change* 30, no. 1 (1999): 1–19, Weiss's "Developmental States in Transition," 21–55, and Stephan Haggard's "The Developmental State Is Dead: Long Live the Developmental State," *Comparative Historical Analysis in Contemporary Political Science* (2015): 39–66. It is more congruent with that of Joseph Wong, "The Adaptive Developmental State in East Asia," *Journal of East Asian Studies* 4, no. 3 (2004): 345–62.

6. When the United States finalized diplomatic ties with the PRC in 1979, the US Congress passed the Taiwan Relations Act to ensure that the United States would provide military equipment to Taiwan and would not engage in negotiations with the PRC at Taiwan's expense or seek to impede Taiwan's continuance as an autonomous political and economic entity. Steven M. Goldstein and Randall Schriver. "An Ucertain Relationship: The United States, Taiwan and the Taiwan Relations Act," *China Quraterly* 165 (2001): 147–72.

7. T. J. Pempel, ed., *The Economic–Security Nexus in Northeast Asia* (Abingdon, Oxfordshire: Routledge, 2013).

8. Michael Yahuda, *The International Politics of the Asia-Pacific*, 3rd ed. (London: Routledge, 2004), chaps. 3 and 4.

9. I. M. Destler, *American Trade Politics* (New York: Columbia University Press, 2005); Stanley D. Nollen and Dennis P. Quinn, "Free Trade, Fair Trade, Strategic Trade, and Protectionism in the U.S. Congress, 1987–88," *International Organization* 48, no. 3 (1994): 491–525; Kenneth Flamm, *Mismanaged Trade: Strategic Policy and the Semiconductor Industry* (Washington, DC: Brookings Institution, 1996).

10. See for example, Steven Berry, James Levinsohn, and Ariel Pakes. "Voluntary Export Restraints on Automobiles: Evaluating a trade policy." *American Economic Review* 89, no. 3 (1999): 400–430.

11. For example, the Clinton administration invoked provisions of Super 301 in 1997 to secure an opening of the Korean market, and particularly access for US automakers, by listing its auto market as Priority Foreign Country Practice. R. W. Stevenson, "U.S. Starts Trade Sanction Process against Koreans and 4 Others," *New York Times*, October 2, 1997: D-1. On beef and oranges in Japan, see Kusano Atsushi, *Nichi-Bei: Massatsu no kôzô* [U.S.-Japan: The structure of friction] (Tokyo: PHP, 1984). See also Laura D'Andrea Tyson, *Who's Bashing Whom? Trade Conflict in High Technology Industries* (Washington, DC: Institute for International Economics, 1992).

12. See, for example, Flamm, *Mismanaged Trade*; Douglas Irwin, "The U.S.-Japan Semiconductor Trade Conflict," in *The Political Economy of Trade Protection*, ed. Anne O. Krueger (Chicago: University of Chicago Press, 1996), 5–14; Tyson, *Who's Bashing Whom?*

13. For an extensive treatment of this influence, see Quinn Slobodian, *Globalization: The End of Empire and the Birth of Neoliberalism* (Cambridge, MA: Harvard University Press, 2018).

14. Robert Solomon and David Solomon, *Money on the Move: The Revolution in International Finance since 1980* (Princeton, NJ: Princeton University Press, 1999), 108–37.

15. Philip Cerny, "The Dynamics of Financial Globalization: Technology, Market Structure, and Policy Response," *Policy Sciences* 27 (1994): 319–20.

16. William Grieder, *One World, Ready or Not: The Manic Logic of Global Capitalism* (New York: Simon and Schuster, 1997), 227. See also G. R. Krippner, *Capitalizing on Crisis* (Cambridge, MA: Harvard University Press, 2011).

17. See, for example, Barry Eichengreen, *Globalizing Capital: A History of the International Monetary System* (Princeton, NJ: Princeton University Press, 2008); Joseph E. Stiglitz, *Globalization and Its Discontents* (London: Penguin, 2002).

18. On the subject see, inter alia, John Ravenhill, "Production Networks in Asia," in *The Oxford Handbook of the International Relations of Asia*, ed. Saadia Pekkanen, John Ravenhill, and Rosemary Foot (Oxford: Oxford University Press, 2014), 348–68; Richard Stubbs, *Rethinking Asia's Economic Miracle: The Political Economy of War, Prosperity, and Crisis* (New York: Macmillan International Higher Education, 2017; Henry Wai-chung Yeung, *Strategic Coupling: East Asian Industrial Transformation in the New Global Economy* (Ithaca, NY: Cornell University Press, 2016), 7.

19. Sven W. Arndt and Henryk Kierzkowski, *Fragmentation: New Production Patterns in the World Economy* (Oxford: Oxford University Press, 2001); Gary Hamilton and Kao Cheng-Shu, *Making Money: How Taiwanese Industrialists Embraced the Global Economy* (Stanford, CA: Stanford University Press, 2017); John Ravenhill, "Production Networks in Asia," 348–68; Stubbs, *Rethinking Asia's Economic Miracle*; Dennis Tachiki, "Between Foreign Direct Investment and Regionalism: The Role of Japanese Production Networks," in *Remapping East Asia: The Construction of a Region*, ed. T. J. Pempel (Ithaca, NY: Cornell University Press, 2005), 149–69; Yeung, *Strategic Coupling*; inter alia.

20. Etel Solingen, "Domestic Coalitions, Internationalization, and War: Then and Now," *International Security* 39, no. 1 (2014): 46.

21. Xiangming Chen, "Taiwan Investments in China and Southeast Asia: 'Go West, but also Go South,'" *Asian Survey* 36, no. 5 (1996): 449.

22. Chen, "Taiwan Investments in China and Southeast Asia," 451.

23. Gary G. Hamilton, ed., *Asian Business Networks*, vol. 64 (Berlin: Walter de Gruyter, 2011).

24. Barry Naughton, *The China Circle: Economics and Technology in the PRC, Taiwan, and Hong Kong* (Washington, DC: Brookings Institution, 1997); see also Peter J. Katzenstein and Takashi Shiraishi, *Network Power* (Ithaca, NY: Cornell University Press, 1997).

25. June-Dong Kim and In-Soo Kang, "Outward FDI and Exports: The Case of South Korea and Japan," *Journal of Asian Economics* 8, no. 1 (1996): 42.

26. Seungjin Kim, "Effects of Outward Foreign Direct Investment on Home Country Performance Evidence from Korea," in *The Role of Foreign Direct Investment in East Asian Economic Development*, ed. Takatoshi Ito and Anne O. Krueger (Chicago: University of Chicago Press, 2000), 296.

27. David D. Hale, "Dodging the Bullet—This Time," *Brookings Review* 16 (1998): 22–25; T. J. Pempel, "Soft Balancing, Hedging, and Institutional Darwinism: The Economic-Security Nexus and East Asian Regionalism," *Journal of East Asian Studies* 10, no. 2 (2010): 216.

28. Willem Thorbecke and Nimesh Salike, "Foreign Direct Investment in East Asia," RIETI Policy Discussion Paper Series 13-P-003: 11, 28,https://www.rieti.go.jp/jp/publications/pdp/13p003.pdf.

29. Thomas Kalinowski and Hyekyung Cho, "The Political Economy of Financial Liberalization in South Korea: State, Big Business, and Foreign Investors," *Asian Survey* 49, no. 2 (2009): 236; see also Yoshimichi Sato and Jun Imai, eds., *Japan's New Inequality: Intersection of Employment Reforms and Welfare Arrangements* (Melbourne: Trans Pacific Press, 2011).

30. T. J. Pempel, *Japan: The Dilemmas of Success* (New York: Foreign Policy Association, 1986).

31. Yasusuke Murakami, "The Age of New Middle Mass Politics: The Case of Japan," *Journal of Japanese Studies* 8, no. 1 (1982): 29–72; see also William W. Kelly, "Rationalization and Nostalgia: Cultural Dynamics of New Middle-Class Japan," *American Ethnologist* 13, no. 4 (1986): 603–18.

32. Robert Wade, *Governing the Market: Economic Theory and the role of Government in East Asian Industrialization* (Princeton: Princeton University Press, 2004), 44–45.

33. Hagan Koo, "From Farm to Factory: Proletarianization in Korea," *American Sociological Review* 56, 5 (October, 1990): 672.

34. OECD, data bank, https://data.oecd.org/.

35. See "GDP per Capita, Countries Compared," *NationMaster*, http://www.nationmaster.com/graph/eco_gdp_percap-economy-gdp-per-capita&date=1962; World Economic Databses, International Monetary Fund, https://www.imf.org/external/pubs/ft/weo/2018/01/weodata/weorept.aspx?sy=1980&ey=2023&scsm=1&ssd=1&sort=country&ds=.&br=1&c=186&s=NGDP_RPCH%2CPPPGDP%2CPPPPC%2CPCPIPCH%2CLUR%2CGGXWDG_NGDP&grp=0&a=&pr.x=17&pr.y=7.

36. See World Economic Databses, International Monetary Fund, https://www.imf.org/external/pubs/ft/weo/2018/01/weodata/weorept.aspx?sy=1980&ey=2023&scsm=1&ssd=1&sort=country&ds=.&br=1&c=528&s=NGDP_RPCH%2CPPPGDP%2CPPPPC%2CPCPIPCH%2CLUR%2CGGXWDG_NGDP&grp=0&a=&pr.x=42&pr.y=9.

37. Hung-mao Tien, "Transformation of an Authoritarian Party State," in *Political Change in Taiwan*, ed. Tun-jen Cheng and Stephan Haggard (Boulder, CO: Lynne Rienner, 1992), 38.

38. *Taiwan Statistic Data Book* (2008), table 14-5a, https://ws.ndc.gov.tw/Download.ashx?u=LzAwMS9hZG1pbmlzdHJhdG9yLzExL3JlbGZpbGUvNTgxNy83MDc2LzEzMDc2LzEzMDczMDVfMS9mMl9fMjAyNy83MDc2LzA2Mzg3MDcxLzY2Mzg3MDc2LzA2MzgwODc3MDc2&n=MjAwOGRhdGFib29rLnBkZg%3d%3d&icon=..pdf.

39. Wade, *Governing the Market*, 44–45.

40. Shelly Rigger, "Mobilizational Authoritarianism and Political Opposition in Taiwan," in *Political Oppositions in Industrializing Asia*, ed. Garry Rodan (London: Routledge, 1996), 309.

41. On such changes in values, see Ronald Inglehart, *Modernization and Postmodernization: Cultural, Economic, and Political Change in 43 Societies* (Princeton, NJ: Princeton University Press, 1997).

42. Tun-jen Cheng and Stephan Haggard, "Regime Transformation in Taiwan: Theoretical and Comparative Perspectives," *Political Change in Taiwan*, ed. Tun-jen Cheng and Stephan Haggard (Boulder, CO: Lynne Rienner, 1992), 38.

43. Dan Slater, *Ordering Power: Contentious Politics and Authoritarian Leviathans in Southeast Asia* (Cambridge: Cambridge University Press, 2010).

44. Hsin-huang Michael Hsiao, "The Labor Movement in Taiwan: A Retrospective and Prospective Look," in *Taiwan: Beyond the Economic Miracle*, ed. Denis Fred Simon and Michael Y. M. Lao (Armonk, NY: M.E. Sharpe, 1993), 154.

45. Hsin-Huang Michael Hsiao, "Emerging Social Movements and the Rise of a Demanding Civil Society in Taiwan," *Australian Journal of Chinese Affairs* 24 (July 1990): 165–66.

46. Slater and Wong, "The Strength to Concede," 724.

47. Slater and Wong, 717–33.

48. Tun-jen Cheng, "Democratizing the Quasi-Leninist Regime," *World Politics*, 41, no. 4 (1989): 482. .

49. Slater and Wong, "The Strength to Concede," 725.

50. Koo, "From Farm to Factory," 678.

51. Seongyi Yun,. "Democratization in South Korea: Social Movements and their Political Opportunity Structures." *Asian Perspective* 21, no. 3(Winter, 1997): 145–171.; Su-Hoon Lee, "Transitional Politics of Korea, 1987–1992: Activation of Civil Society," *Pacific Affairs* 68, no. 3 (Autumn, 1993): 351–67.

52. The experience of the 1968 Olympics in Mexico provided a stark warning of how badly protests and police crackdowns meshed with positive national image enhancement. In a military crackdown on student protests in the city of Tiatellolco and the National Autonomous University of Mexico, hundreds of students and civilians died and thousands were arrested. Although the games went forward, they left the government with a symbolic black eye.

53. T. J. Pempel, "Between Pork and Productivity: The Collapse of the Liberal Democratic Party," *Journal of Japanese Studies* 36, no. 2 (Summer, 2010): 227–54; see also Kent E. Calder, *Crisis and Compensation: Public Policy and Political Stability in Japan, 1949–1986* (Princeton, NJ: Princeton University Press, 1988).

54. See inter alia, Naoki Kobayashi, "The Small and Medium-Sized Enterprises Organization Law," in *Japanese Politics: An Inside View; Readings from Japan*, ed. Hiroshi Itoh (Ithaca, NY: Cornell University Press, 1973); Sheldon Garon and Mike Mochizuki, "Negotiating Social Contracts," in *Postwar Japan as History*, ed. Andrew Gordon (Berkeley: University of California Press, 1993), 145–66.

55. There was a coalition government in Japan in 1993–94, but it hardly showed any socioeconomic coherence because it resulted from a fragile alliance of the highly diverse support groups behind the seven coalitional parties.

56. T. J. Pempel, ed., *Uncommon Democracies: The One-Party Dominant Regimes* (Ithaca, NY: Cornell University Press, 1990).

57. Ethan Scheiner, *Democracy without Competition in Japan: Opposition Failure in a One-party Dominant State* (Cambridge: Cambridge University Press, 2005).

58. See, for example, Gerald Curtis, *Election Campaigning Japanese Style* (New York: Columbia University Press, 1971), 38ff; Russell J. Dalton and Scott E. Flanagan, *Electoral Change in Advanced Industrial Democracies: Realignment or Dealignment?*, vol. 4991 (Princeton, NJ: Princeton University Press, 2017); Ikuo Kabashima and Gill Steel, *Changing Politics in Japan* (Ithaca, NY: Cornell University Press, 2012), chap. 2.

59. See, for example, Peter J. Boettke, Christopher J. Coyne, and Peter T. Leeson, "Institutional Stickiness and the New Development Economics," *American Journal of Economics and Sociology* 67, no. 2 (2008): 331–58; Paul Pierson, "The Limits of Design: Explaining Institutional Origins and Change." *Governance* 13, no. 4 (2000): 475–499; Kathleen Thelen, "Why German Employers Cannot Bring Themselves to Dismantle the German Model," in *Unions, Employers, and Central Banks: Macroeconomic Coordination and Institutional Change in Social Market Economies*, ed. Torben Iversen, Jonas Pontussen, and David Soskice (Cambridge, Cambridge University Press, 2000), 138–72.

60. Keiichi Tsunekawa, "Japan: The Political Economy of Long Stagnation," in *Two Crises, Different Outcomes: East Asia and Global Finance*, ed. T. J. Pempel and Keiichi Tsunekawa (Ithaca, NY: Cornell University Press 2015).

61. Garon and Mochizuki, "Negotiating Social Contracts," 145–66.

62. This pattern began to change in the early 2000s, as noted in Ellis S. Krauss and Benjamin Nyblade, "'Presidentialization' in Japan? The Prime Minister, Media and Elections in Japan," *British Journal of Political Science* 35, no. 2 (2005): 357–68.

63. Internal LDP battles hardly ended with these structural overhauls, however. Tensions continued through the next three LDP prime ministers, opening the path for the opposition DPJ to take complete control of both houses of Parliament and the cabinet between 2009 and 2012. Yet the LDP returned to preeminence in 2012, holding that position until the time of this writing. By then, the commanding electoral machinery so integral to the dominant political machine had long since ceased to click on all cylinders, during which time its contributions to economic transformation dissipated. Efforts to reverse that drift began with Prime Minister Koizumi (2001–2006), and certainly Prime Minister Abe, with his long tenure, exerted strong executive authority, though with less focus on using the revitalized state apparatus toward economic invigoration. Pempel, "Pork and Productivity;" *Japan Decides 2014: The Japanese General Election,* (eds.) Robert J. Pekkanen, Steven R. Reed, and Ethan E. Scheiner (New York: Palgrave Macmillan, 2015).

64. Slater and Wong, "The Strength to Concede," 717–33.

65. Cheng and Haggard, "Regime Transformation in Taiwan," 2.

66. Rigger, "Mobilizational Authoritarianism and Political Opposition in Taiwan," 307.

67. Slater and Wong, "The Strength to Concede," 722.

68. Slater and Wong, 724.

69. James Cotton, "From Authoritarianism to Democracy in South Korea," *Political Studies* 37 (1989): 244–59.

70. Cotton, "From Authoritarianism to Democracy," 251.

71. Slater and Wong, "The Strength to Concede," 727.

72. Kim launched reforms to reduce political corruption and abuses of power, going so far as to permit the criminal prosecution of two of his presidential predecessors, Roh Tae-Woo and Chun Doo-Hwan, for crimes committed while in power

73. Slater and Wong, "The Strength to Concede," 730.

74. Cotton, "From Authoritarianism to Democracy," 245.

75. Haeran Lim, "Democratization and the Transformation Process in East Asian Developmental States: Financial Reform in Korea and Taiwan," *Asian Perspective* 33, no. 1 (2009): 103.

76. Yun-han Chu, "Surviving the East Asian Financial Storm: The Political Foundation of Taiwan's Economic Resilience," in *The Politics of the Asian Economic Crisis,* ed. T. J. Pempel (Ithaca, NY: Cornell University Press, 1999), 184–202; Yun-han Chu, "Unraveling the Enigma of East Asian Economic Resilience: The Case of Taiwan," in *Two Crises, Different Outcomes: East Asia and Global Finance,* ed. T. J. Pempel and Keiichi Tsunekawa (Ithaca, NY: Cornell University Press, 2015), 64–89.

77. At the same time, overseas assembly and production often spurred the export of components integral to foreign assembly.

78. Lim, "Democratization and the Transformation Process in East Asian Developmental States," 85–86.

79. Lim, 91.

80. Ha-Joon Chang, Hong-Jae Park, and Chul Gyue Yoo, "Interpreting the Korean Crisis: Financial Liberalization, Industrial Policy, and Corporate Governance," *Cambridge Journal of Economics* 22 (1998): 735–46. See also Lim, "Democratization and the Transformation Process in East Asian Developmental States," 86–87.

81. Ha-Joon Chang, "Korea: The Misunderstood Crisis," *World Development* 26, no. 8 (1998): 1588.

82. Frank S. Hsiao and Mei-Chu Wang Hsiao, *Economic Development of Emerging East Asia: Catching Up of Taiwan and South Korea* (London: Anthem Press, 2017), 34.

83. Jongryn Mo and Barry R. Weingast, *Korean Political and Economic Development: Crisis, Security and Institution Building* (Cambridge, MA: Harvard University Press, 2013); Gregory W. Noble and John Ravenhill, "The Good, the Bad and the Ugly? Korea, Taiwan, and the Asian Financial Crisis," in *The Asian Financial Crisis and the Architecture of Global Finance,* ed. Gregory W. Noble and John Ravenhill (Cambridge: Cambridge University Press, 2000), 80–107.

84. Meredith Woo-Cumings, "The State, Democracy and the Reform of the Corporate Sector in Korea," in *The Politics of the Asian Financial Crisis*, ed. T. J. Pempel (Ithaca, NY: Cornell University Press, 1999), 117.

85. On surrounding events, see T. J. Pempel, ed., *The Politics of the Asian Economic Crisis* (Ithaca, NY: Cornell University Press, 1999), especially chaps. 2 and 5; Gregory W. Noble and John Ravenhill, eds., *The Asian Financial Crisis and the Architecture of Global Finance* (Cambridge, Cambridge University Press, 2000).

86. Nobel and Ravenhill, *The Asian Financial Crisis*, 261–62.

87. Jongryn Mo, "The Korean Economic System Ten Years after the Crisis," in *Crisis as Catalyst: Asia's Dynamic Political Economy*, ed. Andrew MacIntyre, T. J. Pempel, and John Ravenhill (Ithaca, NY: Cornell University Press, 2008), 254ff.

88. Kim and Roh also promoted a radical shift in foreign policy with economic outreach to the DPRK and efforts to rebalance South Korea's relations with the United States and China. See Byung-Kook Kim, "Between China, America, and North Korea: South Korea's Hedging," in *China's Ascent: Power, Security, and the Future of International Politics*, ed. Robert S. Ross and Zhu Feng (Ithaca, NY: Cornell University Press. 2008), 203–10.

89. David Hundt, "Economic Crisis in Korea and the Degraded Developmental State," *Australian Journal of International Affairs* 68, no. 5 (2014): 499–514.

90. UNCTAD, "Share of World Exports," data set, https://unctadstat.unctad.org/wds/TableViewer/tableView.aspx.

91. See http://www.worldstopexports.com/south-koreas-top-import-partners/.

92. Cal Clark and Alexander C. Tan, *Taiwan's Political Economy: Meeting Challenges, Pursuing Progress* (Boulder, CO: Lynne Rienner, 2012), 17.

93. Clark and Tan, *Taiwan's Political Economy*, 21, 83.

94. Roger D. Huang and Cheng-Yi Shiu, "Local Effects of Foreign Ownership in an Emerging Financial Market: Evidence from Qualified Foreign Institutional Investors in Taiwan," *Financial Management* 38, no. 3 (2009): 567–602.

95. For details, see Huang and Shiu, "Qualified Foreign Institutional Investors in Taiwan."

96. T. J. Chen, "Democratization and Trade Liberalization," in *Taiwan's Economic Success since 1980*, ed. Chao-Cheng Mai and Chien-Sheng Shih (Cheltenham, UK: Edward Elgar, 2001), 319.

97. Lim, "Democratization and the Transformation Process in East Asian Developmental States," 99.

98. Hsiao and Hsiao, *Economic Development of Emerging East Asia*, 34.

99. Yun-han Chu, "The Realignment of Business-Government Relations and Regime Transition in Taiwan," in *Business and Government in Industrializing Asia*, ed. Andrew MacIntyre (Ithaca, NY: Cornell University Press, 1994), 121ff.

100. Daniel You-Ren Yang, Jinn-Yuh Hsu, and Chia-Ho Ching, "Revisiting the Silicon Island? The Geographically Varied 'Strategic Coupling' in the Development of High-Technology Parks in Taiwan," *Regional Studies* 43, no. 3 (2009): 371, 375.

101. UNCTAD, "Share of World Exports," data set, https://unctadstat.unctad.org/wds/TableViewer/tableView.aspx.

102. Da-Nien Liu, "The Trading Relationship between Taiwan and the United States: Current Trends and the Outlook for the Future," Brookings Institution, *Taiwan-U.S. Quarterly Analysis*, November 2016, https://www.brookings.edu/opinions/the-trading-relationship-between-taiwan-and-the-united-states-current-trends-and-the-outlook-for-the-future.

103. See https://www.google.com/url?sa=t&rct=j&q=&esrc=s&source=web&cd=20&ved=0CF8QFjAJOApqFQoTCLT88oPlrsgCFVUxiAodl4cCHQ&url=http%3A%2F%2Fwww.state.gov%2Fdocuments%2Forganization%2F227458.pdf&usg=AFQjCNEEUmvrsnmEQoQpINI_w3PFWPhFpA&sig2=11b3F2iq41-L6z16xp9huQ&cad=rja.

104. Jennifer A. Amyx, *Japan's Financial Crisis: Institutional Rigidity and Reluctant Change* (Princeton, NJ: Princeton University Press, 2004).

105. Noguchi Yukio, *Gyôzaisei kaikaku* [Administrative and Financial Reform] (Tokyo: PHP, 1981); Shindô Muneyuki, *Zaisei hatan to zeisei kaikaku* [Financial Bankruptcy and Financial Reform] (Tokyo: Iwanami Shoten, 1989); T. J. Pempel, "The Unbundling of 'Japan, Inc.': The Changing Dynamics of Japanese Policy Formation," *Journal of Japanese Studies* 13, no. 2 (1987): 297ff.

106. Horiuchi Akiyoshi, "The Big Bang Financial System Reforms: Implications for Corporate Governance," in *Japanese Governance: Beyond Japan, Inc.*, ed. Jennifer Amyx and Peter Drysdale (London: Routledge, 2003), 77–95.

107. *Far Eastern Economic Review*, July 4, 1996, 45.

108. See OECD iLibrary, "OECD International Direct Investment Statistics 2018," https://read.oecd-ilibrary.org/finance-and-investment/oecd-international-direct-investment-statistics-2018_bb55ccaf-en#page16.

109. Yun-han Chu, "Unraveling the Enigma of East Asian Economic Resiliency," in *Two Crises, Different Outcomes: East Asia and Global Finance*, ed. T. J. Pempel and Keiichi Tsunekawa (Ithaca, NY: Cornell University Press, 2015), 64–89.

110. Yasunobu Okabe, "Reacting to Financial Crises: Institutional Path Dependence in Korea and Thailand," in *Two Crises, Different Outcomes*, 90–109.

111. Ulrike Schaede, "From Developmental State to the New Japan: The Strategic Inflection Point in Japanese Business," *Asia Pacific Business Review* 18, no. 2 (2012): 182.

5. China

1. See the World Bank, "The World Bank in China," https://www.worldbank.org/en/country/china/overview. Accessed September 9, 2019.

2. Gordon Gekko was an avaricious financier in the movies, *Wall Street* (1987) and its sequel, *Wall Street 2: Money Never Sleeps* (2010), both directed by Oliver Stone and distributed by 20th Century Fox. The widely quoted phrase from Deng was made in the 1960s as a suggestion that the terminology for an economic system was less critical than whether or not it produced good results.

3. For early assessments of the Chinese economic transformation, see William H. Overholt, *The Rise of China: How Economic Reform Is Creating a New Superpower* (New York: W.W. Norton, 1994), and Mark Seiden, *The Political Economy of Chinese Development* (Armonk, NY: M.E. Sharpe, 1993).

4. My calculations derive from Nicholas R. Lardy, *Markets over Mao: The Rise of Private Business in China* (Washington, DC: Peterson Institute, 2014); Daniel Bell, *The China Model: Political Meritocracy and the Limits of Democracy* (Princeton, NJ: Princeton University Press, 2015); Daniel J. Mitchell, "A Lesson from China on Poverty Reduction and Inequality: How China Provides a Great Example of Why It's Bad to Focus on Inequality," Foundation for Economic Education, June 23, 2017, https://fee.org/articles/a-lesson-from-china-on-poverty-reduction-and-inequality.

5. Seung-Wook Baek, "Does China Follow 'the East Asian Development Model'?" *Journal of Contemporary Asia* 35, no. 4 (2005): 485–98; Mark Beeson, "Developmental States in East Asia: A Comparison of the Japanese and Chinese Experiences," *Asian Perspective* 33, no. 2 (2009): 5–39; David Kerr, "Has China Abandoned Self-Reliance?" *Review of International Political Economy* 14, no. 1 (2007): 77–104.

6. Franz Schurmann, *Ideology and Organization in Communist China* (Berkeley: University of California Press, 1966), 110.

7. Lance L. P. Gore, "The Social Transformation of the Chinese Communist Party: Prospects for Authoritarian Accommodation," *Problems of Post-Communism* 62 (2015): 207.

8. Stein Ringen, *The Perfect Dictatorship: China in the 21st Century* (Hong Kong: Hong Kong University Press, 2016), xi.

9. Schurmann, *Ideology and Organization in Communist China*, especially chaps. 2–5.

10. "Color revolution" is a term collectively applied to a series of typically non-violent, anti-authoritarian revolutionary movements, in particular those that occurred in post-Soviet Eastern Europe and the Middle East between the 1990s and into the 2010s. Usually led by NGOs or student groups, most were associated with a specific color or flower. One of the earliest such color revolutions was the People Power or Yellow Revolution against President Marcos in the Philippines in 1986.

11. Susan Shirk, *The Political Logic of Economic Reform in China* (Berkeley: University of California Press, 1993), 9.

12. See, for example, John Gittings, *The Changing Face of China: From Mao to Market* (Oxford: Oxford University Press, 2006); Robin Porter, *From Mao to Market: China Reconfigured* (New York: Columbia University Press, 2011); Andrew H. Wedeman, *From Mao to Market: Rent Seeking, Local Protectionism, and Marketization in China* (Cambridge: Cambridge University Press, 2003), inter alia.

13. Alvin Y. So, "Guest Editor's Introduction," *Chinese Economy* 35, no. 3 (2002): 6.

14. Susan L. Shirk, *How China Opened Its Door: The Political Success of the PRCs Foreign Trade and Investment Reforms* (Washington, DC: Brookings Institution, 1994).

15. Kellee S. Tsai and Sarah Cook, "Developmental Dilemma in China: Socialist Transition and Late Liberalization," in *Japan and China in the World Political Economy*, ed. Saadia M. Pekkanen and Kellee S. Tsai (Abingdon, England: Routledge, 2005), 49.

16. As quoted in Orville Schell and John Delury, *Wealth and Power: China's Long March to the Twenty-First Century* (New York: Random House, 2013), 264.

17. Bruce J. Dickson, "Cooptation and Corporatism in China: The Logic of Party Adaptation," *Political Science Quarterly* 115, no. 4 (2000): 517–40.

18. Jonathan Unger and Anita Chan, "China, Corporatism, and the East Asian Model," *Australian Journal of Chinese Affairs* 33 (1995): 38.

19. See https://www.nakono.com/tekcarta/databank/tv-sets-average-number-of-tv-sets-per-tv-household/.

20. Central Intelligence Agency, "The Chinese Media: More Autonomous and Diverse—Within Limits—Central Intelligence Agency," 2006, www.cia.gov.

21. Beina Xu and Eleanor Albert, "Media Censorship in China," Council on Foreign Relations backgrounder, February 17, 2017, https://www.cfr.org/backgrounder/media-censorship-china.

22. Committee to Protect Journalists, report "China, Turkey, Saudi Arabia, Egypt are World's Worst Jailers of Journalists," https://cpj.org/reports/2019/12/journalists-jailed-china-turkey-saudi-arabia-egypt/.

23. See Reporters without Borders, "True Face: One of the Worst Free Speech Predators," January 9, 2018, https://rsf.org/en/news/chinese-regimes-true-face-one-worst-free-speech-predators.

24. Schell and Delury, *China's Long March to the Twenty-First Century*, 274.

25. Hu was a senior party leader who had been a major architect of economic and political reforms and a proponent of government transparency. This made him the target of conservative party officials who managed to blame him for 1987 student disruptions and remove him from his position as Party Secretary.

26. The estimate of ten thousand comes from the BBC citing a British diplomat who was allegedly given official Chinese state figures. See BBC, "Tiananmen Square Protest Death Toll 'Was 10,000,'" December 23, 2017, https://www.bbc.com/news/world-asia-china-42465516.

27. Andrew J. Nathan, "The New Tiananmen Papers: Inside the Secret Meeting That Changed China," *Foreign Affairs* 98, no. 4 (July/August 2019): 80–91.

28. Orville Schell and Susan L. Shirk, eds., *Course Correction: Toward an Effective and Sustainable China Policy*, Asia Society Task Force Report (New York: Asia Society, 2019), 12, https://asiasociety.org/center-us-china-relations/course-correction-toward-effective-and-sustainable-china-policy.

29. As quoted in Schell and Shirk, 16.

30. Gilles Guiheux, "The Political 'Participation' of Entrepreneurs: Challenge or Opportunity for the Chinese Communist Party?," *Social Research* 73, no. 1, "Special Issue: China in Transition," Jean-François Huchet (ed.) (Spring, 2006): 224.

31. Guiheux. 219–44..

32. Christopher A. McNally, "Sino-Capitalism: China's Reemergence and the International Political Economy," *World Politics* 64, no. 4 (2012): 741–76.

33. Guiheux, "The Political 'Participation' of Entrepreneurs," 232–33.

34. Guiheux, 210.

35. Guiheux, 205.

36. Guiheux, 208.

37. China, National Bureau of Statistics, annual data, available at http://data.stats.gov.cn/easyquery.htm?cn=C01, as cited in Melanie Hart and Kelly Magsamen, *Limit, Leverage, and Compete: A New Strategy on China* (Washington, DC: Center for American Progress, 2019).

38. "China's R&D Spending Sees Rapid Growth in Past Decades," *China Daily*, September 16, 2018, http://www.chinadaily.com.cn/a/201809/16/WS5b9e1a73a31033b4f4656493.html.

39. Study International Staff, "China Is Set to Beat the US for Top STEM Research: Here's Why," Study International, November 23, 2018, https://www.studyinternational.com/news/china-stem-research/.

40. Andrea Boltho and Maria Weber, "Did China Follow the East Asian Development Model?" Barry Naughton and Kellee S. Tsai, (eds.) *State Capitalism, Institutional Adaptation, and the Chinese Miracle* (Cambridge: Cambridge University Press, 2015): 252; Barry J. Naughton, *The Chinese Economy: Transitions and Growth* (Cambridge, MA: MIT Press, 2006).

41. Julian Gewirtz, *Unlikely Partners: Chinese Reformers, Western Economists, and the Making of Global China* (Cambridge, MA: Harvard University Press, 2018).

42. Gordon White, "Corruption and the Transition from Socialism in China," *Journal of Law and Society* 23 (1996): 151. See also Yan Sun, *Corruption and Market in Contemporary China* (Ithaca, NY: Cornell University Press, 2004); T. Gong, "Dangerous Collusion: Corruption as a Collective Venture in Contemporary China," *Communist and Post-Communist Studies* 35, no. 1 (2002): 85–103; Min Xin Pei, *China's Crony Capitalism: The Dynamics of Regime Decay* (Cambridge, MA: Harvard University Press, 2016).

43. David Barboza, "Billions in Hidden Riches for Family of Chinese Leader," *New York Times*, October 25, 2012, https://www.nytimes.com/2012/10/26/business/global/family-of-wen-jiabao-holds-a-hidden-fortune-in-china.html.

44. Mitchell, "A Lesson from China on Poverty Reduction and Inequality."

45. Ming Wan, *The Political Economy of East Asia: Striving for Wealth and Power* (Washington, DC: CQ Press, 2008), 45.

46. Will Freeman, "The Accuracy of China's 'Mass Incidents,'" *Financial Times*, March 2, 2010, https://infoweb-newsbank-com.libproxy.berkeley.edu/apps/news/openurl?ctx_ver=z39.88-2004&rft_id=info%3Asid/infoweb.newsbank.com&svc_dat=WORLDNEWS&req_dat=0D0CB57AB53DF815&rft_val_format=info%3Aofi/fmt%3Akev%3Amtx%3Actx&rft_dat=document_id%3Anews%252F12E37EA734A29FE8. Barbara Demick, "Protests in China over Local Grievances Surge, and Get a Hearing," *Los Angeles Times*, October 8, 2011, http://articles.latimes.com/2011/oct/08/world/la-fg-china-protests-20111009. On the phenomenon in general, see Kevin J. O'Brien and Lianjiang Li, *Rightful Resistance in Rural China* (Cambridge: Cambridge University Press, 2006).

47. Andrew Gilholm, "Xi Jinping's New Watchdog," *Foreign Affairs*, March 6, 2018, https://www.foreignaffairs.com/articles/china/2018-03-06/xi-jinpings-new-watchdog.

48. For a powerful argument that corrupt business–political ties remain, see Min Xin Pei, *China's Crony Capitalism: The Dynamics of Regime Decay* (Cambridge, MA: Harvard University Press, 2016).

49. Giuseppe Gabusi, "'The Reports of My Death Have Been Greatly Exaggerated': China and the Developmental State 25 Years after Governing the Market," *Pacific Review* 30, no. 2 (2017): 232–59.

50. For details, see William Burr, "Sino-American Relations, 1969: The Sino-Soviet Border War and Steps Toward Rapprochement," *Cold War History* 1, no. 3 (2001): 73–112; Aaron Friedberg, *A Contest for Supremacy* (New York: W.W. Norton, 2011), chap. 3; Evelyn Goh, "Nixon, Kissinger, and the 'Soviet Card' in the U.S. Opening to China, 1971–1974," *Diplomatic History* 29, no. 3 (2005): 475–502.

51. For a detailed discussion, see T. J. Pempel, "Japan Shaping the Regional Order," in *Japan and Asia's Contested Order: The Interplay of Security, Economics, and Identity*, ed. Yul Sohn and T. J. Pempel (London: Palgrave McMillan, 2018).

52. See MOFA (Ministry of Foreign Affairs [Japan]), website, http://www.mofa.go.jp/policy/oda/region/e_asia/china.

53. Keiko Ujikane, "Japan Shifts Investment from China to Southeast Asia," *Bloomberg*, May 30, 2016, http://www.bloomberg.com/news/articles/2016-05-30/southeast-asia-is-winning-more-japanese-investment-than-china.

54. Boltho and Weber, "Did China Follow the East Asian Development Model?," 254–55.

55. Andrew Walter, "Addressing Global Imbalances: Domestic and Global Dynamics," in *China across the Divide: The Domestic and Global in Politics and Society*, ed. Rosemary Foot (Oxford: Oxford University Press, 2013), 153.

56. Joshua Kurlantzick, *Charm Offensive: How China's Soft Power Is Transforming the World* (New Haven, CT: Yale University Press, 2007).

57. M. Taylor Fravel, *Strong Borders, Secure Nation: Cooperation and Conflict in China's Territorial Disputes* (Princeton, NJ: Princeton University Press, 2008).

58. Saadia M. Pekkanen and Kellee S. Tsai, "Late Liberalizers: Comparative Perspectives on Japan and China," in *Japan and China in the World Political Economy*, 21.

59. Beeson, "Developmental States in East Asia," 29; Nicholas R. Lardy, *Integrating China into the Global Economy* (Washington, DC: Brookings Institution, 2002), 104.

60. Margaret M. Pearson, "The Institutional, Political and Global Foundations of China's Trade Liberalization," *Japan and China in the World Political Economy*, eds. Saadia Pekkanen and Kellee Tsai (Abbingtonn: Routledge, 2005), 99.

61. Mary E. Gallagher, "'Reform and Openness': Why China's Economic Reforms Have Delayed Democracy," *World Politics* 54, no. 3 (2002): 368, as cited in Beeson, "Developmental States in East Asia," 27.

62. Kellee S. Tsai and Barry Naughton, "Introduction: State Capitalism and the Chinese Economic Miracle," in *State Capitalism, Institutional Adaptation, and the Chinese Miracle*, ed. Barry Naughton and Kellee S. Tsai (Cambridge: Cambridge University Press, 2015), 14.

63. Tsai and Naughton, "Introduction," 17; see also Boltho and Weber, "Did China Follow the East Asian Development Model?," 240–64.

64. Schell and Delury, *China's Long March to the Twenty-First Century*, 262.

65. Schell and Delury, 273.

66. Julian Gewirtz, *Unlikely Partners: Chinese Reformers, Western Economists, and the Making of Global China* (Cambridge, MA: Harvard University Press, 2018).

67. Shannon Tiezzi, "Lee Kuan Yew: The Father of Modern China," *The Diplomat*, March 24, 2015, https://thediplomat.com/2015/03/lee-kuan-yew-the-father-of-modern-china/.

68. Ezra F. Vogel, *Deng Xiaoping and the Transformation of China* (Cambridge, MA: The Belknap Press of Harvard University Press, 2011), 394.

69. *Nikkei Business*, October 23, 1994, 18, as cited in Gregory W. Noble, *Collective Action in East Asia: How Ruling Parties Shape Industrial Policy* (Ithaca, NY: Cornell University Press, 1998).

70. William H. Overholt, *China's Crisis of Success* (Cambridge: Cambridge University Press, 2018), 11.

71. Overholt, *China's Crisis of Success*, 134.

72. Linda Yueh, *China's Growth: The Making of an Economic Superpower* (Oxford: Oxford University Press, 2013), 1.

73. Ashley J. Tellis, "Pursuing Global Reach: China's Not So Long March toward Preeminence," in *Strategic Asia 2019: China's Expanding Strategic Ambitions*, ed. Ashley J. Tellis, Alison Szalwinski, and Michael Wills (Seattle: National Bureau of Asian Research, 2019), 3.

74. Susan L. Shirk, *The Political Logic of Economic Reform in China* (Berkeley: University of California Press, 1993), 129.

75. Yuen Yuen Ang, "Autocracy with Chinese Characteristics: Beijing's Behind-the-Scenes Reforms," *Foreign Affairs* 97, no. 4 (May/June 2018), https://www.foreignaffairs.com/articles/asia/2018-04-16/autocracy-chinese-characteristics.

76. Porter, *From Mao to Market*, 59–60.

77. Porter, chap. 5.

78. Yi-Feng Tao, "A Catch-up Strategy? China's Policy toward Foreign Direct Investment," in *Japan and China in the World Political Economy*, 136–38.

79. Edith Terry, *How Asia Got Rich: Japan, China and the Asian Miracle* (Armonk, NY: M.E. Sharpe, 2002), 453.

80. Terry, *How Asia Got Rich*, 561.

81. Dwight H. Perkins and Thomas G. Rawski, "Forecasting China's Economic Growth to 2025," in *China's Great Economic Transformation* (eds.) Loren Brandt and Thomas G. Rawski (Cambridge: Cambridge University Press, 2008), 829–86.

82. Simon Pritchard, "Emerging Mainland May Eclipse Land of Setting Sun," *South China Morning Post*, January 11, 2002, as quoted in Terry, *How Asia Got Rich*, 561.

83. Edith Terry, *How Asia Got Rich*, 121.

84. Terry, 449.

85. Boltho and Weber, "Did China Follow the East Asian Development Model?," 253.

86. Yi-feng Tao, "A Catch-up Strategy? China's Policy toward Foreign Direct Investment," in *Japan and China in the World Political Economy*, 124–40.

87. Victor Nee and Sonja Opper, *Capitalism from Below: Markets and Institutional Change in China* (Cambridge, MA: Harvard University Press, 2012).

88. Gabusi, "China and the Developmental State 25 Years After," 242–43.

89. In a 2002 book that he cowrote, then-WTO director-general-designate Supachai Panitchpakdi enthused, "The agreement signaled China's willingness to play by international trade rules and to bring its often opaque and cumbersome government apparatus into harmony with a world order that demands clarity and fairness." Supachai Panitchpakdi quoted in Paul Blustein, "The Untold Story of How George W. Bush Lost China," *Foreign Policy*, October 2, 2019, https://foreignpolicy.com/2019/10/04/the-untold-story-of-how-george-w-bush-lost-china.

90. Nicholas R. Lardy, *Integrating China into the World Economy* (Washington, DC: Brookings Institution, 2002), 93.

91. Lardy, *Integrating China*, 46–55.

92. Shirk, *The Political Logic of Economic Reform in China*, chap. 9.

93. David Zweig, *Freeing China's Farmers: Rural Restructuring in the Reform Era* (Armonk, NY: M.E. Sharpe, 1997), 254.

94. Porter, *From Mao to Market*, 61.

95. Overholt, *China's Crisis of Success*, 37–38.

96. Shirk, *The Political Logic of Economic Reform in China*, 47–48.

97. Barry Naughton, "The Current Wave of State Enterprise Reform in China: A Preliminary Appraisal," *Asian Economic Policy Review* 12, no. 2 (July 2017), https://onlinelibrary.wiley.com/doi/full/10.1111/aepr.12185.

98. Shirk, *The Political Logic of Economic Reform in China*, 15.

99. Kellee S. Tsai, *Capitalism without Democracy: The Private Sector in Contemporary China* (Ithaca, NY: Cornell University Press, 2007).

100. Schell and Delury, *China's Long March to the Twenty-First Century*, 337.

101. Naughton, *The Chinese Economy*, 100.

102. Naughton, 100.

103. Barry Naughton, "China: Domestic Restructuring and a New Role in Asia," in *The Politics of the Asian Economic Crisis*, ed. T. J. Pempel (Ithaca, NY: Cornell University Press, 1999), 203–23. See also Edward Steinfeld, "The Capitalist Embrace: China Ten Years after the Asian Financial Crisis," in *Crisis as Catalyst: Asia's Dynamic Political Economy*, ed. Andrew MacIntyre, T. J. Pempel, and John Ravenhill (Ithaca, NY: Cornell University Press, 2008), 183–205.

104. Naughton, "China: Domestic Restructuring," 220.

105. Naughton, 222.

106. This is often associated with the Fifteenth Party Congress in 1997, but first appeared as party policy by the Central Committee in September 1995. Shaun Breslin, "Government-Industry Relations in China: A Review of the Art of the State," *East Asian Capitalism: Diversity, Continuity, and Change* (eds.) Andrew Walter and Xiaoke Zhang (Oxford: Oxford University Press, 2012), 29–45.

107. Tsai and Cook, "Developmental Dilemma in China," 51–52.

108. Cao Yuanzheng, Qian Yingyi, and B. Weingast, "From Federalism, Chinese Style, to Privatization, Chinese Style," *Economics of Transition* 7, no. 1 (1999): 103–31.

109. See for example, Ian Bremmer, "The Return of State Capitalism." *Survival* 50, no. 3 (2008): 55–64; Andrew B. Kennedy, "China's Search for Renewable Energy: Pragmatic Techno-nationalism," *Asian Survey* 53, no. 5 (2013): 909–930; Ted Fishman. *China, Inc.: How the Rise of the Next Superpower Challenges America and the World* (New York: Simon and Schuster, 2005).

110. Blustein, "The Untold Story of How George W. Bush Lost China." .

111. Lardy, *Markets over Mao*.

112. Naughton, "The Current Wave of State Enterprise Reform."

113. Shaun Breslin, "Government-industry Relations in China : a Review of the Art of the State: 37–38.

114. "China Defines Key National Economic Sectors," *China Daily*, December 18, 2006, https://www.chinadaily.com.cn/china/2006-12/18/content_761953.htm.

115. Kaya Sehrt, "Supporting Sunset Sectors: The Financial System in China's Economic Development," in *Japan and China in the World Political Economy*, 173.

116. Tsai and Naughton, "Introduction," 3.

117. Mikael Mattlin, "Chinese Strategic State-Owned Enterprises and Ownership Control," Brussels Institute of Contemporary China Studies, Asia Paper, vol. 4, no. 6 (2009), 13, http://www.vub.ac.be/biccs/site/assets/files/apapers/Asia%20Paper%204(6).pdf.

118. Yet much of this government money went into the largest SOEs, thereby reversing the moves toward SOE shrinkage. See Barry Naughton, "China and the Two Crises: From 1997 to 2009," in *Two Crises, Different Outcomes: East Asia and Global Finance*, ed. T. J. Pempel and Keiichi Tsunekawa (Ithaca, NY: Cornell University Press, 2015), 110–34.

119. Nicholas R. Lardy, *The State Strikes Back: The End of Economic Reform in China* (Washington, DC: Peterson Institute for International Economics, 2019); Naughton, "China: Domestic Restructuring," 203–23.

120. Min Tang, "From 'Bringing-in' to 'Going-out': Transnationalizing China's Internet Capital through State Policies," *Chinese Journal of Communication* 13, no. 1 (2020): 27–46.

121. Thomas Friedman, "Trump to China: 'I Own You.' Guess Again," *New York Times*, September 25, 2018, https://www.nytimes.com/2018/09/25/opinion/trump-china-trade-economy-tech.html.

122. For details, see inter alia, Jost Wübbeke, Mirjam Meissner, Max J. Zenglein, Jaqueline Ives, and Björn Conrad, "Made in China 2025," *Mercator Institute for China Studies. Papers on China* 2 (2016): 74; Zhu Wang, Chao Chen, Bin Guo, Zhiwen Yu, and Xingshe Zhou. "Internet plus in China." *It Professional* 18, no. 3 (2016): 5–8.

123. Tsai and Naughton, "Introduction," 3.

124. Tsai and Naughton, 77.

6. Regimes and the Regional Order

1. This classic statement is by Peter J. Gourevitch, "The Second Image Reversed: The International Sources of Domestic Politics," *International Organization* 32, no. 4 (1978): 881–912.

2. By "order," I mean the values, norms, and organizing principles that regulate state-to-state behavior. See Amitav Acharya, *Constructing a Security Community in Southeast Asia: ASEAN and the Problem of Regional Order* (New York: Routledge, 2014); G. John Ikenberry, "American Hegemony and East Asian Order," *Australian Journal of International Affairs* 58, no. 3 (2004): 353–67; Evelyn Goh, *The Struggle for Order: Hegemony, Hierarchy, and Transition in Post-Cold War East Asia* (Oxford: Oxford University Press, 2013); David Shambaugh, *China Engages Asia: Reshaping the Regional Order* (Cambridge, MA: MIT Press, 2006), inter alia.

3. Michael Mastanduno, "Incomplete Hegemony: The United States and Security Order in Asia," in *Asian Security Order: Instrumental and Normative Features*, ed. Muthiah Alagappa (Stanford, CA: Stanford University Press, 2003): 141–70.

4. A useful overview of this period is Michael Yahuda's *The International Politics of the Asia-Pacific* (London: Routledge, 1996), section 1, 1–83.

5. On Bandung and the NAM, see David Kimche, *The Afro-Asian Movement: Ideology and Foreign Policy of the Third World* (Jerusalem: Israel Universities Press, 1973), and Natasa Miskovic, Harald Fischer-Tiné, and Nada Boskovska, eds. *The Non-aligned Movement and the Cold War: Delhi-Bandung-Belgrade* (London: Routledge, 2014).

6. As E. H. Carr noted long ago, "power is indivisible" and "military and economic weapons are just different instruments of power." Edward Hallett Carr, *The Twenty Years' Crisis: An Introduction to the Study of International Relations* (New York: Harper and Row, 1939), 117–20. See also Jonathan Kirshner, "The Economic Sins of Modern IR Theory and the Classical Realist Alternative," *World Politics* 67, no. 1 (2015): 155–83.

7. Walter LaFeber, *America, Russia, and the Cold War 1945–2006* (New York: McGraw-Hill Humanities/Social Sciences/Languages, 2008), chap. 3; G. John Ikenberry, *After Victory: Order and Power in International Politics* (Princeton, NJ: Princeton University Press, 2009).

8. Charles Meier, "The Politics of Productivity," in *Between Power and Plenty: The Foreign Economic Policies of Advanced Industrial States*, ed. Peter J. Katzenstein (Madison: University of Wisconsin Press, 1977), 23–49.

9. China's trade patterns changed abruptly after the US instituted its embargo; trade with the U.S. became minimal while two-thirds of China's trade was with the Socialist bloc. See Amy King, *China–Japan Relations after World War Two: Empire, Industry and War, 1949–1971* (Cambridge, Cambridge University Press, 2016), 66.

10. On this issue including its manifestation in the Cold War, see for example, Peter Liberman, "Trading with the Enemy: Security and Relative Economic Gains," *International Security* 21, no. 1 (Summer, 1996): 147–175.

11. Nevertheless, in the period from 1961 to 1990, South Korea spent an average of 4.6 percent of its GDP on defense and security, while Taiwan spent 7.9 percent. See Uk Heo and Karl DeRouen Jr., "Military Expenditures, Technological Change, and Economic Growth in the East Asian NICs," *Journal of Politics* 60, no. 3 (1998): 830–46.

12. Thus, in 1967 a full 15 percent of Singapore's national income derived from US military procurements for Vietnam. See Wen-Qing Ngoei, "Lee Kuan Yew's Singapore Bloomed in the Shadow of the Cold War," *The Diplomat*, March 28, 2017, https://thediplomat.com/2017/03/lee-kuan-yews-singapore-bloomed-in-the-shadow-of-the-cold-war/.

13. David Kang, *Crony Capitalism: Corruption and Development in South Korea and the Philippines* (Cambridge: Cambridge University Press, 2002).

14. Andrew Yeo, *Asia's Regional Architecture: Alliances and Institutions in the Pacific Century* (Stanford, CA: Stanford University Press, 2019), 78–82.

15. The Guam Doctrine or Nixon Doctrine was articulated by President Nixon in a series of statements in 1969. In essence, it meant that the U.S would restrict its military involvement primarily to its alliance partners and would no longer attempt to provide defense for countries around the world. Most countries would thus become responsible for their own security.

16. T. J. Pempel, *The Economy–Security Nexus in Northeast Asia* (London: Routledge, 2014).

17. Aaron L. Friedberg, "Ripe for Rivalry: Prospects for Peace in a Multipolar Asia," *International Security* 18, no. 3 (1993): 5–33.

18. Peter Van Ness, "The North Korean Nuclear Crisis: Four-Plus-Two—An Idea Whose Time Has Come," *Asian Perspective* (2003): 249–75.

19. Barry Buzan and Gerald Segal, "Rethinking East Asian Security," *Survival* 36, no. 2 (1994): 18. See also Mitchell Bernard and John Ravenhill, "Beyond Product Cycles and Flying Geese: Regionalization, Hierarchy, and the Industrialization of East Asia," *World Politics* 47, no. 2 (1995): 171–209; Shaun Breslin et al., *New Regionalisms in the Global Political Economy: Theories and Cases* (London: Routledge, 2007); Christopher M. Dent, "Networking the Region? The Emergence and Impact of Asia-Pacific Bilateral Trade Agreement Projects," *Pacific Review* 16 (2003): 1–28; Walter Hatch and Kozo Yamamura, *Asia in Japan's Embrace: Building a Regional Production Alliance* (Cambridge: Cambridge University Press, 1996. Peter J. Katzenstein, *A World of Regions: Asia and Europe in the American Imperium* (Ithaca, NY: Cornell University Press, 2005) T. J. Pempel, ed., *Remapping East Asia: The Construction of a Region* (Ithaca, NY: Cornell University Press, 2005); Richard Stubbs, "ASEAN Plus Three: Emerging East Asian Regionalism?," *Asian Survey* 42, no. 3 (2002): 440–55, inter alia.

20. Track II dialogues are multilateral nongovernmental meetings normally involving academics, think tank representatives, and government officials attending in an unofficial capacity. The goal of such dialogues is to enhance mutual trust and to advance possible policy options less likely to emerge within official government settings. See, for example, Susan L. Shirk, "The Northeast Asia Cooperation Dialogue: An Experiment in Track II Multilateral Diplomacy," Chung-min Lee and T. J. Pempel, ed., *Security Cooperation in Northeast Asia* (Abingdon, Routledge, 2012), 209–227.

21. Gilbert Rozman, *Northeast Asia's Stunted Regionalism: Bilateral Distrust in the Shadow of Globalization* (Cambridge: Cambridge University Press, 2004).

22. An extensive database of some twenty-eight hundred such bodies is found in Saadia Pekkanen, *Asian Designs: Governance in the Contemporary World Order* (Ithaca, NY: Cornell University Press, 2017); see also Kent Calder and Ming Ye, *The Making of Northeast Asia* (Stanford, CA: Stanford University Press, 2010).

23. Natasha Hamilton-Hart, "Banking Systems a Decade after the Crisis," in *Crisis as Catalyst*, ed. Andrew MacIntyre, T. J. Pempel, and John Ravenhill (Ithaca, NY: Cornell University Press, 2008), 46.

24. T. J. Pempel, "The Race to Connect East Asia: An Unending Steeplechase," *Asian Economic Policy Review* 1 (2006): 239–54; William W. Grimes, "Political Economy of Regional Nesting," *Journal of East Asian Studies* 6 (2006): 353–80; William W. Grimes, *Currency and Contest in East Asia: The Great Power Politics of Financial Regionalism* (Ithaca, NY: Cornell University Press. 2009), inter alia.

25. China and Japan each sought to make the largest contribution to CMIM as a reflection of their greater influence. In a bargain negotiated by Korea, the two gained equal bragging rights as Japan (alone) and China–Hong Kong (in combination) each contributed 32 percent of the fund's total capital.

26. The number of such FTAs ranged as of 2019 from Taiwan's low of 14 and Myanmar's 16 to highs of 40, 39, 42, and 47 for Indonesia, Thailand, Korea, and China. See Asian Regional Integration Center data at https://aric.adb.org/fta-group. Accessed December 14, 2020.

27. Geoff McNicholl, "Demographic Future of East Asian Regional Integration," in *Remapping East Asia: The Construction of a Region*, ed. T. J. Pempel (Ithaca, NY: Cornell University Press, 2005), 54–74.

28. Takashi Shiraishi, "The Third Wave: Southeast Asia and Middle-Class Formation in the Making of a Region," in *Beyond Japan: The Dynamics of East Asian Regionalism*, ed. Peter J. Katzenstein and Takashi Shiraishi (Ithaca, NY: Cornell University Press, 2005), 237.

29. Fravel, *Strong Borders, Secure Nation: Cooperation and Conflict in China's Territorial Disputes* (Princeton, NJ: Princeton University Press, 2008).

30. Joshua Kurlantzick, *Charm Offensive: How China's Soft Power Is Transforming the World* (New Haven, CT: Yale University Press, 2007).

31. Witnessing the first Iraq War also led Chinese military planners to concentrate on enhancing the country's capacity to wage asymmetric war, aimed at preventing any hostile power from gaining dominance in the areas immediately contiguous to Chinese territory.

32. Miles Kahler, "Weak Ties Don't Bind: Asia Needs Stronger Structures to Build Lasting Peace," *Global Asia* 6, no. 2 (2011): 19.

33. Etel Solingen, "Pax Asiatica versus Bella Levantina: The Foundations of War and Peace in East Asia and the Middle East," *American Political Science Review* 101, no. 4 (2007): 757–80.

34. William H. Overholt, *Asia, America, and the Transformation of Geopolitics* (Cambridge: Cambridge University Press, 2007), 18–19. See also Solingen, "Pax Asiatica versus Bella Levantina"; Evelyn Goh, "Conceptualizing the Economic-Security-Identity Nexus in East Asia's Regional Order," in *Japan and Asia's Contested Order*, ed. Yul Sohn and T. J. Pempel (Singapore: Springer, 2018), 17–38; Steve Chan, "An Odd Thing Happened on the Way to Balancing: East Asian States' Reactions to China's Rise," *International Security Review* 12 (2010): 387–412; Timo Kivimaki, "East Asian Relative Peace—Does It Exist? What Is It?," *Pacific Review* 23, no 4 (2010): 503–26.

35. See, for example, Stein Tonnesson, "The East Asia Peace: How Did It Happen? How Deep Is It?," *Global Asia* 10, no. 4 (2015), https://www.globalasia.org/bbs/board.php?bo_table=articles&wr_id=9073.

36. BRI has triggered various concerns. For example, 89 percent of all contractors participating in BRI projects are Chinese companies, unlike projects funded by the World Bank and Asian Development Bank, where 40.8 percent are local, 29 percent are Chinese, and 30.2 percent are foreign. This lack of local involvement attracts criticism. Another worry is that BRI projects will expose partner countries to "debt traps," a view amplified in late 2017 when Sri Lanka handed over the management of its Hambantota Port to a Chinese company after struggling to repay its debt. See, for example, Jonathan E. Hillman "The Belt and Road's Barriers to Participation" CSIS, *Reconnecting Asia* (February 7, 2018), https://reconnectingasia.csis.org/analysis/entries/belt-and-road-barriers-participation/; Wade Shepard, "How China Is Losing Support For Its Belt And Road Initiative, *Fortune*, February 28, 2020, https://www.forbes.com

/sites/wadeshepard/2020/02/28/how-beijing-is-losing-support-for-its-belt-and-road
-initiative/?sh=e25c35021990.

37. See, for example, Richard Weitz, "China-Russia's Anti-NATO?," *The Diplomat,* July 4, 2012, http://thediplomat.com/2012/07/is-the-shanghai-cooperation-org-stuck-in-neutral/.

38. Ian Storey, "China's Missteps in Southeast Asia: Less Charm, More Offensive," *China Brief* 10, no. 25 (December 17, 2010), https://jamestown.org/program/chinas-missteps-in-southeast
-asia-less-charm-more-offensive/.

39. See, for example, Bruce W. Jentleson, *American Foreign Policy: The Dynamics of Choice in the 21st Century,* 4th ed. (New York: Norton, 2010), chap. 2.

40. The literature on this is extensive. For one insightful example, see Jacob S. Hacker and Paul Pierson, *Winner-Take-All Politics: How Washington Made the Rich Richer—and Turned Its Back on the Middle Class* (New York: Simon and Schuster, 2010). On the foreign policy implications, see also Kenneth A. Schultz, "Perils of Polarization for U.S. Foreign Policy," *Washington Quarterly* 40, no. 4, (2017): 7–28.

41. On the complicated story of these negotiations, see, for example, Robert Carlin and John W. Lewis, *Negotiating with North Korea: 1992–2007* (Washington, D.C.: Center for International Security and Cooperation, 2008).

42. Mike Chinoy, *Meltdown: The Inside Story of the North Korean Nuclear Crisis* (New York: St. Martin's Press, 2010); Charles L. Pritchard, *Failed Diplomacy: The Tragic Story of How North Korea Got the Bomb* (Washington, DC: Brookings Institution, 2007); inter alia.

43. I analyze these events in detail in Pempel, "How Bush Bungled Asia," 547–81.

44. See National Committee on US–China Relations, "Robert Zoellick's Responsible Stakeholder Speech," 2005, https://www.ncuscr.org/sites/default/files/migration/Zoellick
_remarks_notes06_winter_spring.pdf. For an example of the pervasiveness of this view, see also Edward S. Steinfeld, *Playing Our Game: Why China's Rise Doesn't Threaten the West* (Oxford: Oxford University Press, 2010).

45. On the "US in decline" literature in China, see Fu Mengzhi, quoted in Geoff Dyer, "The Dragon Stirs," *Financial Times,* September 25, 2009, https://www.ft.com/content/671a76ec-a950
-11de-9b7f-00144feabdc0; Joseph S. Nye Jr., "American and Chinese Power after the Financial Crisis," *Washington Quarterly* 33, no. 4 (2010),https://doi.org/10.1080/0163660X.2010.516634.

46. The Asian Barometer surveys underscore the widespread mutual distrust among the general populations of these three countries. Such attitudes make it extremely problematic for governmental leaders in such countries to initiate cooperative contacts. Naturally enough, mass opinions are subject to some shaping by elites. In this regard, leadership can be a powerful activator or impediment to regionalism. For detailed data, see Inoguchi Takashi et al., *Human Beliefs and Values in Striding Asia* (Tokyo: Asahi Shôten, 2006), 482–85.

47. For example, the United States signed the ASEAN Treaty of Amity and Cooperation, appointed a US ambassador to ASEAN, and pursued behind-the-scenes efforts to encourage regime change in Myanmar. The United States also joined the East Asia Summit and reinvigorated its participation in the ARF and the APEC forum. In addition, the United States stepped up its multilateral cooperation in police, disaster relief, and counterterrorism efforts.

48. Barack Obama, "President Obama: The TPP Would Let America not China Lead the Way on Global Trade," *Washington Post,* May 2, 2016, https://www.washingtonpost.com/opinions
/president-obama-the-tpp-would-let-america-not-china-lead-the-way-on-global-trade/2016/05
/02/680540e4-0fd0-11e6-93ae-50921721165d_story.html?utm_term=.2e5c4a651169.

49. T. J. Pempel, "Trump Swings a Wrecking Ball at U.S.-Asia Relations," *East Asia Forum,* August 27, 2017, http://www.eastasiaforum.org.

50. See, for example, Thomas Franck, "Trump Doubles Down: 'Trade Wars are Good, and Easy to Win'" CNBC, March 2, 2018; White House, "Remarks by President Trump in Press Conference," July 14, 2020, https://www.whitehouse.gov/briefings-statements/remarks-president
-trump-press-conference-071420/; Jim Tankersley, "Trump Hates the Trade Deficit. Most Economists Don't," *New York Times,* March 5, 2018, https://www.nytimes.com/2018/03/05/us/politics
/trade-deficit-tariffs-economists-trump.html.

51. As cited in Christopher Layne, "China's Challenge to U.S. Hegemony," *Current History* 107 (January 2008): 15.

52. White House, *National Security Strategy of the United States of America* (Washington, DC: White House, December 2017), https://www.whitehouse.gov/wp-content/uploads/2017/12 /NSS-Final-12-18-2017-0905.pdf.

53. On the term "China virus," see, for example, BBC, "Coronavirus: Trump grilled on use of term 'Chinese virus," March 18, 2020, https://www.bbc.com/news/av/world-us-canada-51953315. On the "all of government" perspective see Anthony H. Cordesman, "From Competition to Confrontation with China: The Major Shift in U.S. Policy," Center for Strategic and International Studies, *Commentary*, August 3, 2020, https://www.csis.org/analysis/competition-confrontation -china-major-shift-us-policy.

54. See Richard Wike et al., "U.S. Image Suffers as Publics Around World Question Trump's Leadership," Pew Research Center, June 26, 2017, https://www.pewglobal.org/2017 /06/26/u-s-image-suffers-as-publics-around-world-question-trumps-leadership/.

55. The first major articulation of this theory was found in A. F. K. Organski, *World Politics* (New York: Knopf, 1958). See also Richard K. Betts, "Wealth, Power, and Instability: East Asia and the United States after the Cold War," *International Security* 18, no. 3 (1999): 34–77; Barry Buzan, "China in International Society: Is 'Peaceful Rise' Possible?," *Chinese Journal of International Politics* 3, no. 1 (2010): 5–36; Paul Kennedy, *The Rise and Fall of Great Powers* (New York: Vintage, 1987). For a Chinese perspective, see Yan Xuetong, *Ancient Chinese Thought, Modern Chinese Power* (Princeton, NJ: Princeton University Press, 2013).

56. See, for example, Graham Allison, "The Thucydides Trap: Are the U.S. and China Headed for War?" *Atlantic*, September 24, 2015, https://www.theatlantic.com/international /archive/2015/09/united-states-china-war-thucydides-trap/406756/. My own views are in T. J. Pempel, "Thucydides (Clap) Trap: US-China Relations in a Changing Asia-Pacific." *Global Asia* 10, no. 4 (2015): 88–93.

57. Thus, Graham Allison, "The Thucydides Trap," Ibid. drawing on sixteen historical examples of power transitions over five centuries, is the most prominent American proponent, concluding: "war between the United States and China in the decades ahead is not just possible, but much more likely than recognized at the moment. Indeed, judging by the historical record, war is more likely than not." Christopher Layne expresses a similar view: "Throughout the history of the modern international state system, ascending powers have always challenged the position of the dominant (hegemonic) power in the international system—and these challenges have usually culminated in war. See Layne, "China's Challenge to U.S. Hegemony," 16. Slightly more tentative and hinging his predictions on Chinese domestic political developments, Aaron Friedberg writes: "If China stays on its current path . . . without becoming a liberal democracy, the present, muted, rivalry with the United States is likely to blossom into something more open and dangerous." See Aaron Friedberg, *A Contest for Supremacy* (New York: W.W. Norton, 2011). To John Mearsheimer, "China's rise . . . is likely to lead to an intense security competition between China and the United States, with considerable potential for war. . . . China cannot rise peacefully." John Mearsheimer, "The Gathering Storm: China's Challenge to U.S. Power in Asia," *Chinese Journal of International Politics* 3, no. 4 (2010): 382. See also Michael Pillsbury, "China and the United States Are Preparing for War," *Foreign Policy*, November 13, 2014, https:// foreignpolicy.com/2014/11/13/china-and-the-united-states-are-preparing-for-war/, and *The Hundred-Year Marathon* (New York: Henry Holt, 2015).

58. On this general interplay, see T. J. Pempel, ed., *The Economy-Security Nexus in Northeast Asia* (London: Routledge, 2014).

59. T.J. Pempel, "Japan: Working to Shape the Regional Order," in *Japan and Asia's Contested Order: The Interplay of Security, Economics and Identity*, ed. Yul Sohn and T. J. Pempel (London: Palgrave Macmillan, 2019), 193–220.

60. Pempel, "Japan: Working to Shape the Regional Order," 196–97.

61. Richard Javad Heydarian, "Middle Powers Step Up in Asia," *Foreign Policy*, October 24, 2018, https://www.chinausfocus.com/article/2018/1024/17295.html.

62. Seguchi Kiyoyuki, "Japanese Companies' Investments in China Get into Full Swing for the First Time in 13 Years-China's Local Government Attitude toward Attracting Japanese Businesses also Changes from Negative to Positive," Canon Institute for Global Studies, http:// www.canon-igs.org/en/column/network/20181009_5278.html. Accessed September 4, 2019.

Index

Note: Entries in italics refer to figures; entries in bold refer to tables.

CPSIA information can be obtained
at www.ICGtesting.com
Printed in the USA
LVHW111117060821
694612LV00006B/551

9 781501 758805